PSYCHOPATHOLOGY
OF AGING

PSYCHOPATHOLOGY OF AGING

EDITED BY

Oscar J. Kaplan

Department of Psychology
San Diego State University
San Diego, California

1979

ACADEMIC PRESS
A Subsidiary of Harcourt Brace Jovanovich, Publishers
New York   London   Toronto   Sydney   San Francisco

ACADEMIC PRESS, INC.
111 Fifth Avenue, New York, New York 10003

United Kingdom Edition published by
ACADEMIC PRESS, INC. (LONDON) LTD.
24/28 Oval Road, London NW1 7DX

Library of Congress Cataloging in Publication Data
Main entry under title:

Psychopathology of aging.

    Includes bibliographies and index.
    1. Geriatric psychiatry.   I. Kaplan, Oscar J.
[DNLM: 1. Aging.   2. Mental disorders––In old age.
WT150 P9743]
RC451.4.A5P778   618.9'28'9   79–21829
ISBN 0–12–396950–6

PRINTED IN THE UNITED STATES OF AMERICA

79 80 81 82   9 8 7 6 5 4 3 2 1

CONTENTS

Chapter 7
THE OLDER SCHIZOPHRENIC 149
Ivan N. Mensh

Chapter 8
NEUROSIS IN THE OLDER ADULT 167
June E. Blum and Marcella Bakur Weiner

Chapter 9
THE MENTALLY RETARDED IN LATER LIFE 197
Alexander J. Tymchuk

LIST OF CONTRIBUTORS

Numbers in parentheses indicate the pages on which the authors' contributions begin.

June E. Blum (167), Department of Psychiatry, Cornell University Medical College, New York, New York 10021

Warren Breed (289), Scientific Analysis Corporation, San Francisco, California 94123

*Charles V. Ford** (7), Department of Psychiatry and Biobehavioral Sciences, University of California, Los Angeles, Los Angeles, California 90024

Robert H. Gerner (97), Department of Psychiatry, School of Medicine, University of California, Los Angeles, Los Angeles, California 90024

Carol L. Huffine (289), Institute of Human Development, University of California, Berkeley, Berkeley, California 94720

Kay Redfield Jamison (79), Department of Psychiatry, School of Medicine, University of California, Los Angeles, Los Angeles, California 90024

Lissy F. Jarvik (7), Department of Psychiatry and Biobehavioral Sciences, University of California and Brentwood Veterans Administration Medical Center, Los Angeles, California 90024

* *Present Address:* Department of Psychiatry, Vanderbilt University School of Medicine, Nashville, Tennessee 37232

Myra T. Johnson (243), Southern University in New Orleans, Baton Rouge, Louisiana 70813

Oscar J. Kaplan (1, 45), Department of Psychology, San Diego State University, San Diego, California 92182

James J. Kelly (243), School of Social Work, University of Hawaii at Manoa, Honolulu, Hawaii 96822

Charles P. McCreary (259), Department of Psychiatry and Biobehavioral Sciences, University of California, Los Angeles, Los Angeles, California 90024

Ivan N. Mensh (35, 149), Department of Psychiatry and Biobehavioral Sciences, UCLA School of Medicine, Los Angeles, California 90024

Margaret A. Moore (229), Alcoholism and Drug Abuse Institute, University of Washington, Seattle, Washington 98105

*Paul A. Pastor, Jr.*** (211), Alcoholism and Drug Abuse Institute, University of Washington, Seattle, Washington 98105

Marc A. Schuckit (211, 229), Department of Psychiatry, University of California, San Diego, Medical School, and Alcohol Treatment Program, San Diego Veterans Administration Medical Center, San Diego, California 92161

Alexander J. Tymchuk (197), University Affiliated Facility for Training in Mental Retardation, Department of Psychiatry, University of California, Los Angeles, Los Angeles, California 90024

Marcella Bakur Weiner (167), Columbia University, Teacher's College, New York, New York 10027

Eugene Ziskind (271), Department of Psychology, University of California, Los Angeles, Los Angeles, California 90024

** *Present Address:* Center for Law and Justice, University of Washington, Seattle, Washington 98105

PREFACE

In 1945 I wrote in the preface to the first edition of *Mental Disorders in Later Life*, the first book on geriatric psychiatry, that "the aura of inevitability is beginning to lift from these widespread maladies which have been viewed as hopeless in the past." Reviewing the progress that has been made since the 1940s has been an exciting experience. Few major breakthroughs have occurred, but substantial gains have been made in most areas with which this book is concerned.

Research activity since the end of World War II has not been distributed evenly among the topics that constitute geriatric psychiatry. The large investment of time and money in the study of the affective disorders has brought us close to an understanding of the etiologies of these conditions, and much progress has been made in their effective control with psychoactive drugs, electroconvulsive therapy, and psychotherapy. This has benefited older patients. Research on the schizophrenias has produced a huge literature, but it has not yet paid off for older schizophrenics, most of whom date their illness from early life. Very little work has been done in the last decades on the elderly mentally retarded. There had been small interest in the geriatric dementias until the early 1970s, when the increasing number of seniles began to arouse concern.

Problems that formerly were mainly those of the young have come to be prominent in the old. This explains the inclusion of chapters in this book on sociopathy, drug abuse, sex deviation, alcoholism, and criminality.

This book is a series of original essays on selected topics in geriatric psychiatry. It does not pretend to be encyclopedic in its coverage. However, it does seek to define the present frontiers in a number of significant areas.

I am much indebted to all the contributors to this book for their cooperation and good work. In particular, I am indebted to Ivan N. Mensh of the University of California at Los Angeles who not only wrote two of the chapters, but also aided me greatly in the organization of the book. The editorial staff of Academic Press provided valuable counsel and assistance. And last, but not least, I wish to acknowledge the contribution of my wife, who kept the project moving.

Chapter 1

INTRODUCTION

Oscar J. Kaplan

Geriatric psychiatry stands on the threshold of a period of great expansion, both in research and in clinical practice. It is estimated that there will be about 50 million Americans age 65 or over in the year 2030. Older persons are subject to all of the behavior disorders that afflict young adults, as well as being subject to the dementias of later life. As a group, they are under greater stress than other age groups from ill health, low income, inappropriate housing, bereavement and loneliness, and approaching death. On a per capita basis, they are more likely to develop psychiatric or adjustment problems than members of any other age group.

As the number of aged with mental health problems has increased, interest has expanded in how older persons contend with mood disorders, schizophrenia, mental retardation, alcoholism and drug abuse, criminality, senile dementias, sociopathy, sex deviation, and suicide. Although most of these conditions are evident in the young, they are not entirely the same in the context of old age.

Only about 2% of psychiatric clinic outpatients are over age 65, even though persons in this age group now constitute about 11% of the general population. Explanations offered for this discrepancy include lack of interest in geriatric psychiatry by most mental health practitioners, unwillingness of older people with problems to seek professional help, greater tolerance of mild psychopathology by older people and their families, the widespread feeling that the dementias of later life are not treatable, and gerontophobia on the part of therapists.

1

PSYCHOPATHOLOGY OF AGING

I predicted in an interview with the University of California News Bureau in 1941 that the number of seniles in the United States would more than double by 1970. The prediction for 1970 turned out to be a conservative one. It was based on the following assumptions: (*a*) the number of persons over age 65 would more than double during the period 1940–1970; (*b*) no effective program for preventing or treating senile brain diseases would be discovered during this period; and (*c*) the per capita incidence rate of senile brain diseases in the population at risk would not change markedly. These assumptions proved to be correct. Looking at the future, some think the incidence rate will be even higher, because medical advances will enable less hardy individuals to survive into the post-65 age period.

A sharp increase in the number of seniles in the next 20 years now seems inevitable. The number of persons age 65 or over will exceed 30 million by the year 2000. If one goes by the percentages, the most rapidly increasing age group in the country is the age group over 80, the group most vulnerable to senile brain diseases. There is little in the current literature that suggests imminent breakthroughs. Moreover, it appears that the dementias of later life are plural and that, at least in some cases, many different causes may be operating concomitantly. If this analysis is correct, it suggests that we should be doing more planning for the housing and care of a huge population of mentally impaired aged. There is need to invent prosthetic environments that increase the ability of seniles to care for themselves partially and that enhance the quality of their lives. I am unwavering in my faith that the dementias of later life, one by one, will be overcome, but I believe it will take a long time. The dementias of later life have much in common with the various forms of mental retardation. They differ in etiology, and there are no simple, all-encompassing solutions.

In the present state of our knowledge, the descriptions of the dementias of later life are mainly phenomenological. Although it is likely that many cases will prove to be the result of some primary cause, such as slow-growing viruses or aluminum accumulation or genetic defect, a likely possibility is that a high percentage of the cases are of multiple causation and develop over a period of many years. This has led to the formulation of the Kaplan Cumulative Insult Theory, which postulates that some cases of senile dementia are the result of lifelong loss of cortical neurones through both "normal" aging and various pathological processes and events. Insult to the brain may begin even in the prenatal period. These losses do not show up as cognitive deficits until late in life because of the redundancy and immense physiological reserves of the brain. If this theory has merit, anything that helps maintain the integrity of the cerebral cortex during the prenatal period, childhood, adolescence, and early adulthood will pay off in a lower rate of senile dementia.

There are four levels of success that we aspire to with regard to the control of the dementias of later life. On the first level, the greatest success would be to prevent these conditions altogether. Since it is believed that the dementias of later life are caused by the destruction of irreplaceable brain neurons, maintaining the integrity of the cells associated with the higher mental functions obviously has top priority. On the second level, we would hope to restore the status quo ante. This may not be possible if large numbers of brain neurons have been destroyed. However, if it is found that factors such as inadequate oxygenation, nutritional deficiencies, or biochemical aberrations (e.g., those relating to choline acetyltransferase) play significant roles in the dementias of later life, early interventions may bring about improvement. On the third level, we aspire to produce therapeutic programs that will keep seniles from getting worse, enabling them to hold on to the cognitive abilities they still have. On the fourth level, we aspire to slow down the rate of decline. At this time, we do not know how to succeed even at the fourth level.

It is sad to report that there is no regimen known today which, if faithfully followed, could be guaranteed to lower the risk of dementia in later life. However, it appears that measures taken to protect the cardiovascular system may be advantageous, since cerebral blood vessel disease is one of the major factors in senile mental impairment. It has been observed that older people who are in robust physical health are less likely to be senile than those who are in poor health. This suggests that there may be some benefit in programs concerned with the maintenance of overall physical health.

Powerful new tools are now available or are being fashioned to gather the information needed for deeper probing of the dementias of later life. The continuing development of the electron microscope, computerized tomography, electroencephalography, and psychological testing procedures offers promise of more precise data than heretofore has been available. The collective expertise of immunology, neurochemistry, epidemiology, psychopharmacology, genetics, neurology, psychology, biostatistics, and psychiatry is being mustered for a more organized attack on senile brain diseases. The need is particularly urgent to find ways of accurately assessing living patients with noninvasive techniques.

Genetics is one of the most flourishing of the biomedical sciences. The pioneering work of Lissy Jarvik and her associates (see Chapter 2) is opening up new vistas in the psychopathology of later life. Some inherited diseases of the central nervous system (e.g., Huntington's Disease, Joseph's Disease) usually do not become manifest until middle or later life. It would be surprising if genetic factors did not operate as primary or secondary causes in some cases of senile dementia as well as in other disorders of interest to geriatric psychiatry.

In the past, geriatric patients suffering acute, reversible psychotic reactions often were not given proper treatment, resulting in permanent disability or death. It still happens. Chapter 3 summarizes recent research on this subject.

As in the case of mental retardation, psychologists play a major role in measuring the extent of mental impairment in the senile dementias. Psychological testing of seniles is the subject of Chapter 4.

Chapters 5 and 6 in this book deal with the mood disorders as they manifest themselves in the elderly. Depression is the most prevalent psychiatric problem of older people, varying from the borderline lows resembling those seen in "normals" to cases requiring tube feeding. Much progress has been made in managing depression with psychotherapy specifically designed for the aged. One of the most important advances in psychiatry in the last quarter of a century has been the use of lithium carbonate as a prophylactic in bipolar manic-depressive illness. Those who prescribe this or other drugs for older patients often must adjust dosages and should be doubly alert for treating side effects.

Most older schizophrenics now are warehoused in state and private mental hospitals and receive little more than custodial care. Barring spectacular advances, most will end their lives in institutions. Clearly, the schizophrenias confer no immunity against the dementias of later life, and the course of illness may be altered in persons who succumb to brain pathology. It is reasonable to expect that the immense efforts being made to understand the etiologies of what are now termed the schizophrenias eventually will enhance our understanding of older schizophrenics. Chapter 7 deals with recent research on older schizophrenics.

Among the most neglected disorders in geriatric psychiatry have been those that are subsumed under the heading of "neuroses," including such conditions as the hysterias, hypochondriases, anxiety reactions, phobias, obsessions, and compulsions. These difficulties are very widespread in the elderly and often markedly affect the quality of their lives. Chapter 8, which deals with neuroses in the aging, and which is written from the psychodynamic point of view, is one of the most comprehensive pieces ever written on this subject.

Mental retardation afflicts millions of Americans. The retarded are included in the lengthening life duration of the general population, and many will reach their 60s and later ages, particularly those who are only mildly or moderately impaired. There are numerous opportunities for cross-sectional and longitudinal studies with retardates, both biomedical and psychosocial. Life planning for persons in this category is becoming more urgent. Chapter 9 on mental retardation in later life points out that there has been little gain in knowledge about the older retarded since the 1940s.

Alcoholism and drug abuse (see Chapters 10 and 11) already are serious problems among the elderly and seem destined to become even more serious. Medical, psychological, and social factors are involved in these behaviors. The needs that foster substance abuse in the old are similar to those evident in the young, but they are not identical.

Homosexuals as well as heterosexuals face the problems of growing older, but they also face special problems of adjustment (see Chapter 12). As we deal more openly with different life-styles and forms of sexual preference, more studies will be reported on the experiences of persons who are not in the mainstream.

Older persons have been depicted more often as victims than as perpetrators of crime. Most arrests of persons age 50 or over are for drunkenness and related offenses. It is well known that age-specific rates for crimes such as robbery, burglary, rape, and murder drop sharply even after the 20s. As a result, we may look forward to a somewhat less violent country as median age rises in the American population. Nevertheless, as Chapter 13 points out, the number of older criminals is increasing because of the sharp rise in the number of people age 50 or over. The more intensive study of these older offenders is expected to generate information that is both practically useful and theoretically enlightening.

Chapter 14, which deals with older sociopaths is, to the best of our knowledge, the first of its kind. Sociopathy in the young is receiving increasing attention, and its forms in later life also are attracting more interest. Thorough longitudinal studies of sociopaths, from early adulthood to old age, are very much needed. There is, of course, a close but not invariable connection between sociopathy and crime.

Chapter 15 discusses the fact that suicide rates are higher in the old than in the young. They fluctuate with changing economic and social conditions. A rising population of elders will mean a sharp increase in the number of suicides unless we become more effective in prevention. We need more knowledge than we now have if we are to do this job adequately. Still, it must be acknowledged that fullest use is not being made of existing knowledge in preventive programs.

We may be able to alleviate or even cure some of the conditions discussed in this book before we fully understand them. Lithium carbonate is being used beneficially with bipolar manic-depressives even though the biochemistry involved still is being elucidated. Electroconvulsive therapy is being used effectively, even though there is lively controversy about why it is successful. In the experience of medicine, however, there is precedent for following a certain procedure without full understanding of why it works. For example, 162 years intervened between James Lind's discovery that lemon juice is a cure for scurvy and the work of Holst and Frohlich, which established its cause.

A tremendous increase in the number of elderly persons with psychiatric problems is almost certain to occur in the next half century. This increase will accelerate sharply the tempo of research on the topics addressed in this book. Geriatric psychiatry soon will be one of the major divisions of psychiatry.

Chapter 2

GENETIC ASPECTS OF PSYCHOPATHOLOGICAL DISORDERS IN LATER LIFE

Charles V. Ford and Lissy F. Jarvik

From an evolutionist's point of view the study of genetic influences may seem unimportant after that age of life when procreation has effectively ceased. Nonetheless, a good rationale for investigating genetic factors in diseases of old age is provided by the possibility of uncovering genetic relationships among a number of diseases and thereby gaining new understanding of underlying disease processes. For example, as described later in this chapter, there is evidence to suggest that Alzheimer's disease, myeloproliferative disorders, and Down's syndrome are genetically related, and that a common pathological factor may be the disorganization of the microtubules (Heston & Mastri, 1977).

Genetic information is also of clinical use, since a hereditary disease appearing late in life offers the opportunity to identify exogenous factors that might hinder or enhance its development. With such information, there is at least the theoretical possibility of modifying environmental factors for persons at risk in such a way as to favorably alter the course of the disease, if not prevent it altogether. Thus, evidence is emerging that Creutzfeldt-Jakob disease may be the result of a virus that affects only susceptible persons and that genetically determined differences may play an important role in susceptibility (Traub, Gajdusek, & Gibbs, 1977).

Finally, genetic knowledge is a sine qua non in genetic counseling. Although genetic counseling related to problems in senescence may not have the same emotional impact on relatives as that related to disorders

7

appearing in childhood, the increasing sophistication of the public has created increasing demands for genetic information concerning familial diseases at all ages. Huntington disease, as discussed later, is the most prominent example of current interest.

To limit the scope of this chapter it has been necessary to restrict diseases under discussion to those that appear primarily in later life and omit those that develop earlier in life, although the patient may often carry them with him or her into old age (e.g., schizophrenia and neuroses). It has also been necessary to exclude many diseases that may influence the development of psychopatholgy in a secondary manner, such as diabetes mellitus, where fluctuations in blood sugar may have a profound influence on brain function.

GENETIC RESEARCH IN LATER LIFE

Techniques of Genetic Research

Genetic factors in a trait or disease can be investigated by a variety of techniques. The simplest of these is the pedigree where the propositus (index case) is identified and a family tree is constructed showing all of the family relationships and identifying other afflicted members. The pedigree method is useful for examination of rare diseases or for distinctive characteristics. It may offer information as to the mode of genetic transmission. For example, an absence of father–son combination is highly suggestive of a sex-linked trait carried on the X chromosome. A major problem in the use of pedigrees is one of selection. A family is not likely to be called to attention unless the family history is positive and, therefore, isolated or sporadic cases are not evaluated. Thus, selection factors may influence data in the direction of an increased familial incidence.

A second method of genetic investigation is that of investigating family histories after determining a group of index cases. It is assumed that the incidence of a genetically determined disease should be correlated with the closeness of the biological relationship. Primary relatives (parents, siblings, and children) share on the average 50% of the genetic material with the index cases. Secondary relatives (grandparents, aunts and uncles, nephews and nieces, etc.) share on the average 25% of the genetic material. From the combined results of a number of family-history investigations, one can then compute a morbidity risk for different groups of relatives. Usually the emphasis is on siblings and parents. Because many of the relatives will not have lived through the risk period of developing the disease under study, a correction factor may be needed to more accurately estimate the risk of acquiring the illness (see Weinberg's method in Rosenthal, 1970). Such a corrected morbidity risk is only as good as the original data upon which it is based, and, therefore, the correction factor has the possibility of multiplying errors. Family risk studies have the advantage of including more cases, especially those that do not necessarily have a positive family history, than do pedigree studies. A major disadvantage is that secondary cases may be poorly diagnosed, thereby contributing to error. This method also does not clearly discriminate genetic from familial factors in disease.

In many ways the best method of investigating the influence of heredity is by using twins. Comparison of monozygotic (one-egg) twins, who have identical genetic material, with dizygotic (two-egg) twins, who share genetic material to the same degree as do other siblings, allows for the utilization of a natural experiment in evaluating environmental and hereditary factors. This comparison presupposes that environmental factors are the same for twins as for other siblings, a supposition that is true only to some extent, since twins in fact do share a more similar environment, beginning in utero, than do siblings of different ages. Major drawbacks in twin studies include selection, in that concordant twin pairs are more likely to be called to attention than are disconcordant pairs, as well as difficulties in finding sufficient twin pairs for the study of rare illnesses. With older age groups, it becomes an even greater problem to find intact twin pairs because of increasing mortality and geographical dislocation.

Perhaps the best research strategy, in comparing environmental and hereditary factors in disease, is the combination of the various methods utilizing twin family data and data on biological and adoptive relatives of persons who have been adopted during early childhood. Unfortunately, utilization of these methods requires a fairly nonmobile population as well as the availability of good medical and legal records, such as those maintained in the Scandinavian countries.

Problems of Genetic Studies in the Elderly

The preceding techniques of investigation, with the exception of adoption studies, have been used in studying diseases in older age groups. Unfortunately, there are a number of complicating factors that add to the difficulty of determining the influence of heredity in disorders of the senium. The subjects themselves are often poor historians or impaired intellectually. Relatives who may be key informants may have died or been scattered geographically; other relatives may be young and, therefore, may not as yet have manifested the disease in question. Similarly, there may have been relatives who died before having lived through the period of risk for developing the disease.

A major difficulty in studying disease in older age groups is that of accuracy of diagnosis. Other chronic diseases may mimic symptoms or coexistingly complicate the symptomatic expression of the disease under investigation. An example is the difficulty in the clinical differentiation between senile dementia, Alzheimer type, and folate deficiency induced dementia (Strachon & Henderson, 1967). Such diagnostic confusion and errors can cause major statistical problems, particularly with uncommon illnesses and small numbers of index patients.

It is also important to note that genetic disease is not the same as familial disease. Many diseases run in families because of environmental factors, and the elderly who have lived a long time have had an increased risk of exposure to exogenous factors. As a consequence, there may be confusion as to whether genetic or exogenous influences have been the most important in the development of a given disease process.

FUNCTIONAL DISORDERS IN LATER LIFE

The "functional" psychiatric disorders are those in which there is no demonstrable anatomical or pathophysiological change of the brain. They traditionally include the major psychiatric syndromes of affective disorders (including involutional melancholia), schizophrenia, and the neuroses. The "functional" disorders have in the past often been assumed to be psychogenic. Genetic research extending over several decades has indicated significant hereditary components in the major affective disorders (Mendlewicz & Rainer, 1977; Winokur, Cadoret, Dorzab, & Baker, 1971; also see review by Gershon, Dunner, & Goodwin, 1971) and in schizophrenia (Kallmann, 1946; Kety, Rosenthal, Wender, Schulsinger, & Jacobsen, 1976; also see review by Liston & Jarvik, 1976). In the light of this evidence, theories that postulate psychological factors as the exclusive etiology in these disorders will have to be modified and the question will have to be raised whether "functional" is an appropriate descriptive term. The evidence for genetic influence in the development of neurotic disorders is less convincing, although this group is highly heterogeneous and genetic factors may be important in some disorders such as anxiety neurosis (Eysenck & Prell, 1951; Miner, 1973; Slater, 1953).

Because the major affective disorders and schizophrenia have a peak incidence of onset in younger life, investigations have not been primarily concerned with the older age group. However, some studies have been published that provide information and directions for further research. To our knowledge, there has been no reported work relating genetic factors to the development of neuroses in later life.

Affective Disorders

Nosological concepts concerning the affective disorders have undergone considerable change during the past several decades, and this evolution is continuing at the present time. Involutional melancholia was in the past regarded to be a distinct entity. Increasingly the view is expressed that it is not a separate diagnostic classification but rather one of the "endogenous" depressions (such as unipolar or bipolar affective disorder) initially manifesting itself at an older age (Angst & Perris, 1972). Earlier genetic studies regarding "involutional melancholia" must therefore be viewed with the perspective that they may represent a collection of different depressive disorders rather than a specific entity.

Kallmann (1950, 1955) studied patients with "involutional psychosis" (referring to patients in whom compulsive-delusional symptoms, nonperiodical forms of depression, or agitated anxiety states are observed after age 50 or before age 70) and found that the incidence of schizophrenia in relatives of these patients was of about the same magnitude as that of involutional psychosis in relatives of schizophrenics. For involutional psychosis itself, the morbidity rates for siblings was 6.0% ± 1.61%, 6.0% ± 3.36% for dizygotic twins, and 60.9% ± 10.8% for monozygotic twins (Kallmann, 1950). In contrast, he found the rate of manic-depressive psychosis in primary relatives of patients with involutional psychosis to be only .8% (Kallmann, 1955). He suggested that this data indicated that involutional psychosis was related to schizophrenia rather than to manic-depressive psychosis.

From family interviews and a review of the hospital records of a group of Swedish patients, Kay and Roth (1961) found that patients with early onset affective disorders had a significantly higher incidence of first-degree relatives with affective disorders than those patients with a late onset of affective disorders. In contrast to Kallmann, they found the morbidity risk for schizophrenia to be only slightly increased in relatives of patients with late onset affective disorder. They concluded that patients with late onset affective disorder are a heterogeneous group with frequent exogenous or secondary factors playing an etiologic role.

Stenstedt (1959), in an investigation of genetic relationships of involutional melancholia in Swedish patients, made an effort to carefully define the disorder and excluded subjects with known manic-depressive illnesses. In this group of patients the mean age at onset was 57.1 ± .7 years for men and 57.5 ± .5 years for women. Primary relatives did not have an increase in the incidence of involutional melancholia when compared with general population expectancy rates. However, he did find the rate of "endogenous" (including both involutional melancholia and manic-depressive illness) affective disorder in primary relatives to be approximately twice that of expectation for the Swedish general population (6.1% versus 3.0%), with a negative correlation betwen age of the proband and morbidity risk for relatives. In addition, the age of onset of affective disorder in the identified relatives was lower than in the probands. Stenstedt interpreted his data as suggesting that the group of patients diagnosed as "involutional melancholia" is actually made up of patients with exogenous depression or late onset manic-depressive illness.

In a study of English patients, Hopkinson (1964) found that age of initial onset of affective disorders was not related to the nature of the symptom complex, with the exception that agitation was more common in those who became ill at a younger age. However, for primary relatives the morbidity risk was significantly greater if the patient had an initial onset of symptoms before age 50 than after age 50 (20.1% ± 3.6% versus 8.3% ± 1.9%, respectively). For those patients specifically diagnosed as having "involutional melancholia" (diagnostic criteria not specified), the risk of affective illness in primary relates was 10.2% ± 3.4%. The incidence of schizophrenia in first-degree relatives did not exceed the general population expectation for those patients diagnosed as having involutional melancholia. In a subsequent study, Hopkinson and Ley (1969) confirmed that the age of onset of affective illness was a significant variable in predicting morbidity risk for affective illness in first-degree relatives, age 40 being the most significant differentiating age. The authors, quoting Roth (1959), suggested that many of the depressions after age 40 might be secondary to illness or due to other exogenous factors. However, an American study (Woodruff, Pitts, & Winokur, 1964) did not disclose any relationship between medical illness or bereavement and the presence or absence of family history of affective disorders in depressed aged patients. These investigators did find, however, that in patients with onset of affective disorders after age

50 a positive family history of similar disease was less frequent than in patients with an earlier onset of symptoms. They reported that the incidence of schizophrenia in relatives was not above general population expectations irrespective of the age of onset of affective disorder in the probands.

In summary, although genetic factors continue to play a role in the affective disorders appearing for the first time in later life, their influence is apparently less than in those disorders with earlier onset. Genetic studies concerning "involutional melancholia" are difficult to evaluate because diagnostic criteria are not well specified for this disorder, if indeed it is a specific entity.

Paranoid States

Paranoid psychoses of late life (late paraphrenia), in the absence of demonstrable brain pathology, may be the mode of expression of schizophrenia in this age group (Roth, 1955). Because of this proposed association, genetic studies have focused upon the incidence of schizophrenia in the relatives of aged patients with paranoid psychoses. Studying a Swedish patient sample, Kay (1959) found that the morbidity risk for schizophrenia of first-degree relatives of patients with late-life paranoia was between 3.6% and 5.6% (the incidence of affective disorders in this group of relatives was between 2.9% and 3.3%). He concluded that this was a relatively homogeneous group in which genetic factors played a lesser role than in the functional psychoses beginning earlier in life. Exogenous factors did appear to be occasionally decisive for the precipitation of the psychotic state. In a phenomenological study of late paraphrenia, Kay and Roth (1961) found that women outnumbered men seven to one and that many patients developed the illness in a setting of social isolation. This isolation was related to several factors, including a high frequency of deafness and a scarcity of surviving relatives. They postulated that there was an inherited predisposition to late paraphrenia; however, they noted that it was likely to be of less importance than in schizophrenia occurring early in life.

Funding (1961), reviewing paranoid patients over age 50 at a Danish state hospital, found that the overall incidence of nonspecific psychosis in relatives was fairly high. He concluded that paranoid psychosis in later life differs genetically from schizophrenia and manic-depressive illness but that an independent mode of inheritance for late-life paranoia could not be demonstrated. Similarly, using rather nonspecific parameters, Sjögren (1964) found the family history of "mentally sick relatives" of patients with late paraphrenia to be positive 78% of the time as compared with 86% for schizophrenia in a nongeriatric group.

In summary, the scanty data relating to genetic influences in late-life paranoid psychosis suggests a relationship to schizophrenia. It is probable, however, that environmental and other exogenous factors influence the development of the disorder to a greater extent than with more youthful schizophrenics.

INTELLECTUAL DECLINE AND AGING

Loss of intellectual powers in old age is a frequent finding and an almost ubiquitous fear. The extent to which genetic factors may influence this intellectual decline or, on the contrary, contribute to preservation of function has been addressed by Kallmann and co-workers as a part of a longitudinal twin study. In this study, 1602 twin pairs were followed over a period of more than 20 years, and over 100 of them were personally examined on repeated occasions (Jarvik, Blum, & Varma, 1972; Jarvik & Falek, 1963; Kallmann, Feingold, & Bondy, 1951; Kallmann & Sander, 1948, 1949). Early reports indicated that many physical and psychological similarities have a tendency to persist through life and that the average intra-pair difference in life span was significantly less for monozygotic than for dizygotic twins (36.9 months versus 78.3 months; Kallmann & Sander, 1948, 1949). Psychometric testing demonstrated that the greater similarity in intellectual functioning of monozygotic twins, as opposed to dizygotic twins, continued into senescence, although it was noted that severe mental disorders depended upon a combination of environmental and genetic factors (Kallmann *et al.*, 1951). Subsequent followup reports indicated that the greater correlation in intellectual functions of monozygotic twins compared with dizygotic twins continued over a period of at least 20 years. Longevity and psychometric test scores were positively correlated, thereby suggesting a relationship between genetic input for intelligence and genetic input for survival (Jarvik & Falek, 1963; Jarvik, Kallmann, & Falek, 1962; Jarvik *et al.*, 1972).

An associated finding emerging from this study suggested that in the absence of significant physical illness many aspects of intelligence were age stable, and that a "critical loss" on two or three specified subtests was a prognostic indicator of 5-year mortality (Jarvik & Blum, 1971; Jarvik & Falek, 1963).

Apparently unrelated to the phenomenon of "critical loss" was the observation of an increased frequency of aneuploidy (cells with more or less than 46 chromosomes) in cultured peripheral leukocytes and its postulated relationship to glial cell and neuronal functioning (Jarvik, 1965) and performance on psychological tests, particularly those of memory (Jarvik, 1973; Jarvik & Kato, 1969, 1970). Chromosome loss (hypodiploidy) has also been associated with the diagnosis of organic brain syndrome (Jarvik, Altshuler, Kato, & Blumner, 1971) and specifically with senile dementia (Nielsen, 1968) in women, but not in men.

Indeed, there are now over a dozen studies in the literature reporting hypodiploidy to be significantly higher in old as compared with young women, regardless of mental functioning, but not in old as compared with young men. These findings were confirmed in the only longitudinal study on aged subjects, a 6-year followup of octogenarians (Jarvik, Yen, Fu, & Matsuyama, 1976). It is widely assumed that women tend to lose an X chromosome with advancing age, and even though men generally do not show increased hypodiploidy in old age, they do tend to show loss of a G-group chromosome, presumably the Y chromosome. The data, even though reported from various parts of the world, are based on small numbers of individuals and await clarification.

In the only study of aged twins published to date, no significant difference in concordance for hypodiploidy was found between monozygotic co-twins and unrelated pairs, suggesting that genotype was not a prime determinant of aneuploidy in those who survive to a very advanced age (i.e., the ninth decade and beyond) (Jarvik & Kato, 1969).

Finally, relationships are beginning to emerge between mental decline, as measured by psychometric performance, and immunoglobulins (Cohen, Matsuyama, & Jarvik, 1976; Roseman & Buckley, 1975) as well as between immunoglobulins and aneuploidy (Matsuyama, Cohen, & Jarvik, 1978). Again, the data are preliminary and await clarification.

In summary, genetic factors continue to have influence over the preservation of intelligence into senescence. Longevity and intelligence are correlated in a positive manner. Chromosome loss in elderly women appears related to organic brain dysfunction, but this relationship does not hold true for elderly men, who have a lower frequency of chromosome loss than do elderly women. Chromosome loss and changes in immunoglobulins may be related to one another and to impaired intellectual functioning.

PRESENILE DEMENTIAS

Huntington Disease

Huntington disease is a heredo-degenerative disease. Although not generally associated with aging, it is included in this discussion because of the wide variability of age of onset, as well as its importance in differential diagnosis, and the potential need to counsel younger relatives. Previously called "Huntington chorea" it is more appropriately termed "Huntington disease" as symptoms are far more extensive than just the involuntary choreic movements that are not always present (Whittier, 1963). Huntington disease is comparatively rare, with an incidence in the United States and Europe reported at between 2 to 7 per 100,000 population (Heathfield, 1973). The symptoms of Huntington disease frequently begin with a variety of nonspecific dementiform, affective, behavioral, or psychotic symptoms. The diagnosis becomes more apparent after the development of the characteristic choreic movements. Neurological and intellectual deterioration progress after the initial development of symptoms, and there is an average life span of about 16 years from disease onset (Reed & Chandler, 1958).

Because of the variability of symptomatic expression, Huntington disease may mimic other illnesses such as schizophrenia (McHugh & Folstein, 1975; Van Putten & Menkes, 1973), or in the older patient it may be regarded as a dementia associated with aging (Heathfield & MacKenzie, 1971). A positive family history may be suppressed due to perceived social stigma, or it may not be available because parents may have died prematurely. Lack of a positive history means that the diagnosis may not be considered and increases the difficulty of establishing an accurate diagnosis. Because Huntington disease will afflict, on the average, 50% of the offspring of all who develop the disease, it is essential that an accurate diagnosis be established in order that younger relatives alter their childbearing plans if they wish. The mode of inheritance appears clearly to be that of autosomal dominance with full penetrance, assuming that the risk period is survived (Reed & Chandler, 1958).

It is also necessary to differentiate the illness from other neurologic disorders with hyperkinetic symptoms in order that persons are not mistakenly diagnosed as having Huntington disease (Chandler, Reed, & De Jong, 1960). Such a mistake would be tragic, for the patients might thereby fail to receive appropriate therapy and the family members would suffer undue anxiety and fear in relationship to concern over the hereditary nature of the disease.

As mentioned previously, the age of onset can be highly variable, with an age range of 5 to over 70 (Myrianthopoulos, 1966). Reed and Chandler (1958), reporting on 205 patients with Huntington disease in Michigan, found that 12 patients had an onset below age 20 and 2 had an onset above age 65. A similar distribution of age of onset was determined by Heathfield (1967) for English patients with Huntington disease. Although the percentage of patients at the extremes is small, it is notable that the age of onset covers a span of greater than a half century.

Although the work is preliminary, a report by Husby, Li, Davis, Wedege, Kokmen, and Williams (1977) may explain why such a wide age range of disease onset occurs. Serum immunoglobulins type G (IgG) antibodies against normal human caudate nuclear neurons were found in nearly half of 80 Huntington disease probands. This compared with only a 3% prevalence in normal controls and 6% prevalence in patients with a wide variety of other neurological disorders. However, 30% of unaffected spouses and 23.2% of primary relatives also had positive antibodies against caudate neurons. The authors interpreted their data to suggest that an antineuronal antibody might reflect exposure to an agent (such as a virus) or common environmental factor. However, to actually develop the clinical manifestations of Huntington disease, one would have to theoretically possess a specific immunologically reactive gene. Barclay, Hardiwijaja, and Menkes (1977) have found that lymphocytes from patients with Huntington disease, grown in culture in the presence of brain tissue from patients with Huntington disease, produce a migration inhibition factor, a correlate of cellular immune response. The response occurs only rarely with exposure to nondiseased brain tissue. Lymphocytes from donors without the disease do not respond to brain tissue from patients with Huntington disease. These two recent studies provide evidence for the importance of immunological factors in this hereditary disease. Other areas of pathophysiologic research are also being actively investigated and have been reviewed by Heathfield (1973).

Creutzfeldt-Jakob Disease

Creutzfeldt-Jakob disease (CJD) is a rapidly progressive neurological illness with a worldwide distribution. It affects both sexes equally and is relatively rare. The annual incidence for England and Wales has been calculated at approximately .09 per million (Matthews, 1975), although geographical clusters of the illness have been reported (Matthews, 1975; Mayer, Orolin, & Mitrova, 1977). The age of onset is highly variable, and May (1968), in a review of the world literature, found reported cases of CJD as young as 21 years and as old as 79 years. Clinical symptoms are somewhat variable and, therefore, some authors have divided the disease into several subtypes dependent upon the clinical symptomatology (May, 1968; Siedler & Malamud, 1963). In general there is an initial presentation with vague symptoms such as dizziness, irritability, or confusion, which is followed by progressive dementia. Concurrently, there is the development of a variety of other neurological disturbances such as visual difficulties, pyramidal and extrapyramidal findings, myoclonus and cerebellar abnormalities. Death invariably ensues within a relatively short period of time, 90% of the victims dying within 2 years (May, Itabashi, & De Jong, 1968).

Previously considered one of the "big three" presenile dementias, CJD has become the subject of intense interest during the past few years following the discovery that the illness could be transmitted to other animals. The important work of Gajdusek (co-recipient of the 1976 Nobel Prize in Medicine) in recognizing and defining the slow virus infectious nature of Kuru (Gajdusek, 1977) was followed by the intracerebral inoculation of brain material from a patient with CJD into a chimpanzee. The chimpanzee developed spongiform encephalopathy 13 months later (Gibbs, Gajdusek, Asher, Alpers, Beck, Daniel, & Matthews, 1968). After this first successful transmission of CJD there have been numerous other instances where the disease has been transmitted to the chimpanzee or to other animals (Traub *et al.*, 1977).

The interest generated by the neurological disease, Kuru, which was shown to be transmitted by endocannibalism of the Fore natives of New Guinea, has focused epidemiological research upon possible methods of transmission of CJD in humans. One study (Bobowick, Brody, Matthews, Roos, & Gajdusek, 1973) reported a fairly high incidence of index cases who had eaten hog brains in the past; however, this was not significant when compared with their control group. Interestingly, the history of eating raw shell fish, particularly raw oysters, was significant when compared with the controls. Past history of eating hog brains by CJD victims was not confirmed in a subsequent report (Matthews, 1975).

Of considerable interest is the fact that although most cases occur sporadically a certain number are familial (Traub *et al.*, 1977). Pedigrees have been published that demonstrate the illness over several generations of families (Bonduelle, Escourolle, Bouygues, Lormeau,

Ribadeau-Dumas, & Merland, 1971; Ferber, Weisenfeld, Roos, Bobowick, Gibbs, & Gajdusek, 1974; Gajdusek, 1977; May et al., 1968; Rosenthal, Keesey, Crandall, & Brown, 1976). In each of these reports the mode of "transmission" is consistent with an autosomal dominant inheritance. Of particular interest is the family reported by Rosenthal et al. (1976). In this five-generation pedigree there are not only confirmed cases of CJD and other nonconfirmed cases of neurological disease with dementia (presumably CJD), but there are in addition various other neurological syndromes. This particular family has findings consistent with a proposed hypothesis of Traub et al. (1977) that the CJD agent may affect only those persons who have some underlying progressive brain process that allows invasion or activation of the infectious agent. Traub et al. (1977) reported two cases diagnosed as familial Alzheimer's disease where transmission to squirrel monkeys caused typical spongiform encephalopathy characteristic of CJD. They suggest, in line with their hypothesis, that Alzheimer's disease and CJD are different diseases but that the CJD agent might infect a brain already damaged by Alzheimer's disease.

In summary, there is considerable evidence that at least a significant portion of cases of CJD are related to a virus-like agent that can be transmitted to other animals. There is suggestive evidence that when this illness is familial it may be due to a slow virus infection superimposed on a preexisting genetically determined dysfunction.

Pick Disease

The clinical symptoms of Pick disease are so similar to Alzheimer's disease that the two are often grouped together as the presenile dementias (Merritt, 1973). There is minimal evidence that the two diseases can be distinguished clinically (Haase, 1971), although pathologically they are quite distinct. A recent report of techniques that evaluate regional cerebral blood flow gives promise that the presenile dementias can be differentiated premorbidly (Gustafson, Brun, Hagberg, Ingvar, & Risberg, 1977). Clinically, the patients with Pick disease have an insidious onset of difficulty with memory, confusion, and defects in judgment. There is a progressive decline with development of severe dementia, neurological defects, and death (Haase, 1971). Pathological findings consist of cerebral atrophy predominantly of the frontal and temporal lobes and microscopic findings include neuronal loss, gliosis, and the distinctive Pick cell, a neuronal cell with a large argyrophilic cytoplasmic inclusion body (Corsellis, 1976).

Schenk (1959) has for several decades followed a family afflicted with Pick disease. Examination of the pedigree, which now includes five generations, indicates that approximately half of the offspring of afflicted persons are similarly afflicted. There is no sex differentiation, thereby suggesting an autosomal dominant mode of inheritance. Pedigrees of two other families (Malamud & Waggoner, 1943) also suggest a dominant mode of inheritance as well as some specificity for the age of onset and the rate of symptomatic progression.

Sjögren, Sjögren, and Lindgren (1952) in an investigation of Swedish patients with presenile dementia found that the morbidity risk for presenile dementia was higher for relatives of patients diagnosed as having Pick disease (19% ± 5% for parents and 6.8% ± 2.9% for siblings) than was the case for relatives of patients with Alzheimer's disease. They concluded that a dominant major gene with modifying genes was the likely mode of inheritance for Pick disease. Marked geographical differences were found in the distribution of specific forms of presenile dementia, and many of the cases of Pick disease originated from the Stockholm area.

Alzheimer's Disease

The clinical picture of Alzheimer's disease is that of a progressive dementia typified by insidious memory defects with progression to aphasia, agnosia, apraxia, neuromuscular disabilities, incontinence, bedfastness, and death (Haase, 1971). There is a marked similarity to the clinical symptoms of Pick disease, although problems of gait disturbance and extrapyramidal symptoms may be more severe in Alzheimer's disease. Traditionally, disease onset has been regarded as beginning in the presenium with an average life span of only a few years after onset of symptoms. Postmortem examinations of the brains of afflicted persons reveal cortical atrophy and typical histopathological findings of senile plaques, neurofibrillary tangles, and granulovacular degeneration (Corsellis, 1976).

Hereditary factors in the disease have been noted in published pedigrees. For example, Lowenberg and Waggoner (1934) described a family where the father and four of five children were affected. Other pedigrees have similarly demonstrated a very high familial incidence (Bucci, 1963; Feldman, Chandler, Levy, & Glaser, 1963; Heston, Lowther, & Leventhal, 1966; Wheelan, 1959). According to these reports, the ratio between affected males and females is equal, and approximately one-half of the children are affected, suggesting an autosomal dominant mode of inheritance. However, there are potential errors of selection in relying on pedigree information alone in evaluating the genetic influence of a disease, because only those pedigrees that are striking may be called to attention.

A detailed systematic study of presenile dementia in Swedish patients was undertaken by Sjögren *et al.* (1952). With the advantage of the detailed hospital and parish records maintained in Sweden, they investigated the families of 80 well-diagnosed cases. For Alzheimer's disease they computed the morbidity risk (Weinberg method) for the presenile dementia in parents to be 10% ± 4% and for siblings to be 3.8% ± 2.1%, compared with .1% in the general population of Sweden. The incidence of other forms of psychosis or mental retardation in the relatives was not elevated compared with expectations for the general population. These investigators concluded that a multifactorial mode of inheritance was probably operative in Alzheimer's disease.

Reviewing family histories from the hospital records of patients with Alzheimer's disease admitted to the Bel Air Clinic of Geneva from 1901 to 1958 Constantinidis, Garrone, and de Ajuriaguerra (1962) found that the incidence of Alzheimer's disease was comparable to the Scandinavian data for siblings (3.3%), but much lower for parents (1.4%); for children it was 1.6%. Moreover, the Geneva group published pedigrees showing both Alzheimer's disease and senile dementia within a single family (Constantinidis, 1968; Constantinidis, Garrone, Tissot, & de Ajuriaguerra, 1965; Constantinidis, Tissot, Richard, & de Ajuriaguerra, 1972) and suggested a genetic relationship between Alzheimer's disease and senile dementia.

Heston and Mastri (1977), who studied the families of 30 well-documented cases of Alzheimer's disease, found the morbidity risk for parents to be 23% ± 7% and for siblings to be 10% ± 3.6%, a much higher frequency than in either of the previously discussed studies. These investigators, who regard Alzheimer's disease and senile dementia (Alzheimer type) as a single pathological entity, used extensive field investigation including review of hospital and autopsy records to establish the diagnoses of the secondary cases. Of major interest was the fact that they also found that the relatives of the probands had a significantly increased morbidity of both Down's syndrome and hematologic malignancies. Related to this finding are the prior reports indicating that if they survive, all patients with Down's syndrome eventually develop histopathological findings typical of Alzheimer's disease (Olson & Shaw, 1969) and that the incidence of leukemia is increased in mongoloid children (Ager, Schuman, Wallace, Rosenfeld, & Gullen, 1965). Because of these two associations, Heston and Mastri suggested that a genetic common factor in Down's syndrome and Alzheimer's disease may be a defect in the spatial organization of the microtubules.

The associations between Down's syndrome and Alzheimer's disease provide new theoretical speculations as to the underlying mechanisms of certain diseases. However, these associated diseases are too rare to have practical use as genetic markers in order to follow families and identify persons at potential risk. Feldman *et al.* (1963) looked for a genetic marker in the family they studied in detail but were unable to find one by analyzing blood groups, fingerprints, and chromosomes. One promising lead comes from the reports by Op den Velde and Stam (1973a,b) that the gene frequency for a specific haptoglobin (Hp^1) is significantly increased in Alzheimer's disease and senile dementia (.70 in Alzheimer's disease and .49 in senile dementia versus .35 in controls). Finally, the work of Crapper, Krisman, and Dalton (1973) indicates that brains of patients with Alzheimer's disease contain increased amounts of aluminum as compared with normal control cases.

In summary, there is impressive evidence for a significant genetic factor in the etiology of Alzheimer's disease. Review of the pedigrees of afflicted families suggests the mode of inheritance to be that of a dominant autosomal gene, which in some families approaches 100% penetrance. There is associated evidence of a relationship to Down's syndrome and leukemia as well as to senile dementia.

SENILE DEMENTIAS

Repeated Infarct Dementia

Prior opinions that dementia in old age is largely secondary to cerebral arteriosclerosis have been revised in recent years. Neuropathological studies indicate that when dementia occurs secondary to vascular disease, it is because the person has experienced multiple infarcts; neither the mere presence of cerebral arteriosclerosis nor a single "stroke" is generally associated with dementia (Hachinski, Lassen, & Marshall, 1974). Because of these findings, the preferred terminology for dementia secondary to cerebrovascular disease is "repeated infarct dementia." However, since previous terminology included terms such as cerebrovascular disease, arteriosclerotic psychosis, and arteriosclerotic organic brain disease, they will be used in this chapter somewhat interchangeably.

Clinical symptoms of repeated infarct dementia include fluctuation in the severity of intellectual disturbance, focal neurological findings, explosive emotional outbursts and, when compared with senile dementia (Alzheimer type), a greater frequency of syncopal attacks and seizures. The presence or absence of peripheral vascular disease in itself is not a differentiating characteristic (Rothschild, 1941). Mortality is high in those patients with arteriosclerotic psychosis who require hospitalization, and over 70% have died 2 years after hospital admission (Roth, 1955).

Despite the fact that repeated infarct dementia may be overdiagnosed, it remains a significant cause of dementia in the aged, particularly in men. Kay, Beamish, and Roth (1964) found the prevalence of arteriosclerotic organ brain syndrome in Newcastle-upon-Tyne for persons over 65 years of age to be 8.7% for men and 1.0% for women, with an overall prevalence rate of 3.9%. Studying a well-defined Swedish elderly population group, Nielsen (1962) found the prevalence rate of cerebrovascular dementia to be 3.22% for men and 2.47% for women, with an overall prevalence rate of 2.86%. In both the English and Swedish studies the prevalence rate for senile dementia (Alzheimer type) was slightly higher than for repeated infarct dementia.

Akesson (1969), in an investigation of a well-delineated Swedish population, found a relatively low prevalence rate of severe arteriosclerotic dementia for both men and women over age 60. He computed the incidence for severe cerebrovascular dementia for both sexes to be .52% ± .11%. However, in calculating the morbidity risk for siblings age 60 or older, he found the risk to be considerably higher than for the general population (5.6% ± 2.4%).

Reviewing 423 case histories of index cases with cerebrovascular disease, Constantinidis et al. (1962) found the morbidity risk for siblings to be 7.3% and the risk for parents to be 3.9%. They concluded that the mode of inheritance was a dominant gene with about 40% penetrance. The morbidity risk for senile dementia for relatives of patients with cerebrovascular disease was quite low, and the converse was also true. Although not studying vascular disease per se, Larsson, Sjögren, and Jacobson (1963) also found the rate of arteriosclerotic psychosis (as diagnosed by a clinical course characterized by marked fluctuations and focal mental or neurological deterioration) in relatives of patients with senile dementia to be lower than expected for the general population.

Further support for genetic influence in the development of cerebrovascular disease comes from the twin study of Jarvik and co-workers (1971), who found that of female twin pairs, monozygotic pairs had higher concordance rates than did dizygotic pairs.

Vascular disease is multidetermined and currently believed to be related to a number of environmental factors as well as to a number of underlying pathological processes that in themselves have genetic components. Included in the latter are diseases such as familial hyperlipidemia (Motulsky, 1976), hypertension (Page, 1976), and diabetes (Rimoin, 1967). It may be very difficult to separate specific factors relating to repeated infarct dementia from these other illnesses, which affect the development of vascular disease in a more general manner, particularly since the primary cause of brain infarction is usually believed to be caused by thromboembolism rather than in situ thrombosis of cerebral blood vessels (Blackwood, Hallpike, Kocen, & Mair, 1969).

Senile Dementia, Alzheimer Type

Strong evidence for hereditary factors in the development of dementia in the senium was accumulated by Kallmann and his colleagues in the twin study (Kallmann, 1950, 1955) that yielded morbidity risks of 3.4% for parents, 6.5% for siblings, 8.0% for dizygotic twins, and 42.8% for monozygotic twins. Diagnostic criteria were not specified, except that senile psychosis was defined as occurring after age 59.

The important paper of Roth (1955) carefully defined five types of psychoses occurring in senescence. One of these, senile psychosis (senile dementia as used here), he defined as a condition with progressive dementia and disorganization of the personality that could not be attributed to specific causes (e.g., infections, cerebrovascular disease). Mortality was exceptionally high, over 80% of patients having died within 2 years after hospitalization. Subsequent publications by neuropathologists indicate that the histopathological findings of the disease are similar, if not identical, to those of Alzheimer's disease (McMenemey, 1963; Tomlinson, Blessed, & Roth, 1970). However, many of the histopathological features also occur in other diseases such as postencephalitic Parkinsonism (Wisniewski, Terry, & Hirano, 1970).

Using Roth's (1955) specific criteria for diagnosis of probands with senile dementia, Larsson *et al.* (1963) studied the relatives of patients hospitalized in Stockholm with that diagnosis. They supplemented their review of hospital records and parish registries with extensive field investigations and determined that the risk for primary relatives to become afflicted with senile dementia was 4.3 times that for the general population of Sweden. For the general Swedish population the aggregate risk for senile dementia was .4% at age 70 rising to 3.8% at age 85. The aggregate morbidity risk for siblings and parents was 1.7% up to age 70 and 16.3% up to age 85. Larsson *et al.* (1963) also found that the risk for arteriosclerotic psychosis in relatives of probands was actually lower than that for the general population (in agreement with the findings of Constantinidis *et al.*, 1962). They reported no cases of Alzheimer's disease in the relatives and interpreted this as an argument against a genetic connection between the two diseases. However, despite the sophisticated statistical analysis of their data, two major criticisms develop from a review of the data.

The first criticism is that although Larsson *et al.* (1963) did not diagnose any secondary cases of Alzheimer's disease, they did report eight cases of "presenile psychosis" among the group of relatives, and the clinical interpretation of at least one of the cases was compatible with Alzheimer's disease. The second criticism is that they also investigated spouses for the presence of senile dementia and found 5 out of 305 so afflicted as compared with 37 out of 1614 siblings. The uncorrected ratio between siblings and spouses is approximately 1.4:1. This figure appears inconsequential when compared to their calculation indicating that primary relatives of persons with senile dementia have a risk of developing the disease 4.3 times greater than for persons in the general population. The extensive work done by Larsson *et al.* (1963) is frequently quoted and deserves careful and critical review by persons seriously interested in the area of genetic research of senile dementia.

Constantinidis *et al.* (1962), in a nonfield investigation of patients from Bel Air Clinic, Geneva, found the morbidity risk of senile dementia in siblings of index cases to be 6.4% (very similar to Kallmann's 6.0%) and in parents, 7.0% (considerably higher than Kallmann's 3.4%). They noted that the morbidity risk for senile dementia was 7.0% in the parents of patients with Alzheimer's disease and 5.2% in the siblings of patients with Alzheimer's disease. Subsequent communications from this group (Constantinidis, 1968; Constantinidis *et al.*, 1965; Constantinidis *et al.*, 1972) have continued to emphasize the relationship between senile dementia and Alzheimer's disease. They have published several pedigrees showing Alzheimer's disease and senile dementia in the same family. In two families where senile dementia or Alzheimer's disease was found in two successive generations, the dementia began at an earlier age in the second generation and had a more severe course (Constantinidis *et al.*, 1972). They have concluded that there is probably one gene acting to cause both Alzheimer's disease and the "Alzheimerized" form of senile dementia, its expression being modified by inhibitory or facilitating genes.

In a different type of study, Akesson (1969) studied the entire population in a well-defined area of islands off the west coast of Sweden. He made an attempt to identify every single case of severe dementia in a population of 17,303, of which almost one-quarter was over 60 years of age. Incidence and prevalence rates were suprisingly low but showed a marked familial distribution. For senile psychosis, the morbidity risk of similar disease for siblings was 18.4% ± 3.5%, much higher than in any of the previously cited studies. Akesson noted that no subjects were the product of first cousin marriages so that obviously consanguinity could not account for this high morbidity figure. Perhaps the high morbidity risk is related to the fact that only cases of severe dementia were included in the study.

The works reviewed in this section offer strong evidence for a familial incidence of senile dementia but fail to clearly establish a genetic etiology. The only slightly increased risk of siblings as compared with spouses in the Stockholm study would argue for environmental factors, whereas other family studies argue in favor of genetic components. Albert (1968) has argued for exogenous influences in senile dementia and has suggested that what may be inherited is a "special cerebral sensitivity." A recent report from Yugoslavia suggests a relationship between cerebral atrophy and cellular immunological response (Janković, Jakulić, & Horvat, 1977). These investigators found that 60% of their patients had a delayed skin hypersensitivity reaction to human brain protein as opposed to a 2.5% response rate with normal controls and a 35% rate with schizophrenics.

Another area of research that holds considerable promise in elucidating basic pathophysiological processes in dementia is the study of brain enzymes. The work of McGeer and McGeer (1976) has indicated that not only do some of the enzymes associated with neurotransmitters vary quantitatively with age, but there is also a marked variation of such changes in different areas of the brain (e.g., a loss of choline acetyltransferase with age, particularly in the cortex).

Of the major difficulties that complicate genetic research in senile dementia the most obvious is that of diagnostic accuracy. There are multiple syndromes that may be labeled as "senile dementia" (Bergman, 1975), and it is probable that they have different genotypic substrates. In addition, the question of the genetic relationship between Alzheimer's disease and senile dementia continues to be unanswered. Heston and Mastri (1977) believe them to be the same disease and treat their data as such, whereas the most quoted work (Larsson *et al.*, 1963) found no such relationship. Merely choosing an arbitrary age of onset to make the diagnosis is unsatisfactory, for two diseases would very likely have overlapping ages of onset. Sjögren *et al.* (1952) in their work on Alzheimer's disease described patients diagnosed as having Alzheimer's disease with an age of onset over 70 years, whereas Larsson *et al.* (1963) describe patients diagnosed as having senile dementia with onset below age 60! If genetic differences between these two groups do exist, then certainly they must be blurred by indistinct diagnostic criteria.

DIRECTIONS FOR FUTURE RESEARCH

The major advancement of knowledge that at least one, albeit rare, disease of chronic progressive dementia is related to a slow virus places new emphasis on the long-standing concept that the phenotype is determined by both the genotype and environmental factors. The view that diseases influenced by genetic factors are predetermined and thereby unmodifiable is not justified, particularly in the aged. The elderly have survived for many years with whatever genetic predisposition to disease they were born with and, therefore, have had a long-term exposure to both noxious and beneficial environmental factors.

Research must continue to explore the genetic relationships of diseases in senescence with special attention to refinement of diagnosis. This is necessary to clarify more exact genetic risks for the diseases in question as well as to assist in identifying those specific persons at risk in order that therapeutic interventions, when possible, can be made. There needs to be an awareness that the development of a disease may depend upon exposure to certain environmental factors and possibly even co-factors. Expressed as an equation this would be as follows: genetic predisposition + specific noxious environmental factors (+ possible co-factors) = disease expression.

One specific area that requires more attention is that of the relationship of Alzheimer's disease to senile dementia. It would be useful to establish a new case control study for patients with progressive dementia of the Alzheimer type. Family investigations should include not only relatives, but also spouses, because a spouse of many years has shared many environmental factors for that period. Families should be investigated using rigorously defined criteria for diagnosis and field investigated wherever possible. Simultaneously there needs to be an investigation of the subjects to determine the presence of unique patterns in serum proteins, chromosome abnormalities, etc. Identification of a genetic marker(s) would be of major assistance in determining relatives at risk.

With the Alzheimer type of dementia it would be of use to construct a study that would specifically compare the two ends of the spectrum with regard to age of onset (Ostfeld, 1972). This would reduce the error caused by placing index cases into the wrong diagnostic group if, indeed, Alzheimer's disease and senile dementia are two separate entities. Twin family and adoption studies are of potential value in the investigation of diseases where environmental and hereditary influences are being considered. Because this issue is especially important in studying the elderly, it would seem valuable to reestablish longitudinal investigations that would allow for the comparison of various categories of genetic and environmental relationships in diseases of later life.

REFERENCES

Ager, E. A., Schuman, L. M., Wallace, H. M., Rosenfeld, A. B., & Gullen, W. H. An epidemiological study of childhood leukemia. *Journal of Chronic Diseases*, 1965, *18*, 113–132.

Akesson, H. O. A population study of senile and arteriosclerotic psychoses. *Human Heredity*, 1969, *19*, 545–566.

Albert, E. Discussion contribution to "epidemiology and genetics of senile dementia." In C. Müller & L. Ciompi (Eds.), *Senile dementia*. Bern, Switzerland: Hans Huber, 1968. Pp. 65–68.

Angst, J., & Perris, C. The nosology of endogenous depression: Comparison of the results of two studies. *International Journal of Mental Health*, 1972, *1*, 145–158.

Barclay, D. S., Hardiwijaja, S., & Menkes, J. H. Huntington's disease: Delayed hypersensitivity in vitro to human central nervous system antigens. *Science*, 1977, *195*, 314–316.

Bergman, K. The epidemiology of senile dementia. *British Journal of Psychiatry*, 1975, *9*, 100–109.

Blackwood, W., Hallpike, J. F., Kocen, R. S., & Mair, W. P. Atheromatous disease of the carotid arterial system and embolism from the heart in cerebral infarction: A morbid anatomical study. *Brain*, 1969, *92*, 897–910.

Bobowick, A. R., Brody, J. A., Matthews, M. R., Roos, R., & Gajdusek, D. C. Creutzfeldt-Jakob disease: A case control study. *American Journal of Epidemiology*, 1973, *98*, 381–393.

Bonduelle, M., Escourolle, R., Bouygues, P., Lormeau, G., Ribadeau-Dumas, J. L., & Merland, J. J. Maladie de Creutzfeldt-Jakob familiale, observation anatomoclinique. *Revue Neurologique*, 1971, *125*, 197–209.

Bucci, L. A familial organic psychosis of Alzheimer type in six kinship of three generations. *American Journal of Psychiatry*, 1963, *119*, 863–866.

Chandler, J. H., Reed, T. E., & De Jong, R. N. Huntington's chorea in Michigan. *Neurology*, 1960, *10*, 148–153.

Cohen, D., Matsuyama, S. S., & Jarvik, L. F. Immunoglobulin levels and intellectual functioning in the aged. *Experimental Aging Research*, 1976, *2*, 345–348.

Constantinidis, J. The familial incidence of degenerative cerebral lesions, histologic substrate of senile dementia. In C. Müller & L. Ciompi (Eds.), *Senile dementia*. Bern, Switzerland: Hans Huber, 1968. Pp. 62–64.

Constantinidis, J., Garrone, G., & de Ajuriaguerra, J. L'hérédité des démences de l'age avancé. *Encéphale*, 1962, *51*, 301–344.

Constantinidis, J., Garrone, G., Tissot, R., & de Ajuriaguerra, J. L'Incidence familiale des altérations neurofibrillaires corticales d'Alzheimer. *Psychiatria et Neurologia* (Basel), *150*, 235–247.

Constantinidis, J., Tissot, R., Richard, S., & de Ajuriaguerra, J. Le role de l'hérédité dans le développement de la démence présenile d'Alzheimer et la démence sénile Alzheimeirsée (à propos de 9 observations familiales). In C. Perez de Francisco (Ed.), *Dimensiones de al psiquiatria contemporanea.* Mexico: Editorial Fournier, 1972.

Corsellis, J. A. N. Aging and the dementias. In W. Blackwood & J. A. N. Corsellis (Eds.), *Greenfield's neuropathology.* London: Edward Arnold, 1976. Pp. 796–848.

Crapper, D. R., Krisman, S. S., & Dalton, A. J. Brain aluminum distribution in Alzheimer's disease and experimental neurofibrillary degeneration. *Science,* 1973, *180,* 511–513.

Eysenck, H. J., & Prell, D. B. The inheritance of neuroticism: An experimental study. *Journal of Mental Science,* 1951, *97,* 441–465.

Feldman, R. G., Chandler, K. A., Levy, L. L., & Glaser, G. H. Familial Alzheimer's disease. *Neurology,* 1963, *13,* 811–824.

Ferber, R. A., Weisenfeld, S. L., Roos, R. P., Bobowick, A. R., Gibbs, C. J., & Gajdusek, D. C. Familial Creutzfeldt-Jakob disease: Transmission of the familial disease to primates. In A. Subriana, J. M. Espadaler, & E. H. Burrows (Eds.), *Proceedings of the 10th International Congress of Neurology, Barcelona.* Amsterdam: Excerpta Medica International Congress Series, 1974. Pp. 358–380.

Funding, T. Genetics of paranoid psychoses in later life. *Acta Psychiatrica Scandinavica,* 1961, *37,* 267–282.

Gajdusek, D. C. Unconventional viruses and the origin and disappearance of Kuru. *Science,* 1977, *197,* 943–960.

Gershon, E. S., Dunner, D. L., & Goodwin, F. K. Toward a biology of affective disorders: Genetic contributions. *Archives of General Psychiatry,* 1971, *25,* 1–15.

Gibbs, C. J., Gajdusek, D. C., Asher, D. M., Alpers, M. P., Beck, E., Daniel, P. M., & Matthews, W. B. Creutzfeldt-Jakob disease (spongiform encephalopathy) transmission to the chimpanzee. *Science,* 1968, *161,* 388–389.

Gustafson, L., Brun, A., Hagberg, B., Ingvar, D. H., & Risberg, J. Presenile dementia: A prospective, clinical neurophysiological and neuropathological investigation. *Abstracts, VI World Congress of Psychiatry, Honolulu,* August 28–September 3, 1977, p. 79.

Haase, G. R. Diseases presenting as dementia. In C. E. Wells (Ed.), *Dementia.* Philadelphia: Dairs, 1971. Pp. 163–207.

Hachinski, V. C., Lassen, N. A., & Marshall, J. Multi-infarct dementia: A cause of mental deterioration in the elderly. *Lancet,* 1974, *2,* 207–210.

Heathfield, K. W. G. Huntington's chorea: Investigation into the prevalence of this disease in the area covered by the Northeast Metropolitan Regional Hospital Board. *Brain,* 1967, *90,* 203–232.

Heathfield, K. W. G. Huntington's chorea: A centenary review. *Postgraduate Medical Journal,* 1973, *49,* 32–45.

Heathfield, K, W. G., & MacKenzie, I. C. K. Huntington's chorea in Bedfordshire, England. *Guy's Hospital, London, Reports,* 1971, *120,* 295–309.

Heston, L. L., Lowther, D. L. W., & Leventhal, C. M. Alzheimer's disease: A family study. *Archives of Neurology,* 1966, *15,* 225–233.

Heston, L. L., & Mastri, A. R. The genetics of Alzheimer's disease: Associations with hematologic malignancy and Down's syndrome. *Archives of General Psychiatry,* 1977, *34,* 976–981.

Hopkinson, G. A genetic study of affective illness in patients over 50. *British Journal of Psychiatry,* 1964, *110,* 244–254.

Hopkinson, G., & Ley, P. A genetic study of affective disorder. *British Journal of Psychiatry,* 1969, *115,* 917–922.

Husby, G., Li, L., Davis, L. E., Wedege, E., Kokmen, E., & Williams, R. C. Antibodies to human caudate nucleus neurons in Huntington's chorea. *Journal of Clinical Investigation*, 1977, *59*, 922–932.

Janković, B. D., Jakulić, S., & Horvat, J. Cerebral atrophy: An immunological disorder? *Lancet II*, July 30, 1977, pp. 219–220.

Jarvik, L. F. Chromosome changes and aging. In R. Kasterbaum (Ed.), *Contributions to the psychobiology of aging*. New York: Springer, 1965. Pp. 87–98.

Jarvik, L. F. Memory loss and its possible relationship to chromosome changes. In C. Eisdorfer (Ed.), *Psychopharmacology and aging*. New York: Plenum Press, 1973. Pp. 145–150.

Jarvik, L. F., Altshuler, K. Z., Kato, T., & Blumner, B. Organic brain syndrome and chromosome loss in aged twins. *Diseases of the Nervous System*, 1971, *32*, 159–170.

Jarvik, L. F., & Blum, J. E. Cognitive decline as predictors of mortality in twin pairs: A twenty-year longitudinal study of aging. In E. Palmore & F. C. Jeffers (Eds.), *Prediction of life span*. Lexington, Massachusetts: Heath Lexington, 1971. Pp. 199–211.

Jarvik, L. F., Blum, J. E., & Varma, A. O. Genetic components and intellectual functioning during senescence: A 20-year study of aging twins. *Behavioral Genetics*, 1972, *2*, 159–171.

Jarvik, L. F., & Falek, A. Intellectual stability and survival in the aged. *Journal of Gerontology*, 1963, *18*, 173–176.

Jarvik, L. F., Kallmann, F. J., & Falek, A. Intellectual changes in aged twins. *Journal of Gerontology*, 1962, *17*, 289–294.

Jarvik, L. F., & Kato, T. Chromosomes and mental changes in octogenarians (preliminary findings). *British Journal of Psychiatry*, 1969, *115*, 1193–1194.

Jarvik, L. F., & Kato, T. Chromosome examinations in aged twins. *American Journal of Human Genetics*, 1970, *22*, 562–573.

Jarvik, L. F., Yen, F. S., Fu, T. K., & Matsuyama, S. S. Chromosomes in old age: A six-year longitudinal study. *Human Genetics*, 1976, *33*, 17–22.

Kallmann, F. J. The genetic theory of schizophrenia. *American Journal of Psychiatry*, 1946, *103*, 309–322.

Kallmann, F. J. The genetics of psychoses: An analysis of 1232 twin index families. *Congrès International de Psychiatrie, Rapports* (Vol. 6) Paris: Herman, 1950. Pp. 1–27.

Kallmann, F. J. Genetic aspects of mental disorders in later life. In O. J. Kaplan (Ed.), *Mental disorders in later life* (2nd ed.). Stanford, California: Stanford University Press, 1955. Pp. 26–46.

Kallmann, F. J., Feingold, L., & Bondy, E. Comparative adaptational, social, and psychometric data on the life histories of senescent twin pairs. *American Journal of Human Genetics*, 1951, *3*, 65–73.

Kallmann, F. J., & Sander, G. Twin studies on aging and longevity. *Journal of Heredity*, 1948, *39*, 349–357.

Kallmann, F. J., & Sander, G. Twin studies on senescence. *American Journal of Psychiatry*, 1949, *106*, 29–36.

Kay, D. Observations on the natural history and genetics of old age psychoses: A Stockholm material 1931–1937. *Procedures of the Royal Society of Medicine*, 1959, *52*, 791–794.

Kay, D. W. K., Beamish, P., & Roth, M. Old age mental disorders in Newcastle-upon-Tyne, Part I: A study of prevalence. *British Journal of Psychiatry*, 1964, *110*, 146–158.

Kay, D., & Roth, M. Environmental and hereditary factors in the schizophrenias of old age (late paraphrenia) and their bearing on the general problem of causation in schizophrenia. *Journal of Mental Science*, 1961, *107*, 649–676.

Kety, S. S., Rosenthal, D., Wender, P. H., Schulsinger, F., & Jacobsen, B. Mental illness in the biological and adoptive families of adopted individuals who have become schizophrenic. *Behavior Genetics,* 1976, *6,* 219–225.

Larsson, T., Sjögren, T., & Jacobson, G. Senile dementia: A clinical sociomedical and genetic study. *Acta Psychiatrica Scandinavica* (Suppl. 167), 1963, *39,* 1–259.

Liston, E. H., & Jarvik, L. F. The genetics of schizophrenia. In M. A. Sperber & L. F. Jarvik (Eds.), *Psychiatry and genetics.* New York: Basic Books, 1976. Pp. 76–94.

Lowenberg, K., & Waggoner, R. W. Familial organic psychosis (Alzheimer's type). *Archives of Neurology and Psychiatry,* 1934, *31,* 737–767.

Malamud, N., & Waggoner, R. W. Genealogic and clinicopathologic study of Pick's disease. *Archives of Neurology and Psychiatry,* 1943, *50,* 288–303.

Matsuyama, S. S., Cohen, D., & Jarvik, L. F. Hypodiploidy and serum immunoglobulin concentrations in the elderly. *Mechanisms of Aging and Development* 1978, *8,* 407–412.

Matthews, W. B. Epidemiology of Creutzfeldt-Jakob disease in England and Wales. *Journal of Neurology, Neurosurgery and Psychiatry,* 1975, *38,* 210–213.

May, W. W. Creutzfeldt-Jakob disease: 1. Survey of the literature and clinical diagnosis. *Acta Neurologica Scandinavica,* 1968, *44,* 1–32.

May, W. W., Itabashi, H. H., & De Jong, R. N. Creutzfeldt-Jakob disease: II. Clinical pathologic and genetic study of a family. *Archives of Neurology,* 1968, *19,* 137–149.

Mayer, V., Orolin, D., & Mitrova, E. Cluster of Creutzfeldt-Jakob disease and presenile dementia. *Lancet II,* 1977, 256.

McGeer, E., & McGeer, P. L. Neurotransmitter metabolism in the aging brain. In R. D. Terry & S. Gershon (Eds.), *Neurobiology of aging.* New York: Raven Press, 1976. Pp. 389–403.

McHugh, P. R., & Folstein, M. F. Psychiatric syndrome of Huntington's chorea: A clinical and phenomenologic study. In D. F. Benson & D. Blumer (Eds.), *Psychiatric aspects of neurologic disease.* New York: Grune & Stratton, 1975. Pp. 267–285.

McMenemey, W. H. The dementias and progressive diseases of the basal ganglia. In W. Blackwood, W. H. McMenemey, A. Meyer, R. M. Norman, & D. S. Russell (Eds.), *Greenfield's neuropathology.* London: Edward Arnold, 1963. Pp. 520–576.

Mendlewicz, J., & Rainer, J. D. Adoption study supporting genetic transmission in manic-depressive illness. *Nature,* 1977, *268,* 327–329.

Merritt, H. H. *A textbook of neurology* (5th ed.). Philadelphia: Lea and Febiger, 1973. Pp. 442–445.

Miner, G. D. The evidence for genetic components in the neuroses: A review. *Archives of General Psychiatry,* 1973, *29,* 111–118.

Motulsky, A. G. Current concepts in genetics: The genetic hyperlipidemias. *New England Journal of Medicine,* 1976, *294,* 823–827.

Myrianthopoulos, N. C. Huntington's chorea: Review article. *Journal of Medical Genetics,* 1966, *3,* 298–314.

Nielsen, J. Geronto–psychiatric period—prevalence investigation in a geographically delineated population. *Acta Psychiatrica Scandinavica,* 1962, *38,* 307–330.

Nielsen, J. Chromosomes in senile dementia. In C. Müller & L. Ciompi (Eds.), *Senile dementia.* Bern, Switzerland: Hans Huber, 1968. Pp. 59–62.

Olson, M. I., & Shaw, C. M. Presenile dementia and Alzheimer's disease in mongolism. *Brain,* 1969, *92,* 147–156.

Op den Velde, W., & Stam, F. C. Haptoglobin types in Alzheimer's disease and senile dementia. *British Journal of Psychiatry,* 1973, *122,* 331–336. (a)

Op den Velde, W., & Stam, F. C. Haptoglobin types and subtypes in Alzheimer's disease and senile dementia. *Humangenetik,* 1973, *20,* 25–30. (b)

Ostfeld, A. M. The aging brain, Alzheimer's disease and senile dementia—discussants perspective. In A. M. Ostfeld & D. C. Gibson (Eds.), *Epidemiology of aging.* Washington, D. C.: U.S. Government Printing Office, 1972. Pp. 129–135.

Page, L. B. Epidemiologic evidence on the etiology of human hypertension and its possible prevention. *American Heart Journal,* 1976, *91,* 527–534.

Reed, T. E., & Chandler, J. H. Huntington's chorea in Michigan: Demography and genetics. *American Journal of Human Genetics,* 1958, *10,* 201–225.

Rimoin, D. L. The genetics of diabetes mellitus. *Diabetes,* 1967, *16,* 346–351.

Roseman, J. M., & Buckley, C. E. Inverse relationship between serum IgG concentrations and measures of intelligence in elderly persons. *Nature,* 1975, *254,* 55–56.

Rosenthal, D. *Genetic theory and abnormal behavior.* New York: McGraw-Hill, 1970, Pp. 38–42.

Rosenthal, N. P., Keesey, J., Crandall, B., & Brown, W. J. Familial neurological disease associated with spongiform encephalopathy. *Archives of Neurology,* 1976, *33,* 252–259.

Roth, M. The natural history of mental disorder in old age. *Journal of Mental Science,* 1955, *101,* 281–301.

Roth, M. The phenomenology of depressive states. *Canadian Psychiatric Association Journal,* 1959, *4* (special supplement), S32–S53.

Rothschild, D. The clinical differentiation of senile and arteriosclerotic psychoses. *American Journal of Psychiatry,* 1941, *98,* 324–333.

Schenk, V. W. D. Reexamination of a family with Pick's disease. *Annals of Human Genetics,* 1959, *23,* 325–333.

Siedler, H., & Malamud, N. Creutzfeldt-Jakob disease: Clinicopathologic report of 15 cases and review of the literature (with special reference to 9 related disorders designated as subacute spongiform encephalopathy). *Journal of Neuropathology and Experimental Neurology,* 1963, *22,* 381–402.

Sjögren, H. Paraphrenic, melancholic and psychoneurotic states in the presenile–senile period of life. *Acta Psychiatrica Scandinavica* (supplement), 1964, *176,* 1–63.

Sjögren, T., Sjogren, H., & Lindgren, A. G. H. Morbus Alzheimer and Morbus Pick. *Acta Psychiatrica et Neurologica Scandinavica* (supplement), 1952, *82,* 1–152.

Slater, E. *Psychotic and neurotic illness in twins.* Medical Research Council Special Report Series, Number 278. London: Her Majesty's Stationery Office, 1953.

Stenstedt, A. Involutional melancholia: An etiologic, clinical and social study of endogenous depression in later life, with special reference to genetic factors. *Acta Psychiatrica et Neurologica Scandinavica* (supplement), 1959, *127,* 1–71.

Strachon, R. W., & Henderson, J. G. Dementia and folate deficiency. *Quarterly Journal of Medicine,* 1967, *36,* 189–204.

Tomlinson, B. E., Blessed, G., & Roth, M. Observations on the brains of demented old people. *Journal of the Neurological Sciences,* 1970, *11,* 205–242.

Traub, R., Gajdusek, D. C., & Gibbs, C. J. Transmissable virus dementia: The relation of transmissable spongiform encephalopathy to Creutzfeldt-Jakob disease. In W. L. Smith & M. Kinsbourne (Eds.), *Aging and dementia.* New York: Spectrum, 1977. Pp. 91–146.

Van Putten, T., & Menkes, J. H. Huntington's disease masquerading as chronic schizophrenia. *Diseases of the Nervous System,* 1973, *34,* 54–56.

Wheelan, L. Familial Alzheimer's disease. *Annals of Human Genetics,* 1959, *23,* 300–310.

Whittier, J. E. Research on Huntington's chorea: Problems of privilege and confidentiality. *Journal of Forensic Science,* 1963, *8,* 568–575.

Winokur, G., Cadoret, R., Dorzab, J., & Baker, M. Depressive disease: A genetic study. *Archives of General Psychiatry,* 1971, *24,* 135–144.

Wisniewski, H., Terry, R. D., & Hirano, A. Neurofibrillary pathology. *Journal of Neuropathology and Experimental Neurology*, 1970, *29*, 163–176.

Woodruff, R., Pitts, F. N., & Winokur, G. Affective disorder: II. A comparison of patients with endogenous depressions with and without family history of affective disorder. *Journal of Nervous and Mental Disorders*, 1964, *139*, 49–52.

Chapter 3

ACUTE, REVERSIBLE, PSYCHOTIC REACTIONS IN GERIATRIC PATIENTS

Ivan N. Mensh

INTRODUCTION

As noted in Chapter 7 on schizophrenia, Fann, Wheless, and Richman (1976) have stated that "Psychoses other than those associated with senility or arteriosclerosis are seldom diagnosed in patients over 65 years of age." Further, Redick, Kramer, and Taube (1973) reported for 1969 that resident patients 65 years and older, in state and county mental hospitals, private mental hospitals, and Veterans Administration hospitals, diagnosed either as schizophrenic or with organic brain disorder, comprised 78%, 58% and 88% of the total numbers of patients, respectively. Against the background of these huge proportions and those older patients diagnosed as suffering from affective or depressive disorders, the numbers of acute, psychotic patients seem relatively small. However, the latter group, because of the acute nature of their illness, infrequently appear among the patient populations cited here. Restricting the focus still further to those patients whose subsequent histories reflect the reversible character of their acute psychotic reactions, their identification and their numbers are not easily specified. For example, this focus excludes the "agitated, delusional hallucinating (patient with) . . . the symptomatic intensity of a core psychotic process" (schizophrenia occuring late in life) characterized by Fann *et al.* (1976).

Janzarik (1963) observed that "Again and again we can observe psychoses resulting from intoxications, encephalitises, and other or-

35

ganic illnesses which cannot be distinguished from schizophrenia. With old age, these diagnostic difficulties increase." Fann *et al.* (1976) caution use of the phenothiazines: "Because geriatric patients have a special susceptibility to phenothiazine-induced states of confusion and delirium, these states can be mistaken . . . for an increase in the intensity of psychiatric symptoms; as a result, the physician might increase the dosage of the offending agent."

Simon and Neal's report (1963) of an early phase of the San Francisco General Hospital receiving wards, for over 530 patients admitted who were 60 or older and had no previous psychiatric hospitalization (235 other patients in this age range who were admitted in the 1959–1962 study period were excluded because of previous hospitalization for psychiatric disorder), showed 55% with acute brain syndrome. Thus, because of the nature of acute illness, the general hospital, perhaps after evaluation in office practice in the community, will be the principal site where acute, reversible, psychotic reactions are seen, evaluated, and treated. Yet, there is the occasional report of acute reactions in patients brought to psychiatric hospitals. For example, Vorsamis, Zuchowski, and Maini (1972) did a 6-year followup study of 130 patients, 65 years or older, admitted to a 60-bed acute treatment unit. Arteriosclerosis and related diseases accounted for 58%, schizophrenia and affective psychoses for 30.5%, and "acute confusions" 11.5% of the admissions. The followup indicated a survival rate of 50–60% for the schizophrenic and affective psychoses, but less than 10% for the other patients.

Kral (1973) reviewed some of his experience in a long-term followup of 1200 residents and patients in a home and hospital for the aged, mental hospital, and comprehensive geriatric clinic. His findings demonstrated the numerical and practical importance of confusional states, confirming Roth's observations based on hospitalized patients and complementing Roth's finding that, among nonhospitalized old people, neurotic conditions are the most frequent. Kral's study indicated only about 30% of the admissions to mental hospitals were for senile and arteriosclerotic dementia, even in the highly selected sample entering the mental hospital, while the "functional psychoses, particularly endogenous depression, form a considerable proportion of the mental disorders of the aged."

PHYSICAL ILLNESS AND ACUTE PSYCHOLOGICAL STATES

Dunn and Arie (1973) are typical of the investigators who remark on the role of physical illness in acute psychological states. Even with a history of "chronic delusional states without progressive dementia, usually paranoid . . . common in old people" it is only with the occurrence of a severe physical illness that "the delusional state may become more severe or come to the notice of the doctor for the first time." Dunn and Arie recommend phenothiazines to relieve the persecutory states, but the caution cited by Janzarik (1963) should be observed.

Kay, Bergmann, Foster, McKechnie, and Roth (1970), beginning in 1960, followed nearly 300 elderly, 65 and older, living at home, and a second sample, beginning in 1964, of over 460 community-living elderly. The followup revealed functional syndromes "of at least moderate severity" in 12%, most of whom were diagnosed affective disorders or neuroses. "Unlike patients with chronic brain disorder, the [patients with] functional syndromes did not show markedly different patterns of hospital usage from normal subjects." Dunn and Arie (1973) note, however, that "Even when there is no obvious mental impairment the aged brain tends to have less 'reserve,' that it is much more readily upset than the younger brain by drugs or illness." And Verwoerdt observes (1976) that "Psychotic reactions commonly seen with chronic brain syndrome are paranoid states and depressions, with or without agitation."

Krakowski and Langlais (1974) see "organic etiological factors" as the principal variables in "precipitating acute psychiatric emergencies." As expected, the range is wide—metabolic and endocrine, general and systemic, and nutritional disorders, as well as psychotropic and other drugs. They agree with Kral (cited earlier) that "chronic deteriorative processes ending in senile dementia or psychosis associated with cerebral arteriosclerosis . . . are less frequent than previously estimated." What is the extent of acute, reversible, psychiatric reactions is not known, however, as indicated by Post (1973) and Bergmann (1971), in spite of a number of surveys of elderly people living in their own homes, in several countries. The following data suggest the following "approximate" percentages:

Acute organic psychoses	Not known
Chronic organic psychoses	3–6%
"Early or dubious" organic psychoses	5–10%
Affective psychoses	1–3%
"Late" schizophrenia	.5–1%
Character disorders and neuroses	12–20+%

Post specifies further that "when broken down by age groups (past age 60 or 65), the incidence of organic psychoses increases considerably during the eighth and ninth decades, while functional psychiatric conditions are recognized increasingly rarely."

Although Beck (1967) has concentrated his studies on depression, his wide experience is also significant for the present discussion. He reviews "conditions that specifically impair the normal functioning of the nervous system . . . [acute brain syndromes] such as those associated with alcohol, drugs, head trauma, or post-ictal states [following a stroke or seizure]. . . . Depression [is] a manifestation of the physiological disturbance created by structural disease or toxic agents . . . [or] a psychological reaction to being acutely or choronically ill. . . ."

The most comprehensive manual is, of course, the *Diagnostic and Statistical Manual of Mental Disorders* (American Psychiatric Association, 1968). In Section II, Organic Brain Syndromes, acute disorders are defined as reversible, whereas chronic disorders are defined as permanent. The acute brain syndromes may be associated with the following: acute alcohol intoxication; pathologic intoxication ("acute brain syndrome of psychotic proportion after a small intake of alcohol"); acute conditions caused by infections, including meningitis and brain abscess; psychosis with cerebrovascular circulatory disturbance, other than cerebral arteriosclerosis; cerebral thrombosis or embolism; arterial hypertension; cardiac and cardiorenal disease; primary and metastic neoplasms; posttraumatic conditions, following severe head injury or brain surgery; endocrine, metabolic, and nutritional disorders; systemic infection, pneumonia, acute fever, typhoid fever, malaria; drugs, hormones, gases, heavy metals, and other intoxicants.

An elaboration of some of these conditions appears in Freedman, Kaplan, and Sadock (1973). These writers discuss, for example, acute brain syndrome in association with excessive alcohol intake, poor nutrition (often a concomitant of alcoholism and of the later years), and a physical illness. Prognosis is good, Freedman *et al.*. suggest, for the acute periods and for discharge from hospital, but "many have repeated hospital admissions until the development of [a] chronic brain syndrome makes long-term care necessary."

Nobbs (1973) warns, however, that "Misplacement of physically ill patients in mental hospitals produces mortality nearly three times that of correctly placed psychiatric cases. The mortality of misplaced psychiatry cases in geriatric units is more than twice that of the correctly placed medical cases. Among survivors, misplaced patients were less often discharged than properly placed patients." Mensh (1959) earlier had investigated the problem of confounding mental illness with physical illness among elderly patients.

With this caution in mind we can turn to Agate's (1970) urging that "The recognition of mental change as part of the picture of physical diseases has an importance which cannot be overstated. As a sign of acute physical illness in old age, mental change is more significant than a rise of temperature or pulse rate, and often it gives useful warning of a more insidious disease." He further states that a sudden change in mental state should be assumed to be related to a physical cause, even with such symptoms as clouding of consciousness, disorientation and misinterpretation of both internal and external stimuli, hallucination or delusion, rambling speech, restlessness and wakefulness, "noisily irrational" behavior, and either resistance to aid offered or pleas for help where there is no apparent need. Agate (1970) observed that acute infections, both minor and major, may produce profound mental disturbance and that drugs may add to the very disturbance for which they are prescribed. Further, since the rationale for treating a confusional episode is the treatment of the disease believed to be associated with the symptoms, the sedative effects and depressive response of the patient may do more harm than good.

Agate's concern with acute confusional episodes among elderly patients arises because these often are "attributed loosely to 'toxic-infective' causes, when other causes are clearly of equal importance, notably cerebral ischaemia and ionic imbalance in conditions of disturbed water and salt metabolism." Confusion also may follow anesthesia or major surgery, even minor surgery, and has been reported, Agate notes, following simple cataract extraction. Evaluating the mental state is significant in the course of the patient's illness because "the mortality amongst old people admitted to hospital with physical disease ushered in by a mental change is one-half as high again as it is for those who are admitted in a state of mental clarity." Complicating the picture, however, are the observations that, on occasion, the acute confusion appears after the peak of the precipitating illness has passed; for those patients who do survive but are not among the majority who appear to "recover their mental balance completely," there may be severe cerebral damage or "the acute confusional episode was in reality a sign of senile or arteriosclerotic dementia with an unusual onset"; and, Agate (1970) continues, "Even when the many organic possibilities are considered and excluded, a proportion of acute delirious and confusional states go unexplained."

Hamilton and Cowdry (1976) also associate acute brain syndrome with a rapid onset of impairment of consciousness, or impairment developing at the time of a physical illness or in conjunction with medication, alcohol intake, or changes in nutrition, hydration, or other metabolic function, where the physical state of the patient may involve toxemia or circulatory changes. Their experience leads them to conclude that "The toxic basis for a brain syndrome is often a drug or a combination of drugs . . . sedatives for nervous tension, hypnotics for sleep, phenothiazines for tranquility, and anti-depressants for depression . . . antihistamines, reserpine, and antihypertensives. . . . Bromides . . . still are used and abused."

Although Hamilton and Cowdry (1976) also note the frequency of confusion, drowsiness in daytime, and restlessness at night, they find the presence of hallucinations only on occasion but emphasize the frequent occurrence of fluctuating symptoms, alternating periods of lucidity and confusion and disorientation. A patient's awareness of an abnormal state may be followed by fear and anxiety. These authors highlight the difficulties in understanding acute brain syndrome because of the wide variety of medical conditions which may not be immediately apparent at the time of the physical examination. These conditions may include respiratory, circulatory, inflammatory or other infections, or neoplasms.

The significance of rapid onset in diagnosing acute brain syndrome is for Butler (1971) much less important than the reversibility of the changes. He notes that, in England, the syndrome is recognized much more often than in the United States. For example, in a study of patients in "a major municipal hospital, 13% . . . had acute brain syndromes and 33% had mixed acute and chronic disorders." The importance of the discrimination between acute and chronic brain syndromes lies in the disposition of the patient. "If a reversible brain syndrome is assumed to be a chronic brain disorder, the older person is apt to be transferred to the nursing home or mental hospital without active treatment and without hope of discharge."

Butler (1971) agrees with Hamilton and Cowdry (1976) on the significance of a "fluctuating state of awareness, from stupor to acute delirium," but Butler reports that hallucinations are not uncommon, "especially visual rather than auditory, and with evidence of misidentification [of persons] . . . as [a] son . . . [or] brother." He emphasizes that the first clue to the acute disorder may be in psychiatric symptoms, in connection with or following "febrile, debilitating, or exhausting illnesses." Butler (1971) also notes the association of acute, reversible disorders with medication by "Tranquilizers, bromides, barbiturates, thiocyanates, gases, even hormones . . . [f]or example, cortisone [and] steroids." As have other writers, Butler points out how common poor nourishment is among the elderly and how nutritional defects may result in acute brain syndrome, as well as such other etiological agents as arteriosclerosis, reduced kidney function, and the side effects of drugs (as he puts it, "untoward responses to drugs even at modest levels"), including the effects of prolonged use of tranquilizers to allay anxiety before surgery and agitation caused by the pharmacological action of barbiturates. "The older person may misinterpret . . . side effects. . . . They may believe that the side effects verify their fears of aging and deterioration [1971]."

The frequency of accidents and falls among elderly individuals also prompts Butler (1971) to suggest evaluation of this etiological possibility for an acute brain syndrome. Among pedestrian fatalities and fatal falls, persons over 65 account for 75% of the latter and 30% of pedestrian deaths. Thus, Butler points out that there is need to examine patients for head traumas or subdural hematoma, following falls due to weakness or incoordination, especially in alcoholics. Butler also sees the possibilities of "ischemic attacks . . . marked by aphasia or paralysis. . . . Little strokes . . . [are] probably quite frequent." Vitamin deficiencies, congestive heart failure, and chronic respiratory disease such as respiratory and other infections are seen by Butler as among the other common causes of a reversible brain syndrome.

Verwoerdt (1976) also evaluates an organic brain syndrome as acute when it is reversible. "When secondary to somatic illness, it tends to be reversible; a physical illness may also cause an acute exacerbation of an already existing chronic brain syndrome." In the latter case, Verwoerdt warns, "serial episodes of an acute brain syndrome often represent a step-like progression to the chronic form."

Finally, there is the plea by Segal (1975) for more systematic study of organic brain syndromes. "Of all mental illnesses, organic psychosis has been the most severely neglected by researchers. Yet, patients with organic psychosis [sometimes called organic brain syndrome] fill about one-quarter of the total mental hospital beds in the country."

SUMMARY

Psychological symptoms, sudden changes in behavior, acute physical illnesses are characteristics which demand intensive study in older patients, particularly to determine whether the syndrome is reversible, that is, whether it is possible to return the patient to the premorbid state. This determination is significant, for it helps us to assess whether there is the likelihood of a favorable outcome, or whether the patient is suffering from a chronic brain syndrome and faces the likelihood of death. The range of variables that have preceded acute brain syndromes is enormous. Most of these variables have been noted in this chapter, and investigators report the difficulty in establishing the important antecedents, noting that treatment, symptomatic by its nature, is far less of a problem than is diagnosis. Thus, careful examination and taking a careful history from the patient and other informants may be far more significant in the diagnosis and treatment of the acute brain syndrome, and, therefore, the outcome of the acute state, than is generally true for most of the ills that afflict the elderly. Finally, psychological symptoms and behavioral changes may constitute the first clues of acute brain syndrome developing from one or more of the multiple causes that have been identified.

REFERENCES

Agate, J. *The practice of geriatrics* (2nd ed.). London: Heinemann, 1970.

American Psychiatric Association. *Diagnostic and statistical manual of mental disorders* (DSM-II). Washington, D.C.: American Psychiatric Association, 1968.

Beck, A. T. *Depression: Causes and treatment.* Philadelphia: Univ. of Pennsylvania Press, 1967.

Bergmann, K. The neuroses of old age. In D. W. K. Kay, M. Roth, & A. Walk (Eds.), *Recent developments in psychogeriatrics.* Ashford, Kent: Royal Medico–Psychological Association, 1971.

Butler, R. N. Clinical psychiatry in late life. In I. Rossurair (Ed.), *Clinical geriatrics.* Philadelphia: Lippincott, 1971.

Dunn, T., & Arie, T. Mental disturbance in the ill old person. *British Medical Journal,* 1973, 4, 413–416.

Fann, W. E., Wheless, J. C., & Richman, B. W. Treating the aged with psychotropic drugs. *Gerontologist,* 1976, 16, 322–328.

Freedman, A. M., Kaplan, H. I., & Sadock, B. J. *Modern synopsis of psychiatry.* Baltimore, Maryland: Williams & Wilkins, 1973.

Hamilton, J. A., & Cowdry, E. V., Jr. Psychiatric aspects. In F. U. Steinberg (Ed.), *Cowdry's The care of the geriatric patient.* St. Louis, Missouri: Mosby, 1976.

Janzarik, W. Diagnostic and nosological aspects. In R. H. Williams, C. Tibbits, & W. Donahue (Eds.), *Processes of aging: I.* New York: Atherton, 1963.

Kay, D. W. K., Bergmann, K., Foster, E. M., McKechnie, A. A., & Roth, M. Mental illness and hospital usage in the elderly: A random sample followed up. *Comprehensive Psychiatry,* 1970, 11, 26–35.

Krakowski, A. J., & Langlais, L. M. Acute psychiatric emergencies in a geriatric hospital. *Psychosomatics,* 1974, 15, 72–75.

Kral, V. A. Psychiatric problems in the aged: A reconsideration. *Canadian Medical Association Journal,* 1973, 108, 584–590.

Mensh, I. N. Psychiatric diagnosis in the institutionalized aged. *Geriatrics,* 1959, 14, 511–517.

Nobbs, K. L. G. Mental disorders in the elderly. In K. K. Hazell, K. L. G. Nobbs, W. A. Hurr, & W. F. Anderson (Eds.), *Social and medical problems of the elderly* (3rd ed.). London: Hutchinson, 1973.

Post, F. Psychiatric disorders. In J. C. Brockelhurst (Ed.), *Textbook of geriatric medicine and gerontology*. London: Churchill Livingstone, 1973.

Redick, R. W., Kramer, M., & Taube, C. A. Epidemiology of mental illness and utilization of psychiatric facilities among older persons. In E. W. Busse & E. Pfeiffer (Eds.), *Mental illness in later life*. Washington, D.C.: American Psychiatric Association, 1973.

Segal, J. (Ed.). *Research in the service of mental health*. Washington, D.C.: Department of Health, Education and Welfare Publication No. (ADM) 75–236, 1975.

Simon, A., & Neal, M. W. Patterns of geriatric mental illness. In R. H. Williams, C. Tibbits, & W. Donahue (Eds.), *Processes of aging: I*. New York: Atherton, 1963.

Verwoerdt, A. *Clinical geropsychiatry*. Baltimore, Maryland: Williams & Wilkins, 1976.

Vorsamis, J., Zuchowski, T., & Maini, K. F. Survival rates and causes of death in geriatric psychiatric patients: A six-year follow-up study. *Canadian Psychiatric Association Journal*, 1972, *17*, 17–22.

Chapter 4

PSYCHOLOGICAL TESTING OF SENILES

Oscar J. Kaplan

A number of books have appeared recently on Alzheimer's disease and kindred subjects, among which are books by Katzman, Terry, and Dick (1978), Storandt, Siegler, and Elias (1978), Nandy (1978), Miller (1977), Smith and Kinsbourne (1977), Nandy and Sherwin (1977), Slaby and Wyatt (1974), Pearce and Miller (1973), Wells (1971), and Wolstenholme and O'Connor (1970). As clinical and research interest in the dementias of later life has heightened, the literature on psychological testing of those in this category has sharply expanded. This chapter will critically review this literature.

It is not surprising that a strong effort is being made to find more precise ways of assessing the psychological status of those with senile brain disease. At this stage in our knowledge, psychological measures are more useful than evaluations of brain pathology in living patients in estimating the extent of dementia.

NOSOLOGY AND ETIOLOGY

The nosology and nomenclature of the dementias of later life are still evolving. It is currently fashionable to include what used to be called "senile dementia" or "senile psychosis with chronic brain syndrome" under the heading of "Alzheimer's disease." These are brain conditions characterized by marked loss of neurons, granulovacuolar changes, neuritic or senile plaques, and neurofibrillary tangles. The

45

distinction between Alzheimer's disease and senile dementia, in which brain vascular pathology is minimal, is mainly fixed by time of onset. Vascular dementia in the elderly is very common, and dementia of mixed type (both vascular and nonvascular) is markedly underdiagnosed. No doubt, what now is called Alzheimer's disease someday will be split up into more meaningful categories on the basis of etiology. For the purposes of this chapter, the terms *senile dementia, chronic brain syndrome*, and *Alzheimer's disease* will be used interchangeably. The broader terms of *senile brain disease* or *dementias of later life*, of course, include not only Alzheimer's disease, but also comprehend conditions mainly of vascular origin, Creutzfeldt-Jakob disease, as well as many other disorders.

Opinion is not unanimous that the histopathology of Alzheimer's disease and senile dementia are qualitatively similar and that they are essentially the same. Sourander and Sjögren (1970) declare that the difference in location of senile plaques indicates that Alzheimer's disease is not an early manifestation of senile dementia.

The etiologies of the senile dementias are still very obscure. Some of the possible routes to brain malfunction or damage in the elderly include cerebral blood vessel disease, cardiac insufficiency, intracranial neoplasms, low pressure hydrocephalus, head trauma, "slow viruses" (Creutzfeldt-Jakob disease), genetic defects, thyrotoxicosis, excessive accumulation in neurons of elements such as mercury or aluminum, immunologic disorders, dietary deficiencies, toxic drugs, electrolyte disturbances, drug abuse, diminished production of acetylcholine and other derangements in nervous system biochemistry, anemia, and untreated syphilis. Many of these conditions are or will be treatable. These and countless other factors are etiologically involved in the later life dementias, and many no doubt operate concomitantly in the same individual. Apparently all humans suffer continuing attrition of neurons. According to Vogel (1977), the human central nervous system has about 20 billion neurons at age 30, and it loses approximately .8% each year thereafter, even in the absence of active pathology.

Senile plaques and neurofibrillary tangles are not age specific, nor are they peculiar to the dementias of later life. Lauter and Meyer (1968) point out that senile plaques have been found in Lissauer's type of general paralysis, Down's syndrome, amaurotic family idiocy, cerebral injuries, and in various systemic atrophies even in infancy. Neurofibrillary tangles have been observed in myxoedema, Lissauer's type of general paralysis, cerebral injuries, postencephalitic Parkinsonism, and pugilistic dementia. It appears that senile plaques and neurofibrillary tangles may occur because of either endogenous or exogenous processes or both.

Vogel (1977) observes that the brains of some who have lived beyond age 70 have been free of senile plaques, neurofibrillary tangles, and granulovacuolar degeneration. Unfortunately, psychometric data is not available on such persons.

The problems involved in classifying the mental disorders of old age and unraveling their etiology have been delineated by Roth (1971). Precise knowledge of the etiology and neuropathology of the condition he is assessing can be helpful to a psychometrician, but psychological testing can be illuminating even in the absence of such knowledge. This has been demonstrated in the field of mental retardation.

USES OF TESTS FOR SENILES

Severe senile dementia is almost as easy to diagnose as it is to establish that a one-legged man has one leg. This was brought home dramatically to me and my associates when we were developing the Psychological Abilities Scale for Seniles (PASS) at the Edgemoor Geriatric Hospital (Santee, California), a test that will be described later in this chapter. This institution had locked wards for the more impaired seniles (Grades 4 and 5 on the PASS) and open wards for the minimally impaired (Grades 1–3 on the PASS). With one exception, without access to test results of any kind, the hospital staff had appropriately segregated the patients in terms of our ratings. The one exception was that of a woman who scored in Grade 2 on the PASS who had gained admission to the locked ward by feigning severe dementia in order to obtain a private room and to escape an unpleasant situation she faced in the open ward. Psychologists and psychiatrists usually have no difficulty in making a correct diagnosis of senile dementia after asking a few simple questions dealing with recent and remote memory and time and place orientation. Sophisticated psychological testing, however, is needed to meet other needs.

Almost never is a senile first identified as a result of poor performance on a psychological test. Sometimes the complaint presented when an older person or his family seeks professional advice is the loss of a long-practiced skill involving both short-term and long-term memory, such as the ability to dial a telephone accurately, or to tell time correctly, or to pass the written part of an automobile driver's examination even after repeated attempts. Deterioration in self-care is often associated with developing dementia. Such losses may indicate serious impairment since they relate to abilities that have been practiced for many years. In these and other instances of apparent decline, the alert tester will not rule out the possibility that poor performance is due to psychiatric difficulties, sensory impairments, poor motivation, or a combination of these and other factors.

Valid and reliable psychological tests for seniles have many potential applications, among which are the following:

1. They can be used in determining the effectiveness of therapeutic interventions of various kinds, such as the use of new drugs, exercise programs, and specially designed educational activities. Very precise measurements usually are needed in such studies.
2. They can be used in longitudinal investigations of the speed and course of the dementia process in the elderly, in elucidating the changing structure of intellect as people deteriorate, in relating psychological variables to biomedical ones, and in providing other information needed for a fuller understanding of the basic nature of Alzheimer's disease and similar conditions.
3. If administered to individuals regularly over a period of many years, tests can be used to identify early those who are slipping into senile mental decline. This may make possible more effective interventions as our knowledge of etiology enlarges.
4. Tests, in conjunction with other kinds of assessments, eventually may be helpful in accomplishing more accurate differential diagnoses in elderly persons with psychiatric problems. This may lead to more suitable and efficacious treatment. For example, one of the penalties for misdiagnosing elderly patients with affect disorders as senile dements may be premature death. Copeland and his associates (1975) found that such misdiagnoses and accompanying neglect led to a mortality rate comparable with that of brain syndrome patients. Clinical acumen and trials with antidepressive drugs may be needed to tie down a diagnosis of mood disorder in an older person who does poorly on mental tests.
5. Results of psychological testing can be used in making decisions about the assignment of patients within an institution or placement in the community. They can be used in designing prosthetic environments appropriate for particular patients.
6. There is growing interest in the psychological assessment of elderly persons for legal purposes, such as in the making of decisions on the control of property, independent living, and the enjoyment of certain privileges. Gunn (1977) points out that competence need not be expressed in all-or-none terms, but should relate to specific behaviors such as managing one's own

financial affairs, driving an automobile, practicing medicine, or caring for one's own person with ordinary prudence. Aker, Walsh, and Beam (1977) have summarized the literature on the medical and legal aspects of determining the mental capacity of the aging. The existing psychological tests may provide useful information on surviving levels of competence but may be insufficient for arriving at final appraisals, particularly in borderline cases of specific behaviors.

Although most of the emphasis in psychometric studies of dementia in the elderly has focused on institutionalized and severely impaired persons, the largest number are mildly impaired and still llving in the community. If living alone, they frequently are malnourished and lack proper medical and other kinds of care. Certainly they are incapable of the same level of self-care that was possible for them earlier in their lives. Often their marginal competence makes them easy prey for unscrupulous insurance and other kinds of salesmen. Sometimes they sell their homes far below market value, particularly in times of rapid price change.

The protection of these individuals, who are on the borderline between "normal" aging and diminished capacity of such magnitude as to make proper judgments in business affairs dubious, will become a growing social concern. Difficult legal questions are involved. A further complication is that law suits brought to redress grievances often linger for several years in civil courts, and by the time the case is brought to trial the complainant is either dead or unable to press the charges. There is need for tests and other measures that are able to identify these marginally impaired persons. The justice system may need to be revised to take cognizance of this problem.

The psychologists who have developed tests for infants and for the severely mentally retarded have demonstrated that it is possible to test intelligence at the lowest levels. "Nontestable" seniles are those for whom no appropriate tests have been developed. Of course, tests for persons at the lowest levels of performance must be extremely simple and must emphasize recognition rather than recall in measurement of memory abilities.

POPULATION HETEROGENEITY

Ideally, a research psychologist would like to work with a "pure" population of Alzheimer's patients (or some other type of senile dementia) in various stages of decline, free of all other pathology, and with comparable life histories. Such a population, of course, does not exist. This presents problems to those who seek psychological characterizations of the dementias of later life. Since the populations of seniles who have been tested are very diverse, results must be interpreted with these differences in mind.

Institutions differ markedly in their criteria for admission and often change their criteria over time. In our studies in four southern California institutions, we found substantial differences among seniles; this was mainly the result of intake policy. At Metropolitan State Hospital (Norwalk), a facility for the mentally ill, patients usually exhibited severe behavior problems in addition to cognitive deficit. Those at the Veterans Administration Domiciliary (West Los Angeles) were predominantly single males with a life-long history of marginal adjustment. Patients at Rancho Los Amigos Hospital (Downey) tended to be physically sicker than those we worked with in the other institutions. Our subjects at Edgemoor Geriatric Hosptial (Santee) were predominantly female and without surviving relatives and were mainly ambulatory. Seniles who are married and who are members of more affluent families are more likely to remain in their homes. They usually show up in institutional populations only when they have markedly deteriorated and cannot be cared for at home because of medical and/or behavioral reasons. For obvious reasons, almost all of the psychological literature on senile brain disease is based on institutionalized persons. It is unfortunate that most published articles fail to describe the institution's intake policy and do not supply demographic data on those tested.

Quality of research differs greatly in the published studies on the fate of cognitive functions in seniles. There are few studies that are based on large, representative samples and that recognize or incorporate the principles of good experimental design. This is not intended as criticism, since good studies are hard to carry through even when adequate funds are available because of the heterogeneity of populations available for investigation.

FACTORS INFLUENCING TEST PERFORMANCE

Many factors, in addition to the test used, influence test results obtained with seniles. Tests must be administered individually, sometimes on a ward. There is need for skill and patience on the part of the examiner, particularly in the more deteriorated cases.

Use of standardized psychological tests as a regular part of a geriatric admission examination is challenged by Comfort (1978). He points out that questions about name, address, age, year of birth, date of birth, next-of-kin, and past or present occupation are asked routinely in the course of the admission process and that detailed testing is indicated only if there is failure on such items. If testing is required, it should be included as part of the nervous system examination insofar as possible. Many older people, particularly those with minimal brain damage, are defensive about their intellectual status and may be threatened by formal testing.

Motivation always is of primary importance in psychological testing, whether the subject is a child or a senile. The degree of rapport established by the examiner with the subject may profoundly influence test results. There are examiners who hate testing seniles, and even though they may be professional enough to attempt to conceal their dislike for the task, it cannot help but influence their relationship with their subjects. It has been our experience that older persons are especially responsive when the examiner is an attractive, friendly young person of the opposite sex. Institutionalized seniles usually are an abandoned group, leading humdrum, meaningless lives. Being tested may be perceived as a major event. If the test situation is properly handled, and if it is not seen as threatening or humiliating, it may be fully accepted and a full effort may be induced.

Severe impairment of vision or hearing often requires the elimination of test items dependent upon these senses. Sometimes it is possible to develop substitute items that address similar psychological functions. Properly fitted hearing aids and glasses make many patients testable. It is disturbing that so many older persons lack these prosthetic devices.

It is well known that both institutionalized and noninstitutionalized older people frequently take a number of medications on a regular basis. Although those over age 65 now constitute about 11% of the United States population, they consume about 25% of all drugs sold in the country. The average elderly person uses six or seven different drugs at any one time. Many of the drugs widely used by the elderly are psychoactive, including many that are not prescribed for psychiatric purposes. In some cases, the drugs may aid test performance and in others they may interfere with it.

The stress of the test situation may lower test performance. In this connection, Eisdorfer, Nowlin, and Wilkie (1970) have reported improvement of test performance in the elderly by giving a beta-blocking agent that affected autonomic nervous system activity.

Wilkie and Eisdorfer (1971) found that elevated diastolic blood pressure rather than age per se was a significant factor in the mental decline of older subjects. The subjects were in the 60–69 age bracket at the beginning of the study and were followed for 10 years. The Wechsler Adult Intelligence Scale (WAIS) was used to assess mental status. Variations in blood pressure in hypertensive patients may account for some of the variance in test results at different times with the same instrument.

Often patients are tested immediately after admission to an institution and at a time when they have not fully adjusted to a major change in their routine and life circumstances. This is a period of such severe stress for many that they do not survive it. Therefore, it is not surprising that test results obtained at such a time sometimes are spuriously low.

It is well known that depression in the elderly may masquerade as senile brain disease. Often prescription of an antidepressant drug may bring about dramatic improvement in test performance in appropriate cases. A history of depressive or manic-depressive illness is not incompatible with the development of senile brain disease, and fluctuations in an underlying affective illness may affect test performance.

Kaplan, Rumbaugh, Mitchell, and Thomas (1963) investigated the effects of testing at different times of day (morning and afternoon) and of practice (test–retest) on the psychological performance of seniles at different levels of functioning (grades). Eighty subjects residing in the Edgemoor Geriatric Hospital (Santee, California) were given a battery of six tests from the Psychological Abilities Scale for Seniles (PASS): Vocabulary, New Learning, Numbers, "C" Picture (an alternate form of the "B" Picture), Structured Association, and Weight Discrimination. Data were subjected to analysis of variance.

Ages of patients ranged from 59 to 97 years. Mean ages, by sex and level, were as follows: males—Grade 1, 80 years; Grade 2, 79.6 years; Grade 3, 74.2 years; Grades 4 and 5, 74.1 years; and females—Grade 1, 78.8 years; Grade 2, 77.5 years; Grade 3, 78.9 years; Grades 4 and 5, 80.3 years. Most of the patients in Grades 3–5 were in locked wards to prevent them from wandering away. Half of the subjects at each grade were men.

Subjects in the four performance levels (grades) were systematically tested in the morning and afternoon to ascertain the effect that time of day might have upon their test results. The tests were given again on the day following the initial examination to define the effect of test–retest according to time and level.

The principal findings in this study (Kaplan *et al.*, 1963) were:

1. Performance on all psychological tests in the battery varied significantly with level (grade).
2. In the one instance of test–retest effect, gain was greater in the higher levels (grades) than in the lower ones.
3. Time of day was of no significance, even in its interaction with level, except in one instance.
4. No significant interaction between time of day and test–retest was found.
5. In general, sex differences were inconsequential.

The results were somewhat surprising, since it appeared that afternoon performance would be lower than morning performance because of fatigue, particularly in patients functioning at lower levels.

Evidence that elderly subjects are not unusually susceptible to test fatigue has been offered by Cunningham, Sepkoski, and Opel (1978). Intelligence test performance was based on tests of verbal comprehension, number facility, perceptual speed, and word fluency. The effects of fatigue were studied by using breaks between tests, by varying the number of previous tests, and by using a modified form of the Finding A's test as a pretest fatigue producer.

In evaluating test results, consideration must be given to the person's current life situation. If the person examined is not reading newspapers, listening to the radio, or watching television, one can hardly expect such a person to be knowledgeable about current events. If no calendars are displayed and if daily activities are not related to month or day of the week, inability to correctly answer questions dealing with such matters is not conclusive proof of time disorientation. Social isolation and sensory deprivation may markedly affect test performance.

As is true in psychological testing generally, more confidence can be placed in higher scores than in lower ones. This assumes that the higher scores have been honestly earned and that there are no undue practice effects or special advantages leading to spurious ratings. Of course, poor scores frequently represent accurately the surviving abilities of subjects. Spuriously low scores, as previously discussed, may be due to inadequate motivation, sensory defect, inappropriate test, examiner deficiencies, etc.

Although good psychological tests are an indispensable part of the armamentarium of geriatric psychiatry, they cannot be depended upon to do the job of diagnosis and assessment alone. In appraising an elderly patient, consideration also must be given to life history, medical findings, and current behavior in nontest situations. For example, if the person tested has a history of affective illness, this would warrant a hard search for current signs of depression. If the person tested has a lifelong history of mental retardation, this knowledge is extremely valuable to an examiner in evaluating the test results. If the person examined is consuming substantial quantities of alcohol, this may at least partially account for episodic drops in test performance. Good medical histories are equally useful and may make the examiner aware of factors leading to diminished effort and/or transient confusion.

Seniles differ markedly in their early adult intelligence level, and in their social, vocational, and educational histories. They number among them former university presidents and captains of industry as well as unskilled laborers and long-term mental patients. Too little attention has been given in clinical practice and in research studies to the earlier life of patients in interpreting test results. Such consideration is particularly important in making decisions in individual cases. The ability of seniles to cope is a function of not only the extent of their mental impairment, but also their life history.

Detailed, extensive case histories are needed if one is to evaluate remote memory. For example, in the absence of dependable information on birthdate, family composition, and education, it is not possible to determine the authenticity of respondent answers. Retrospective falsification, which often is not deliberate, is something the psychologist must contend with. Dependable information is needed to check and authenticate the answers given by subjects.

CONSTRUCTING PSYCHOLOGICAL TESTS FOR SENILES

The task of constructing psychological tests for seniles is essentially the same as that in developing instruments for use with other populations. Nevertheless, the special characteristics of seniles must be taken into account in test design. Special effort must be made to develop tests consisting of familiar material interesting to the subject. The high incidence of visual problems among the elderly, some of which cannot be corrected by glasses, makes it important to use large-size letters in any material that is to be read by subjects. Above all, opportunities for success must be maximized through inclusion of some items that can be passed even by the most deteriorated.

In many tests now used with seniles, the person being tested is frequently given tasks remote from his or her daily life or material never previously encountered. Although success on such measures indicates proficiency, failure does not necessarily spell incompetence. For example, asking a senile to memorize a long list of digits is not likely to be an attractive task. Being questioned about a story built around a photograph may be much more interesting. Some of the so-called memory problems of the senile may be partly problems of encoding.

Learning and memory, simplistically defined, are the principal bases for psychological life. Impairment of the ability to learn from current experiences is a staggering handicap. Inability to utilize past experiences in the solution of current problems is, if anything, even more disabling, since the gains of a lifetime are not available in dealing with the problems of everyday living. Memory is the keystone of intelligence, binding us to our past and enabling us to exploit it for present ends. Much of the content of tests used with seniles consists of items that examine short-term and long-term memory. Psychologists, in developing tests, must take into account the three stages of memory: encoding, storage, and retrieval.

Kral (1978) distinguished between "benign" and "malignant" forgetfulness, which essentially is the difference between memory deficit in advanced "normal" aging and Alzheimer's disease. In "benign" forgetfulness, the afflicted person is unable to recall parts of an experience (e.g., a place, date, or name) but is cognizant of the experience; information that cannot be recalled may be retrievable at a later time, and forgotten material is more likely to pertain to remote rather than recent events. Kral emphasizes that this distinction between "benign" and "malignant" forgetfulness does not necessarily mean that two neuropathological processes are involved.

As persons grow older, retrieval of stored information becomes more difficult. Loss of this ability is particularly noticeable as individuals become senile. Many who are unable to deal with material at the recall level are able to succeed at the recognition level. Although loss in ability to retrieve information and express it at the recall level should be noted, to fail to provide opportunity for success at the recognition level may result in incorrect appraisals.

✦ Most tests used with seniles give little attention to judgment, which benefits heavily from experience. In this connection, one is reminded of the words of La Rochefoucauld: "Everybody complains of his lack of memory, but nobody of his want of judgment."

More than 40 years ago, Lorge (1936) recognized the importance of speed in intelligence test performance. When he made adjustments for speed on the New England data collected by Jones and Conrad, the declining curve flattened into a plateau around age 40. Any test that requires speed will penalize a senile even more than a "normal" older person.

Intelligence is a construct, and each test author defines intelligence by the way in which he or she develops the test. Some tests emphasize speed or power more than others. Apart from making gross distinctions, such as between dements and nondements, global scores have little value and indeed may mislead. More attention needs to be paid to subscores and to mental factors, particularly in research-oriented investigations. For example, older persons usually pick up more points on information and vocabulary tests (crystallized intelligence) than on items that are novel (fluid intelligence). Two individuals may receive the same total score but may differ appreciably in abilities. Tests that yield summary scores by an additive procedure do not take into account the fact that not all abilities deteriorate at the same rate.

Employing the Wechsler Adult Intelligence Scale (WAIS), Wechsler (1958) found that the verbal subtests were more resistant to decline with age than the performance items. This is not surprising, since the verbal subtests are heavily weighted with vocabulary and other highly practiced abilities.

Babcock (1930) developed the Test of Mental Efficiency based upon the assumption that there is little change in vocabulary level until the end of life and that earliest acquired material is the last to be lost. She constructed a Deterioration Index by using achievement on the Terman vocabulary list as a measure of early adult mental status and a series of speed and learning tests to assess current efficiency, noting the difference between these two sets of scores. The validity of Babcock's Deterioration Index is questionable, since it is known that severely impaired seniles may experience marked loss in ability to define words.

Savage (1977), in describing the structure of intellect in the aged, breaks down cognitive functioning into level and learning components that are orthogonal, or independent of one another. There are both verbal and performance aspects of these two components. "Intellectual level of functioning" refers to acquired abilities such as vocabulary and general information and appears to be more resistant to both "normal" aging and cerebral pathology than "learning ability." "Intellectual level of functioning" has much in common with Cattell's (1963) concept of "crystallized intelligence," and "learning ability" closely resembles what is connoted by the term "fluid intelligence." "Learning ability" or "fluid intelligence" is highly vulnerable to neuropathology in the aged.

Kinsbourne (1974) has shown that the more heavily weighted a test is with material of the "fluid intelligence" type, the more difficult it is for older people. Items of the "crystallized intelligence" type have limited power to discriminate between young and old adult age groups. Many test items require the application of varying amounts of both "fluid" and "crystallized" intelligence.

Caird (1965) studied memory disorder and psychological test performance in aged psychiatric patients. As anticipated, those diagnosed as suffering from arteriosclerotic or senile dementia had more difficulty than "functional" patients on tasks requiring efficient short-term memory and "fluid" ability. "Crystallized" ability and long-term memory were less efficient in distinguishing between these groups.

Heimann (1968) points out that different factors may lead to lowered test performance in different older individuals, such as a drop in speed, diminished visual acuity, or lessened reasoning ability. Heimann describes Wechsler's model as additive, with performance expressed as the sum of the performances on each of the tests. There is the implied assumption that deterioration occurs in the abilities measured by each of the tests. Validity of Wechsler's additive model is in question, says Heimann, when "variance among the results of the variables increases instead of decreasing [p. 39]."

Investigating the predictive power of an adaptation of the Bender Visual Motor Gestalt Test, Inglis, Colwell, and Post (1960) showed that the prognostic strength of this instrument is limited, even though it effectively differentiates between elderly "functional" and "organic" psychiatric patients. The authors argue that "psychological tests must be directly validated for the purpose to which they are being put."

Studies by Botwinick and Birren (1951) and Dorken and Greenbloom (1953) show that tests that are most likely to show decline with advancing age are not necessarily the most efficient in separating the seniles from the "normals." Vocabulary and general information tests, for example, may be more useful for this purpose. Botwinick (1967) has pointed out that tests or subtests that yielded significant differences in performance as between "normal" young and old adults were not always equally efficient in differentiating between the "normal" old and the demented old.

It is extremely helpful to have two or more forms of the same test for use with the elderly, particularly if it is established that they are of comparable difficulty. It makes it possible to reduce practice effects that may be important in those who still are relatively well preserved. No doubt the time will come when each individual will be followed through life, tested periodically, and given special attention if there is an unexplained and substantial drop in intelligence test performance. Such tests, indeed, might accompany regular medical examinations.

As sophistication increases in the construction of psychological scales for seniles, more of them will be developed by factor-analytic procedures. Spitzer (1967) deals with the properties of such scales.

PSYCHOLOGICAL TESTS USED WITH SENILES

A large body of literature on psychological tests for seniles and related subjects has appeared during the last several decades, most of it since the late 1960s. Earlier work has been summarized by Kaplan (1956).

No attempt is made in this chapter to mention or describe all the tests that are used with seniles. The number is very large. However, those discussed in this section are representative.

Most of the tests being used with seniles were developed with other populations in mind. The most widely used is probably the Wechsler Adult Intelligence Scale (WAIS). The verbal scores on this examination derive from the six subtests: Information, Comprehension, Arithmetic, Similarities, Digit Span, and Vocabulary. The five performance subtests are Digit Symbol, Picture Completion, Block Design, Picture Arrangement, and Object Assembly. These subtests are grouped as "Hold" or "Don't Hold" tests on the basis of their resistance to decline with age. The "Hold" subtests are Information, Comprehension, Vocabulary, Object Assembly, and Picture Completion. The "Don't Hold" subtests are Picture Arrangement, Arithmetic, Block Design, Digit Span, Similarities, and Digit Symbol. Comparison of the "Hold" and "Don't Hold" scores yields a "Deterioration Quotient."

Pfeiffer (1975) has developed a short portable status questionnaire for assessment of organic brain deficit in elderly patients and has described a multidimensional functional assessment program for this age group. Plutchik, Conte, Lieberman, Bakur, Grossman, and Lehrman (1970) and Plutchik, Conte, and Lieberman (1971) have published information about the development of a scale (GIES) for assessment of cognitive and perceptual functioning in geriatric patients. Jastak and Jastak (1965) have developed the Wide Range Achievement Test, which has been used with elderly subjects. Kahn, Goldfarb, Pollack, and Peck (1960) have made available brief objective measures for determining the mental status of the aged.

Robinson (1975) has discussed the usefulness of the Intellectual Rating Scale in assessing the mental status of elderly persons. It allows a normal conversational approach in which scored items are interspersed with others that are affable and nonthreatening. Arithmetical problems are presented late in the examination. The results permit assignment to mildly, moderately, and severely impaired categories.

Arguing for the use of short screening tests with the elderly at the time of their first office visit, Canter (1978) specifically recommends the use of the Mini-Mental State Test (Folstein, Folstein, & McHugh, 1975), the Symbol Digit Modalities Test (Smith, 1976), and the Background Interference Procedure (BIP) Bender Test (Canter, 1968). Persons showing substantial impairment on these tests may be reexamined with other psychological instruments and/or referred for such procedures as the computerized tomographic brain scan (CAT) and electroencephalography.

Lowenthal and Berkman (1967) made use of the Kent E-G-Y in their study of aging and mental disorder in San Francisco. This simple 10-item test was developed by Kent (1946) and originally was intended to estimate the intelligence level of the subject, so that examination with longer and more sophisticated tests could begin at the proper place. Psychologists working on this project with a hospitalized sample found a high correlation ($r = .80$) between the E-G-Y and the WAIS.

Mattis (1976) has developed two tests that are useful with elderly subjects: the Mattis Organic Mental Syndrome Screening Examination (MOMSSE) and the Mattis Dementia Rating Scale (MDRS). The MDRS yields scores in the following categories: attention, initiation and perseveration change (verbal and motor), construction, conceptualization, and memory.

Hersch, Kral, and Palmer (1978) have reported on the clinical value of the London Psychogeriatric Rating Scale (LPRS). The LPRS is composed of a 36-item questionnaire, which divides into four subscales: Mental Disorganization–Confusion, Physical Disability, Socially Irritating Behavior, and Disengagement. Ratings are made by members of the ward staff. Predictive validity of the LPRS has been established in terms of ward placement, outcome, diagnosis, and effectiveness of treatment programs.

Birkett and Boltuch (1977) studied the effectiveness of two tests in differentiating between elderly patients with organic brain damage (neurologic disease, chiefly stroke) and those with functional disorders (present since youth). The Maudsley Tests of the Sensorium (employed by clinicians to evaluate orientation and visual memory) and the Kendall Memory for Design Test (used by psychologists to measure visual memory) were compared and both were found to be effective in differentiating functional from organic disorders. The difference in the effectiveness of these two tests was not statistically significant.

Branconnier and Cole (1978) combined 10 neuropsychological test scores and items from the Profile of Mood States (POMS) into an Impairment Index. Among the neuropsychological tests used were the Wechsler Memory Scale, Sperling's Perceptual Trace, the Bender Visual Motor Gestalt Test, and Gottschaldt's Hidden Figures Test. The battery was used in evaluating a drug administered to seniles with mild organic brain impairment. The Impairment Index picked up changes after drug administration that were not evident to the participating psychiatrists.

Errors in diagnosing senile confusion occurred with the Face–Hand Test (FHT), Mental Status Questionnaire (MSQ), and staff ratings in a study reported by Brink, Capri, De Neeve, Janakes, and Oliveira (1978). Although the FHT, MSQ, and staff ratings in the main were in agreement, some lucid and alert patients with limited brain damage received low FHT scores and some poorly educated immigrants were given spuriously low MSQ scores.

THE PSYCHOLOGICAL ABILITIES SCALE FOR SENILES

Kaplan, Thomas, and Thomas have developed a Psychological Abilities Scale for Seniles (PASS) and a related instrument known as the Grade Assessment Questionnaire (GAQ).[1] These tests have not yet been published but a very large amount of information dealing with psychological functioning of seniles has been collected with them. The PASS consists of original items in 11 categories: Reading Errors, "B" Picture, Vocabulary, Clocks, Structured Association, Photo Identification, New Learning, Weight Discrimination, Numbers, Calendar, and Blocks. These are briefly described in the boxed material on page 62–63. The study is one of the most systematic and extensive ever undertaken on cognitive functioning in seniles.

The first step in the research program was to develop a Grade Assessment Questionnaire (GAQ) on the basis of which subjects were assigned to a grade of from 1 to 5. Those in Grade 1 were the least impaired and those in Grade 5 were the most impaired. The GAQ not only yields a total score that translates into grade, but it also provides subscores on Remote Memory, Recent Memory, Place Orientation, Time Orientation, and Current Events. Typical questions are the following: What is the name of this city? Do you have any children? How many children do you have? What are (is) their (his/her) name(s)? What is the capital city of the United States? Why do we celebrate the Fourth

[1] Work on this project was supported in part by NIMH Grant M-2919.

of July in the United States? What time is it on this watch (clock)? What was the last meal you ate: breakfast, lunch, or supper?

Grade is determined by the percentage of correct responses on items attempted. Some items cannot be included in every examination. For example, if information is lacking on marital history or number of children, such items must be eliminated. If a person being tested has a physical impairment that prevents him or her from writing a simple sentence, it must be eliminated. Therefore, the percentage of correct items may be based on different numbers of items in different cases. The percentage equivalents for the five grades on the GAQ are: Grade 1, 90% and above; Grade 2, 70–89%; Grade 3, 46–69%; Grade 4, 26–45%; Grade 5, 0–25%.

On the basis of total scores on the GAQ, 300 senile patients were selected in four Southern California institutions: Edgemoor Geriatric Hospital (Santee), Rancho Los Amigos Hospital (Downey), Metropolitan State Hospital (Norwalk), and a small private institution. Most of the patients were residents of the Edgemoor Geriatric Hospital. Of the sample of 300, 60 persons qualified for each of the five grades. Half of the persons in each grade were men. In addition, a control group of 60 subjects (half men, half women) age 65 and older and living in their own homes were used as controls. Thirty of these subjects were outpatients of the San Diego County Hospital and were examined while visiting the hospital; the remaining 30 subjects were recruited for the project by the County Welfare Department and were tested in their own homes by appointment.

Table 4.1 summarizes the intercorrelations of test scores and other variables for the total population under study. It shows high correlations between almost all of the PASS tests and grade. Sex and time of day of testing are not particularly influential in reference to test performance. It is interesting to note that the New Learning test correlated .84 with grade, the highest correlation for any of the psychological tests. This item measures immediate memory, flexibility, and other abilities. The influence of differences in educational attainment is minimized in this test. The data are being subjected to factor analysis and there are indications that six or seven factors will be identified.

Although it is true that "crystallized" intelligence test items and recall of early life experiences hold up better than "fluid" intelligence test items and recent life experiences in older dementia patients, those who are very severely impaired do poorly on all kinds of items. For example, some of those who are in Grade 5 on our Grade Assessment Questionnaire often cannot remember names of spouses, names of

DESCRIPTION OF PASS TESTS

Reading Errors Examinee is asked to read a simple paragraph and is checked for number of errors.

"B" Picture A colored picture of a living room containing a large number of objects whose names begin with a variety of letters is presented to the subject. The subject is asked to name as many objects as possible beginning with the letter "b", such as boy, bat, brick, and ball. A minimum of 3 minutes is allowed. If at least one correct response is given in the third minute, the test is continued until an additional minute elapses in which there is no correct response. All correct responses are given equal credit.

Vocabulary Subject is asked to select a synonym for the word to be defined from a list of four printed alternative words.

Clocks Subject is shown four clocks, each representing a different time, and is asked to tell the times represented.

Structured Association The subject is asked to name as many animals as possible and is allowed to continue until a full minute elapses in which no acceptable response occurs. A minimum of 3 minutes is permitted each subject.

Photo Identification Photographs are shown to the person being tested. Typical question: "I have some pictures to show you. This is a boy named David. The lady's name is Mrs. Martin and this man is Mr. Taylor. Now remember (*point to each*) this is David, this is Mrs. Martin and this is Mr. Taylor. Which one did I call David?" Respondent is asked to select the correct photograph.

New Learning Subject is asked to learn the names of five symbols. Ten large cards are presented in a fixed sequence. Each card presents a symbol representing an object. For example, the most concrete symbol is a drawing of the sun and its rays. The most abstract symbol is a triangle representing a boat. Other symbols stand for a loaf of bread, a fish, and a cow. First, a series of 5 cards containing both the symbols and printed names are presented. Then 5 cards are shown on which only the symbols appear, and the subject is asked to recall the names of the symbols. The examiner speaks the name of each symbol each time a card is presented during the training period and asks the subject to repeat it. The deck of 10 cards is presented twice during the training period. The score is the number of names correctly recalled with the 5 cards that have only symbols on them.

Weight Discrimination A series of five weights, in containers of different colors, is presented to the subject. The containers weigh 20,

40, 60, 80, and 100 grams. The subject is first required to identify the heaviest and lightest weights. If successful, he is asked to attempt finer discriminations. He is also asked to arrange the weights in a line from the lightest to the heaviest.

Numbers Arithmetical problems of graded difficulty are presented both orally and visually in the form of printed cards.

Calendar Seven questions are asked about the month of December using a calendar that the subject can study. Typical question: "What day of the week is the second?" "Sunday is the 10th. What day will the next Thursday be?"

Blocks Eight interlocking blocks of four colors (yellow, red, blue, green) are used in this test, which consists of several tasks, each individually scored. First, the subject is asked to name the color of each block. The blocks then are united and the subject is asked a series of questions, such as: "How many blocks are touching the top yellow one?" Then the subject is told: "I am going to take away one of the blocks and later I will ask you the color of the block I took away." Then a block is removed and the subject is asked to restore the original pattern from memory.

children, or year of birth. Curiously, some who are unable to recall these elementary facts still may remember the name of the religion in which they were reared. This may be because religious experience antedates the establishment of families and is more strongly entrenched.

Table 4.2 summarizes a multiple regression analysis in which grade was predicted from the linear combination of 10 tests. The analysis demonstrated that the regression was very substantial ($R^2 = .8291$). The largest regression coefficient was obtained for New Learning ($p < .001$), and significant coefficients also were found for "B" Picture, Photo Identification, and Blocks ($p < .05$). Although the zero order correlation for the Calendar test is among the higher ones, this variable seems to lose some of its weight in the regression analysis due to its association with other variables.

Reliabilities for selected tests in the PASS battery are shown in Table 4.3. With the exception of the Clocks item, all other items show high reliabilities. It has been found that some subjects who failed the Clocks item are able to tell time correctly when shown an actual watch or clock, indicating some inadequacy in the item or possibly a neurological defect.

In 1962, D. Mitchell (personal communication), using the GAQ of

TABLE 4.1

Intercorrelations of Test Scores and Other Variables (Psychological Abilities Scale for Seniles)[a]

		−1	2	−3	−4	5	6	7	8	9	10	11	−12[b]
Sex	−1	—	−044	049	165	011	−014	−019	020	075	−024	022	−060
Time of day	2	−044	—	159	007	015	054	000	013	004	020	069	022
Examination length	−3	049	159	—	−028	333	375	287	170	378	318	322	143
Locomotor status	−4	165	007	−028	—	230	288	145	149	228	344	214	102
Percentage correct (GAQ)	5	001	015	333	230	—	955	943	661	890	898	791	568
Grade (GAQ)	6	−014	054	375	288	955	—	887	625	867	910	804	526
Remote memory	7	−019	000	287	145	943	887	—	608	773	776	668	610
Recent memory	8	020	013	170	149	661	625	608	—	534	589	452	357
Place orientation	9	075	004	378	228	890	867	773	534	—	807	726	472
Time orientation	10	−024	020	318	344	898	910	776	589	807	—	782	421
Current events	11	022	069	322	214	791	804	668	452	726	782	—	403
Reading errors	−12	060	022	143	102	568	526	610	357	472	421	403	—
"B" picture	13	−075	011	340	252	806	795	764	543	733	744	656	587
Vocabulary	14	−110	−009	218	138	754	720	736	574	652	656	579	609
Clocks	15	116	123	346	202	742	718	720	542	688	665	547	578
Structured Association	16	−061	032	305	224	742	758	689	501	677	735	647	438
Photo identification	17	−022	−022	277	094	820	802	778	548	749	754	674	532
New learning	18	021	042	324	176	845	844	774	559	775	813	740	456
Weight discrimination	19	−024	−054	129	206	700	651	710	477	593	576	487	576
Number test 1	20	019	−017	231	204	772	755	755	537	707	674	580	622
Number test 2	21	113	−041	272	229	713	719	664	501	667	659	593	508
Number total	22	077	−030	264	228	758	756	721	532	704	685	610	568
Calendar	23	−004	−009	341	151	830	814	808	595	779	723	635	622
Block 1	24	066	−021	215	204	601	598	587	432	551	565	474	456
Blocks 2	25	−064	−015	234	207	747	736	751	515	628	659	574	590
Blocks total	26	−039	−017	247	221	769	759	769	534	657	687	594	603

[a] Decimal points have been omitted; $r_{.05} = .11$; $r_{.01} = .15$.

[b] Variables 1, 3, 4, and 12 have been reflected so that the high values go with male (1), rate of work on the tests (3), good locomotor status (4), and low number of errors in reading (12).

the PASS, investigated the relationship between grade and self-care abilities at the Edgemoor Geriatric Hospital. Her subjects were 60 women on a locked ward, 20 women in each of three grades: 3, 4, and 5. Persons with physical disabilities that interfered with self-care were excluded from the investigation. She used a specially designed check list that yielded scores on five categories: personal hygiene,

TABLE 4.1 (Continued)

13	14	15	16	17	18	19	20	21	22	23	24	25	26
−075	−110	116	−060	−022	021	−024	019	113	077	−004	066	−064	−039
011	−009	023	032	−022	042	−054	−017	−041	−030	−009	−021	−015	−017
340	218	346	305	277	324	129	231	272	264	341	215	234	247
252	138	202	224	094	176	206	204	230	228	151	204	207	221
806	754	742	742	820	845	700	772	713	758	830	601	717	769
795	720	718	758	802	844	651	755	710	756	814	598	736	759
764	736	720	689	778	774	710	755	664	721	808	587	751	769
543	574	542	501	548	559	477	537	501	532	595	432	515	534
733	653	688	677	749	775	593	707	667	704	779	551	628	657
744	656	665	735	754	813	576	674	659	685	723	565	659	687
656	579	547	647	674	740	487	589	593	610	635	474	574	594
587	609	587	438	532	456	576	622	508	568	622	456	590	603
—	735	719	743	722	722	620	727	700	730	789	618	699	732
735	—	642	709	674	636	609	784	740	779	744	553	710	726
719	642	—	654	646	664	606	715	681	715	779	595	672	704
743	709	654	—	689	715	527	694	690	714	729	577	667	696
722	674	646	689	—	796	610	692	651	687	767	539	662	683
722	636	664	715	796	—	581	673	649	679	754	555	638	667
620	609	606	527	610	581	—	617	546	592	676	519	623	645
727	784	715	694	692	673	617	—	881	955	821	662	745	781
700	740	681	690	651	649	546	881	—	981	757	627	666	707
730	779	715	714	687	679	592	955	981	—	806	660	719	759
789	744	779	729	767	754	676	821	757	806	—	659	739	776
618	553	595	577	539	555	519	662	627	660	659	—	603	738
699	710	672	667	662	638	623	745	666	719	739	603	—	983
732	726	704	696	683	667	645	781	707	759	776	739	983	—

undressing–dressing, eating behavior, care of room, and ward orientation. The GAQ discriminated between Grade 4 and Grade 5 on each of the five self-care categories at the 1% level of confidence. The only significant difference when a similar comparison was made between women in Grades 3 and 4 was in ward orientation, which was significant at the 5% level.

Preliminary findings on the standardization sample of the PASS indicate that there is a relationship between recumbency and the rate at

TABLE 4.2
Multiple Regression Predicting Grade from Ten Tests

Tests	Regression weight (B_j)	T ratio	Regression weight (B_j)	r_{1j}	$B_j r_{1j}$	Partial $r_{1j.2....}$
"B" pictures	.045	2.94	.135	.795	.107	.167
Vocabulary	.002	.39	.017	.720	.012	.022
Clocks	.026	.56	.023	.718	.016	.032
Structured association	.020	2.02	.084	.758	.064	.116
Photo identification	.065	2.88	.129	.802	.103	.164
New learning	.156	7.87	.350	.844	.296	.413
Weight discrimination	.029	1.67	.058	.651	.038	.096
Number skills	.011	1.29	.061	.756	.046	.074
Calendar	.042	1.58	.087	.814	.070	.091
Blocks	.037	2.29	.100	.759	.076	.131

$R^2 = .8291; r = .91.$

which mental decline proceeds. When senile patients become bedfast, they go downhill more rapidly, both physically and in terms of test performance. Their life expectancy usually is reduced. These adverse outcomes may occur because it is the sicker patients who are kept in bed. However, it now is widely held that recumbency is to be avoided when possible. Doctors usually get their patients out of bed as soon as possible after surgery. Ambulatory patients no doubt have more opportunities for psychological stimulation. Unfortunately, in many institu-

TABLE 4.3
Psychological Abilities Scale for Seniles

Test	Reliabilities for selected tests		
	Males $(N = 90)$	Females $(N = 90)$	Total $(N = 180)$
Vocabulary[a]	.97	.95	.96
Photo identification[a]	.88	.91	.90
Calendar[a]	.82	.88	.88
Number facts[a]	.93	.93	.94
Number reasoning[a]	.94	.90	.92
Number skills total[a]	.95	.92	.93
New Learning[b]	.87	.87	.87
Clocks[b]	.43	.47	.45

[a] Split halves reliabilities with Spearman–Brown correction (Formula 14.1, in Guilford, 1954).
[b] Kuder-Richardson formula for reliability (Formula 17.21, in Guilford, 1956).

tions patients are kept in bed for the convenience of the staff. There is need for further study of the relationship between exercise and the preservation of mental abilities.

Kaplan, Brown, Thomas, and Thomas (1966) found high correlations between grade on the GAQ of the PASS and the extent of brain damage at autopsy on senile patients at the Rancho Los Amigos Hospital (Downey, California).

The distribution of dementia by grades is not equal. As a general rule, the more severe the impairment, the fewer the cases. In our experience, the most difficult to find are Grade 5 men.

NEUROPATHOLOGICAL–PSYCHOLOGICAL
INTERRELATIONSHIPS

A number of investigators have reported interrelationships between psychological test results and neuropathological findings in seniles. In the main, they agree that there is a high correlation between amount of brain damage and extent of cognitive deficit.

The correlation between extent of brain damage and psychological deficit has been emphasized by Blessed, Tomlinson, and Roth (1968) They found that when the amount of damaged tissue in cerebrovascular disease exceeds 50 cubic centimeters there is a sharp proportional increase in dementia symptoms. A quantitative relationship also was found between the number of senile plaques and stages of dementia. Roth, Tomlinson, and Blessed (1966) see the possibility of identifying and quantifying the psychological defects that correlate best with measures of cerebral impairment.

Utilizing criteria developed by Martin Roth, Corsellis (1962) assigned clinical diagnoses to 300 mental patients over the age of 65 who came to autopsy. Parenchymatous atrophy and cerebrovascular change in each brain was graded. Vascular changes were more pronounced in those who were labeled as in the arteriosclerotic dementia category, and senile plaques and neurofibrillary tangles were seen more frequently in those classified as senile dements. Many of the patients had both vascular and nonvascular pathology. Significantly, those who had been classified as "functional psychotics" (affective psychosis, late paraphrenia) showed less brain damage than those in the organic group.

Reviewing the literature on the relationship between cerebral atrophy and intellectual impairment, Wang (1977) cites evidence that neuropathology in the aged produces greater cognitive deficit than in the young. Premorbid personality also influences the relationship between brain damage and intellectual functioning; those who had a history of adaptive versatility earlier in life fared better than those who did not. When cerebral loss was small, individual variations in impairment were greater than when cerebral pathology was extensive. This makes sense, since when neuropathology is massive, even outstanding adjustment in early and middle adulthood cannot compensate for the biological deficit.

Studies that purport to show that there are significant differences in the performance of those with cerebral arteriosclerosis with psychosis and senile dementia have been questioned because of the difficulty of differentiating between these conditions in living patients. Postmortem studies have shown appreciable error in diagnoses when checked against postmortem findings. Indeed, a substantial number of patients have neuropathological postmortem reports that place them in the "mixed type" category (Malamud, 1965). Moreover, since in most cases of both vascular and nonvascular dementia impairment increases with time, it is difficult to match groups in terms of initial status.

Rothschild (1956) argued that there is not a 1:1 relationship between brain damage and psychological impairment, and he noted that different persons with essentially the same neuropathology may test or behave quite differently. He called for more attention to such factors as life history, personality, and environmental demands in reconciling neuropathological and psychometric findings. Rothschild's position is more defensible when the data relate to a sample of persons in the early or milder grades of senile dementia than when the data derive from a broad spectrum of impaired individuals including many who are severely afflicted.

There are a small number of puzzling cases in which autopsy reveals appreciable brain damage without a history of marked psychological deficit in life. This may be due to the location of the damaged neurons, as well as a result of the makeup and distribution of surviving neurons or other factors.

Goldstein and Scheerer (1941) have demonstrated the relationship between brain impairment and diminished ability to think abstractly. Concretization of thought is measured in items such as the WAIS Similarities subtest in which the subject is asked how an apple and an orange are alike.

Lauter and Meyer (1968) do not regard senile dementia as only "an accelerated and intensified senile involution," citing the results of psychological investigations. Senile dementia and related conditions are the outcome of pathological processes.

It has been claimed that brain pathology simulating that seen in Alzheimer's disease appears around age 35 in many persons with Down's syndrome. Ohara (1973) studied such changes in the brains of eight patients with the aid of the electron microscope. Malamud (1964) found neuropathologic changes characteristic of Alzheimer's disease in all 20 of a group of Down's syndrome patients who died in the age range 37–66. Owens, Dawson, and Losin (1971) have commented on the early appearance of physical and mental aging symptoms in Down's syndrome. Demaine and Silverstein (1978) tested two groups of mentally retarded patients with Form L, M, or L–M of the Stanford–Binet (Terman & Merrill, 1937, 1960). One group consisted of 189 Down's syndrome patients, the total hospital population in this category. The second group was a control group made up of retarded individuals with other diagnoses, matched with the Down's syndrome patients on mental age (MA) and chronological age (CA) at the time of initial testing.

Using a semilongitudinal method of analysis, Demaine and Silverstein (1978) developed curves for subjects in the CA range 4–50. Curves for both the Down's syndrome group and the control group showed a strong linear trend during the 4–16 years period, after which both curves remained fairly level through age 50. Unfortunately, neuropathological data is not available on the subjects. There were few Down's syndrome patients in the older age brackets, and it may be that those who developed Alzheimer's changes tended to die sooner than the others. This topic deserves further study.

Ellis, McCulloch, and Corley (1974) declare that "in Down's syndrome, the reward for survival beyond age 40 is presenile dementia [p. 101]. Senile plaques and neurofibrillary tangles, identical with those seen in Alzheimer's disease, were found in a 54-year-old woman at autopsy. Evidence for accelerated aging in Down's syndrome is provided in a study by Schneider and Epstein (1972), which reported a lowered replication rate and life span in cultured skin fibroblasts from patients of this kind.

Another interesting disorder is progeria in which advanced signs of aging are seen in children. Rosenfeld (1976) observes that although progeria mimics many of the symptoms of old age, symptoms of senile dementia are absent. This is in agreement with reports by physicians who have treated progeria patients. Kaplan (1963) corresponded with physicians throughout the world who had published articles on progeria, asking if their patients had been given psychological tests, and if not, he sought their clinical judgment with regard to the survival of cognitive functions. No psychological tests had been administered, but there was consensus that there was no striking impairment of intellectual abilities. As was to be expected, depression was present almost invariably.

Attempts to localize and otherwise characterize brain damage through psychological tests have been considered and evaluated by Benton (1967), Burgemeister (1962), and Meyer (1957). Clearly, this is extremely difficult to do in the present state of our knowledge. Mattis (1976) also has reviewed the literature on the neuropsychological examination of the mentally impaired aged, citing difficulties in localizing lesions on the basis of psychological testing. Fuld (1978) believes that psychological testing may be helpful in accomplishing the differential diagnosis of Alzheimer's disease from other dementias of later life.

Since the etiologies of the senile dementias are still largely obscure, psychological testing can offer little help in differential diagnosis. Moreover, there is reason to believe that often multiple causes are involved in the same individual. It may make little difference whether neurons have been destroyed by blood vessel disease, toxic substances, slow-growing viruses, or because of other causes. The critical factors affecting psychological test results may be the number of neurons destroyed and where they are located.

Physiological and biochemical aberrations may be involved in the senile dementias and may help to account for the fluctuations in test performance that are so frequently observed. Kolata (1979) reviews several investigations that indicate that Alzheimer's disease may be due, in part, to a lack of acetylcholine. Wang, Obrist, and Busse (1970) have reported on the relationship among impaired intellectual function, reduced cerebral blood flow, and cerebral oxygen consumption. Many other investigators have confirmed the relationship between impaired intellectual functioning and reduced cerebral blood flow and oxygen consumption (Butler, Dastur, & Perlin, 1965; Hedland et al., 1964; Klee, 1964; Lassen, Munck, & Tottey, 1957; Wang, Obrist, & Busse, 1970). O'Brien (1977) has summarized the literature on vascular disease and dementia in the elderly. Although acknowledging that the etiological importance of blood vessel impairment as a cause of cognitive deficit in the aged has been somewhat exaggerated, he insists that it deserves serious attention as a primary or contributory factor.

In the past, much of the neuropathological work on the senile dementias has been gross. With the increasing use of the electron microscope, more subtle changes are being reported. Berry (1975) states that the average number of synapses in one mammalian cortical neuron is about 10^4 or 10^5 and that it is at the synaptic level that some of the earliest demonstrable ultrastructural changes in dementias occur. The psychological correlates of such changes are deserving of study, but the task will be a difficult one.

It is natural to overlook or minimize functional disorder in what is mainly an organic dementia. Alzheimer's disease may be superimposed upon manic-depressive illness, schizophrenia, or a neurosis, and these preexisting conditions may influence test performance. Morgan (1967) is critical of the view that memory disorder in senile psychosis is due entirely to nonpsychogenic learning decay based on organic brain deterioration. He contends than an interference model of senile learning fits in better with the facts than do decay models.

Irreversible brain damage is not necessarily associated with progressive mental deterioration, although this does occur in some cases. In some cases, mental status is remarkably stable for many years.

PSYCHOLOGICAL TEST PERFORMANCE AS A DEATH PREDICTOR

Dropping psychological test scores in seniles frequently are harbingers of approaching death. A sizable literature supports this finding, and the search for the details of the relationship now is attracting many investigators. It is our experience, based on a limited number of cases, that the most severely mentally deteriorated have a higher mortality rate than those who have suffered less psychological decline, but there are conspicuous exceptions. The case comes to mind of a senile woman who declined gradually but consistently over a period of 15 years, dying, very severely impaired, at age 94. Rapid decline is more prognostic with regard to early death than slow decline.

Institutionalized aged persons who did poorly on four selected indicators—psychiatric examination, psychological testing, medical assessment, and incontinence—had a death rate of 52% within 1 year, according to a report by Goldfarb, Fisch, and Gerber (1966). Kay, Norris, and Post (1956) also have examined indicators of early death and recovery in geriatric mental patients. Müller, Grad, and Engelsmann (1975), in a 5-year followup study, found that psychological test results were good predictors of survival in a geriatric population.

Commenting on the "terminal drop hypothesis," Siegler (1975) presents data indicating that a sharp fall in cognitive functions may be an indication of approaching death. Wang and Whanger (1971) have explored the relationship between brain impairment and longevity. In a later paper, Wang and Busse (1974) report that when older persons with and without dementia are matched by age, longevity differences between the two groups are markedly diminished. Most seniles are in their 70s or older and hence are more vulnerable to death.

Go, Todorov, Elston, and Constantinidis (1978) studied 982 patients admitted to a psychiatric clinic over a 10-year period. The life expectancy of patients with dementia was one-third that of controls. Among Alzheimer's disease patients, those with neurofibrillary tangles in the neocortex had the longest survival times, whereas those not showing this kind of neuropathology had the shortest survival times.

A 6-year followup of 130 geriatric psychiatric patients showed that the lowest survival rates were among those with organic brain syndromes (Varsamis, Zuchowski, & Maini, 1972). The survival rate varied between those with senile and those with arteriosclerotic dementias. The leading cause of death in those with dementias was bronchopneumonia.

Botwinick, West, and Storandt (1978) have described brief behavioral measures that successfully predicted survival of apparently healthy men and women in the age range 60–89 during a 5-year period. The battery consisted of 18 tasks as well as eight measures of social activity, health, and demographic characteristics.

A statistically significant difference in mortality among women in a home for the aged as between those who had chronic brain syndrome (CBS) and those not so diagnosed was found by Peck, Wolloch, and Rodstein (1978). Those who had CBS died sooner, even if their medical examinations on admission showed them to be in "good" physical condition, exceeding that of women without CBS judged to be in "poor" health. CBS was not a significant factor in mortality in men in this population.

Jarvik, Kallman, and Falek (1962), in their study of intellectual changes in aged twins, did a followup of them after 9 years with the Wechsler Adult Intelligence Scale. There was little change during the 9-year period among the subjects, but those who died had lower scores on the vocabulary and similarities subtests and on three of the performance items.

The sharp drop in cognitive functions that precedes death in some seniles may be due in part to lowered energy level, poorer motivation, distracting pain, and other factors associated with ill health.

REFERENCES

Aker, J. B., Walsh, A. C., & Beam, J. R. *Mental capacity: Medical and legal aspects of the aging.* Colorado Springs, Colo.: Shepard's, Inc., 1977.

Babcock, H. An experiment in the measurement of mental deterioration. *Archives of Psychology* (New York), 1930, No. 117.

Benton, A. Psychological tests for brain damage. In A. M. Freedman & H. I. Kaplan (Eds.), *Comprehensive textbook of psychiatry*. Baltimore, Md.: Williams & Wilkins, 1967.

Berry, R. G. Pathology of dementia. In J. G. Howells (Ed.), *Modern perspectives in the Psychiatry of old age*. New York: Brunner-Mazel, 1975. Pp. 51–83.

Birkett, D. P., & Boltuch, B. Measuring dementia. *Journal of the American Geriatrics Society*, 1977, 25, 153–156.

Blessed, G., Tomlinson, B. E., & Roth, M. The association between quantitative measures of dementia and of senile change in the cerebral grey matter of elderly subjects. *British Journal of Psychiatry*, 1968, 114, 797–811.

Botwinick, J. *Cognitive processes in maturity and old age*. New York: Springer, 1967.

Botwinick, J., & Birren, J. E. Differential decline in the Wechsler–Bellevue subtests in the senile psychoses. *Journal of Gerontology*, 1951, 6, 365–368.

Botwinick, J., West, R., & Storandt, M. Predicting death from behavioral test performance. *Journal of Gerontology*, 1978, 33, 755–762.

Branconnier, R. J., & Cole, J. O. The impairment index as a symptom-independent parameter of drug efficacy in geriatric psychopharmacology. *Journal of Gerontology*, 1978, 33, 217–223.

Brink, T. L., Capri, D., De Neeve, V., Janakes, C., & Oliveira, C. Senile confusion: Limitations of assessment by the Face–Hand Test, Mental Status Questionnaire, and staff ratings. *Journal of the American Geriatrics Society*, 1978, 26, 380–382.

Burgemeister, B. B. *Psychological techniques in neurological diagnosis*. New York: Harper & Row, 1962.

Butler, R. H., Dastur, D. K., & Perlin, S. Relationships of senile manifestations and chronic brain syndromes to cerebral circulation and metabolism. *Journal of Psychiatric Research*, 1965, 3, 229–238.

Caird, W. K. Memory disorder and psychological test performance in aged psychiatric patients. *Diseases of the Nervous System*, 1965, 26, 499–505.

Canter, A. BIP bender test for the detection of organic brain disorder: Modified scoring method and replication. *Journal of Consulting Clinical Psychology*, 1968, 32, 522–526.

Canter, A. How to do office-based screening for organic brain disorders. *Geriatrics*, 1978, 33, 86–91.

Cattell, R. B. The theory of fluid and crystallized intelligence: A critical experiment. *Journal of Educational Psychology*, 1963, 54, 1–22.

Comfort, A. Non-threatening mental testing of the elderly, *Journal of the American Geriatrics Society*, 1978, 26, 261–262.

Copeland, J. R. M. *et al.* Cross-national study of diagnosis of the mental disorders: A comparison of the diagnoses of elderly psychiatric patients admitted to mental hospitals serving Queens County, New York, and the former Borough of Camberwell, London. *British Journal of Psychiatry*, 1975, 126, 11–20.

Corsellis, J. A. N. *Mental illness and the aging brain* (Maudsley Monograph No. 9). London: Oxford Univ. Press, 1962.

Cunningham, W. R., Sepkoski, C. M., & Opel, M. R. Fatigue effects on intelligence test performance in the elderly. *Journal of Gerontology*, 1978, 33, 541–545.

Demaine, G. C., & Silverstein, A. B. MA changes in institutionalized Down's syndrome persons: A semilongitudinal approach. *American Journal of Mental Deficiency*, 1978, 82, 429–432.

Dorken, H., & Greenbloom, G. C. Psychological investigation of senile dementia. *Geriatrics*, 1953, 8, 324–333.

Eisdorfer, C., Nowlin, J., & Wilkie, F. Improvement of learning in the aged by modification of autonomic nervous system activity. *Science,* 1970, *170,* 1327–1329.

Ellis, W. G., McCulloch, J. R., & Corley, C. L. Presenile dementia in Down's syndrome. *Neurology,* 1974, *24,* 101–106.

Folstein, M. F., Folstein, S. E., & McHugh, P. R. Mini-mental state: A practical method for grading the cognitive state of patients for the clinician. *Journal of Psychiatric Research,* 1975, *12,* 189–198.

Fuld, P. A. Psychological testing in the differential diagnosis of the dementias. In R. Katzman, R. D. Terry, & K. L. Bick (Eds.), *Alzheimer's disease: Senile dementia and related disorders.* New York: Raven Press, 1978. Pp. 185–193.

Go, R. C. P., Todorov, A. B., Elston, R. C., & Constantinidis, J. The malignancy of dementias. *Annals of Neurology,* 1978, *3,* 559–561.

Goldfarb, A. I., Fisch, M., & Gerber, I. E. Predictors of mortality in the institutionalized aged. *Diseases of the Nervous System,* 1966, *27,* 21–29.

Goldstein, K., & Scheerer, M. Abstract and concrete behavior: An experimental study with special tests. *Psychological Monographs,* 1941, *53,* 151.

Guilford, J. P. *Psychometric methods* (2nd ed.). New York: McGraw Hill, 1954.

Guilford, J. P. *Fundamental statistics in psychology and education* (3rd ed.). New York: McGraw Hill, 1956.

Gunn, A. E. Mental impairment in the elderly: Medico-legal assessment. *Journal of the American Geriatrics Society,* 1977, *25,* 193–197.

Hedland, S. *et al.* Cerebral blood circulation in dementia. *Acta Psychiatrica Scandinavica,* 1964, *40,* 77–106.

Heimann, H. Psychometry of advanced age. In C. Müller & L. Ciompi (Eds.), *Senile dementia.* Baltimore, Maryland: Williams & Wilkins, 1968. Pp. 38–40.

Hersch, E. L., Kral, V. A., & Palmer, R. B. Clinical value of the London Psychogeriatric Rating Scale. *Journal of the American Geriatrics Society,* 1978, *26,* 348–354.

Horn, J. L. Psychometric studies of aging and intelligence. In S. Gershon & A. Raskin (Eds.), *Genesis and treatment of psychologic disorders in the elderly.* New York: Raven Press, 1976. Pp. 19–43.

Inglis, J., Colwell, C., & Post, F. An evaluation of the predictive power of a test known to differentiate between elderly "functional" and "organic" psychiatric patients. *Journal of Mental Science,* 1960, *106,* 1486–1492.

Jarvik, L. F., Kallman, F. J., & Falek, A. Intellectual changes in aged twins. *Journal of Gerontology,* 1962, *17,* 289–294.

Jastak, J. F., & Jastak, S. R. *The Wide Range Achievement Test.* Wilmington, Delaware: Guidance Associates, 1965.

Kahn, R. L., Goldfarb, A. I., Pollack, M., & Peck, A. Brief objective measures for the determinations of mental status in the aged. *American Journal of Psychiatry,* 1960, *117,* 326–328.

Kaplan, O. J. (Ed.), *Mental disorders in later life* (2nd ed.). Stanford, California: Stanford Univ. Press, 1956.

Kaplan, O. J. Personal correspondance, 1963.

Kaplan, O. J., Brown, W. J., Thomas, E., & Thomas, P. Neuropathological–psychological correlations in organic brain syndromes in the elderly. *Proceedings of the 7th International Congress of Gerontology.* Vienna: International Association of Gerontology, 1966. P. 350.

Kaplan, O. J., Rumbaugh, D. M., Mitchell, D. C., & Thomas, E. D. Effects of level of surviving abilities, time of day, and test–retest upon psychological performance in seniles. *Journal of Gerontology,* 1963, *18,* 55–59.

Katzman, R., Terry, R. D., & Bick, K. L. (Eds.). *Alzheimer's disease: Senile dementia and related disorders.* New York: Raven Press, 1978.

Kay, D. W. K., Norris, V., & Post, F. Prognosis in psychiatric disorders of the elderly. An attempt to define indicators of early death and early recovery. *Journal of Mental Science,* 1956, *102,* 129–140.

Kent, G. H. *Kent E-G-Y test: Series of emergency scales* (Manual). New York: Psychological Corp., 1946.

Kinsbourne, M. Cognitive deficit and the aging brain: A behavioral analysis. *International Journal of Aging and Human Development,* 1974, *5,* 41–49.

Klee, A. The relationship between clinical evaluation of mental deterioration, psychological test results, and the cerebral metabolic rate of oxygen. *Acta Neurologica Scandinavica,* 1964, *40,* 337.

Kolata, G. B. Mental disorders: A new approach to treatment? *Science,* 1979, *203,* 36–38.

Kral, V. A. Memory loss in the aged. *Diseases of the Nervous System,* 1966, *27,* 51–54.

Kral, V. A. Benign senescent forgetfulness. In R. Katzman, R. D. Terry, & K. L. Bick (Eds.), *Alzheimer's disease: Senile dementia and related disorders.* New York: Raven Press, 1978. Pp. 47–51.

Lassen, N. A., Munck, O., & Tottey, E. R. Mental function and cerebral oxygen consumption in organic dementia. *Archives of Neurology and Psychiatry,* 1957, *77,* 126–133.

Lauter, H., & Meyer, J. E. Clinical and nosological concepts of senile dementia. In C. Muller & L. Ciompi (Eds.), *Senile dementia.* Baltimore, Maryland: Williams & Wilkins, 1968. Pp. 13–26.

Lorge, I. The influence of the test upon the nature of mental decline as a function of age. *Journal of Educational Psychology,* 1936, *27,* 100–110.

Lowenthal, M. F., & Berkman, P. L. *Aging and mental disorder in San Francisco.* San Francisco: Jossey-Bass, 1967.

Malamud, N. Neuropathology. In H. A. Stevens & R. Heber (Eds.), *Mental retardation.* Chicago: Univ. of Chicago Press, 1964. Pp. 429–452.

Malamud, N. A comparative study of the neuropathologic findings in senile psychoses and in "normal" senility. *Journal of the American Geriatrics Society,* 1965, *13,* 113–117.

Mattis, S. Mental status examination for organic mental syndrome in the elderly. In L. Bellak & T. B. Karasu (Eds.), *Geriatric psychiatry.* New York: Grune & Stratton, 1976. Pp. 77–121.

Meyer, V. Critique of psychological approaches to brain damage. *Journal of Mental Science,* 1957, *103,* 80–109.

Miller, M. *Abnormal aging: The psychology of senile and presenile dementia.* New York: John Wiley & Sons, 1977.

Morgan, R. F. Memory and the senile psychoses: A follow-up note. *Psychological Reports,* 1967, *20,* 733–734.

Müller, H. F., Grad, B., & Engelsmann, F. Biological and psychological predictors of survival in a psycho-geriatric population. *Journal of Gerontology,* 1975, *30,* 47–52.

Nandy, K. (Ed.). *Senile dementia: A biomedical approach.* New York: Elsevier–North Holland Biomedical Press, 1978.

Nandy, K., & Sherwin, I. (Eds.). *The aging brain and senile dementia.* New York: Plenum Press, 1977.

O'Brien, M. D. Vascular disease and dementia in the elderly. In W. L. Smith & M. Kinsbourne (Eds.), *Aging and dementia.* New York: Spectrum Publications, 1977. Pp. 77–90.

Ohara, P. T. Electron microscopical study of the brain in Down's syndrome. *Brain,* 1973, *95,* 681–684.

Owens, D., Dawson, J. C., & Losin, S. Alzheimer's disease in Down's syndrome. *American Journal of Mental Deficiency*, 1971, *75*, 606–612.

Pearce, J., & Miller, E. *Clincial aspects of dementia*. London: Bailliere, Tindall, 1973.

Peck, A., Wolloch, L., & Rodstein, M. Mortality of the aged with chronic brain syndrome: further observations in a five-year study. *Journal of the American Geriatrics Society*, 1978, *26*, 170–176.

Pfeiffer, E. A short portable mental status questionnaire for the assessment of organic brain deficit in elderly patients. *Journal of the American Geriatrics Society*, 1975, *23*, 433–441.

Pfeiffer, E. *Multidimensional functional assessment: The OARS methodology*. Durham, North Carolina: Center for the Study of Aging and Human Development, 1975.

Plutchik, R., Conte, H., & Lieberman, M. Development of a scale (GIES) for assessment of cognitive and perceptual functioning in geriatric patients. *Journal of the American Geriatrics Society*, 1971, *19*, 614–623.

Plutchik, R., Conte, H., Lieberman, M., Bakur, M., Grossman, J., & Lehrman, N. Reliability and validity of a scale for assessing the funtioning of geriatric patients. *Journal of the American Geriatrics Society*, 1970, *18*, 491–500.

Robinson, R. A. The assessment center. In J. G. Howells (Ed.), *Modern perspectives in the psychiatry of old age*. New York: Brunner/Mazel, 1975. Pp. 379–396.

Rosenfeld, A. *Prolongevity*. New York: Alfred A. Knopf, 1976. P. 102.

Roth, M. Classification and etiology in mental disorders of old age. In D. W. K. Kay & A. Walk (Eds.), *Recent developments in psychogeriatrics* (Special publication no. 6), *British Journal of Psychiatry*, Ashford, Kent, Headley, 1971.

Roth, M., Tomlinson, B. E., & Blessed, G. Correlation between scores for dementia and counts of "senile plaques" in cerebral gray matter of elderly subjects. *Nature*, 1966, *209*, 109–110.

Rothschild, D. Senile psychoses and psychoses with cerebral arteriosclerosis. In O. J. Kaplan (Ed.), *Mental disorders in later life* (2nd ed.). Stanford, California: Stanford Univ. Press, 1956. Pp. 289–331.

Savage, R. D. Intellect and personality in the aged. In W. L. Smith & M. Kinsbourne (Eds.), *Aging and dementia*. New York: Spectrum Publications, 1977. Pp. 173–188.

Schneider, H., & Epstein, C. J. Replication rate and life-span of cultured fibroblasts in Down's syndrome. *Proceedings of the Society for Experimental Biology and Medicine*, 1972, *141*, 1092.

Siegler, I. C. The terminal drop hypothesis: Fact or artifact. *Experimental Aging Research*, 1975, *1*, 169–185.

Slaby, A. E., & Wyatt, R. J. *Dementia in the presenium*. Springfield, Illinois: Charles C Thomas, 1974.

Smith, A. *Symbol digit modalities test manual*. Los Angeles: Western Psychological Services, 1976.

Smith, W. L., & Kinsbourne, M. (Eds.). *Aging and dementia*. New York: Spectrum Publications, 1977.

Sourander, P., & Sjögren, H. The concept of Alzheimer's disease and its clinical implications. In G. E. W. Wolstenholme & M. O'Connor (Eds.), *Alzheimer's disease and related conditions*. London: Churchill, 1970.

Spitzer, R. L., Fleiss, J. L., Endicott, J., & Cohen, J. Mental status schedule: Properties of factor-analytically derived scales. *Archives of General Psychiatry*, 1967, *16*, 479–493.

Storandt, M., Siegler, I. C., & Elias, M. E. (Eds.). *The clinical psychology of aging*. New York: Plenum Press, 1978.

Terman, L. M., & Merrill, M. A. *Measuring intelligence*. Boston: Houghton Mifflin, 1937.

Terman, L. M., & Merrill, M. A. Stanford-Binet intelligence scale: Manual for the third revision, Form L-M. Boston: Houghton Mifflin, 1960.

Varsamis, M. B., Zuchowski, T., & Maini, K. K. Survival rates and causes of death in geriatric psychiatric patients. *Canadian Psychiatric Association Journal,* 1972, *17,* 17–22.

Vogel, F. S. The brain and time. In E. W. Busse & E. Pfeiffer (Eds.), *Behavior and adaptation in late life* (2nd ed.). Boston: Little, Brown, 1977. Pp. 228–239.

Wang, H. S. Organic brain syndromes. In E. W. Busse & E. Pfeiffer (Eds.), *Behavior and adaptation in late life* (2nd ed). Boston: Little, Brown, 1977, Pp. 240–263.

Wang, H. S., & Busse, E. W. Brain impairment and longevity in community aged persons. In E. Palmore (Ed.), *Normal aging. II.* Durham, North Carolina: Duke Univ. Press, 1974. Pp. 263–268.

Wang, H. S., Obrist, W. D., & Brusse, E. W. Neurophysiological correlates of the intellectual function of elderly persons living in the community. *American Journal of Psychiatry,* 1970, *126,* 1205–1212.

Wang, H. S., & Whanger, A. Brain impairment and longevity. In E. Palmore & F. Jeffers (Eds.), *Prediction of life span—recent findings.* Lexington, Massachusetts: D. C. Heath, 1971. Pp. 95–105.

Wechsler, D. *The measurement and appraisal of adult intelligence.* Baltimore, Maryland: Williams & Wilkins, 1958.

Wells, C. E. (Ed.). *Dementia.* Philadelphia, Pennsylvania: Davis, 1971.

Wilkie, F., & Eisdorfer, C. Intelligence and blood pressure in the aged. *Science,* 1971, *172,* 959–962.

Wolstenholme, G. E. W., & O'Connor, M. (Eds.). *Alzheimer's disease and related conditions.* London: Churchill, 1970.

Chapter 5

MANIC-DEPRESSIVE ILLNESS IN THE ELDERLY

Kay Redfield Jamison

*Wrapt in the wave of the music, with weariness
more than of earth,
The moil of my centuries filled me; and gone
like a sea-covered stone
Were the memories of the whole of my sorrow
and the memories of the whole of my mirth
And a softness came from the starlight and filled
me full to the bone.*

—W. B. YEATS, *The Wanderings of Oisin*[1]

INTRODUCTION

History

Severe, cyclic disorders of mood were observed and described by ancient poets and physicians such as Homer, Plutarch, and Hippocrates. Although these writers discussed both depression ("melancholia") and mania in great detail, the occurrence of mania and depression in the same person was not systemically investigated until 1684, when Bonet described *folie mania-comelancolique.* Then, in the eighteenth century, Falret studied a group of patients over a period of years and noted the tendency for some of the patients to have recurrent bouts of both elation and despair; he also noted the tendency for this particular illness, which he called *la folie circulaire,* to occur much more often within children and parents of these patients than in the relatives of persons displaying no signs of the illness. In the 1890s, Kraepelin published a monograph on manic-depressive illness in which he described patients in different stages of their illness and presented his view that these stages of mania and depression "only represent manifestations of a single morbid process." Although the

[1] Reprinted with permission of Macmillan Publishing Co., Inc. from *Collected Poems* by William Butler Yeats. Copyright 1906 by Macmillan Publishing Co., Inc. and renewed 1934 by William Butler Yeats.

PSYCHOPATHOLOGY OF AGING

advances in the study of mood disorders have been remarkable since Kraepelin's time—particularly since 1960—his description (1921) of manic-depressive illness remains among the best available:

[Depressed stage, maniacal-depressive insanity]:
She spoke and ate but little, stared into space, and hardly slept at all. She also took a knife to be with her at night, and expressed ideas of suicide. . . . For the past three months, she said, she had no rest, and had been absent-minded and forgetful. The patient spoke little of her own accord, and generally lay still in bed with a downcast expression. She was obliged to think for a disproportionately long time over the answers to simple questions, was not quite clear about the chronological order of her experience, and hardly knew at all where she was. All her expressions and movements were slow and hesitating, as if she did not quite know what she ought to say and do. She was low-spirited, and in particular cried a great deal when she had visitors. . . . The patient calls herself the greatest of sinners.

[Maniacal excitement]:
She does not sit down, but walks about quickly, examines briefly what she sees, interferes unceremoniously with the students, and tries to be familiar with them. No sooner is she induced to sit down than she quickly springs up again, flings away her shoes, unties her apron, and begins to sing and dance. The next minute she stops, claps her hands, goes to the blackboard, seizes the chalk, and begins to write her name. . . . During the whole time the patient chatters almost incessantly, though the purport of her rapid headlong talk is scarcely intelligible, and quite disconnected. Still, one can sometimes follow up her erratic thoughts. Her mood is extremely merry, she laughs and titters continuously between her talk, but easily becomes angry on slight provocation, and then breaks out into a torrent of the nastiest abuse, only to be tranquil a minute after with a happy laugh [pp. 22, 27].

Epidemiology

In order to estimate the number of persons who have manic-depressive illness, it is necessary to be aware of a few of the major limitations on the accuracy of frequently cited statistics. These limitations include diagnostic inconsistencies, availability of psychiatric services outside the hospital, the expansion of preventive and early intervention measures, effects of mass communication on public knowledge of psychiatric disorders, and cultural differences in both diagnostic practice and symptom presentation. An interesting example of the latter cultural differences can be found in Kramer's work (1965, 1969) comparing rates of manic-depressive illness in the United States and in the United Kingdom. Kramer's initial work indicated that the first admission rate for manic-depressive illness was 18 times as high for public hospitals in the United Kingdom as in the United States and 9 times as high when the figures for public and private hospitals were combined. However, when diagnostic interviewing techniques were standardized between the two countries, much of the discrepancy dissolved (although significant and, as yet, unexplained differences remain), underscoring the importance of the research methods used in obtaining such results (Becker, 1974; Perris, 1976).

With these restrictions kept in mind, what are the general estimates for the prevalence of manic-depressive illness? Cohen (1975) and Ripley (1977) state that the lifetime period rate of manic psychoses, worldwide, is 3 to 4 per 1000. Using highly inclusive diagnostic criteria Winokur, Clayton, and Reich (1969) estimate the lifetime risk at approximately 2% for males and 3% for females. As might be expected, epidemiological data are far less precise and comprehensive for manic-depressive illness in the elderly. Pitt (1974) states that manic illness accounts for no more than 1 in 20 admissions to the general psychogeriatric ward, whereas depressive illness is responsible for almost half. Post (1976) noted that studies of patients over 60 indicated 50% of the admissions were for affective disorders, but that manic-depressive illness was only a small fraction of those disorders. In an earlier investigation Post (1965) estimated that only between 5% and 10% of elderly people referred for the treatment of affective disorders exhibit the excited or elated phase. Kay, Beamish, and Roth (1964), in a study of prevalence of old-age mental disorders in Newcastle upon Tyne, found that manic-depressive illness occurs in about 14 per 1000 for those 65 years or older. Nielsen (1963) found, in the same age group, virtually the same prevalence of the illness (1.2%). Both the Kay *et al.* (1964) study and Nielsen's study found that the great majority of patients were being treated at home or in old-age homes rather than in the hospital. It will be interesting to see in future years if the advent of lithium will ultimately increase the incidence of elderly manic-depressives by lowering the illness's high attendant suicide rate (which has been responsible for a significant proportion of premature deaths in patients with bipolar illness).

Demographic Correlates

As in unipolar depression, women appear somewhat more likely than men to get manic-depressive illness. Recent statistics indicate that the ratio of female to male unipolar depressives is approximately 3:1, while the corresponding ratio for bipolar illness is only half of that, or 1.5:1. However, possibly due to a greater life span in women and a higher suicide rate in men, the ratio of female to male manic-depressives over the age of 65 is approximately 2:1 (Kay *et al.*, 1964; Nielsen, 1963). Manic-depressive illness has often been presented as an illness of later life, but the scientific literature belies this. Kraepelin described "circular madness" in a 14-year-old girl and estimated that approximately 60% of first "attacks" occurred between the ages of 20 and 35. Winokur *et al.* (1969) reported that one-third of their bipolar patients experienced their first episode prior to age 20; Perris (1968) reported that 40%

occurred between ages 15 and 25; and Wertham (1929) reported that 20% of 2000 manic episodes began before the age of 20. Carlson, Davenport, and Jamison (1977) compared bipolar patients whose illness began before age 20 with a group whose first episode occurred after 45; the results indicated that age of onset was not a factor in the course and prognosis of the illness. In general, the onset of manic-depressive illness after the age of 65 is quite rare, and indeed, some authors question whether or not a late-life manic episode is a true expression of manic-depressive illness or a separate entity altogether (Roth, 1955; Verwoerdt, 1976). Kraepelin (1921) observed that 93% of the patients he studied had their first episodes prior to the age of 60, and Grof, Angst, and Haines (1973) noted that of their cohort, 88% were first ill before the age of 50. Thus, for any given elderly patient experiencing a manic episode, the odds are overwhelming that the attack will represent a recurrence rather than a first event; this is consistent, of course, with the recurrent nature of the illness itself.

CLINICAL DESCRIPTION AND DIAGNOSIS

The general characteristics, signs, and symptoms of major depressive disorders are well described by Gerner in Chapter 6 of this book; therefore, the focus here will be primarily on the clinical description and diagnosis of mania and hypomania. In all recent diagnostic systems, bipolar and unipolar illnesses have been distinguished due to their highly different natural histories, genetic, biological, and pharmacological features. A few of these differences are summarized in Table 5.1.

On the basis of an extended series of clinical research studies, investigators at Washington University in St. Louis devised a series of inclusionary and exclusionary criteria for various disorders, including manic-depressive illness (Feighner, Robins, & Guze, 1972). This work led to the development of standardized diagnostic criteria for psychiatric disorders. Basically, the inclusion criteria for the mood disorders comprise the following: (a) necessity for a given *mood state*; (b) a certain number and type of *behavioral changes*; (c) a particular minimal level of *disturbance severity*; and (d) a specified minimal *duration* of illness. Exclusionary criteria are the presence of other, preexisting psychiatric illness or a life-threatening medical illness. Table 5.2 shows the research diagnostic criteria for manic-depressive illness.

The Diagnostic and Statistical Manual of Mental Disorders (DSM-III, April 1977 draft), based on the research criteria listed in Table 5.2,

TABLE 5.1

Characteristics of Bipolar and Unipolar Patients

	Bipolar	Unipolar
Clinical features	Retarded in psychomotor activity; postpartum episodes; lower ratings of anxiety and physical complaints	Agitated (sometimes retarded) in psychomotor activity; higher ratings of anxiety and physical complaints
Family history	+ Mania, + depression, + suicide + alcoholism, + 2-generation affective illness; mania in primary relative 4–10%	− Mania, + depression, − alcoholism, + sociopathy; mania in primary relative .29–.35%
Proportion female	59%	64–68%
Onset	Average age *younger*, mean age of onset 28.7	Average age *older*, mean age of onset 37.3
Follow-Up	Average number of episodes *more* (>3 episodes per lifetime); episodes last 3–6 months	Average number of episodes *fewer* (usually 1–2 episodes in lifetime); episodes last 6–9 months
Suicide	*Higher* rate	*Lower* rate
Socioeconomic status	Significantly higher educational and occupational achievements compared with matched unipolars	Significantly lower socioeconomic status
Divorce rate	Higher	Lower
Premorbid personality	Active and sociable; intelligent, shy, active, good judgment; *not* insecure, ambitious, thrifty, or promiscuous	Insecure, obsessional, sensitive; shy, conscientious, sensitive with good judgment; *not* insecure, intelligent, egocentric, or promiscuous
Biochemistry	Subnormal steroid output; lower platelet MAO activity	Above normal steroid output; normal platelet MAO activity
Neurophysiology	"Augmenter" on evoked potentials; lower threshold for response to flicker stimuli; lower sedation threshold	"Reducer" on evoked potentials; higher threshold for response to flicker stimuli; higher sedation threshold
Pharmacology	Lithium-carbonate-responsive; may switch to hypomania if on tricyclic antidepressant; lithium useful as antidepressant	Less likely to respond to lithium; more likely to respond to tricyclic antidepressant

Source: Material in this table is based on Akiskal and McKinney, 1975; Grof *et al.*, 1973; Winokur, 1978.

TABLE 5.2
Research Diagnostic Criteria for Manic-Depressive Illness

Criteria	Mania	Depression
Mood	Euphoria or irritability (may alternate with depressive mood)	Dysphoria
Behavioral changes	At least three of the following: 1. Hyperactivity 2. Push of speech, increased talking 3. Flight of ideas 4. Inflated self-esteem, grandiosity 5. Decreased need for sleep 6. Distractibility 7. Markedly increased activities (e.g., hypersexuality, buying sprees, reckless driving)	At least five of the following: 1. Anorexia or weight change (usually loss) 2. Sleep disorder 3. Loss of energy, fatigability 4. Psychomotor agitation or retardation 5. Loss of interest in usual activities (sex, work) 6. Self-reproach or guilt 7. Decreased concentration 8. Recurrent thoughts of death or suicide
Severity of disturbance	At least one of the following: 1. Meaningful conversation impossible 2. Serious impairment socially (family, work, home) 3. In absence of 1 or 2, hospitalization	Sought help from someone during the dysphoric period or had impaired functioning socially (family, home, work)
Duration	At least 1 week (or any duration if hospitalized)	At least 2–4 weeks
Exclusionary	Presence of other preexisting psychiatric illness or life-threatening medical illness	Presence of other preexisting psychiatric illness or life-threatening medical illness

Source: Spitzer, Endicott, and Robins, 1975.

defines the essential feature of the manic episode as "a distinct period when the predominant mood is either elevated, expansive, or irritable and is associated with other symptoms of the manic syndrome. These symptoms may include hyperactivity, excessive involvement in activities without recognizing the high potential for painful consequences, pressure of speech, flight of ideas, inflated self-esteem, decreased need for sleep, and distractibility [p. E-9]." These episodes typically begin suddenly, rapidly escalate and vary in length from days to a few months. Hypomanic disorders are characterized by many of the signs and symptoms of the manic disorder, but psychotic symptomatology is not present, fewer symptoms are required for the diagnosis, and the severity of impairment is less. Similarities of family history and response to lithium treatment among those with bipolar I (bipolar depression with mania), bipolar II (bipolar depression with hypomania), and certain well-defined cyclothymic disorders have been suggested (e.g., Akiskal, Djenderedjian, Rosenthal, & Khani, 1977).

The research criteria outline "classical manic-depressive illness" and its variants. How, then, does bipolar illness present itself in the elderly? Are there idiosyncratic features that make an accurate diagnosis more difficult to make? What factors should be kept in mind in taking a history and doing a differential diagnosis? Although there has been virtually no systematic research on presenting symptoms of mania in the elderly, clinical observations have been made by several investigations (e.g., Pitt, 1974; Post, 1965; Verwoerdt, 1976). Pitt (1974) has noted that mania in the elderly does have certain distinctive features:

1. *Confusion* at the outset may lead to a misdiagnosis of delirium. A prior affective history and an absence of physical findings makes the differential relatively straightforward.
2. *Paranoid* features are often more pronounced.
3. *Mixed affect* or *lability of affect* may be more present in the elderly. Concomitant depression may lead to "miserable mania" where there may be pressured speech and flight of ideas, but with morbid content.

Such dysphoric presentations of mania and rapid cycling of moods may occur, of course, in the younger manic patient, but they seem to be more characteristic of older bipolar patients. Pitt also remarks that true flight of ideas is often replaced by circumstantiality and increased talkativeness. Post (1965) also notes the relative decrease in flight of ideas, with speech characterized by repetition and anecdotal punctuation. He, too, comments on the increased irritability and relative decreased euphoric aspects of the mood disorder; this he attributes to the greater admixture of depression with mania, leading to both the lability of mood and the dysphoria. This dysphoria, combined with increased psychomotor output, occasionally makes the differential diagnosis between a manic disorder and an agitated depression a difficult one. Thus, Verwoerdt (1976) remarks: "Patients with agitated depression may report that they feel unable to resist the surge of energy that compels them to be active, and also that 'going so fast' lifts their spirits and makes them feel good. Typically, there is a pattern of decreased sleep; the appetite may be up or down, but since the patient usually 'does not have time to sit down and eat,' weight loss is common."

The differential diagnosis of a manic disorder must rule out: (*a*) *agitated depression* (cited previously); (*b*) *organic brain syndrome*; (*c*) *drug-induced psychoses* (e.g., alcohol, steroids, amphetamines); (*d*) *hyperthyroidism*; (*e*) *schizoaffective schizophrenia*; (*f*) *catatonic excitement*; (*g*) *delirium secondary to cerebral infection* and other organic states; and (*h*) *psychogenic manic reaction.* As is always the case in clinical psychiatry, a thorough psychiatric history and examination are essential. It is particularly important to ascertain the patient's own affective history in an attempt to document prior episodes, duration of those episodes, phasing of epidsodes (e.g., has a manic episode always been followed by a depressive episode? If so, has it required treatment or presented a risk of suicide?), and response to treatment. It is also extremely important both to document a family history of affective illness to aid in the differential and to obtain corroborating information from the patient's family members or friends. Often, it is only those close to the patient who can recall subtle or not-so-subtle behavioral and cognitive changes, document possible substance abuse patterns, and remember the nature of the onset of the illness. Because cognitive changes are pathognomonic of both severe affective illness and organic brain disease, it is important to inquire about the patient's cognitive functioning before the acute exacerbation of symptoms. Particularly important to note are recent and remote memory impairments and a decreased ability to learn new material. A more gradual insidious decline in intellectual functioning would be, of course, more consistent with dementia, although nothing precludes the coexistence of dementia with manic-depressive illness. When the patient is able to undergo psychological testing, it is often useful to order a full-scale organicity work-up. This can give useful information on current cognitive status but, more importantly, it can serve as a baseline measure for future evaluations.

The natural history of single episodes of mania, and the course of recurrent manic and depressive episodes over many years, have been described by a few investigators. Carlson and Goodwin (1973) studied acute, untreated, manic episodes in a relatively young population of patients. They found three basic stages characterizing the accelerating course; the first two stages were seen in all of their patients, the third and most severe in only 70%. These stages, with their mood, cognitive, and behavioral features described, are shown in Table 5.3. Unfortunately, no comparable study has been done in elderly patients. Their research demonstrates again the importance of a longitudinal analysis of behavior in making a diagnosis; for example, they found that pa-

TABLE 5.3
Stages of Mania

	Stage I	Stage II	Stage III
Mood	Lability of affect; euphoria predominates; irritability if demands not satisfied	Increased dysphoria and depression; open hostility and anger	Clearly dysphoric; panic-stricken; hopeless
Cognition	Expansivity, grandiosity, overconfidence; thoughts coherent but occasionally tangential; sexual and religious preoccupation; racing thoughts	Flight of ideas; disorganization of cognitive state; delusions	Incoherent, definite loosening of associations; bizarre and idiosyncratic delusions; hallucinations in one-third of patients; disorientation to time and place, occasional ideas of reference
Behavior	Increased psychomotor activity; increased initiation and rate of speech; increased spending, smoking, telephone use	Continued increased psychomotor acceleration; increased pressured speech; occasional assaultive behavior	Frenzied and frequently bizarre psychomotor activity

Source: Adapted from Carlson and Goodwin, 1973.

tients in Stage III mania were frequently indistinguishable, in clinical presentation, from paranoid schizophrenics. However, good premorbid functioning and a positive family history of primary affective disorder were highly correlated with the accurate diagnosis of bipolar illness and response to lithium. No relationship was found between the level of psychotic disorganization during the acute manic episode and the level of functioning at follow-up.

In a follow-up study of approximately 400 bipolar patients Grof, Angst, and Haines (1973) found that: (*a*) virtually every patient experienced a recurrence of the illness (99%); (*b*) a certain stability existed, after the first several episodes, in terms of duration between attacks; (*c*) the best predictor of course for a current episode was the course of past episodes; and (*d*) the length of episode plus its remission is longer in those patients with an earlier onset of the illness. The course of mania in the elderly, like its symptomatology, has not been systematically investigated. However, Post (1965) states that:

> In manic disorders the outlook is well known and varies little. Patients tend to remain disturbed somewhat longer than is the case at an earlier age, but most attacks subside within a few weeks, and they rarely last longer than six months. In the elderly, attacks tend to be frequent, most commonly every 1–2 years. Later illnesses are not necessarily more severe or prolonged than first ones, and the intervals between them do not always become shorter.

In his earlier monograph, Post (1962) noted that first onset of affective illness in the involutional period carried with it a less favorable prognosis than earlier onset illness; late onset also displayed significantly less genetic loading for manic-depressive illness. Of the 100 patients with affective illness studied, 19% made virtually complete recoveries, 35% had a considerably longer course of illness, 28% failed to recover completely to previous levels of personality functioning, and 18% showed considerable social deterioration and remained mentally ill most of the time. The following were correlates of good prognosis: age below 70; positive family history of affective disorders; recovery from earlier attacks before the age of 50, especially when these had led to hospital admissions; extroverted personality; social ties and activities extending beyond the family; absence of dysthymic or cyclothymic trends; severe affective symptoms including so-called schizophreniform features. It can be seen that many of the variables correlating with favorable prognosis are also associated with symptoms and histories of manic-depressive illness, although the data were not broken down this way, nor were the more recently developed diagnostic criteria used.

TREATMENT

Depression

The standard treatment modalities for depression (tricyclic antidepressants, monoamine oxidase inhibitors, electroconvulsant therapy, sleep deprivation, neuroleptics, and psychotherapy) are thoroughly discussed in Chapter 6 and thus will be only briefly mentioned here. It is important to stress the necessity for acquiring comprehensive and reliable information, whenever possible, about an individual's past treatments and responses to them. Generally a patient with manic-depressive illness will have had several episodes of depression and it should be possible to piece together a clinical picture of duration, severity, suicide risk, and effectiveness of different treatment interventions. Where a person has clearly responded to a simple variation in lithium level or a course of tricyclics, the therapeutic task is a relatively straightforward one. However, it is essential to determine, in instances where a patient cites a failure to respond to a particular medication, that an adequate clinical trial was involved in the nonresponse, that is, that the patient was treated at a therapeutic level for a sufficient period of time. A comprehensive clinical history should also ascertain the extent of the patient's compliance with the treatment program, and hospitalization should be considered for those who, for whatever reasons (conscious or unconscious resistance, marked confusion, or suicidality), are unable to adhere to a therapeutic regime.

Goodwin (1977) has developed a drug "decision tree" prototype for the clinical psychopharmacology of major depressive disorders (see Figure 5.1). This prototype is particularly applicable for patients who have no personal or family history of response to a given medication. Thus, as Goodwin states, decisions about treatment in bipolar I depression really concern the usage of medications *in addition to lithium*; for some bipolar I patients, lithium alone will be sufficient and for others it will act as a "cover" against precipitation of manic episodes by antidepressants. In any event, most of these patients will have been on lithium for prophylactic purposes.

Suicide is, of course, a major problem in manic-depressive illness and suicidal ideation and expression should always be taken very seriously. The suicide rate for persons with bipolar illness is higher than for any other psychiatric or nonpsychiatric group; Guze and Rob-

Bipolar Illness	
Bipolar I	Bipolar II
Lithium	Imipramine–Amitriptyline
↓	↓
Lithium and imipramine	Lithium
↓	↓
Lithium and amitriptyline	Lithium and IMI–AMI
↓	↓
Lithium and MAO inhibitors	Lithium and MAOI
↓	↓
Lithium and MAOI and IMI	Lithium and MAOI and IMI–AMI
↓	
Lithium and MAOI and AMI	

FIGURE 5.1 Drug decision tree prototype for bipolar depressive illness. (From Goodwin, 1977.)

ins (1970) reviewed 17 outcome studies of patients with primary affective disorders and found suicide to be the eventual cause of death in 15% of those with manic-depressive illness. Barraclough (1972) found that of 100 cases of suicide in a retrospective study, "21 had histories of recurrent affective illness of sufficient frequency and severity to have qualified them hypothetically for lithium therapy." Suicide rates as a function of age in bipolar illness are not known, but rate of suicide, of course, increases with age *in general*. However, there are many exceptions to this general statement, and it may be that of those patients with a sufficiently virulent form of manic-depressive illness the majority will have committed suicide prior to reaching old age. This could result in: (*a*) an actual decrease in bipolar suicide past the age of 65; or (*b*) no overall change due to the averaging out of a generally higher suicide rate past 65 with a relatively lower bipolar rate. Yet another possibility, although not systematically investigated, is a "burn out" phenomenon where, after a given number of episodes, there may be an extinction or decrease in the number and severity of episodes (Grof, Angst, & Haines, 1973).

As in any instance where suicide is a possibility, an assessment of the patient's lethality, means, and current social support system is essential. Where safe treatment cannot be instituted or continued on an outpatient basis, the patient should be hospitalized and, when necessary, placed on suicide observation and watched continuously. Reasonable common-sense precautions with respect to prescriptions should be followed; thus, only small amounts of antidepressants, lithium, and hypnotics should be prescribed until it is clear that the risk of suicide has greatly diminished. Suicide can be a problem in mania as well as in depression and, due to the increased lability of affect and dysphoric features in older manic patients, clinicians should be particularly attentive to this problem.

Mania

In the years since the mid-1960s we have witnessed the introduction of lithium as a highly effective treatment for acute manic episodes (often in conjunction with the temporary use of neuroleptics and hospitalization) and as a prophylactic measure against recurrent manic and depressive episodes in bipolar illness. In acute mania and hypomania, marked clinical improvement is seen within 3–14 days in approximately 75% of patients (Goodwin & Ebert, 1973). A review of six well-controlled clinical studies of lithium prophylaxis showed that the overall relapse rate (in bipolar patients) for manic or depressive episodes was 85% among 175 patients given a placebo, but only 30% among 174 patients maintained on lithium (Johnson, 1975). The mechanism of action of lithium remains unclear, although several possibilities have been suggested: (*a*) change in electrolyte balance across membranes; (*b*) correction of intracellular sodium imbalance; (*c*) changes in acetylcholine synthesis and release; and (*d*) inhibition of the release of norepinephrine and dopamine at the synapse, as well as changes in the uptake and retention rates of catecholamine neurotransmitters at presynaptic terminals (Baldessarini & Lipinski, 1975; Fieve, 1977).

In acute mania, adjunctive treatments are frequently used until the lithium has reached a therapeutic level. Thus, hospitalization is often necessary to protect the patient (occasionally to protect others) and to ensure the institution of adequate treatment; frequently chlorpromazine or haloperidol is used for more immediate symptom relief. In those instances where cardiac or renal impairment rules out the use of lithium, and where the patient does not respond or adversely responds to neuroleptics, electroconvulsive therapy is an effective treatment for most patients.

The major contraindications for lithium therapy are few—certain types of renal dysfunction and heart disease as well as illnesses affecting sodium balance or requiring the use of diuretics. Common mild and generally transient side effects from lithium include tremor (which usually requires no intervention but can be treated with Propranolol), gastrointestinal distress including nausea, vomiting, and diarrhea, and mild lethargy and fatigue. More serious symptoms are primarily central nervous system in origin and usually indicate lithium toxicity: hyperreflexia, confusion, slurred speech, dizziness, somnolence, stupor, seizures, and rarely, death. Long-term complications from lithium include functional hypothyroidism, nontoxic goiter, and weight gain (commonly 10–15 pounds). Hypothyroidism can, of course, present as dementia in older patients; thyroid functioning should be closely watched in patients on maintenance lithium in this age group. Baseline, prelithium laboratory data should include protein-bound iodine, serum creatinine, urinalysis, blood urea nitrogen, EKG, and serum electrolytes.

As with other psychopharmacologic agents, lithium dosage levels for older patients are generally much lower than those prescribed for younger patients. Hewick, Newbury, Hopwood, Naylor, and Moody (1977) found that the mean weight-related daily dose of lithium prescribed decreased by about 50% between the third and eighth decades; this dosage reduction was seen as necessary to compensate for an age-related decrease in lithium excretion and reduce lithium side effects to a level comparable to that acceptable in younger patients. However, the authors noted that interindividual variation was great, and they estimated that age contributed only 14% to the total interpatient variance.

Foster, Gershell, and Goldfarb (1977), while noting that lithium appears to be as useful in the control of manic states in the older as in younger patients, observe that severe reactions to lithium can develop very rapidly in the elderly, sometimes within 15 minutes of the initial dose. Lithium has a longer half-life in the elderly (36–48 hours versus 24 hours in younger adults), at least partially due to renal aging, which results in linear 30% decrease in glomerular filtration rate in normal subjects 30–80 years old. Foster *et al.* state that there are no reports of serious side effects in the elderly when the dosage has been less than 900 mg daily and when the serum levels were maintained under 1.0 mEq/liter. All of the common signs of lithium toxicity are seen in the elderly; however, the predominant feature of toxicity in this age group appears to be an acute organic brain syndrome characterized by extreme neuromuscular irritability and impaired consciousness, occasionally leading to coma. Due to severe adverse reactions in a few of their elderly patients Foster *et al.* (1977) recommend the following:

> Our present dosage regimen is suitable for initiation in a hospital or ambulatory setting. A test dose of 50–75 mg of lithium carbonate is given; if no adverse effects occur within three hours we continue that dose as tolerated two or three more times at 4-hour intervals to an amount not exceeding 300 mg on the first day. This daily dose is then increased by 75–150 mg every other day until a daily dosage of 450–600 mg is reached on day 5 of treatment. The dosage is held at this point for about four to six days in anticipation of therapeutic response often signaled by a diuresis. If no diuresis occurs by the eleventh day, the lithium dose is increased another 150 mg to a daily dosage range now of 600–750 mg and a serum lithium level is obtained. The target blood lithium levels we expect are in the range of 0.4 to 0.6 or 0.7 mEq/liter. The maximum daily lithium doses we employ are usually 900 mg although rarely doses of 1200 mg have been briefly prescribed. The serum lithium levels we use are much lower and in a more tightly restricted range than the literature generally advises. We have had no serious toxic problems at these levels with generally excellent therapeutic responses.

Others, of course, would argue that a higher serum level would have to be maintained, but definitive outcome studies in this age group have not been done.

Maintenance

The efficacy of lithium as a prophylactic measure against recurrent depressive and manic episodes in bipolar illness has been well documented (Fieve, 1977; Gerbino, Oleshansky, & Gershon, 1978) and will not be reviewed here. Unless medically contraindicated, most patients with manic-depressive illness are generally maintained on lithium. Regular serum lithium levels should be obtained in order to encourage and ascertain compliance as well as to ensure that the patient's lithium level is within a clinically effective range. Adjunctive psychotherapy is frequently useful due to the tumultuous and highly disruptive nature of bipolar illness. With an increasing number of clinics specializing in the treatment of mood disorders, many patients can be seen more economically and efficiently than has been true in the past. Such clinics for affective disorders (or lithium clinics) usually provide diagnostic services, lithium maintenance programs, and individual, group, and conjoint psychotherapy. Compliance in lithium treatment is a problem (Foster *et al.* 1977; Goodwin & Ebert, 1977; Jamison, Gerner, & Goodwin, 1979) and quite close supervision of some patients is essential in order to increase the probability of clinical success.

REFERENCES

Akiskal, H. S., Djenderedjian, A. H., Rosenthal, R. H., & Khani, M. K. Cyclothymic disorder: Validating criteria for inclusion in the bipolar affective group. *American Journal of Psychiatry*, 1977, *134*, 1227–1233.

Akiskal, H. S., & McKinney, W. T. Overview of recent research in depression. *Archives of General Psychiatry*, 1975, *32*, 285–305.

Angst, J., Baastrup, P., Grof, P., *et al.* The course of monopolar depression and bipolar psychoses. *Folia Psychiatrica, Neurologica et Neurochirurgica Neerlandica*, 1973, *76*, 489–500.

Baldessarini, R. J., & Lipinski, J. F. Lithium Salts: 1970–1975. *Annals of Internal Medicine*, 1975, *83*, 527–533.

Barraclough, B. Suicide prevention, recurrent affective disorder and lithium. *British Journal of Psychiatry*, 1972, *121*, 391–392.

Beck, A. T. *Depression: Causes and treatment*. Philadelphia: Univ. of Pennsylvania Press, 1967.

Becker, J. *Depression: Theory and research*. New York: Wiley, 1974.

Carlson, G. A., Davenport, Y. B., & Jamison, K. A comparison of outcome in adolescent and late-onset bipolar manic-depressive illness. *American Journal of Psychiatry*, 1977, *134*, 919–922.

Carlson, G. A., & Goodwin, F. K. The stages of mania. *Archives of General Psychiatry*, 1973, *28*, 221–228.

Cohen, R. A. Manic-depressive illness. In A. M. Freedman, H. I. Kaplan, & B. J. Sadock (Eds.), *Comprehensive textbook of psychiatry-II*. Baltimore, Maryland: Williams & Wilkins, 1975.

Diagnostic and statistical manual of mental disorders (3rd ed.). New York: American Psychiatric Association, April 1977.

Feighner, J. P., Robins, E., Guze, S. B., *et al.* Diagnostic criteria for use in psychiatric research. *Archives of General Psychiatry*, 1972, *26*, 57–63.

Fieve, R. R. Lithium: An overview. In G. D. Burrows (Ed.), *Handbook of studies on depression*. Amsterdam: Excerpta Medica, 1977. Pp. 217–227.

Foster, J. R., Gershell, W. J., & Goldfarb, A. I. Lithium treatment in the elderly. *Journal of Gerontology*, 1977, *32*, 299–302.

Gerbino, L., Oleshansky, M., & Gershon, S. Clinical use and mode of action of lithium. In M. A. Lipton, A. Di Mascio, & K. F. Killam (Eds.), *Psychopharmacology: A generation of progress*. New York: Raven Press, 1978. Pp. 1261–1275.

Goodwin, F. K. Diagnosis of affective disorders. In M. E. Jarvik (Ed.), *Psychopharmacology in the practice of medicine*. New York: Appleton, 1977. Pp. 219–228.

Goodwin, F. K., & Ebert, M. H. Lithium in mania. In S. Gershon & B. Shopsin (Eds.), *Lithium: Its role in psychiatric research and treatment*. New York: Plenum Press, 1973. Pp. 237–252.

Goodwin, F. K., & Ebert, M. H. Recent advances in drug treatment of affective disorders. In M. Jarvik (Ed.), *Psychopharmacology in the practice of medicine*. New York: Appleton, 1977.

Grof, P., Angst, J., & Haines, T. The clinical course of depression: Practical issues. In J. Angst (Ed.), *Classification and prediction of outcome in depression*. New York: F. K. Shatlauer. Verlag, 1973.

Guze, S. B., & Robins, E. Suicide and primary affective disorders. *British Journal of Psychiatry*, 1970, *117*, 437–438.

Hewick, D. C., Newbury, P., Hopwood, S., Naylor, G., & Moody, J. Age as a factor affecting lithium therapy. *British Journal of Clinical Pharmacology*, 1977, *4*, 201–205.

Jamison, K. R., Gerner, R. H., & Goodwin, F. K. Patient and physician attitudes toward lithium. *Archives of General Psychiatry*, 1979, *36*, 866–869.

Johnson, F. N. (Ed.). *Lithium research and therapy*. New York: Academic Press, 1975.

Kay, D. W. K., Beamish, P., & Roth, M. Old age mental disorders in Newcastle upon Tyne. *British Journal of Psychiatry*, 1964, *110*, 146–158.

Kraepelin, E. *Manic depressive insanity and paranoia*. Edinburgh: E & S Livingston, 1921.

Kramer, M. Classification of mental disorders for epidemiological and medical care purposes: Current status, problems, and needs. In M. M. Katz, J. O. Cole, & W. E. Barton (Eds.), *The role and methodology of classification in psychiatry and psychopathology* (U.S. Public Health Service Publication No. 1584). Washington, D.C.: U.S. Government Printing Office, 1965.

Kramer, M. Cross-national study of diagnosis of the mental disorders: Origin of the problem. *American Journal of Psychiatry*, 1969, *125* (Suppl. No. 10), 1–12.

Nielsen, J. Geronto-psychiatric period-prevalence investigation in a geographically delimited population. *Acta Psychiat. Scand.*, 1963, *38*, 307–330.

Perris, C. The course of depressive psychoses. *Acta Psychiat. Scand.*, 1968, *44*, 234–248.

Perris, C. Frequency and hereditary aspects of depression. In D. M. Gallant & G. M. Simpson (Eds.), *Depression: Behavioral, biochemical, diagnostic, and treatment concepts*. New York: Spectrum Publications, 1976. Pp. 75–107.

Pitt, B. *Psychogeriatrics*. Edinburgh: Churchill-Livingston, 1974.

Pokorny, A. D., & Prien, R. F. Lithium in treatment and prevention of affective disorder. *Diseases of the Nervous System*, 1974, *35*, 327–333.

Post, F. *The significance of affective symptoms in old age*. London: Oxford Univ. Press, 1962.

Post, F. *The clinical psychiatry of late life*. Oxford: Pergamon, 1965.

Post, F. Diagnosis of depression in geriatric patients and treatment modalities appropriate for the population. In D. M. Gallant & G. M. Simpson (Eds.), *Depression: Behavioral, biochemical, diagnostic, and treatment concepts*. New York: Spectrum Publications, 1976. Pp. 205–231.

Ripley, H. S. Depression and the life span—epidemiology. In G. Usdin (Ed.), *Depression: Clinical, biological, and psychological perspectives*. New York: Brunner/Mazel, 1977.

Roth, M. The natural history of mental disorders in old age. *Journal of Mental Science*, 1955, *101*, 281–301.

Spitzer, R. L., Endicott, J., & Robins, E. Clinical criteria for psychiatric diagnosis and DSM-III. *American Journal of Psychiatry*, 1975, *132*, 1187–1192.

Verwoerdt, A. *Clinical geropsychiatry*. Baltimore, Maryland: Williams & Wilkins, 1976.

Wertham, F. L. A group of benign chronic psychoses: Prolonged manic excitements. *American Journal of Psychiatry*, 1929, *86*, 17–78.

Winokur, G. Mania, depression: Family studies, genetics, and relation to treatment. In M. Lipton, A. Di Mascio, & K. Killiam (Eds.), *Psychopharmacology: A generation of progress*. New York: Raven Press, 1978.

Winokur, G., Clayton, P. J., & Reich, T. *Manic-depressive illness*. St. Louis, Missouri: C. V. Mosby, 1969.

Yeats, W. B. *The celtic twilight*. New York: Signet Classics, 1962.

Chapter 6
DEPRESSION IN THE ELDERLY

Robert H. Gerner

INTRODUCTION

Grow old along with me. The best is yet to be.
—Robert Browning

Unfortunately, this invitation to the senium is often not the fortune of many. Approximately 33% of those older than 60 have depressive symptoms, and their lives are consequently colored gray and dysphoric (Dovenmuehle, Reckless, & Newman, 1970). Depressive illness is responsible for up to 45% of new admissions of those over 65 to mental hospitals (Myers, Sheldon, & Robinson, 1963; Tongas & Gibson, 1969). One cannot overemphasize the very real, practical need to accurately diagnose depression, since it can be effectively treated in the vast majority of instances. If untreated, the morbidity from factors other than suicide is significantly increased (Avery & Winokur, 1976; Davis, Fann, El-Yousef, Janowsky, 1973, p. 113; Post, 1972, p. 46). In contrast to depression in the young, depression in the elderly usually does not eventually lift in a spontaneous manner. Rather, it worsens and after approximately 2 years becomes much more resistant to effective treatment (Jarvik, 1978).

DIAGNOSIS

Over the past few years, a very extensive effort has derived reliable methods to diagnose depression. Several systems are currently used or

97

scheduled for use in the United States: Research Diagnostic Criteria (Spitzer, Endicott, & Robins, 1975), those of Feighner (1972), and the developing Diagnostic and Statistical Manual (DSM) III (Spitzer, 1978). Additionally, there are computer diagnostic programs (Duckworth & Kedward, 1978). In contrast to earlier diagnostic systems, where reliability was poor, the use of these present methods results in reliable diagnoses. All of these systems use both history and present mental status in determining the diagnosis. The final diagnosis does not depend on psychodynamic formulations nor on theoretical etiologies, but rather on a constellation of relatively clear signs and symptoms. Such a system has been shown to have a high degree of reliability among clinicians and is superior to the older American system of diagnosis based in part on psychodynamic variables (Cooper, Kendell, Gurland, Sartorius, & Farkas, 1969). It is pertinent that in the United States the diagnosis of organic mental syndrome is made more frequently in the geriatric age group, and functional psychoses, at a lower frequency, compared with the United Kingdom (Cooper, Gurland, Sharpe, Copeland, & Simon, 1972; Copeland, Kelleher, Kellett, Gourlay, Cowan, Barron, Kurianski, & Stiller, 1975). This suggests that there is an overdiagnosis of organicity in this country at the expense of the more treatable and better prognosis functional disorders.

The concept of depression as an illness as opposed to a normal variant of mood has been recently reviewed (Katz & Hirshfeld, 1978; Winokur, 1973a). *Primary depression* occurs in the absence of other premorbid psychiatric medical illnesses that are associated with the development of depression. In *secondary depression*, the full range of depressive signs and symptoms occur, but on a background of another psychiatric diagnosis such as alcoholism or schizophrenia. Depression associated with the occurrence of manic or hypomanic episodes is part of *bipolar* illness (see Chapter 5 of this volume). Various authors have defined *unipolar* depression by either absence of mania and/or by virtue of an arbitrary number of past episodes. Since it has been estimated that 50% of patients with an initial depressive episode will have another (Spitzer *et al.*, 1975), it may be of greater utility to diagnose depression as either single episode or recurrent. This chapter will address itself to unipolar primary depression, both single and recurrent.

Unipolar Depression

Two additional useful subtypes of depression are *agitated* and *retarded*. Although all patients cannot be fitted into this dichotomy, it has been of value both for research and for clinical practice (Gershon, 1978; Kupfer, Pickar, Himmelhoch, & Detre, 1975; Schildkraut, 1978). However, it should be borne in mind that the full range of symptoms can be seen within a single patient (El-Islam, 1973). Ratings of anxiety in depressed unipolar patients covary such that severe anxiety is typically seen in all depressions. When symptoms of depression are present, the diagnosis of depression is more appropriate (Mendels, Weinstein, & Cochrane, 1972; Murray & Blackburn, 1974). Use of appropriate diagnostic tools can prevent contamination by nondepressed patients with anxiety alone (Roth, Gurney, Garside, & Kerr, 1972).

The following criteria for primary depression have been adapted from those that have been proposed for the DSM III (Spitzer, 1978).

1. The essential feature of a depression is a dysphoric, depressive mood manifested by any of the following: sadness, hopelessness, "feeling low," discouraged, blue, empty and without feeling, weepiness, irritable, and worried. Only sophisticated individuals are likely to report feeling "depressed." An absence of capacity for pleasure manifested by loss of interest in former activities is typically present. The mood is reported as different from that following the death of a loved one.

2. Poor appetite, or weight loss of more than 1 pound per week when not dieting, or increased appetite are also typical. The former is more characteristic of agitated depression and the latter, of retarded type.

3. There is often an alteration of sleep pattern. Insomnia, especially with frequent awakenings during the night or early in the morning not solely due to urgency to urinate, with difficulty returning to sleep, is present in agitated depression. Increased sleep, often manifested by difficulty in getting up in the morning, is typical of retarded depression.

4. There is loss of the subjective sense of energy, or easy fatigability.

5. Objective psychomotor agitation or retardation are usually present.

6. There is objective or subjective difficulty with concentration or thinking, which may be manifested as inattention, apathy, indecisiveness, or blocking. Patients will often report that they are unable to read the newspaper or a book without losing their place, or notice that they are unable to remember what they just read, yet they may worry or ruminate about minor matters and not be able to come to closure with what used to be insignificant daily problems.

7. There is verifiable loss of interest in previously pleasurable activities, including sexual drive.

8. Self-reproach or guilt of unrealistic proportion or in an obsessional manner is present.

9. The person has thoughts of suicide or death, or the equivalent ("Everyone would be better off without me," "I wish I wouldn't wake up," "I could sleep forever," "I see myself dying or falling seriously ill").

Additionally, depression may vary quantitatively and range from mild to severe for any given episode. In *moderate depression* there is less reactivity to the environment in that it does not remit temporarily in the face of positive events. Diurnal variation is usually subjectively present, and mood is often worse in the morning. However, evidence of diurnal variation is often absent (Williams, Barlow, & Agras, 1975). Carrying out daily chores is done only with difficulty and by consciously forcing oneself. The patient may still be able to "put on an act" and go out if pushed, but typically prefers to withdraw rather than engage in social intercourse.

Severely depressed individuals will be unable to function alone and will need help to provide food or maintain personal hygiene. Psychotic symptoms may be present in the form of delusions that are usually nihilistic or guilt ridden, or there may be hallucination of critical voices. Communication may be difficult or impossible due to muteness or difficulty in comprehension. Schizophrenia must not be present, nor any other known organic mental disorder that can cause depression. Psychosis or thought disorder may be present in psychotic depression. In view of this one should be extremely wary of making a new diagnosis of schizophrenia in those over 60, since its average age of onset is in the late teens or early 20s.

Age-Related Symptoms

These diagnostic guidelines are not specifically formulated for the older population, and there are a number of reports that age per se results in some variation of symptoms (Fisch, Goldfarb, Shahinian, & Post, 1962). Older depressives exhibit more physical symptoms and complaints, express less guilt, and report feeling "depressed" to a lesser extent than the young (Busse, 1969; Salzman, Schader, & Harmatz, 1975; Schwab, Holzer, & Warheit, 1973; Spicer, Hare, & Slater, 1973; Whitehead, 1974, p. 42). Apathy is much more prominent than in younger-age groups (Levin, 1963). Paranoid symptoms ranging from suspiciousness and irritability to frank delusions remain more frequent in the elderly. The constellation of agitation, depression, and paranoia has been diagnosed as involutional depression, although there is evidence that this is not a distinct entity (Rosenthal, 1974, p. 694).

Pseudodementia

Pseudodementia is a term originated by Kiloh (1971), but it is not a diagnosis. This refers to a presentation of depression in an elderly individual where symptoms and signs of dementia are significant enough to suggest the diagnosis of dementia. Symptoms of moderate or severe depression may easily mimic dementia: Cognition and memory are decreased, and apathy, loss of ability to care for self, delusions, confused behavior, insomnia, and agitation, are often present in both (Blusewicz, Dustman, Schenkenberg, & Beck, 1977). In fact, both may coexist. As noted previously, there are suggestions that pseudodementia may often be misdiagnosed as dementia in America. Careful questioning of family or staff may elicit a history of depressive symptoms occurring prior to the apparent dementia. The distinction is crucial since large numbers are affected by both. Perhaps 10% of the population over 60 will develop dementia, and 25%, depression. Over 50% of geriatric patients in mental hospitals are diagnosed as having organic mental syndrome (OMS) (Riley & Foner, 1968), and as much as 10–20% of the elderly population may be affected by OMS (Fisch, Goldfarb, & Shahinian, 1968). Post (1972, 1975) found that patients who had definite organic impairment in addition to depressive signs had a poor prognosis and did not evolve into a pure depression. However, the presence of doubtfully impaired central nervous system function was of no prognostic significance. Confusion or severe symptomatology was a predictor of good outcome. Post found that cerebral arteriosclerosis was significantly associated with the depressive affective syndrome, and he suggests that in some patients, the former may be of etiological importance.

Although repeated psychological testing may show a progressive and indisputable picture of dementia after several months, the problem cases are not easily resolved by psychological testing (Miller, 1977). Use of computed tomography to make a diagnosis of dementia is fraught with problems. The aged may have readings of gross atrophy but have perfectly normal functioning on psychometric test preformance (Feinberg, Jernigan, Zatz, Price, & Feinberg,1979). Since the diagnosis of dementia cannot be absolutely accurate, and since depression is usually reversible if treated—but may result in chronic institutionalization, sensory deprivation, mental decompensation, or death if untreated—

one should aggressively overtreat the syndrome in order not to miss the individuals with depression. This position has been previously advocated (Snowdon, 1972). When the two conditions coexist, the depressive component is often responsive to treatment. Specific use of antidepressants in dementia is currently being investigated in a Veterans Administration collaborative study.

Masked Depression

Masked depression, "depression sine depression," or depressive equivalent, may represent one-third or more of individuals with depression. It has not been rigorously studied and may possibly represent a "missed depression" because an adequate history and examination are not done or are resisted by the patient. Lesser (1974, p. 61) reports that one-third of several hundred depressives he saw over a 7-year period were of the masked type, and that the syndrome appears to be more frequent in the aged. Usually the patient presents a multitude of somatic complaints that do not respond to symptomatic treatment. This may result in more drastic approaches. Krietman (1965) reported that one-third of patients with such depressions had unnecessary surgery. These individuals must be differentiated from Briquet's syndrome, which also presents with a multisymptomatic picture, although it usually has onset in the third decade. Most elderly who are diagnosed as hypochondriacal were not overly focused on physical symptoms previously (Charaton, 1975). Although they may have had an obsessive life style and habitually used the soma as a medium of communicating their emotional state (Dasberg & Assad, 1968). Hence, the development of somatic concerns or symptoms that do not correspond to known diseases suggests that a thorough affective history should be taken. Presence of other depressive signs and symptoms might then lead to a diagnosis of depression. However, the high frequency of physical illness among the elderly makes the diagnosis of masked depression difficult and challenging (Ibor, 1972; Kielholz & Basle, 1973).

The diagnosis may be resisted by the patient, who desires a more "respectable" physical illness (see the section on evaluation in this chapter). Adequate recognition and treatment of this group is essential, since they have a very high suicide risk—up to two-thirds are morbidly preoccupied with suicidal thoughts (Hochstetter, 1959, p. 59). Unfortunately, this group of patients is usually capable of alienating even the most compassionate family and physicians with their interminable complaints. This can result in an unconscious sadistic withholding of proper diagnosis or treatment.

Characterological Depression

Chronic characterological depression (Schildkraut, 1978) does not represent a change from a premorbid level of functioning. If carefully interviewed, the patient gives a history of chronic interpersonal dependency needs that are repeatedly frustrated, and he or she lacks the signs and symptoms of depression for a sustained duration of time. This entity, which may respond to pharmacotherapy (Schildkraut & Klein, 1975, p. 46), is more properly considered under personality disorders (Verwoerdt, 1976, pp. 84–95).

Grief

Grief, in contrast to depression, is a normal emotion. Its absence in appropriate circumstances is viewed as pathological. The response to acute loss may produce many symptoms similar to those of depression with the distinction that the feeling of loss is intensely felt, in contrast to the blank desert of depression and its refractoriness to environmental intervention. Additionally, suicidal ideation is extremely rare in grief alone (Bornstein & Clayton, 1972). The course of grief is a gradual improvement over time (Greenblatt, 1978). By 3 months, only 50% of widows still showed depression symptoms, and by 13 months, only 17% (Bornstein, Clayton, Halikas, Maurice, & Robins, 1973), and 14% in another study (Parker, 1970). Individuals with severe anniversary reactions may be at risk for developing clinical depression, however (Bornstein & Clayton, 1972). Widowhood does not appear to be a good model for clinical affective disorder, but rather there is an affective response to the clear-cut loss (Bornstein *et al.*, 1973).

Dichotomous Subgroups

The terms *neurotic, psychotic, reactive,* and *endogenous* are posited subcategories of depression. They implicitly suggest etiologies, and for some, a course of treatment. Unfortunately, they are not used in a systematic manner throughout the literature, and they may prejudice us in our approach to the patient's evaluation and treatment. No matter what the label, the patient still has the same range of problems to be managed. It has been suggested that these terms be abandoned since they do not enhance communication (Lewis, 1971; Mendels, 1965; Van Praag, 1977, p. 8).

There is controversy regarding the existence of a neurotic–psychotic dichotomy. Most studies investigating this have used a multifactorial model to analyze signs and symptoms. Some have found a continuous model to fit best, suggesting that there is no inherent distinction of neurotic or psychotic depression in the young nor the aged (Foulds, 1973; Kendell & Gourley, 1970; Post, 1972; Zubin & Fleiss, 1970), whereas others have found a suggestion that there may be distinct categories of the two illnesses (Kiloh, Andrews, Neilson, & Bianchi, 1972). Although Klerman (1976) and Gurland (1976) hold the view that neurotic depressions are more common in old age, this position is not supported by large epidemiologic studies (see the section on epidemiology in this chapter).

The existence of a distinct endogenous–reactive dichotomy is not substantiated by biochemical studies nor by retrospective studies. Busse (1970, p. 87) found that 85% of his subjects over 60 had the onset of depressive episodes traced to specific stimuli. However, Post (1972), who found precipitating factors in 78% of his elderly depressives, also found that there was no significant difference in precipitating factors and a psychotic, intermediate, or neurotic presentation. Factorial analysis of ratings and symptoms of normals, as well as reactive and endogenous depressives, shows a continuous distribution that argues against a bimodal model (Costello, Christensen, & Rogers, 1974). It is obvious that one cannot separate individuals from their surroundings and that it is best to help patients deal more effectively with the events that are meaningful to them. Even those patients who clearly have a depressive illness that is an "endogenous" and genetically determined type, may have the course significantly affected by life events that are particularly meaningful to them (Post, Stoddard, Gillin, Buchsbaum, Runkle, Black, & Bunney, 1977).

SUICIDE

Suicidal ideation usually is a symptom of depression and does not merely reflect an existential position. Some 55% of elderly suicides, as opposed to 40% of younger ones, were found to have occurred when the person was in a depressed state, according to one British study (Sainsbury, 1962). As mentioned earlier, suicidal ideation may be very subtle, but it must be given serious attention. The rate is highest for hypochondriacal depressed individuals and for males. The probability of suicide during depression is much greater after age 40 (Robins, Murphy, Wilderson, Glassner, & Kayes, 1959). The danger is so great with the aged that they should be immediately evaluated, since the elderly may be more willing to commit suicide than seek professional help. Baraclough (1971) found that completed suicides in the elderly occurred most often early in the depression, within 6 months of onset, whereas referral to a psychiatrist usually was not made until the depression had lasted 1 year. However, the suicide rate is clearly related to age only in white males (Silverman, 1968, p. 150), where it increases linearly as a function of age. The peak ages for women are 45 to 54 years.

Some "rational suicides" may rarely occur (i.e., in the face of imminent painful death). These should not necessarily be dealt with in the same manner as depression. However, depression or other psychiatric illnesses must be thoroughly considered, and the patient should definitely be evaluated by a psychiatrist, and preferably a second opinion should be obtained.

EPIDEMIOLOGY

There is a large range of estimates of both rate and prevalence for depression in the elderly. A recent study found that in a community sample of persons over 65, 33% of the males and 42% of the females needed psychiatric or social help (Goldstein, 1973). Since about one-half of geropsychiatric outpatients appear to have depression (Charatan, 1975; Roth, 1955), this suggests that a very significant proportion of the geriatric age group may suffer from depression. About 30% of the general community population over 60 showed the symptoms of depression (Dovenmuehle, Reckless, & Newman, 1970), and 21% of the total sample had disabling depression (Dovenmuehle & McGough, 1970). This agrees with community studies in Newcastle, which showed the prevalence of affective illness and neurosis in those over 65 to be 26% (Pitt, 1974, p. 51). Pfeiffer and Busse (1973) found significant depressive symptoms in 65% of a population over 60. Essen-Moller and Hagnell (1961) found the highest rates for depression in those above 60 years. This is striking because of nearly complete ascertainment and a sample of 2550. The incidence of depression in the geriatric population has also been reported to range from 1–7% (Gurland, 1976, 2–3%; Juel-Nielson, 1961, 1.2–3.7%; Kay, Beamish, & Roth, 1964, 3%; Parsons, 1965, 7%). Prevalence in the general population approximates 3% (Winokur, 1973a), with a lifetime risk of 10–20% (Klerman, 1976).

The rate of depression differs considerably in the elderly if one considers a neurotic–psychotic dichotomy. Spicer, Hare, and Slater (1973) found that neurotic depression declined for both males and females from the third decade. Psychotic depression and nonneurotic depression increased with age in males, peaking at age 60 (approximately 55 per 100,000 and 120 per 100,000 respectively, at a rate approximately two and one-half times that at age 20). In females, psychotic depression increases to age 50 (80 per 100,000) and remains even until age 65 when it declines. Other nonneurotic depression decreased slightly from 180 per 100,000 at age 35 to 160 per 100,000 at age 65 and then decreased rapidly. Weeke, Bille, Videbech, Dupont, and Juel-Nielsen (1975) also found that psychogenic depression and neurotic depression decreased with age, and that psychotic depression increased with age to 50 years and then gradually and unevenly declined. Thus, age appears to be highly correlated with the diagnostic type in these and other similar studies, neurotic depression being higher in the young and psychotic depression higher in the aged (Nielsen, Homma, & Biør-Henriksen, 1977; Pederson, Barry, & Babigan, 1972; Silverman, 1968, p. 79).

Similar to younger age groups, older females have a higher incidence of depression than males. If the rates for all types of depression in the Weeke *et al.* (1975) study are grouped, the highest rate for males is found at age 50 to 55 (approximately 2.2 per 1000) with very little variation from age 45 through 64. For females, the highest rates were from age 20 through 39 (about 4.6 per 1000). An apparent difference in the studies demonstrating a large amount of depression in the aged from those that show a much smaller rate can be explained in part by methodology. The community studies that showed much depression were prevalence studies, and with an illness that has a long duration, prevalence will exceed the incidence. Perhaps more importantly, the community studies sought out individuals for determination of their affective symptoms, whereas the other studies (Spicer *et al.*, 1973; Weeke *et al.*, 1975) worked with data derived from identified patients.

Within the older age group, the incidence of depression varies considerably depending on level of social functioning. Busse, Barnes, Silverman, Thaler, and Frost (1955) found that 48% of a population over 60 who were not working and who were attending an outpatient clinic for physical disorders had depression, while 44% of that age group who were not outpatients and who were in good physical health, but were nonactive, were depressed. Only 25% of those who were active and continuing some work were depressed. Of course, it is quite possible that the lack of depression can explain the increase in activity rather than vice versa. In some studies, high social class is associated with less depression in those over age 60 (Dovenmuehle & McGough, 1970, p. 98; Schwab, 1976), but not in others (Simon, 1970).

GENETICS

Although several workers have developed genetic models for depression, no one has systematically evaluated this in the aged population. In any genetic study there are considerable difficulties in obtaining a reliable family history (Andreasen, Endicott, Spitzer, & Winokur, 1977). Gershon (1978) has reviewed the genetics of the affective disorders as a whole and concludes that the bipolar group may be a relatively homogeneous entity, but he notes that the unipolar group is probably heterogeneous as far as genetic types go, although patients with recurrent retarded depression may be related to those with bipolar disease. This distinction is supported by psychometric tests (Donnelly, Murphy, & Goodwin, 1976). A dichotomy within unipolars that is presumed to relate to genetic factors, and that is based on drug response, has been proposed (Kupfer *et al.*, 1975), one group being a tricyclic responder and the other a lithium responder. A dichotomy of genetic factors is consistent with the study of Kiloh *et al.* (1972), who used factor-analytic techniques and found that psychotic depressions fit a unitary model separate from a "neurotic" group that appeared to be heterogeneous. However, Post (1972) found that a family history of depression was not significantly correlated with the severity of the illness or a neurotic–psychotic dichotomy, and that precipitating events appeared to be more important in the genetically predisposed. This is especially interesting since he was working with an older age group, and one might expect that genetic predisposition would be weaker in the later onset depressions. Similar findings in wider age groups were reported by Thompson and Hendric (1972).

ETIOLOGIES

It is important to understand that the etiology of an illness does not necessarily carry with it an implication for treatment. It is very difficult to demonstrate an etiology, and one must go further than simply making correlations obtained retrospectively. Retrospective collection of data is probably not a valid methodology to determine etiology (Hudgens, Robins, & Delong, 1970). An adequate theory of etiologies should not only provide an explanation for the onset of a phenomenon, but also have a clinically useful predictive value. While there are several interesting hypotheses, there is currently no adequate etiological explanation for unipolar depression, either psychodynamic or biological.

Although it is my view that it is an error to dichotomize the psyche and the soma, psychogenic and biological etiologies will be discussed separately. However, an attempt at unification will be made in a preliminary manner.

Psychogenic Etiologies: Losses and Stresses

One has to ultimately explain the mechanism for the onset of depression at a late age in an individual who previously has coped without depression. The events that are relatively unique to the aged are the increased number of losses and other similar stressors that have been implicated in causing depression (Paykel, 1969). However, many older persons adapt to losses without becoming depressed, as shown by the studies of Bornstein *et al.* (1973). There is even evidence that the premorbid occurrence of stressful life events to the onset of the depression is nonetiological in nature and is not significantly different than the norm (Hudgens, Morrison, & Barcha, 1967). If that is true, then one would have to ascertain the relationship of particular personalities to life events and subsequent healthy or nonhealthy outcomes. A study that accounts for premorbid personality, life events, and current losses in relationship to depression or other illnesses has not yet been carried out in this age group.

There are many losses that are particularly obvious in this age group. Some are unavoidable and are particularly related to the factors of age.

1. *Role*. Particularly pertinent in this age group is the loss of the role as an individual vis-à-vis career, brought about either by retirement or infirmity. Additionally, the role as supporter of children and family and as being absolutely necessary for the survival of others diminishes as the children grow and establish themselves as independent entities.

2. *Power*. There is significant loss of political power in individuals in the older age group, both literally through decrease in influence with elected officials, but also because power emanates from respect, and in our society, younger individuals have a negative attitude toward individuals in their senium. In addition, retired individuals no longer enjoy the power that accompanies their senior positions at work. At retirement, one typically passes from a respected experienced member of the team to an unemployed status and one's business acumen is not sought out.

3. *Socioeconomic changes*. Older individuals are threatened with or

actually undergo a loss of wealth as measured by money, place of abode, and economic status (Walther, 1975). In our society, age itself is accorded a lower social status. This appears to be specifically linked to depression in the elderly: Within a given age group, lower social status is significantly related to increased levels of depression (Schwab *et al.*, 1973). Loss of social status secondarily results in loss of self-esteem. It may result in lack of places to experience new stimuli, because one is invited to fewer social events that often were connected with work or people one met at work. Thus, there is a general loss of control over events that affect one's own life (Niederehe, 1977).

There is a loss of ability to undo things that one has regretted. Although this is often a fantasied loss, since we can rarely change the past, there is a very real loss of potential to engage and accomplish new tasks prior to one's death.

4. *Health.* There is a general loss of health and somatic function. There is a decrease in the speed of memory recall and acquisition of new information, a decrease in endurance, and increased physical limitations in activities relative to one's youth, even without the occurrence of severe illnesses that are always a realistic threat (Coleman, 1969). Loss of physical health is significantly related to onset of depression (Post, 1975; Simon, 1970).

5. *Past losses.* There is a loss of friends, acquaintances, and relatives who made up one's own intimate world in later years, subsequently leaving one increasingly a stranger in the present. The loss of a spouse is one of the most stressful (Holmes & Rahe, 1967; Paykel, Prusoff, & Uhlenhuth, 1971). A resurgence of the memories of one's parents, their aging years, and their death occurs at this age. It is possible that defenses raised to deal with inadequate grieving for parental loss may not be adequate in older life, resulting in a recrudescence of the conflict. The loss of one's parents in the early years of life appears to be related to the development of severe depression when one reaches older age (Brown, Harris, & Copeland, 1977; McDonald, 1969; Post, 1972, p. 400).

6. *Death.* Finally, there is the anticipation of the loss of one's own life, which can be viewed separately and as distinctly different from fear of death.

All these losses are blows to one's narcissistic needs. Individuals who have a general personality style of perceiving and evaluating their environment negatively are probably more predisposed to become depressed (Lunghi, 1977). Blows may be weathered or not, depending on both their number and intensity, and the personality and its vulnerability to specific losses. There is some evidence that certain premorbid personality characteristics are associated with depression. Those with rigid personalities and compulsiveness appear to have a greater chance of becoming depressed (Kendell & Discipio, 1970). This personality type may be psychogenetic, but there is also clear evidence that it may be heritable in a strict sense (Woodruff, Goodwin, & Guze, 1974, p. 84). It seems likely that individuals with less healthy narcissism would be more vulnerable to depression, regardless of the degree narcissism is constitutionally determined. Individuals whose self-concept depends on qualities that are diminished with age may be especially vulnerable to depression (physical appearance, social power or standing, and idealized future). Unfortunately, this has not been tested.

Stresses in a general sense vary with the adaptational ability of individuals to subsequently influence their futures. Paykel *et al.* (1969) have found that some of the variation in the onset of depression can be accounted for by life events, but not all, and presumably other factors contribute variously to the onset (Niederehe, 1977). Even the loss of the spouse is not significantly associated with the development of depression (Post, 1975). Only 14% of widows by 13 months after the spouse's death appeared to have continued depressive signs (Bornstein & Clayton, 1972).

In any given individual's personality, adaptability to stress depends on a number of factors that decline with age. With less money, there will be a decrease in its useful derivations, such as opportunities for personalized health care, easy transportation, and varied cultural experiences. The support of family and friends becomes less available, either through death or illness of parents and siblings, or through geographic distance from children and grandchildren. Finally, there will be diminished intrapersonal adaptability due to a normal decline in sophisticated brain functions. Diminished resources may result in movement from a familiar neighborhood to an unfamiliar "retirement city" or less expensive section of the city. Additionally, societal laws penalize working for those past "retirement age." This substantially diminishes the opportunity for interpersonal relationships and exchanges that are often secondary to work. This may result secondarily in a social deprivation syndrome. This syndrome is characterized by withdrawn behavior, negativism, chronic complaints to those who will listen, apathy, and pessimism at the possibility of engaging in new and meaningful activities. To some extent, it may appear to be indistinguishable from depression. However, it may be differentiated from clinical depression, since such a syndrome will show a response to structured activities and resocialization.

Biological Etiologies

There are three major biochemical hypotheses regarding depressive disorders:

1. *The catecholamine hypothesis* states that a relative decrease in the catecholamine neurotransmitters, norepinephrine or dopamine, at critical synapses in the brain will result in depression (Schildkraut, 1978; Van Praag, 1977a).

2. *The indolamine hypothesis* (Murphy, Campbell, & Costa, 1978; Van Praag, 1977a,b) is similar, except that serotonin is the specific neurotransmitter implicated. A variant of this, the permissive hypothesis (Prange, 1974), combines the two. Individuals who are predisposed to depression may have a relatively low functional level of serotonin. Clinical depression develops when there is a decrease in catecholamines.

3. *The cholinergic hypothesis* (Davis, 1975) suggests that an inverse relationship exists between acetylcholine and the catecholamine, dopamine. An alteration of this relationship that favors an increase in the acetylcholine–catecholamine ratio is accompanied by depressive symptoms.

Extensive investigational efforts have been carried out both to substantiate these hypotheses and to elucidate possible mechanisms (Freedman, 1975). There are large bodies of evidence that substantiate each of these theories, suggesting that either they can be integrated into one unitary theory of depression, or that there are biochemical subtypes of major depressions. The latter option is supported to some extent by a bimodal distribution of cerebro-spinal fluid (CSF) 5-hydroxyindoleacetic acid (5-HIAA), the metabolite of serotonin (Asberg, Thoren, Traskman, Bertilsson, & Ringberger, 1976). This may account for the trend for low CSF 5-HIAA in depressed patients as a group (Goodwin & Post, 1975, pp. 299–332). Two groups are evident when one looks at CSF 5-HIAA, and treatment response differs. The group with low 5-HIAA responds to serotonin precursors and not to the usual tricyclics, whereas the higher 5-HIAA group does not respond to the precursors (Van Praag, 1977b).

Studies of the cerebro-spinal fluid and urine metabolites of norepinephrine, 3-methoxy-4-hydroxy-phenylglycol (MHPG), suggest that there may be a decrease in norepinephrine metabolism in some depressions and for the group as a whole (Goodwin & Post, 1975; Maas, Fawcett, & Dekirmenjian, 1968; Schildkraut, 1973; Taube *et al.*, 1978).

The validity of such findings is supported by the differential treatment response to antidepressants depending on the biochemical picture of the patient's CSF (Banki, 1977; Goodwin & Post, 1975) or urine (Beckman & Goodman, 1975; Maas, Fawcett, & Dekirmenjian, 1972; Schildkraut, 1973). Low MHPG depressions may respond to imipramine, whereas relatively higher MHPG depressions may respond to amitriptyline.

Monoamine oxidase (MAO) and catechol-O-methyltransferase (COMT) are enzymes responsible for the degradation of catecholamines intracellularly and extracellularly, respectively. If these enzymes are relatively increased, one would expect that a depletion of catecholamines might occur, resulting in depression. COMT has been reported to be both increased (Gershon, 1978) and decreased, with most favoring the latter (Briggs & Briggs, 1973; Cohn, Dunner, & Axelrod, 1970; Dunner, Cohn, Gershon, & Goodwin, 1971). Platelet MAO is thought to reflect brain MAO levels. Platelet MAO appears to be more consistently increased in depression, although significant increases are not present for the depressive group as a whole. This suggests that subgroup differences may exist. Unipolar patients have higher MAO activity than bipolar depressant patients (Murphy & Weiss, 1972; Murphy & Wyatt, 1975; Nies, Robinson, Harris, & Lamborn, 1974). Platelet MAO increases linearly with age, suggesting that the metabolism of some neurotransmitters may be increased with the result that levels might decrease to critical "depressive" levels (Nies et al., 1971; Nies, Robinson, Davis, & Ravaris, 1973). Unfortunately, studies relating older normal and older depressive MAO levels and CSF neurotransmitter metabolites have not been carried out.

It is possible that the aging brain may sustain loss of enough of these critical neurotransmitters, which may result in depression, similar to Parkinson's disease resulting from the loss of a similar neurotransmitter, dopamine. There is a great deal of evidence to suggest that this may be an important factor (Ordy, Kaack, & Brizzee, 1975). McGreer, McGreer, and Wade (1971) (McGreer & McGreer, 1975) found a decrease in the neurotransmitter norepinephrine and its synthetic enzymes associated with age. A decrease in serotonin in the forebrain and hypothalamus, and norepinephrine in the hypothalamic region, occurs with age (Samorajski, 1977), suggesting that transmitter levels are diminished differentially in certain parts of the brain. It is just these transmitters, of course, that have been implicated in the etiology of depression.

As noted previously, stress is often associated temporally with the onset of depression. However, a mechanism for stress mediating depression has not been rigorously demonstrated. Short-term and severe stress has been shown to result in a decrease of brain norepinephrine levels, whereas levels of serotonin, acetylcholine, and dopamine were not so susceptible to stress. Moderate stress may, on the contrary, result in increased norepinephrine levels (Ordy & Scheide, 1973; Samorajski, 1975). The pathophysiology of this is not clear, although it is known that stress greatly effects a multitude of neurotransmitter regulatory enzymes (Yuwiler, 1976).

A little studied but potentially important area in this age group is chronobiological changes and their relationship to affective disorders. Cahn, Folk, and Huston (1968) have demonstrated the dissociation of certain biorhythms occurring more frequently in older males and in depressed males as compared with a younger group.

A number of biological concomitants of depression are routinely found, although age itself has not been the focus of study. Cortisol levels are elevated throughout the day during a depressive episode, and they return to normal levels only with resolution. This is thought to be inherently related to the depressive illness and possible disturbance at the hypothalamic level and not due to nonspecific factors such as stress or hospitalization (Carpenter & Bunney, 1971; Sachar, 1975a). There are marked changes in the sleep patterns during depression to an extent that sleep electroencephalograms can be an effective diagnostic tool (Karacan, Williams, & Salis, 1977; Kupfer, Foster, Koble, McPartland, & Fulrich, 1978): There is a decrease in rapid eye movement (REM) latency, more awakenings during sleep, and an increase in REM density. Growth hormone response to L-dopa is decreased with age in males, and growth hormone response to hypoglycemia is decreased in depressed women. Lutenizing hormone response (mediated by norepinephrine) is also decreased in depressed women (Sachar, Altman, Gruen, Glassman, Halpern, & Sassin, 1975; Sachar, 1975b).

Depression Secondary to Other Illnesses

Depression can emerge during or as an initial symptom of a large number of conditions. Often the relationship to an underlying pathological process is not initially evident. The general rule that one must suspect a disease to diagnose it applies to depressive symptoms also. Since the depressive symptoms can exactly duplicate those found in patients without gross medical etiologies, an alert attitude for underlying illness is warranted (Smith, Barish, Correa, & Williams, 1972).

Endocrine Dysfunctions

Hyper- and hypothyroidism can both result in depressive symptoms (Green, 1974). These levels do not need to be out of "normal limits" in order to engender symptoms. A decrease in thyroid function and insensitivity of the pituitary to hypothalamic releasing factors has been suggested by Lipton (1976) as mechanisms to account for the high frequency of elderly depressions. Unfortunately, there are few studies that have dealt systematically with both thyroid disorders and depression. Hypothyroidism is especially common in patients who have been treated with antithyroid drugs.

MENOPAUSE. There are a number of reasons to think that depression might follow menopause, which is a normal event. The decrease in estrogens, which inhibit monoamine oxidase, and which have other effects in the brain as well, certainly suggests this. Response in some menopausal depressed women to estrogens is clinically dramatic and cannot be denied by anyone who has seen it (Verwoerdt, 1976, p. 191). However, if there were a clear menopausal depression, one would expect to see the depressive rates for women to suddenly increase after age 40 to 45. Weeke *et al.* (1975) did not find this in their study of quinquinial age groups, nor did Schwab *et al.* (1973). Winokur (1973b) also did not find that depression following menopause was greater than would be expected. However, Lehman (1971) cites a report in Germany that there was an increase in the rate of depression in the years following menopause. A systematic prospective study in this important area clearly needs to be attempted. Trials of estrogens in depressed women have shown some promise as effective antidepressants, but further well-controlled studies are needed (Klaiber, Broverman, Vogel, Kobayashi, & Moriarty, 1972).

HYPERCALCEMIA. Hypercalcemia from any cause can exactly mimic depression. The mechanism is not clear, but calcium ions do affect tyrosine hydroxylase activity (the rate-limiting step in the synthesis of catecholamines) and membrane coupling, which is necessary for neurotransmitter release (Phillis, 1974). Carman, Post, Goodwin, and Bunney (1977) have shown that serum calcium and the CSF calcium decrease as patients improve from depression treated with electroconvulsive therapy (ECT).

Central Nervous System Etiologies

POST HEAD INJURY. The percentage of patients who develop depression after head injuries is not known, but it has been noted in several cases (Lishman, 1973). This may be pertinent to the aged since they are susceptible to head injuries from falls.

NORMAL PRESSURE HYDROCEPHALUS. Although the fully developed symptoms are dementia, incontinence, and ataxia (Bellak & Karasu, 1976, p. 236), I have seen early forms presenting with depressive symptomatologies that partially responded to antidepressants, similar to other dementias.

PARKINSON'S DISEASE. Parkinson's disease is associated with the loss of dopaminergic neurons in the nigrostriatal pathway. In addition to extrapyramidal symptoms, there is not infrequently a depression. One must note that Parkinsonian faces look depressed but may not necessarily reflect depression. The problems of depression in Parkinson's disease may range from 35% to 65% (Robins, 1976). Lebensohn and Jenkins (1975) have reported beneficial effects on depression in Parkinson's disease treated with ECT. Others have suggested that there may be a genetically based association between Parkinson's disease and depression (Stern, Hurtig, Mendels, & Balaban, 1978).

PERNICIOUS ANEMIA AND FOLATE DEFICIENCY. Pernicious anemia and folate deficiency are associated with depression in an unknown percentage of cases. Approximately 1 out of every 200 persons over 60 has pernicious anemia (Herbert, 1975, p. 1404). The term *megaloblastic madness* has been applied to this entity. The specific pathophysiology is not well understood, but presumably it is similar to the degeneration of the dorsal and lateral columns of the spinal cord.

POST-VIRAL ENCEPHALOPATHY. Post-viral encephalopathy has been associated with illnesses mimicking functional psychoses (Wilson, 1976). I have seen three older individuals over the past year who developed an onset of depression immediately after apparent complete recovery from a viral encephalitis.

DEMENTIA. Depression occurs as a symptom of dementia in 25% of cases (Roth, 1955). It can also occur following a stroke. The type of rehabilitation the patient receives following a stroke may greatly influence recovery from such insults, both at a gross behavioral and at a neuronal level (Walker & Hertzog, 1975). Ciompi (1968) has suggested that this depression may be a reaction to intellectual loss and that it will tend to disappear as the intellect deteriorates. Mild central nervous system deficits normally increase with age and can be expected to become more manifest with the additional handicap of depression.

Neoplasms

PANCREATIC CARCINOMA. Pancreatic carcinoma is especially associated with depression as a symptom prior to other symptoms of the disease process. This occult tumor's most frequent symptoms are pain in the upper right quadrant; mild epigastric pain radiating to the lower back; or paroxysmal pain perceived over wide areas of the abdomen, back, and chest. The pain is usually worse at night and not related to diet (Kowlessar, 1975).

BRAIN TUMORS. Brain tumors, especially in the frontal lobe, may exactly mimic depression and can grow to a surprising extent before they become obvious. They are often accompanied by frontal release signs and a loss of behavioral inhibition due to diminished cortical inhibitory influences (Gilroy & Meyer, 1975). This entity does not occur frequently enough to warrant a full work-up (including computer axial tomographic (CAT) scan) in all patients with depression, but they should definitely have a thorough neurological examination.

OTHER TUMORS. Depression is mentioned as an associated symptom for many tumors. It may reflect fatigue or depression per se. The lack of intensive studies in this area preclude specific statements.

Alcohol

Depression is associated with alcohol dependence to a degree much greater than chance (see Schuckit & Pastor, Chapter 10 of this volume; Bennet, 1973). Although its abuse in the aged may be less than in middle age, it is still an important entity (Mayfield, 1974). Many patients use alcohol to self-medicate a depression that is subsequently hidden by the alcohol use. Evaluation for depression cannot be carried out well in an intoxicated individual or those undergoing withdrawal. A detailed history is very important to separate primary alcoholism from depression and requires an active history taken from family and friends. This is no small task since the focus of many lay persons is on the less abstract entity of alcoholism. "Alcoholism" should not be treated as such until a thorough evaluation of an affective disorder is carried out.

Iatrogenic Disorders

Unfortunately iatrogenic disorders are a serious cause of psychiatric problems in the elderly. Learoyd (1972) found that 16% of individuals over 65 who were admitted to a psychogeriatric unit were there solely due to the adverse effects of psychotropic drugs. The major tranquilizers, especially, cause a syndrome of apathy, sluggishness, and poor concentration that can mimic depression or dementia. Confusion in this age group can be caused by most drugs, even when careful attention is paid to their dosage (Davis *et al.*, 1973).

ANTIHYPERTENSIVES, RESERPINE. Reserpine is especially dangerous in that it can induce suicidal depression in "normals." The incidence of drug-induced depression is especially high in patients with past history of depression. The pathophysiology of this is known: Reserpine depletes catecholamines and serotonin from presynaptic neurons. It should not be given to patients with a history of depression (Ambrosino, 1974). Although some authors have suggested that alphamethyldopa and guanethidine do not cause depression (Snaith & McCoubrie, 1974), I have seen several cases where both agents were clearly associated with the onset of depression. Suggestions that they do not cross the blood–brain barrier need to be reconsidered, since this barrier is not completely intact around the hypothalamus. It is suggested that patients who have depressive symptoms should be switched to another antihypertensive and their depression treated.

STIMULANTS. All the stimulants that are used for their activating or anorexigenic properties can produce a "rebound" depression following withdrawal that may last for weeks or months (Harding, 1972). Usually such depressions will respond to antidepressant medication. Simply stopping the stimulant alone will not resolve the depression.

Treatment of the underlying illness or condition should always be appropriately carried out, but one should not necessarily expect that depression will resolve when this is done. Once in progress from whatever cause, depressions tend to continue for a course of months or years. Aggressive treatment should be carried out in these cases as indicated in the treatment section of this chapter.

EVALUATION

Evaluation and treatment should be carried out when the physician suspects that depression may be present. One should not wait for spontaneous reports by patients or their families, since symptom reporting and actual perception of symptoms by patients may differ by race or by socioeconomic status. White Americans report symptoms to mental health professionals to a much greater extent than do either blacks or Mexican-Americans (Scott & Gaitz, 1975). The treatment that is chosen should not depend on the orientation of the individual doing the evaluation, but rather on the patient and on known evidence relating to response. There is no legitimate rationale to choose a unitary treatment method over multimodality treatment methods (Docherty, Marder, VanKammen, & Siris, 1977). This applies also to distinctions relative to qualitative forms of the illness (mild, moderate, or severe). There is no clear uniform evidence that the severity of the illness dictates in any way the most effective type of therapy.

Because multiple etiologies can cause an identical clinical picture and the appropriate treatment may vary immensely, it is absolutely necessary that patients be evaluated by a physician who understands the relationship of physical illness to the brain. All patients with possible complaints of a depressive nature should be referred to a physician, whether it be an internist, psychiatrist, or neurologist, for thorough evaluation. The evaluation must be complete in every case and the often practiced routine of nonmedical mental-health workers asking the patient if they had a "physical" is not adequate. The presence of signs that suggest dementia does not mean that a complete work-up is not necessary. Some 80% of individuals with dementia can have a specific etiology defined and, in a number of cases, this is treatable (Duckworth & Kedward, 1978; Seltzer & Sherwin, 1978; Wells, 1978). In certain individuals who are in a severely withdrawn state, the use of amytal, given intravenously, may be helpful in differentiating functional versus organic confusion (Ward, Rowlett, & Burke, 1978). The utility of this technique may be limited in an older age group because barbiturates can have paradoxical effects in older individuals and can cause confusion. Use of psychological testing may be particularly useful in documenting clear organic cases, but many doubtful cases will remain. All medications not clearly related to vital functions should be withdrawn to allow determination of a baseline state and relieve the patient of possible pharmacological factors relating to their condition.

The following tests should be considered routine and should be carried out during evaluation for depressed persons, both as a diagnostic tool and as a pretreatment baseline in case medications are used: complete blood count, VDRL, T–3, T–4, SGOT, creatinine, sodium, potassium, calcium (it is often less expensive to obtain an SMA–12 and –6 rather than specific tests), urinalysis, electrocardiogram, ophthalmological examination for narrow occludable chamber angle or frank glaucoma (this is necessary if tricyclics or neuroleptics with anticholinergic activity may be used). Further tests may be required if there is reason to suspect specific pathology. Preliminary evidence suggests that use of the dexamethasone suppression test may soon be considered a diagnostic tool when positive. Negative results do not reliably indicate the absence of depression, but a positive result highly correlates with specific depressive illness. Studies relative to this specific age group, however, have not been done. The dexamethasone suppression test involves giving 1 mg of dexamethasone orally between 10:30 and 11:00 P.M. and obtaining plasma samples for cortisol determination between 8:00 and 10:00 A.M. the following morning. A test is positive if the cortisol is greater than 5 mcg% (Brown, Johnston, & Mayfield, 1979; Stokes, Stoll, Mattson, & Sollod, 1976).

Evaluation should also include a complete review of systems, past medical history, present and past medications, past psychiatric history, and family history with special attention to psychiatric problems. The psychiatric history should specifically include the items of a standard diagnosis (see the section on diagnosis in this chapter), and the history should also be obtained from friends or family who are considered to be reliable. One's diagnostic ability is improved a great deal by obtaining historical information from individuals other than the patient alone, and there should be no hesitation at being insistent on having access to these people.

Mental status examination should be carefully done. One should expect performance to be good and not rationalize a few mistakes as "old age" as opposed to possible signs of organic impairment.

Resistance to Evaluation or Treatment

Patient Resistance

There are several factors involved in patient resistance to evaluation or treatment.

1. The patient may view him or herself as becoming senile, or attribute their defects to "old age," and see old age as being hopeless. People view old age in their own historic context, along with mental illness, and therefore may conceive of mental illness or dysfunction as equivalent to that described in the "snake pit," the poor farm, or in stories of senile relatives in the past.

2. Depression per se results in a negativistic outlook, and along with fatigue and hopelessness, will render a patient difficult to reach even with a great deal of effort.

3. Hypochondriacal concern with total focus on the soma often will preclude psychiatric work-up, either because the patient will not be

seen by a psychiatrist or because the patient refuses, believing the mythology that psychiatrists deal with things that are "imaginary" and "in the head."

4. There are possible secondary gains to not getting better, such as keeping the family bound to the patient or finally receiving attention when previously one was isolated due to social or geographic factors. The concept of secondary gain, however, should not be overutilized and should definitely not be rationalized as a reason not to undertake appropriate treatment.

5. Many patients who have an agitated depression are too anxious to get out of their house and have agoraphobic symptoms. They also may have great difficulty in tolerating change or the stresses associated with a visit to a new doctor or hospital.

6. Some individuals will have guilt over the way they treated their own aging parents and may see their suffering as a deserved retribution.

All of these items and many others should be dealt with in a straightforward manner and not allowed to impede work-up or treatment. An active team involvement with the patient and family may be necessary and is warranted.

Physician Resistance

Physician resistance to evaluation and treatment of individuals in this age group has been present for many years. Freud (1904) said that older people were not amenable to analysis. This may or may not be true, but there is no reason for modern physicians or therapists to excuse lack of care in such a population. We may have the prejudice of ageism or be too quick to see a diagnosis of organic brain syndrome and consequently jump to a conclusion that the case is hopeless. Psychiatrists, as a group, do not deal with individuals over 65. A recent survey (Finkel, 1978) found that 56% of psychiatrists did not see any individuals over 65 in their practice, and only 2% of psychiatrists' patients were over 65 (Feigenbaum, 1974). One suggests that in addition to other factors, there may be a prejudice that older individuals cannot change, especially through the use of dynamic psychiatry. In addition, there may be a lack of vicarious gratification in treating older patients, for it is unlikely that they will become famous or live glorious lives that the therapist can be proud of. There may be a fear in most physicians of age per se and loss of brain function and performance. Finally, there may be countertransference from their relationships with their own parents.

Family Resistance

Frequently there will be family resistance to evaluation and treatment. This may stem from dislike for a patient who has been irritable, negativistic, and depressed for many months or years. In many families, there is a prejudice regarding age, and the patient is not recognized as ill, but rather, "just old." In such instances, the family may be reluctant to spend the money or time that is necessary in order to have a complete and thorough work-up. Younger relatives may act out anger from past unresolved conflicts, or they may act out a fear of age or mental illness and, in an effort to deny such possibilities, attempt to get their parents quickly put out of sight.

Societal Resistance

Lastly, there appears to be a general societal resistance to adequate evaluation and treatment of older individuals. A recent study (Redlich & Kellert, 1978) has shown that over the last 25 years, community psychiatric facilities have come to serve fewer older individuals rather than more. Society is very reluctant to spend money on the health care of the aged, especially as it pertains to psychiatric illness (Kerschner & Hirshfield, 1975). Medicare will pay only for 190 days of psychiatric inpatient care in a lifetime. This trend occurs in the face of an increase in the incidence of psychiatric illness in this age group. This prejudice against psychiatric care for the aged may be related to the concept of psychiatry as equivalent to psychotherapy and a belief that the aged cannot benefit from "talking therapy," or it may be the result of an ignorance of the advances in the medical treatment of many psychiatric illnesses, especially depression.

PROGNOSIS

Good prognosis to all treatments is related to several factors: first onset of affective symptomatology prior to age 70; a positive family history for affective disorders; recovery from previous depressions; extroversion; multiple interests; severe symptomatology; confusion or irrationality; and emotionality. Poor prognosis is related to concomitant serious physical illness (especially in females), dependency-obsessiveness, and clear organic signs (Ciompi, 1969; Epstein, 1976; Post, 1975).

THERAPY

Somatic Therapies

Medications and other somatic therapies have a primary place in the treatment of affective disorders. Although about 20% of depression does not readily respond to treatment (Ananth & Ruskin, 1974; Greenblatt, Grosser, & Wechler, 1964), true treatment-resistant depression is not common (Freyhan, 1974; Walcher, 1974) and may reflect lack of a thorough trial (Kotin, Post, & Goodwin, 1973; Sethna, 1974).

Medication

General caveats with special reference to the elderly age group must be borne in mind. The elderly do not have the same response to the same medication or dose as the young. The age and sex differences may be very marked (Bressler & Palmer, 1974; Learoyd, 1972; Salzman *et al.*, 1975; Stotsky, 1975). In older aged individuals, there is alteration of absorption of the drug, and excretion is prolonged due to diminished renal blood flow, irregular filtration rate, and tubular secretion. There is also a decrease in cardiac output and consequently an increase in circulation time. In addition, there is loss of muscle in relationship to fatty tissue, and since most psychoactive drugs are lipid soluble they tend to accumulate to a greater extent. The total binding of drug to plasma protein will be decreased since plasma protein decreases with age (Verwoerdt, 1976). Metabolism by the liver may be altered resulting in a longer half-life of the medication (Bressler & Palmer, 1974). Finally, the target organ, the brain, has changed from a younger state. Neurons may have dropped out in a variable pattern, and one can expect that various synthetic and feedback systems may be differentially altered, resulting in "paradoxical" effects. As a rule of thumb the doses used in the aged should be reduced to one-third or one-half of that used in the younger adult population. Seldom does one have reason to push a dose rapidly up to high levels.

ANTIDEPRESSANTS. Tricyclics are the primary antidepressants to be considered. Their posited mechanism of action is to inhibit the re-uptake of essential catecholamines or serotonin and thus permit the neurotransmitter to have a greater biological activity at the postsynaptic receptor. These agents can be set on a continuum by side effects and by central neurotransmitter effects. One ought to take advantage of each when prescribing for an individual patient (see Table 6.1).

It is crucial to note that a standard oral dose produces tremendous

TABLE 6.1

Central Neurotransmitter Effects, Side Effects, and Clinical Indications for Tricyclic Antidepressants[a]

	Usual initial dose in elderly (in milligrams)	Upper limit (milligrams a day)	Relative activity		Depressive type	Anticholinergic effect	Sedative effect
			Serotonergic	Noradrenergic			
Amitriptyline	25–50	300	marked	none	agitated	high	high
Doxepin	25–50	300	similar to amitriptyline		agitated		
Nortriptyline	10	100	moderate	moderate		continuum	
Imipramine	25–50	300	moderate	moderate	both		
Protriptyline	5	40	little	marked	retarded		
Desipramine	25–50	300	none	marked	retarded	low	low

[a] Adapted from Goodwin, 1977; Maas, 1975; Snyder & Yamamura, 1977; U'Prichard, Greenberg, Sheehan, & Snyder, 1978.

interindividual variation in plasma levels. Differences up to 30-fold are commonly reported. Recent studies suggest that the same dose results in higher plasma levels in the aged than in younger subjects (Friedel, 1978; Nies, Robinson, Friedman, Green, Cooper, Ravaris, & Ives, 1977), although earlier preliminary studies did not indicate this (Asberg, Evans, & Sjoquist, 1971). The tricyclics may take 2–3 weeks to reach a steady state plasma level on a given dose in this age group. Therapeutic response depends upon achievement of a plasma level in the therapeutic range (Braithwaite *et al.*, 1972). The plasma level of nortriptyline has a narrow therapeutic range (Asberg, Cronholm, Sjoquist, & Tuck, 1971), and levels higher or lower than this are associated with a lack of response. This "therapeutic window" may also be present with protriptyline and desipramine, although controversy exists in these areas (Biggs & Ziegler, 1977; Glassman & Perel, 1978). Plasma levels of imipramine appear to show response threshold occurring at approximately 180 nanograms/ml. Higher levels may be associated with better response, but a leveling out of response occurs at levels greater than this. The clinical relationship of tricyclic plasma levels has been extensively reviewed by Glassman and Perel (1978).

It appears likely that measurement of plasma levels of tricyclics will be a necessary and routine part of their use in the near future. However, in addition to the determination of the primary medication, one must measure and take into account the metabolites. Amitriptyline is metabolized to nortriptyline, and imipramine to desipramine (Goodwin, 1977). The clinical relevance of these plasma profiles is currently being examined and the relationship of specific plasma level response to the aged is under investigation.

Since plasma levels can vary so widely, any individual may respond to a relatively low dose. In this age group, it is recommended that one initiate therapy at the lowest range of the usual adult daily doses and slowly increase this every 2 to 3 days. This is particularly important with nortriptyline, since it is easy to exceed the therapeutic plasma level. With this medication it is best to decrease the dose if some positive response has not been achieved in 2 to 3 weeks. If a response is not seen in a week, the dose may then be increased.

For the tricyclics without a therapeutic window, one should slowly increase the dosage every 3 to 5 days. The rate of increase can be diminished or halted if side effects become difficult or if response occurs. Except for the more potent nortriptyline and protriptyline, the usual minimally effective dose will be 75 mg per day. However, some individuals will respond to as little as 20 mg per day. An adequate trial constitutes 4 weeks of treatment at the highest dose tolerated. After a response has been obtained, the medication should be continued for several months and then tapered off over 2 to 3 months. If depressive symptoms emerge, the antidepressant should be re-instituted for several more months. Many individuals may require a maintenance treatment with antidepressants in order to remain functional (Davis, 1976; Klerman, 1978). Although it is commonly said that it takes 3 weeks or more at a therapeutic dose before an antidepressant effect is seen, in my experience one can often detect clinically relevant improvement in some signs of depression during the second week. Often agitation and problems with sleep are found to improve first, with a subjective improvement in depression and depressive mood occurring later (Haskell, DiMascio, & Prusoff, 1975).

Clinical lore has suggested that amitriptyline or doxepin are preferable for agitated depression and that imipramine or desipramine are preferable for retarded depression. This lore has been supported by several studies (Grof, Saxena, & Cantor, 1974; Hollister & Overall, 1965; Raskin, 1974). Predictors of tricyclic response have been extensively reviewed by Bielski and Friedel (1976). Tricyclic response has been reported to be better with endogenous as compared with neurotic depression in some studies (Raskin & Crook, 1976) but not in others (Haskell *et al.*, 1975). Although in younger patients the whole daily dose may be given at night, it may be wiser in the aged to divide the daily dose to one-third in the morning and two-thirds at night. In addition to decreasing high plasma levels that could have cardiotoxic or central nervous system (CNS) toxic effects, many individuals find that protriptyline and desipramine interfere with sleep if given in the evening. If one tricyclic fails to alleviate adequately the depression, then it is best to switch to another with effects at the other end of the pharmacological spectrum (see Table 6.1).

In females who do not respond to an adequate trial of tricyclics, triiodothyronine (T_3) can be used to potentiate their effect (Coppen, Whybrow, Noguepa, Maggs, & Prange, 1972; Prange, Wilson, Knox, McClure, & Lipton, 1970). Presumably, the mechanism is by increasing the sensitivity of the postsynaptic receptor, adenylate cyclase. The usual dose is initially 25 micrograms daily and may be increased to 50 micrograms for 2 weeks. This should be done with consideration of cardiac functions, for T_3 may increase arrhythmias in suceptible individuals, and hence use with a digitalis preparation is contraindicated.

Adverse effects occur with all the tricyclics and are either mediated through anticholinergic or adrenergic activity. All the side effects are potentially more dangerous in the older age group and care should be taken to elicit information about such effects each time the patient is seen.

The following potentially dangerous side effects should be systematically kept in mind (Bassuk & Schoonouer, 1977; Prange, 1973):

1. Precipitation of glaucoma crisis in patients with glaucoma or with a narrow occludable chamber angle can occur. However, certain types of glaucoma are not contraindications to tricyclics. Consultation with an ophthalmologist is indicated.

2. Urinary obstruction can occur, especially in males if they have a marginally enlarged prostate.

3. Adynamic ileus may be precipitated secondary to anticholinergic effect on the gut.

4. Orthostatic hypotension may result in falls or arrhythmias. Patients should be instructed to rise slowly from a supine or sitting position. The less sedating tricyclics may produce less hypotension. Hypotension should be especially considered in individuals taking antihypertensives concomitantly, and the dose of antihypertensives may be lowered during treatment with tricyclics.

5. Psychoses may be induced: (a) anticholinergic psychosis identical to atropine psychosis may occur and may be rapidly, but only acutely, reversed by 1–2 mg of physostigmine, intravenously (Muñoz, 1976); (b) mania may be precipitated in patients with or without a bipolar history (Bunney, 1978); (c) psychoses of a nonspecific nature may also be induced. Withdrawal of the tricyclic is indicated in all of the preceding, and the use of antipsychotics may be useful in b and c. Reinstitution of tricyclic treatment may be done in a, but at a lower dose.

6. Cardiac arrhythmias secondary to alteration of conduction and repolarization are important possible side effects. Monitoring the cardiac function in susceptible individuals with a cardiogram may be necessary until a stable dose has been reached. Amitriptyline is considered the most dangerous tricyclic (Avery et al., 1976; Bigger, Kantor, Glassman, & Perel, 1978; Davies, 1965; de Groot, 1974; Grof et al., 1974; Jefferson, 1975; Vohra & Burrows, 1974; Vohra, Burrows, & Sloman, 1975), although others, including imipramine are also implicated. Doxepin is considered to be relatively safer and as efficacious as amitriptyline (Friedel, 1978; Pelc, 1975; Prange, 1973). Acute cardiotoxic and other anticholinergic effects can often be reversed by physostigmine (Bassuk & Schoonouer, 1977). The incidence of sudden death with tricyclic treatment is not great enough to withhold treatment to an

individual suffering depression. Depression, itself, is associated with an increased mortality and the quality of life is clearly inferior. Desipramine, and to a lesser extent, imipramine, occasionally cause palpitations, presumably mediated through the noradrenergic effects.

Bothersome side effects that are unusual or not life threatening include dry mouth, constipation, tremor, increased sweating, impotence, fatigue, hesitancy at micturition, blurred vision, drowsiness for several days during the initial phase of treatment, allergic skin reactions, and edema. Cholestatic jaundice and agranulocytosis are very rare. The bothersome effects should be discussed openly with the patient and active efforts directed toward alleviating them to increase the compliance to treatment. Decreasing the dose or changing to another medication is the usual course of action. If necessary, bethanachol, 10–75 mg per day may be used to counteract the peripheral anticholinergic effects of the tricyclics (Everett, 1975). Sympathomimetic effects (sweating, palpitations, etc.) may respond to propranolol 10–80 mg per day in divided doses (Benkert, 1978).

INTERACTIONS WITH OTHER MEDICATIONS. All the tricyclics will interfere with hypotensive action of guanethidine. They will interact synergistically with the hypotensive effects of diuretics, methyldopa, and reserpine. Tricyclics have the following effects when combined with other medications:

Clonidine—paradoxical increase in blood pressure
Adrenergic agents—enhanced pressor effects, arrhythmias
Oral anticoagulants—enhance effect
Thyroid hormones—enhanced effect
Neuroleptics—increase in plasma levels
L-Dopa—may interfere with absorption
Antipyrine—possible enhanced toxicity
Narcotic analgesics—increased effect
Quinidine—potentiation of quinidine effect

The effect of other drugs on tricyclic effects are as follows:

Barbiturates—decreased plasma levels
Thyroid medications—enhanced effect
Neuroleptics—increase in plasma levels
Estrogens—may enhance tricyclic effects
Narcotics—increased tricyclic effects
Amphetamines—increased tricyclic plasma levels

NEW ANTIDEPRESSANTS. The adverse side effects of tricyclics have motivated the development of compounds that are less anticholinergic. Currently, at least three compounds are in clinical trials in the United States: (*a*) trazadone, which is a serotonergic tetracyclic; (*b*) viloxazine, which is probably active by blocking the re-uptake of catecholamines; and (*c*) nomafensine, which has dopaminergic properties. The efficacy of at least the first two compounds in the aging is of great interest and appears promising.

NEUROLEPTICS. Neuroleptics may be used in combination or alone with tricyclic antidepressants. There is evidence that concomitant use results in increased plasma levels of both agents and, hence, lower than expected doses may work. Neuroleptics are of greatest usefulness in severe agitated or psychotic depressions. They may only be needed to control symptoms during initial weeks of treatment, until the tricyclics have had time to work. Chronic treatment should be used judiciously, since the elderly are more susceptible to drug-induced dyskinesias (Paulson, 1973). Although thioridazine is usually considered the first choice of the neuroleptics (Kurland, 1976; Thompson, 1972), there are no data to suggest that others are not equally efficacious (Brodie *et al.*, 1975; Davis *et al.*, 1973; Raskin, 1974; Stotsky, 1975; Tsuang, Lu, Stotsky, & Cole, 1971). The anticholinergic effects of thioridazine may result in anticholinergic toxicity (Heiman, 1971; Snyder & Yamamura, 1977). Side effects of the neuroleptic should be taken into account in an individual case. The more sedating (thioridazine and chlorpromazine) may be useful for patients with anxiety and insomnia. The more potent (haloperidol, fluphenazine, thiothixene, etc.) may be indicated when psychosis is more prominent, although they may also be efficacious in neurotic depressions (Goldstein & Banas, 1968). Very small doses may result in symptom improvement. Doses should be slowly increased with the neuroleptics as with the tricyclics.

ANXIOLYTICS AND HYPNOTICS. Because agitation, anxiety, and insomnia are frequent concomitants to depression, there is a rationale for specific drug treatment for these symptoms. However, reduction of these symptoms alone does not constitute adequate treatment and antidepressants should be used also. Clinical experience suggests that anxiolytics and hypnotics usually do not produce as complete a response of anxiety or insomnia as the use of an appropriate antidepressant for an effective duration, although diazepam may be superior to the neuroleptic thioridazine to reduce anxiety associated with depression (Rosenthal & Bowden, 1973). After response is obtained to antidepressants, the anxiolytics and the hypnotics often can be discontinued. One should not casually rely on these agents for maintenance treatment. All will tend to exacerbate any preexisting confusion and decrease mentation. If the anxiety stems from difficulty coping secondary to decreased cognitive function, then anxiolytics may make the situation worse (Salzman, Shader, & Harmatz, 1975).

Barbiturates and related compounds are to be avoided in the elderly. Both accidental and intentional overdosage can easily be fatal. Paradoxical reactions are common with these agents. They disturb sleep and are a poor choice for a hypnotic. Finally, they induce hepatic microsomal enzymes that can decrease the plasma level of a number of other drugs. I feel similarly with regard to glutethimide (Doridan), ethchlorvynol (Placidyl), methyprylon (Noludar), meprobamate, methaqualone (Quaalude), and related compounds. The benzodiazepines and related compounds (oxazepam, diazepam, chlordiazepoxide, lorazepam and flurazepam) should be the first anxiolytics and hypnotics used in the aged (Davis *et al.*, 1973). They all may produce drowsiness and if doses are too high, ataxia, decreased cognition, or paradoxical disinhibition of emotion may occur. This latter problem is important to take into account, since it often (erroneously) leads to increased use of "tranquilizers" instead of a decreased dose. Some clinicians prefer oxazepam to others because of its relatively short half-life of 10 to 14 hours, compared with diazepam's 20 to 42 hours (Greenblatt & Shader, 1975; Gulevich, 1977). Lorazepam also has a short half-life. Deaths from overdosage on benzodiazepines are very rare. Benzodiazepines, chloral hydrate, and triclofos (half-life 11 hours) are useful hypnotics and do not disturb sleep as do the barbiturates.

Comparisons of tricyclic antidepressants, minor tranquilizers, and neuroleptics suggest that the minor tranquilizers are not as efficacious in the older age group (Henry, Overall, & Markette, 1971), and that retarded depression responds better to appropriate tricyclics, whereas agitated depression responds about equally to tricyclics and neuroleptics (Downing & Rickels, 1972; Glick, 1973; Goldberg & Finnerty, 1972; Haskell, McNair, Fisher, & Kahn, 1974; Hollister & Overall, 1965; Paykel, Price, Gillan, Palmai, & Chesser, 1968).

ADDITIONAL ANTIDEPRESSANT MODALITIES. *Lithium* is now considered to be useful in the prophylaxis of recurrent unipolar depression (Davis, 1976). It may also be useful in the acute treatment of depression (Watanabe, Ishino, & Otsuki, 1975). Prophylactic use in the aged should be predicated either on the diagnosis of bipolar illness or frequent recurring unipolar depression (Cox, 1977). It is probably safer as a maintenance medication than as a tricyclic, although there are few studies related to this age group (Van der Velde, 1971). The only absolute contraindication is the concomitant use of a diuretic, which may result in lithium toxicity. *Caffeine* in the form of one to two cups of coffee in the morning has commonly been used to self-medicate for fatigue. I have seen several aged individuals in the diagnostic criteria of retarded depression respond dramatically to two morning cups of coffee. Presumably this could be mediated by xanthene and caffeine, which may increase receptor sensitivity to neurotransmitters.

Monoamine oxidase inhibitors (MAOIs) can be used alone or in combination with tricyclics. MAOIs are effective, especially when depression is associated with phobias and anxiety, although it is widely agreed that they are not as efficacious as the tricyclics (Kay, Garside, & Fahy, 1970). Use should be confined to individuals who have failed to respond to adequate trials of two or more tricyclics and who are able to maintain the low monoamine diet and regimen (abstinence from sympathomimetic agents such as nasal decongestants). MAOIs inhibitors may be especially indicated in phobic depressions (Kay *et al.*, 1970). The fear that American psychiatrists have about these compounds is not supported by major studies (Raskin, 1972; Schuckit, Robins, & Feighner, 1971; Tyrer, 1976).

Both *L-Dopa*, a precursor to dopamine and norepinephrine, and *L-tryptophan* or L-5-hydroxytryptophan, which are precursors of serotonin, have an antidepressant effect in a minority of patients. The lack of clinically available tests to predict response suggests that currently the use of such agents should be relegated to treatment-resistant cases in a setting where special consent has been obtained. L-Dopa appears to be only infrequently effective in retarded depression and may induce mania in susceptible individuals (Brodie, 1973; Murphy, Goodwin, Brodie, & Bunney, 1973). The serotonin precursor, L-tryptophan, may be useful in a subgroup of depressions with low CSF 5-HIAA (Coppen, Shaw, Herzberg, & Maggs, 1967; Coppen, Whybrow, Noguepa, Maggs, & Prange, 1972; Van Praag & Korf, 1973; Rao, 1972). L-tryptophan needs to be given with pyridoxine and a decarboxylase inhibitor to prevent peripheral metabolism; gastrointestinal symptoms are frequent, and the drug is very expensive.

Amphetamines and other stimulants should be used as antidepressants only with the greatest of consideration (Lehman & Aban, 1975; Salzman *et al.*, 1975; Schmidt, 1974). Less severe depressions are more likely to respond to these agents than the psychotically ill (Kiloh, Neilson, & Andrews, 1974), and females are more likely to respond than males (Salzman *et al.*, 1975). An extended release preparation provides a more even effect and may be safer. Approximately 5–10 mg of D-amphetamine in the morning may alleviate depressive symptoms and improve cognition for several hours, sometimes dramatically (Gilbert, Donnelly, Zimmer, & Kubis, 1973). Continued daily use will lead to tolerance, and withdrawal produces severe depression. Use with tricyclics results in increased tricyclic plasma levels and thus suggests that the tricyclic dosage might preferably have been increased rather than adding a stimulant. There are infrequent instances where, after an extensive and thorough trial of other antidepressants, stimulants are the only agents that are effective, and in such cases they should not be withheld. Although stimulants are not specifically cardiotoxic, the cardiovascular status should be evaluated systematically during such treatment.

Gerovital has been subjected to a number of open and blind trials and may be an effective antidepressant, possibly through its activity as a monoamine oxidase inhibitor. At present, it appears to be less useful than standard treatments (Cohen & Ditman, 1974; Jarvik & Milne, 1975).

Vasodilators have not been assessed in relationship to antidepressant effects. *Amantadine* has been reported to be useful specifically in treatment of the elderly and bears consideration for further study (Chierichetti, Ferrari, Sala, & Vibelli, 1977).

Electroconvulsive therapy (ECT) is the best antidepressant treatment that has been developed and is considerably safer than medication or no treatment (Avery *et al.*, 1976; Fink, 1979). It is the first treatment of choice for delusional or psychotic depressions and may be life-saving (Glassman, Kantor, & Shostak, 1975; Wilson & Major, 1973). Although several states have passed laws inhibiting the use of ECT, one must consider that each patient deserves the best treatment for the individual illness. At times this medical axiom may conflict with the law. The only contraindication to ECT is a space occupying lesion in the cranium. When given with light anesthesia and succinylcholine, there is very, very slight risk of physical harm (Fink, 1978), and ECT can be given an outpatient as well as an inpatient (Merrill, 1977). Temporary memory loss that may occur with ECT can be diminished to such an extent that often it is not detectable. This can be done by using unilateral treatment to the right hemisphere and by giving the treatments every other day. Older individuals as a group respond more quickly than younger people. Often only four to six treatments are required. After improvement, antidepressant medication should be given for several months to maintain the improvement and prevent relapse. Both pure depression and depressive spectrum disease respond to ECT (Van Valkenburg, Lowry, Winokur, & Cadoret, 1977). The response may be dramatic in the extreme, even in "chronic depression" that is accompanied by organic signs in a patient who has not responded to a medication. ECT should not be delayed as the "treatment of last resort."

Sleep deprivation for one night is an extremely useful adjunct to the antidepressant medications. The procedure is simple to carry out and merely involves missing one complete night of sleep. The patient is asked to stay awake, with supervision from breakfast on Day 1 through 10 P.M. on Day 2. The onset of antidepressant effects occurs from about noon on Day 2 in about 50% of the patients and are related to alterations in neurotransmitter metabolism and biorhythms (Gerner, Post, & Bunney, 1979; Post, Kotin, & Goodwin, 1976). The effect may be dramatic with full remission of the depression for 1 to 7 days. The severely depressed appear to have a more robust response. Nonresponders and patients who relapse may be redeprived every 3 to 5 days until response is obtained. This method is in relatively widespread use in Europe and can be carried out on an outpatient basis if supervision is possible. Sleep deprivation may decrease the response latency of the antidepressants when carried out at the beginning of medication.

Neurosurgery should be considered for patients who do not respond after 2 to 3 years of aggressive treatment. It carries a small morbid risk and can result in a much higher quality of life. Consultation with several colleagues is suggested and detailed explanation should be offered the patient and family by an expert in the field. As with ECT, the real "informed" part of the consent may deal with assuaging irrational fears and prejudices that have been popularized (Bailey, Dowling, & Davies, 1973; Bridges, Goktepe, & Maratos, 1973).

Hospitalization

Hospitalization should be considered for the following reasons:

1. More thorough evaluation is needed.
2. Prevention of suicide—for patients who have thoughts or wishes of death or suicide, or who think they or others would be better off if they were not around—may be necessary. The burden rests on giving a well thought out, rational reason as to why such individuals should not initially receive treatment in the hospital.
3. Monitoring somatic parameters such as EKG or renal function during institution of pharmacotherapy is necessary.
4. There is need for provision of treatment that cannot be carried out effectively on an outpatient, depending on the patient's condition or social circumstances. This may include ECT and

aggressive pharmacotherapy, such as use of monoamine oxidase inhibitors and tricyclics.

5. It may be necessary to alleviate negative social factors such as intense family discord and/or to initiate family therapy.
6. There is a need to initiate social rehabilitation.

The risk of developing an institutional syndrome is unlikely because of the generally short periods of stay in the hospital, and this risk should not be a major reason to avoid hospitalization. The institutional syndrome was observed to occur only after many months or years of hospitalization prior to effective therapies (Barton, 1966; Gruenberg, Kasins, & Huxley, 1962). A greater danger is precipitation of disorientation in a marginally compensated patient. Change in daily routine and physical surrounding requires a considerable degree of adaptational ability. This ability is decreased with age and may be lessened by depression. Repeated orientation should be carried out several times a day by staff to lessen this undesirable effect.

Nonsomatic Therapy and Techniques for Outpatients

In addition to an empathetic, receptive approach, which should always be a part of a therapeutic relationship, it is especially important to consider counseling the family of the elderly. They may have many misunderstandings or myths that need to be cleared up. Older individuals may, as a group, benefit more from frequent visits for a relatively shorter period of time (e.g., 30 minutes as opposed to 60). This is especially true in the depressed group who may find it difficult to sit still or who may be embarrassed by feeling that they have nothing to say. Active followup is a vital part of treatment of individuals with depression, and individuals who do not show up for appointments should be paid home visits and not allowed to drop out of treatment. Individuals on medications who may be a bit confused, will benefit greatly from use of a standard pill box that has all 7 days of the week marked on separate compartments.

There is, unfortunately, very little hard data on psychotherapy with depression in the aged, although, there are a number of well-written guidelines (Goldfarb, 1975). Extensive reviews of the literature by Lieberman (1975), Luborsky, Singer, and Luborsky (1975), and Cristol (1972) agree that there are no studies of psychotherapy in depression that meet minimal scientific standards. Three groups have examined an interaction of antidepressants, diazepam, and placebo with psychotherapy, both individual and group (Covi, Lipman, Derogatis,

Smith, & Pattison, 1974; Friedman, 1975; Klerman, DiMascio, Weissman, Prusoff, & Paykel, 1974; Lipman & Covi, 1976; Lipman, Covi, & Smith, 1975; Weissman, Klerman, Paykel, Prusoff, & Hanson, 1974). All groups found a main antidepressant effect with medication, with minimal or no effect of psychotherapy on symptoms or relapse. However, all three groups found a positive effect of psychotherapy on various aspects of social functioning and interpersonal relationships, and only one group reported such effects with medication. Paykel, DiMascio, Haskell, and Prusoff (1975) have demonstrated that early withdrawal from antidepressant medication may result in a recrudescence of depression that will not be prevented by continued psychotherapy. Psychotherapy should never be carried out to the exclusion of somatic therapy if somatic therapies are indicated (Weissman, 1978). Indications for specific psychotherapy beyond empathy and a sympathetic, supportive, and optimistic outlook are anecdotal. Most reports suggest that both individual therapy and group therapies should be directive and active and not carried out with a passive therapist approach (Post, 1965). Group therapy may be especially useful for withdrawn patients. Passivity of the therapist may be interpreted by the patient as a refusal on the therapist's part to allow the patient to depend on them. This will, in turn, make the patient more anxious and dependent. Rather, it is useful to allow the patient to see the therapist as a parental surrogate. Once this is achieved, one is in a position to suggest actions to the patient that may break into the vicious cycle of negativism and failure. A cognitive stance of dealing positively with problems should be constantly reinforced. Ultimately, the patient may discover ways to gain effective control over many aspects of life. Age does not mean that there are no particular fears or conflicts that ought to be explored in psychotherapy in a more traditional sense.

A frequent complaint of older individuals is that they are categorized and stereotyped and not respected as individuals. Some care must be used in avoiding terms that are laden with negative connotations for this particular age group ("geriatric" and "elderly" are often offensive). Counseling of the family not to treat the patient as a fifth wheel nor to use the third person when talking to the patient or in their presence is absolutely crucial. Additionally, the family should be told not to exclude the patient from decision making.

Social therapies seem to be particularly important with individuals of this age group who are depressed. Active efforts to increase the contact with the environment should be carried out, but only as tolerated. To some extent it is important not to pursue these too actively in the beginning because the patient may panic or will necessarily fail.

Initial rejection of therapeutic intervention and negativism should not result in the patient being left alone (Post, 1975). Involvement with the environment is important because it may break a cycle of depressive behavior and inactivity which, if continued, worsens existing depression. There is also evidence that brain function at the cellular level improves with new contacts with a varied environment in contrast to the myth that the older brain cannot grow and change (Walker & Herzog, 1975).

REFERENCES

Ambrosino, S. V. Depressive reactions associated with reserpine. *New York State Journal of Medicine*, 1974, *74*, 860–864.

Ananth, J., & Ruskin, R. Treatment of intractable depression. *International Pharmacopsychiatry*, 1974, *9*, 218–229.

Andreasen, M. C., Endicott, J., Spitzer, R. L., & Winokur, G. The family history method using diagnostic criteria. *Archives of General Psychiatry*, 1977, *34*, 1229–1235.

Asberg, M., Cronholm, B., Sjoquist, F., & Tuck, D. Relationship between plasma level and therapeutic effect of nortriptyline. *British Medical Journal*, 1971, *3*, 331–334.

Asberg, M., Evans, D. A., Sjoquist, F. Genetic control of nortriptyline kinetics in man. *Journal of Medical Genetics*, 1971, *8*, 129–135.

Asberg, M., Thoren, P., Traskman, L., Bertilsson, L., & Ringberger, V. "Serotonin Depression." A biochemical subgroup within the affective disorders. *Science*, 1976, *191*, 478–480.

Avery, D., & Winokur, G. Mortality in depressed patients treated with electroconvulsive therapy and antidepressants. *Archives of General Psychiatry*, 1976, *33*, 1029–1037.

Bailey, H. R., Dowling, J. L., & Davies, E. The control of affective illness by cingulotractotomy: A review of 150 cases. *The Medical Journal of Australia*, 1973, *2*, 366–371.

Banki, C. M. Cerebrospinal fluid amine metabolites after combined amitriptyline–triiodothyronine treatment of depressed women. *European Journal of Clinical Pharmacology*, 1977, *11*, 311–315.

Barraclough, B. M. Suicide in the elderly. *Recent developments in psychogeriatrics. British Journal of Psychiatry*, Special Publication No. 6. Ashford, Vent: Headley Bros., 1971.

Barton, R. *Institutional neurosis*. Bristol: John Wright, 1966.

Bassuk, E. L., & Schoonouer, S. C. *The practitioner's guide to psychoactive drugs*. New York: Plenum Press, 1977.

Beckman, H., & Goodwin, F. K. Antidepressant response to tricyclics and urinary MHPG in unipolar patients. *Archives of General Psychiatry*, 1975, *32*, 17–21.

Bellak, L., & Karasu, T. B. *Geriatric Psychiatry*. New York: Grune & Stratton, 1976.

Benkert, O. Indikationen für Beta-Rezeptorenblocker in der Psychiatric. *Internist*, 1978, *19*, 1202–1204.

Bennett, A. E. Psychiatric management of geriatric depressive disorders. *Diseases of the Nervous System*, 1973, *34*, 222–225.

Bielski, R. J., & Friedel, R. O. Prediction of tricyclic antidepressant response. *Archives of General Psychiatry*, 1976, *33*, 1479–1489.

Bigger, J. T., Kantor, S. J., Glassman, A. H., & Perel, J. M. Cardiovascular effects of tricyclic antidepressant drugs. In M. A. Lipton, A. DiMascio, & K. F. Killam (Eds.),

Psychopharmacology: A generation of progress. New York: Raven Press, 1978. Pp. 1033–1046.

Biggs, J. T., & Ziegler, V. E. Protriptyline plasma levels and antidepressant response. *Clinical Pharmacology Therapeutics,* 1977, *22,* 269–273.

Blusewicz, M. J., Dustman, R. E., Schenkenberg, T., & Beck, E. C. Neuropsychological correlates of chronic alcoholism and aging. *Journal of Nervous and Mental Disease,* 1977, *165,* 348–355.

Bornstein, P. E., & Clayton, P. J. The anniversary reaction. *Journal of Nervous and Mental Disease,* 1972, *33,* 470–472.

Bornstein, P. E., Clayton, P. J., Halikas, J. A., Maurice, W. L., & Robins, E. The depression of widowhood after thirteen months. *British Journal of Psychiatry,* 1973, *122,* 561–566.

Braithwaite, R. A., Goulding, R., Theano, G., Bailey, J., & Coppen, A. Plasma concentration of amitriptyline and clinical response. *Lancet,* 1972, *1,* 1298–1300.

Bressler, R., & Palmer, J. Drug interactions in the aged. In W. E. Fann & G. L. Maddox (Eds.), *Drug issues in geropsychiatry.* Baltimore, Maryland: William & Wilkins, 1974. Pp. 49–60.

Bridges, P. K., Goktepe, E. O., & Maratos, J. A comparative review of patients with obsessional neurosis and with depression treated by psychosurgery. *British Journal of Psychiatry,* 1973, *123,* 663–674.

Briggs, M. H., & Briggs, M. Hormonal influence on erythrocyte catechol-O-methyltransferase activity in humans. *Experentia,* 1973, *29,* 279–280.

Brodie, K. H. Affective changes associated with L-DOPA therapy. C. Eisdorfer & W. E. Fann (Eds.), *Psychopharmacology and aging.* New York: Plenum Press, 1973. Pp. 97–104.

Brodie, K. H., McGhie, N. H., McGhie, R. L., O'Hara, H., Valle-Jones, J. C., & Schiff, A. A. A double-blind comparative study of fluphenazine/nortriptyline and promazine. *The Practitioner,* 1975, *215,* 660–664.

Brown, G. W., Harris, T., & Copeland, J. R. Depression and loss. *British Journal of Psychiatry,* 1977, *130,* 1–18.

Brown, W. A., Johnston, R., & Mayfield, D. The 24-hour dexamethasone suppression test in a clinical setting: Relationship to diagnosis, symptoms, and response to treatment. *American Journal of Psychiatry,* 1979, *136,* 543–547.

Bunney, W. E. Psychopharmacology of the switch process in affective illness. In M. A. Lipton, A. DiMascio, & K. F. Killam (Eds.), *Psychopharmacology: A generation of progress.* New York: Raven Press, 1978. Pp. 1249–1260.

Busse, E. W. Psychopathology. In J. E. Birren (Ed.), *Handbook of aging and individual.* Chicago: Univ. of Chicago Press, 1969. Pp. 389–391.

Busse, E. W. Psychoneurotic reactions and defense mechanisims in the aged. In E. Palmore (Ed.), *Normal aging.* Durham, North Carolina: Duke Univ. Press, 1970. Pp. 84–90.

Busse, E. W., Barnes, R. H., Silverman, H. J., Thaler, M., & Frost, L. L. Studies of the process of aging, X. The strength and weaknesses of psychic functioning in the aged. *American Journal of Psychiatry,* 1955, *111,* 896–901.

Cahn, H. A., Folk, G. E., & Huston, P. E. Age comparison of human day–night physiological differences. *Aerospace Medicine,* 1968, *39,* 608–610.

Carman, J. S., Post, R. M., Goodwin, F. K., & Bunney, W. E. Calcium and electroconvulsive therapy of severe depressive illness. *Biological Psychiatry,* 1977, *12,* 5–18.

Carpenter, W. T., & Bunney, W. E. Adrenal cortical activity in depressive illness. *American Journal of Psychiatry,* 1971, *128,* 31–40.

Charatan, F. B. Depression in old age. *New York State Journal of Medicine*, 1975, *75*, 2505–2509.

Chierichetti, S. M., Ferrari, P., Sala, P., & Vibelli, C. Effects of amantadine on mental status of elderly patients; A double-blind comparison with placebo. *Current Therapeutic Research*, 1977, *22*, 158–165.

Ciompi, L. On the relations between depression, brain damage, and the aging process. In C. Muller & L. Ciompi (Eds.), *Senile dementia*. Berne: Hans Huber, 1968.

Ciompi, L. Follow-up studies on the evolution of former neurotic and depressive states in old age. *Journal of Geriatric Psychiatry*, 1969, *3*, 90–106.

Cohen, S., & Ditman, K. S. Gerovital II$_3$ in the treatment of the depressed aging patient. *Psychosomatics*, 1974, *15*, 15–19.

Cohn, C. K., Dunner, D. L., & Axelrod, J. Reduced catechol-O-methyltransferase activity in red blood cells of women with primary affective disorder. *Science*, 1970, *170*, 1323–1324.

Coleman, J. Severe emotional disturbance associated with physical illness I. Double-blind study. *Psychosomatics*, 1969, *10*, 32–35.

Cooper, J. E., Gurland, B. J., Sharpe, L., Copeland, J. R. M., & Simon, R. *Psychiatric diagnosis in New York and London: A comparative study of mental hospital admissions*. London: Maudsley Monograph, Oxford Press, 1972.

Cooper, J. E., Kendell, R. E., Gurland, B. J., Sartorius, N., & Farkas, T. Cross-national study of diagnosis of the mental disorders: Some results from the first comparative investigation. *American Journal of Psychiatry*, 1969, *125*, 21–29.

Copeland, J. R. M., Kelleher, M. J., Kellett, J. M., Gourlay, A. J., Cowan, D. W., Barron, G., Kurianski, J., & Stiller, P. Cross-national study of diagnosis of the mental disorders: A comparison of the diagnosis of elderly psychiatric patients admitted to mental hospitals serving Queens County, New York, and the former Borough of Camberwell, London. *British Journal of Psychiatry*, 1975, *126*, 11–20.

Coppen, A., Shaw, D. M., Herzberg, B., & Maggs, R. Tryptophan in the treatment of depression. *Lancet*, 1967, *2*, 1178–1180.

Coppen, A., Whybrow, P. C., Noguepa, R., Maggs, R., & Prange, A. J. The comparative antidepressant value of L-Tryptophan and imipramine with and without attempted potentiation by tiothyronine. *Archives in General Psychiatry*, 1972, *26*, 234–241.

Costello, C. G., Christensen, S. J., & Rogers, T. B. The relationships between measures of general depression and the endogenous versus reactive classification. *Canadian Psychiatric Association Journal*, 1974, *19*, 259–265.

Covi, L., Lipman, R., Derogatis, L., Smith, V., & Pattison, J. Drugs and group psychotherapy in neurotic depression. *American Journal of Psychiatry*, 1974, *131*, 191–198.

Cox, J. R., Pearson, R. E., & Brand, H. L. Lithium in depression. *Gerontology*, 1977, *23*, 219–235.

Cristol, A. H. Studies of outcome of psychotherapy. *Comprehensive Psychiatry*, 1972, *13*, 189–200.

Dasberg, H., & Assad, M. Somatic manifestations of psychotic depression. *Diseases of the Nervous System*, 1968, *29*, 399–404.

Davies, B. M. Depressive illness in the elderly patient. *Postgraduate Medicine*, 1965, *38*, 314–320.

Davis, J. M. Critique of single amine theories: Evidence of a cholinergic influence in the major mental illnesses. In D. X. Freedman (Ed.), *Biology of the major psychoses*. New York: Raven Press, 1975. Pp. 333–346.

Davis, J. M. Overview: Maintenance therapy in psychiatry: II. Affective disorders. *The American Journal of Psychiatry*, 1976, *133*, 1–13.

Davis, J. M., Fann, W. E., El-Yousef, M. K., & Janowsky, D. Clinical problems in treating the aged with psychotropic drugs. In C. Eisdorfer & W. E. Fann (Eds.), *Psychopharmacology and aging*. New York: Plenum Press, 1973. Pp. 41–54.

de Groot, M. H. L. The clinical use of psychotherapeutic drugs in the elderly. *Drugs*, 1974, *8*, 132–138.

Docherty, J. P., Marder, S. R., VanKammen, D., & Siris, S. G. Psychotherapy and pharmacology: Conceptual issues. *American Journal of Psychiatry*, 1977, *134*, 529–533.

Donnelly, E. F., Murphy, D. L., & Goodwin, F. K. Cross-sectional and longitudinal comparisons of bipolar and unipolar depressed groups on the MMPI. *Journal of Consulting and Clinical Psychology*, 1976, *44*, 233–237.

Dovenmuehle, R. H., & McGough, W. E. Aging, culture, and affect: Predisposing factors. *Normal aging*. Durham, North Carolina: Duke Univ. Press, 1970. Pp. 98–107.

Dovenmuehle, R. H., Reckless, J. B., & Newman, G. Depressive reactions in the elderly. *Normal aging*. Durham, North Carolina: Duke Univ. Press, 1970. Pp. 90–97.

Downing, R. W., & Rickels, K. Predictors of amitriptyline response in outpatient depressives. *The Journal of Nervous and Mental Disease*, 1972, *154*, 248–263.

Duckworth, G. S., & Kedward, H. Man or machine in psychiatric diagnosis. *American Journal of Psychiatry*, 1978, *135*, 64–68.

Dunner, D. L., Cohn, C. K., Gershon, E. S., & Goodwin, F. K. Differential catechol-O-methyltransferase activity in unipolar and bipolar affective illness. *Archives of General Psychiatry*, 1971, *25*, 348–353.

El-Islam, M. F. Is response to antidepressants an aid to the differentiation of response-specific types of depression? *British Journal of Psychiatry*, 1973, *123*, 509–511.

Epstein, L. J. Depression in the elderly. *Journal of Gerontology*, 1976, *31*, 278–282.

Essen-Moller, E., & Hagnell, O. The frequency and risk of depression within a rural population group in Scandia. *Acta Psychiatrica Scandinavica*, 1961, Suppl. *162*, 28–32.

Everett, H. C. The use of bethanechol chloride with tricyclic antidepressants. *American Journal of Psychiatry*, 1975, *132*, 1202–1204.

Feigenbaum, E. M. Geriatric psychopathology—internal or external? *Journal of the American Geriatrics Society*, 1974, *22*, 49–55.

Feighner, J. P., Robins, E., Guze, S. P., Woodruff, R. A., Winokur, A., & Muñoz, R. Diagnostic criteria for use in psychiatric research. *Archives of General Psychiatry*, 1972, *26*, 57–63.

Feinberg, I., Jernigan, T., Zatz, L., Price, L. J., & Fein, G. *Relation of computed tomography measures of brain atrophy to psychometric performance in well-functioning elderly persons*. Paper presented at the American Psychiatric Association Annual Meeting, Chicago, May 1979.

Fink, M. Efficacy and safety of induced seizures (EST) in man. *Comprehensive Psychiatry*, 1978, *19*, 1–18.

Fink, M. *Convulsive therapy: Theory and practice*. New York: Raven Press, 1979.

Finkel, S. I. Geriatric psychiatry training for the general psychiatry resident. *American Journal of Psychiatry*, 1978, *135*, 101–103.

Fisch, M., Goldfarb, A., & Shahinian, S. Chronic brain syndrome in the community aged. *Archives of General Psychiatry*, 1968, *18*, 739–745.

Fisch, M., Goldfarb, A., Shahinian, S., & Post, F. *The significance of affective symptoms in old age*. London: Oxford, 1962.

Foulds, G. A. The relationship between the depressive illnesses. *British Journal of Psychiatry*, 1973, *122*, 531–533.

Freedman, D. X. (Ed.). *Biology of the major psychoses*. New York: Raven Press, 1975.

Freud, S. On psychotherapy (1904). In J. Strachey (Ed.), *The complete psychological works of Sigmund Freud* (Vol. 3). London: Hogarth Press, 1963.

Freyhan, F. A. Contributions to the definition of therapy resistance and of the therapy-resistant depressions. *Pharmakopsychiatry*, 1974, *7*, 70–75.

Friedel, R. O. Pharmacokinetics in the geropsychiatric patient. In M. A. Lipton, A. DiMascio, & K. F. Killam (Eds.), *Psychopharmacology: A generation of progress*. New York: Raven Press, 1978. Pp. 1499–1506.

Friedman, A. S. Interaction of drug therapy with marital therapy in depressive patients. *Archives of General Psychiatry*, 1975, *32*, 619–637.

Gerner, R. H., Post, R. M., & Bunney, W. E. Biological and behavioral effects of one night's sleep deprivation in depressed patients and normals. *Journal of Psychiatric Research*, 1979, *15*, 21–40.

Gershon, E. S. The search for genetic markers in affective disorders. In M. A. Lipton, A. DiMascio, & K. F. Killam (Eds.), *Psychopharmacology: A generation of progress*. New York: Raven Press, 1978. Pp. 1223–1234.

Gilbert, J. G., Donnelly, K. J., Zimmer, L. E., & Kubis, J. F. Effect of magnesium pemoline and methylphenidate on memory improvement and mood in normal aging subjects. *International Journal of Aging and Human Development*, 1973, *4*, 35–51.

Gilroy, J., & Meyer, J. S. *Medical neurology*. New York: Macmillan, 1975.

Glassman, A. H., Kantor, S. J., & Shostak, M. Depression, delusions & drug response. *American Journal of Psychiatry*, 1975, *132*, 716–719.

Glassman, A. H., & Perel, J. M. Tricyclic blood levels and clinical outcome. A review of the art. In M. A. Lipton, A. DiMascio, & K. F. Killam (Eds.), *Psychopharmacology: A generation of progress*. New York: Raven Press, 1978. Pp. 917–922.

Glick, B. S. Comparison of doxepin and thioridazine in outpatients. *Diseases of the Nervous System*, 1973, *34*, 37–39.

Goldberg, H. L., & Finnerty, R. J. The use of doxepin in the treatment of symptoms of anxiety neurosis and accompanying depression: A collaborative controlled study. *American Journal of Psychiatry*, 1972, *129*, 74–77.

Goldfarb, A. I. Depression in the old and aged. In F. F. Flach (Ed.), *The nature and treatment of depression*. New York: John Wiley, 1975. Pp. 119–114.

Goldstein, B. J., & Banas, F. A. Clinical evaluation of thiothixene in the treatment of hospitalized depressed patients. *Current Therapeutic Research*, 1968, *10*, 453–456.

Goldstein, S. Community psychiatry and the elderly. *Canadian Medical Association Journal*, 1973, *108*, 579–583.

Goodwin, F. K. Drug treatment of affective disorders: General principles. In M. E. Jarvik (Ed.), *Psychopharmacology and the practice of medicine*. New York: Appleton-Century-Crofts, 1977. Pp. 243–244.

Goodwin, F. K., & Post, R. M. Studies of amine metabolites in affective illness and schizophrenia: A comparative analysis. In D. X. Freedman (Ed.), *The biology of the major psychoses*. New York: Raven Press, 1975. Pp. 299–332.

Green, M. F. Endocrinology in the elderly. In W. F. Anderson & T. Judge (Eds.), *Geriatric medicine*. New York: Academic Press, 1974. Pp. 153–170.

Greenblatt, M. The grieving spouse. *American Journal of Psychiatry*, 1978, *135*, 43–47.

Greenblatt, M., Grosser, G. H., & Wechler, H. Differential response of hospitalized depressed patients to somatic therapy. *American Journal of Psychiatry*, 1964, *121*, 935–945.

Greenblatt, M., & Shader, R. I. Psychotropic drugs in the general hospital. In R. Shader (Ed.), *Manual of psychiatric therapeutics*. Boston: Little, Brown, 1975. Pp. 1–26.

Grof, P. B., Saxena, B., & Cantor, R. Doxepin versus amitriptyline in depression: A sequential double blind study. *Current Therapeutic Research*, 1974, *16*, 470–476.

Gruenberg, E. M., Kasins, R. V., & Huxley, M. Objective appraisal of deterioration of a group of long-stay hospital patients. *Milbank Memorial Fund Quarterly*, 1962, *40*, 90.

Gulevich, G. Psychopharmacological treatment of the aged. In J. D. Barchas, P. A. Berger, R. D. Ciaranello, & G. R. Elliot (Eds.), *Psychopharmacology: From theory to practice*. New York: Oxford, 1977. Pp. 448–465.

Gurland, B. J. The comparative frequency of depression in various adult age groups. *Journal of Gerontology*, 1976, *31*, 283–292.

Harding, T. Depression following fenfluramine withdrawal. *The British Journal of Psychiatry*, 1972, *121*, 338–339.

Haskell, D. S., DiMascio, A., & Prusoff, B. Rapidity of symptom reduction in depressions treated with amitriptyline. *Journal of Nervous and Mental Disease*, 1975, *160*, 24–33.

Haskell, D. S., McNair, D. M., Fisher, S., & Kahn, R. J. A controlled outpatient trial of perphenazine-amitriptyline and chlorpromazine. *The Journal of Clinical Pharmacology*, 1974, *14*, 536–542.

Heiman, E. M. Cardiac toxicity with thioridazine–tricyclic antidepressant combination. *Journal of Nervous and Mental Disease*, 1971, *165*, 139–143.

Henry, B. W., Overall, J. E., & Markette, J. R. Comparison of major drug therapies for alleviation of anxiety and depression. *Diseases of the Nervous System*, 1971, *32*, 655–667.

Herbert, V. Megaloblastic anemias. In P. B. Beeson & W. McDermott (Eds.), *Textbook of medicine* (14th ed.). Philadelphia: Saunders, 1975.

Hochstetter, W. Depression syndromes. *Proceedings of the Royal Virchow Society*, 1959, *18*, 116–128.

Hollister, L. E., & Overall, J. E. Reflections on the specificity of action anti-depressants. *Psychosomatics*, 1965, *6*, 361–370.

Holmes, T. H., & Rahe, R. H. The social readjustment rating scale. *Journal of Psychosomatics Research*, 1967, *11*, 213–218.

Hudgens, R. W., Morrison, J. R., & Barchha, R. G. Life events and onset of primary affective disorders. *Archives of General Psychiatry*, 1967, *16*, 134–145.

Hudgens, R. W., Robins, E., & Delong, W. B. The reporting of recent stress in the lives of psychiatric patients—a study of 80 hospitalized patients and 103 informants reporting the presence or absence of specified types of stress. *British Journal of Psychiatry*, 1970, *117*, 635–643.

Ibor, J. J. L. Masked depressions. *British Journal of Psychiatry*, 1972, *120*, 245–258.

Jarvik, L. Personal communication, January 1978, Department of Psychiatry, University of California at Los Angeles.

Jarvik, L. F., & Milne, J. F. Gerovital-H$_3$: A review of the literature. In S. Gershon & A. Raskin (Eds.), *Aging* (Vol. 2). New York: Raven Press, 1975. Pp. 203–228.

Jefferson, J. W. A review of the cardiovascular effects and toxicity of tricyclic antidepressants. *Psychosomatic Medicine*, 1975, *37*, 160–179.

Juel-Nielson, N. Frequency of depressive states within geographically delimited population groups. 3. Incidence (the Aarhus County investigation). *Acta Psychiatrica Scandinavica*, 1961, Suppl. *162*, 69–80.

Karacan, I., Williams, R. L., & Salis, P. J. Sleep and sleep abnormalities in depression. In W. E. Fann, Z. Karacan, A. D., Pokorney, & R. L. Williams (Eds.), *Phenomenology and treatment of depression*. New York: Spectrum, 1977. Pp. 167–186.

Katz, M. M., & Hirshfeld, R. M. A. Phenomenology and classification of depression. In

M. A. Lipton, A. DiMascio, & K. F. Killam (Eds.), *Psychopharmacology: A generation of progress*. New York: Raven Press, 1978. Pp. 1185–1196.

Kay, D. W. K., Beamish, P., & Roth, M. Old age mental disorders. Newcastle-upon-Tyne: A study of prevalence. *British Journal of Psychiatry*, 1964, *110*, 146–159.

Kay, D. W. K., Garside, R. F., & Fahy, T. J. A double-blind trial of phenelzine and amitriptyline in depressed outpatients. A possible differential effect of the drugs on symptoms. *British Journal of Psychiatry*, 1970, *123*, 63–67.

Kendell, R. E., & Discipio, W. J. Obsessional symptoms and obsessional personality traits in patients with depressive illnesses. *Psychological Medicine*, 1970, *1*, 65–72.

Kendell, R. E., & Gourlay, J. The clinical distinction between psychotic and neurotic depressions. *British Journal of Psychiatry*, 1970, *117*, 257–266.

Kerschner, P. A., & Hirshfield, I. S. Public policy and aging: Analytic approaches. In R. A. Woodruff & J. E. Birren (Eds.), *Aging: Scientific perspectives and social issues*. New York: Van Nostrand, 1975. Pp. 352–373.

Kielholz, P. (Ed.). *Masked depression*. Vienna: Hans Huber, 1973.

Kiloh, L. G. Pseudo-dementia. *Acta Psychiatrica Scandinavica*, 1971, *61*, 336–351.

Kiloh, L. G., Andrews, G., Neilson, M., & Bianchi, G. N. The relationship of the syndromes called endogenous and neurotic depression. *British Journal of Psychiatry*, 1972, *121*, 183–196.

Kiloh, L. G., Neilson, M., & Andrews, G. Response of depressed patients to methylamphetamine. *British Journal of Psychiatry*, 1974, *125*, 469–496.

Klaiber, E. L., Broverman, D. M., Vogel, W., Kobayashi, Y., & Moriarty, D. Effects of estrogen therapy on plasma MAO activity and EEG driving responses of depressed women. *American Journal of Psychiatry*, 1972, *128*, 1492–1498.

Klerman, G. L. Age and clinical depression: Today's youth in the twenty-first century. *Journal of Gerontology*, 1976, *31*, 318–323.

Klerman, G. L. Long-term treatment of affective disorders. In M. A. Lipton, A. DiMascio, & K. F. Killam (Eds.), *Psychopharmacology: A generation of progress*. New York: Raven Press, 1978. Pp. 1303–1312.

Klerman, G. L., DiMascio, A., Weissman, M. M., Prusoff, B., & Paykel, E. S. Treatment of depression by drugs and psychotherapy. *American Journal of Psychiatry*, 1974, *131*, 186–191.

Kotin, J., Post, R. M., & Goodwin, F. K. Drug treatment of depressed patients referred for hospitalization. *American Journal of Psychiatry*, 1973, *130*, 1139–1141.

Kowlessar, O. D. *Carcinoma of the pancreas*. In P. B. Beeson & W. McDermott (Eds.), *Textbook of medicine*. Philadelphia: Saunders, 1975.

Krietman, N., Salsbury, P., Pearce, K., & Costain, W. R. Hypochondriasis and depression in outpatients of a general hospital. *British Journal of Psychiatry*, 1965, *111*, 607.

Kupfer, D. J., Foster, F. G., Coble, P., McPartland, R. J., & Fulrich, R. The application of EEG sleep for the differential diagnosis of affective disorders. *American Journal of Psychiatry*, 1978, *135*, 69–74.

Kupfer, D. J., Pickar, D., Himmelhoch, J. M., & Detre, T. P. Are there two types of unipolar depression? *Archives of General Psychiatry*, 1975, *32*, 866–871.

Kurland, M. L. Neurotic depression—an empirical guide to two specific drug treatments. *Diseases of the Nervous System*, 1976, *37*, 424–431.

Learoyd, B. M. Psychotropic drugs and the elderly patient. *The Medical Journal of Australia*, 1, 1972, 1131–1133.

Lebensohn, Z. M., & Jenkins, R. Improvement of Parkinsonism in depressed patients treated with ECT. *American Journal of Psychiatry*, 1975, *132*, 283–285.

Lehman, H. E. Epidemiology of depressive disorders. In R. R. Fieve (Ed.), *Depression in the 1970s*. Amsterdam: Excerpta Medica, 1971. Pp. 21–30.

Lehman, H. E., & Aban, T. Central nervous system stimulants and anabolic substances in geropsychiatric therapy. In S. Gershon & A. Raskin (Eds.), *Aging* (Vol. 2). New York: Raven Press, 1975. Pp. 179–202.

Lesser, S. *Masked depression*. New York: Aronson, 1974. Pp. 53–74.

Levin, S. Depression in the aged: A study of the salient external factors. *Geriatrics*, 1963, *18*, 302–307.

Lewis, A. J. "Endogenous" & "exogenous"; a useful dichotomy. *Psychological Medicine*, 1971, *1*, 191–195.

Lieberman, M. *Survey and evaluation of the literature on verbal psychotherapy of depressive disorders*. Report prepared for the Clinical Research Branch, National Institute of Mental Health, Rockville, Md., 1975.

Lipman, R., & Covi, L. Outpatient treatment of neurotic depression: Medication and group psychotherapy. In R. L. Spitzer & D. F. Klein (Eds.), *Evaluation of psychological therapies*. Baltimore, Maryland: Johns Hopkins, 1976. Pp. 178–218.

Lipman, R., Covi, L., & Smith, V. Prediction of response to drug and group psychotherapy in depressed outpatients. *Psychopharmacology Bulletin*, 1975, *11* Abstract 38.

Lipton, M. A. Age differentiation in depression: Biochemical aspects. *Journal of Gerontology*, 1976, *31*, 293–299.

Lishman, W. A. The psychiatric sequelae of head injury: A review. *Psychological Medicine*, 1973, *3*, 304–318.

Luborsky, L., Singer, B., & Luborsky, L. Comparative studies of psychotherapies. *Archives of General Psychiatry*, 1975, *32*, 995–1008.

Lunghi, M. E. The stability of mood and social perception measures in a sample of depressive inpatients. *British Journal of Psychiatry*, 1977, *130*, 598–604.

Maas, J. W. Biogenic amines and depression. *Archives of General Psychiatry*, 1975, *32*, 1357–1361.

Maas, J. W., Fawcett, J. A., & Dekirmenjian, H. 3-methoxy-4-hydroxyphenyl glycol (MHPG) excretion in depressive states. *Archives of General Psychiatry*, 1968, *19*, 129–135.

Maas, J. W., Fawcett, J. A., & Dekirmenjian, H. Catecholamine metabolism, depressive illness, and drug response. *Archives of General Psychiatry*, 1972, *26*, 252–262.

Mayfield, D. G. Alcohol problems in the aging patient. In W. E. Fann & G. L. Maddox (Eds.), *Drug issues in geropsychiatry*. Baltimore, Md.: Williams & Wilkins, 1974. Pp. 35–39.

McDonald, C. Parental deprivation and psychiatric illness in old age. *Australian–New Zealand Journal of Psychiatry*, 1969, *3*, 401–403.

McGreer, E., & McGreer, P. L. Neurotransmitter metabolism in the aging brain. In R. D. Terry & S. Gershon (Eds.), *Aging* (Vol. 3). New York: Raven Press, 1975. Pp. 389–403.

McGreer, E. G., McGreer, P. L., & Wade, J. A. Distribution of tyrosine hydroxylase in human and animal brain. *Journal of Neurochemistry*, 1971, *18*, 1647–1658.

Mendels, J. Electro-convulsive therapy and depression. II. Significance of endogenous and reactive syndromes. *British Journal of Psychiatry*, 1965, *111*, 682–686.

Mendels, J., Weinstein, N., & Cochrane, C. The relationship between depression and anxiety. *Archives of General Psychiatry*, 1972, *27*, 649–653.

Miller, E. *Abnormal aging: The psychology of senile and presenile dementia*. New York: Wiley, 1977.

Muñoz, R. A. Treatment of tricyclic intoxication. *American Journal of Psychiatry*, 1976, *133*, 1085–1087.

Murphy, D. L., Campbell, I., & Costa, J. L. Current status of the indoleamine hypothesis of affective disorders. In M. A. Lipton, A. DiMascio, & K. F. Killam (Eds.), *Psychopharmacology: A generation of progress*. New York: Raven Press, 1978. Pp. 1235–1248.

Murphy, D. L., Goodwin, F. K., Brodie, K. H., & Bunney, W. E. L-Dopa, dopamine and hypomania. *American Journal of Psychiatry*, 1973, *130*, 79–82.

Murphy, D. L., Shiling, D. J., & Murray, R. M. Psychoactive drug responder subgroups: Possible contributions to psychiatric classification. In M. A. Lipton, A. DiMascio, & K. F. Killam (Eds.), *Psychopharmacology: A generation of progress*. New York: Raven Press, 1978. Pp. 807–820.

Murphy, D. L., & Weiss, R. Reduced monoamine oxidase activity in blood platelets from bipolar depressed patients. *American Journal of Psychiatry*, 1972, *128*, 1351–1357.

Murphy, D. L., & Wyatt, R. J. Neurotransmitter-related enzymes in the major psychiatric disorders: I. Catechol-O-methyltransferase monoamine oxidase in the affective disorders, and factors affecting some beheviorly correlated enzyme activities. In D. X. Freedman (Ed.), *Biology of the major psychoses*. New York: Raven Press, 1975. Pp. 277–288.

Murray, L. G., & Blackburn, I. M. Personality differences in patients with depressive illness and anxiety neurosis. *Acta Psychiatrica Scandinavica*, 1974, *50*, 183–191.

Myers, J. M., Sheldon, D., & Robinson, S. S. A study of 138 elderly first admissions. *American Journal of Psychiatry*, 1963, *120*, 244–249.

Neiderehe, G. *Interaction of stressful events with locus of control in depressions of later life*. Paper presented at 30th annual scientific meeting of the Gerontological Society, San Francisco, November 20, 1977.

Nielsen, J., Homma, A., & Biør-Henriksen, R. Follow-up 15 years after a gerontopsychiatric prevalence study in Samsø. 1. Geriatric service by the general practitioners, the local hospital and the community psychiatric clinic. *Comprehensive Psychiatry*, 1977, *18*, 533–544.

Nies, A., Robinson, D. S., Ravaris, C. L., & Davis, J. M. Amines and monoamine oxidase in relation to aging and depression in man. *Psychosomatic Medicine*, 1971, *33*, 470–475.

Nies, A., Robinson, D. S., Davis, J. M., & Ravaris, L. Changes in monoamine oxidase with aging. In C. Eisdorfer & W. E. Fann (Eds.), *Psychopharmacology and aging*. New York: Plenum Press, 1973. Pp. 41–54.

Nies, A., Robinson, D., Friedman, M. J., Green, R., Cooper, B., Ravaris, C. L., & Ives, J. O. Relationship between age and tricyclic antidepressant plasma levels. *American Journal of Psychiatry*, 1977, *134*, 790–793.

Nies, A., Robinson, D. S., Harris, L. S., & Lamborn, K. R. Comparison of monoamine oxidase substrate activities in twins, schizophrenics, depression, and controls. *Advanced Biochemistry Psychopharmacology*, 1974, *12*, 59–70.

Ordy, J. M., Kaack, B., & Brizzee, K. R. Life-span neurochemical changes in the human and nonhuman primate brain. In H. Brody, D. Harman, & J. M. Ordy (Eds.), *Aging* (Vol. 1). New York: Raven Press, 1975. Pp. 133–189.

Ordy, J. M., & Schiede, O. A. Univariate and multivariate models for evaluating long term changes in neurobiological development, maturity and aging. In D. H. Ford (Ed.), *Progress in brain research* (Vol. 40): *Neurobiological aspects of maturation and aging*. New York: Elsevier, 1973. Pp. 25–51a.

Parker, C. M. The first year of bereavement: A longitudinal study of the reaction of London widows to the death of their husbands. *Psychiatry*, 1970, *33*, 444–467.

Parsons, P. L. Mental health of Swansea's old folk. *British Journal of Preventative Social Medicine*, 1965, *19*, 43–47.

Paulson, G. W. Dyskinesia in the aging. In C. Eisdorfer & W. E. Fann (Eds.), *Psychopharmacology and aging*. New York: Plenum Press, 1973. Pp. 83–88.

Paykel, E. S., DiMascio, A., Haskell, D., & Prusoff, B. A. Effects of maintenance amitriptyline and psychotherapy on symptoms of depression. *Psychological Medicine*, 1975, *5*, 67–77.

Paykel, E. S., Myers, J. K., Dienelt, M. N., Klerman, G. L., Lindenthal, J. J., & Pepper, M. P. Life events and depression. *Archives of General Psychiatry*, 1969, *21*, 735–760.

Paykel, E. S., Price, J. S., Gillan, R. U., Palmai, G., & Chesser, E. S. A comparative trial of imipramine and chlorpromazine in depressed patients. *British Journal of Psychiatry*, 1968, *114*, 1281–1287.

Paykel, E. S., Prusoff, B. A., & Uhlenhuth, E. H. Scaling life events. *Archives of General Psychiatry*, 1971, *25*, 340–347.

Pederson, A. M., Barry, D. J., & Babigan, H. M. Epidemiological considerations of psychotic depression. *Archives of General Psychiatry*, 1972, *27*, 193–197.

Pelc, I. Doxepin I. M. in the treatment of depression and anxiety. *Current Therapeutic Research*, 1975, *17*, 467–477.

Pfeiffer, E., & Busse, E. W. Mental disorders in later life—affective disorders; paranoid, neurotic, and situational reactions. In E. W. Busse, & E. Pfeiffer (Eds.), *Mental illness in later life*. Washington, D.C.: American Psychiatric Association, 1973.

Phillis, J. W. The role of calcium in the central effects of biogenic amines. *Life Sciences*, 1974, *14*, 1189–1201.

Pitt, B. *Psychogeriatrics*. London: Churchill Livingstone, 1974.

Post, F. *The clinical psychiatry of late life*. Oxford: Pergamon, 1965.

Post, F. The management and nature of depressive illness in late life: A follow-through study. *British Journal of Psychiatry*, 1972, *121*, 389–395.

Post, F. Dementia, depression, and pseudo-dementia. In D. F. Benson & D. Blumer (Eds.), *Psychiatric aspects of neurologic disease*. New York: Grune & Stratton, 1975. Pp. 99–120.

Post, R., Kotin, J., & Goodwin, F. K. Effects of sleep deprivation on mood and central amine metabolism in depressed patients. *Archives of General Psychiatry*, 1976, *33*, 627–632.

Post, R. M., Stoddard, F. J., Gillin, J. C., Buchsbaum, M. S., Runkle, D. C., Black, K. E., & Bunney, W. E. Alterations in motor activity, sleep, and biochemistry in a cycling manic-depressive patient. *Archives of General Psychiatry*, 1977, *34*, 470–477.

Prange, A. J. Use of antidepressant drugs in the elderly patient. In C. Eisdorfer & W. E. Fann (Eds.), *Psychopharmacology and aging*. New York: Plenum Press, 1973. Pp. 225–238.

Prange, A. J. L-tryptophan in mania: A contribution to a permissive hypothesis of affective disorders. *Archives of General Psychiatry*, 1974, *31*, 56–62.

Prange, A. J., Wilson, I. C., Knox, A., McClure, T. K., & Lipton, M. A. Enhancement of imipramine by thyroid stimulating hormone: Clinical and theoretical implications. *American Journal of Psychiatry*, 1970, *127*, 191–199.

Rao, C. K. Combined therapy of E.C.T. and amitriptyline and l-tryptophan in the treatment of severe depression. *The British Journal of Psychiatry*, 1972, *120*, 127–128.

Raskin, A. Adverse reactions to phenelzine: Results of a nine-hospital depression study. *Journal of Clinical Pharmacology*, 1972, *12*, 22–25.

Raskin, A. A guide for drug use in depressive disorders. *American Journal of Psychiatry,* 1974, *131,* 181–185.

Raskin, A., & Crook, T. H. The endogenous–neurotic distinction as a predictor of response to antidepressant drugs. *Psychological Medicine,* 1976, *6,* 59–70.

Redlich, R., & Kellert, S. R. Trends in American mental health. *American Journal of Psychiatry,* 1978, *135,* 22–28.

Riley, M. W., & Foner, A. *Aging and society.* New York: Russell Sage Foundation, 1968.

Robins, A. H. Depression in patients with Parkinsonism. *British Journal of Psychiatry,* 1976, *128,* 141–145.

Robins, E., Murphy, G. E., Wilderson, R. H., Glassner, S., & Kayes, J. Some clinical consideration in the prevention of suicide based on a study of 134 successful suicides. *American Journal of Public Health,* 1959, *49,* 888–898.

Robinson, D. S., Davis, J. M., Nies, A., Ravaris, C. L., & Sylvester, D. Relaxation of sex and aging to monoamine oxidase activity of human brain, plasma, and platelets. *Archives of General Psychiatry,* 1971, *24,* 536–539.

Rosenthal, S. H. Involutional depression. In S. Arieti (Ed.), *American handbook of psychiatry* (Vol. 3). New York: Basic Books, 1974. Pp. 694–709.

Rosenthal, S. H., & Bowden, C. L. A double-blind comparison of thioridazine (mellaril) versus diazepam (valium) in patients with chronic mixed anxiety and depressive symptoms. *Current Therapeutic Research,* 1973, *15,* 261–267.

Roth, M. The natural history of mental disorder in old age. *The Journal of Mental Science,* 1955, *101,* 281–301.

Roth, M., Gurney, C., Garside, R. F., & Kerr, T. A. Studies in the classification of affective disorders. The relationship between anxiety states and depressive illness—I. *British Journal of Psychiatry,* 1972, *121,* 147–161.

Sachar, E. J. Hormonal changes in stress and mental illness. *Hospital Practice,* 1975, *10,* 49–65. (a)

Sachar, E. J. A neuroendocrine strategy in the psychobiological study of depressive illness. In J. Mendels (Ed.), *The psychobiology of depression.* New York: Spectrum, 1975. P. 123. (b)

Sachar, E. J., Altman, N., Gruen, P. H., Glassman, A., Halpern, F. S., & Sassin, J. Human growth hormone response to levodopa. Relation to menopause, depression, and plasma dopa concentration. *Archives of General Psychiatry,* 1975, *32,* 502–503.

Sainsbury, P. Suicide in later life. *Gerontology Clinics,* 1962, *4,* 161–170.

Salzman, C., & Shader, R. Responses to psychotropic drugs in the normal elderly. In C. Eisdorfer & W. E. Fann (Eds.), *Psychopharmacology and aging.* New York: Plenum Press, 1973. Pp. 41–54.

Salzman, C., Shader, R. I., & Harmatz, J. S. Response of the elderly to psychotropic drugs: Predictable or idiosyncratic? In S. Gershon & A. Raskin (Eds.), *Aging* (Vol. 2). New York: Raven Press, 1975. Pp. 259–272.

Samorajski, T. Age-related changes in brain biogenic amines. In H. Brody, D. Harman, & J. M. Ordy (Eds.), *Aging* (Vol. 1). New York: Raven Press, 1975. Pp. 199–214.

Samorajski, T. Central neurotransmitter substances and aging: A review. *Journal of the American Geriatrics Society,* 1977, *25,* 337–340.

Schildkraut, J. J. Norepinephrine metabolites as biochemical criteria for classifying depressive disorders and predicting responses to treatment: Preliminary findings. *American Journal of Psychiatry,* 1973, *130,* 695–698.

Schildkraut, J. J. Current status of the catecholamine hypothesis of affective disorders. In M. A. Lipton, A. DiMascio, & K. F. Killam (Eds.), *Psychopharmacology: A generation of progress.* New York: Raven Press, 1978. Pp. 1249–1260.

Schildkraut, J. J., & Klein, D. F. The classification and treatment of depression disorders. In R. I. Shader (Ed.), *Manual of psychiatric therapeutics*. Boston: Little, Brown, 1975.

Schmidt, C. W. Psychiatric problems of the aged. *Journal of the American Geriatrics Society*, 1974, *22*, 355–359.

Schuckit, M., Robins, E., & Feighner, J. Combination therapy in the treatment of depression. *Archives of General Psychiatry*, 1971, *24*, 509–514.

Schwab, J. J. Depression among the aged. *Southern Medical Journal*, 1976, *69*, 1039–1041.

Schwab, J. J., Holzer, C. E., & Warheit, G. J. Depressive symptomatology and age. *Psychosomatics*, 1973, *14*, 135–141.

Scott, J., & Gaitz, C. M. Ethnic and age differences in mental health measurements. *Diseases of the Nervous System*, 1975, *36*, 389–393.

Seltzer, B., & Sherwin, I. "Organic brain syndromes": An empirical study and critical review. *American Journal of Psychiatry*, 1978, *135*, 13–21.

Sethna, E. R. A study of refractory cases of depressive illnesses and their response to combined antidepressant treatment. *British Journal of Psychiatry*, 1974, *124*, 265–272.

Silverman, C. *The epidemiology of depression*. Baltimore, Maryland: Johns Hopkins Press, 1968.

Simon, A. Physical and socio-psychologic stress in the geriatric mentally ill. *Comprehensive Psychiatry*, 1970, *11*, 242–247.

Smith, C. K., Barish, J., Correa, J., & Williams, R. H. Psychiatric disturbance in endocrinology disease. *Psychosomatic Medicine*, 1972, *34*, 69–86.

Snaith, R. P., & McCoubrie, M. Antihypertensive drugs and depression. *Psychological Medicine*, 1974, *4*, 393–398.

Snowdon, J. When is dementia presenile? *British Medical Journal*, 1972, *3*, 465.

Snyder, S. H., & Yamamura, H. I. Antidepressants and the muscarinic acetylcholic receptor. *Archives of General Psychiatry*, 1977, *34*, 236–239.

Spicer, C. C., Hare, H., & Slater, E. Neurotic and psychotic forms of depressive illness: Evidence from age-incidence in a national sample. *British Journal of Psychiatry*, 1973, *123*, 535–541.

Spitzer, R. L. *DSM III* (3rd ed.). Washington, D.C.: American Psychiatric Association, 1978.

Spitzer, R. L., Endicott, J., & Robins, E. *Research diagnostic criteria (RDC) for a selected group of functional disorders* (2nd ed.). New York: Biometrics Research, New York State Psychiatric Institute, 1975.

Stern, S. L., Hurtig, H. I., Mendels, J., & Balaban, D. Psychiatric illness in relatives of patients with Parkinson's disease: A preliminary report. *American Journal of Psychiatry*, *143*, 443–444.

Stokes, P. E., Stoll, P. M., Mattson, M. R., & Sollod, R. N. Diagnosis and psychopathology in psychiatric patients resistant to dexamethasome. In E. J. Sachar (Ed.), *Hormones, behavior and psychopathology*. New York: Raven Press, 1976. Pp. 225–230.

Stotsky, B. A. Psychoactive drugs for geriatric patients with psychiatric disorders. In S. Gershon & A. Raskin (Eds.), *Aging* (Vol. 2). New York: Raven Press, 1975. Pp. 229–258.

Taube, S. L., Kirstein, L. S., Sweeney, D. R., Heninger, G. R., & Maas, J. W. Urinary 3-methoxy-4-hydroxyphenylglycol and psychiatric diagnosis. *American Journal of Psychiatry*, 1978, *135*, 78–82.

Thompson, K. C., & Hendric, H. C. Environmental stress in primary depressive illness. *Archives of General Psychiatry*, 1972, *26*, 130–132.

Thompson, W. Thioridazine as an antidepressant. *The Practitioner*, 1972, *209*, 95–102.

Tongas, P. N., & Gibson, R. S. *A study of older patients admitted to the Sheppard and Enoch Pratt Hospital, 1966–1968.* Towson, Maryland: Research Department, Sheppard and Enoch Pratt Hospital, 1969.

Tsuang, M. M., Lu, L. M., Stotsky, B., & Cole, J. O. Haloperidol versus thioridazine for hospitalized psychogeriatric patients: A double-blind study. *American Geriatric Society Journal*, 1971, *19*, 593–600.

Tyrer, P. Towards rational therapy with monoamine oxidase inhibitors. *British Journal of Psychiatry*, 1976, *128*, 354–360.

U'Prichard, D. C., Greenberg, D. A., Sheehan, P. P., & Snyder, S. H. Tricyclic antidepressants: Therapeutic properties and affinity for alpha-noradrenergic receptor binding sites in the brain. *Science*, 1978, *199*, 197–198.

Van der Velde, C. D. Toxicity of lithium carbonate in elderly patients. *American Journal of Psychiatry*, 1971, *127*, 1075–1077.

Van Praag, H. M. *Depression and schizophrenia.* New York: Spectrum, 1977. (a)

Van Praag, H. M. Significance of biochemical parameter in the diagnosis, treatment, and prevention of depression disorders. *Biological Psychiatry*, 1977, *12*, 101–132. (b)

Van Praag, H. M., & Korf, J. 5-hydroxytryptophan as antidepressive: The predictive value of the probenecid test. In M. Lader & R. Garcia (Eds.), *Aspects of depression.* Barcelona: World Psychiatric Association, 1973. Pp. 149–156.

Van Valkenburg, C., Lowry, M., Winokur, G., & Cadoret, R. Depression spectrum disease versus pure depressive disease. *Journal of Nervous Mental Disease*, 1977, *165*, 341–347.

Verwoerdt, A. *Clinical geropsychiatry.* Baltimore, Maryland: Williams & Wilkins, 1976.

Vohra, J., & Burrows, G. D. Cardiovascular complications of tricyclic antidepressant overdosage. *Drugs*, 1974, *8*, 432–437.

Vohra, J., Burrows, & Sloman, G. Assessment of cardiovascular side effects of therapeutic doses of tricyclic antidepressant drugs. *Australian–New Zealand Journal of Medicine*, 1975, *5*, 207–210.

Walcher, W. Influence-possibilities on therapy-resistant late depressions. *Pharmakopsychiatry*, 1974, *7*, 207–210.

Walker, J., & Hertzog, C. Aging, brain function, and behavior. In D. S. Woodruff & J. E. Birren (Eds.), *Aging: Scientific perspectives and social issues.* New York: Van Nostrand, 1975. Pp. 152–178.

Walther, R. J. Economics and the older population. In D. S. Woodruff & J. E. Birren, (Eds.), *Aging: Scientific perspectives and social issues.* New York: Van Nostrand, 1975. Pp. 336–351.

Ward, N. G., Rowlett, D. B., & Burke, P. Sodium amylobarbitone in the differential diagnosis of confusion. *American Journal of Psychiatry*, 1978, *135*, 75–77.

Watanabe, S., Ishino, H., & Otsuki, S. Double-blind comparison of lithium carbonate and imipramine in treatment of depression. *Archives of General Psychiatry*, 1975, *32*, 659–668.

Weeke, A., Bille, M., Videbech, T., Dupont, A., & Juel-Nielsen, N. Incidence of depressive syndromes in a Danish county. *Acta Psychiatrica Scandinavica*, 1975, *51*, 28–41.

Weissman, M. Psychotherapy and its relevance to the pharmacology of affective disorders: From ideology to evidence. In M. A. Lipton, A. DiMascio, & K. F. Killam (Eds.), *Psychopharmacology: A generation of progress.* New York: Raven, 1978. Pp. 1313–1321.

Weissman, M. M., Klerman, G. L., Paykel, E. S., Prusoff, B., & Hanson, B. Treatment effects on the social adjustment of depressed patients. *Archives of General Psychiatry*, 1974, *31*, 771–778.

Wells, C. E. Chronic brain disease: An overview. *American Journal of Psychiatry*, 1978, *135*, 1–12.

Whitehead, J. A. *Psychiatric disorders in old age*. New York: Springer, 1974. P. 42.

Williams, J. G., Barlow, D. H., & Agras, W. S. Diurnal variation in depression—is it there? *Journal of Nervous and Mental Disease*, 1975, *161*, 59–62.

Wilson, L. G. Viral encephalopathy mimicking functional psychosis. *American Journal of Psychiatry*, 1976, *133*, 165–170.

Wilson, W. P., & Major, L. F. Electroshock and the aged patient. In C. Eisdorfer & W. E. Fann (Eds.), *Psychopharmacology and aging*. New York: Plenum Press, 1973. Pp. 239–244.

Winokur, G. The types of affective disorders. *The Journal of Nervous and Mental Disease*, 1973, *156*, 82–96. (a)

Winokur, G. Depression in the menopause. *American Journal of Psychiatry*, 1973, *130*, 92–93. (b)

Woodruff, R. A., Goodwin, D. W., & Guze, S. B. *Psychiatric Diagnosis*. New York: Oxford, 1974.

Yuwiler, A. Stress, anxiety, and endocrine function. In R. G. Grenell & S. Gabay (Eds.), *Biological foundations of psychiatry*. New York: Raven Press, 1976. Pp. 889–893.

Zubin, J., & Fleiss, J. Current biometric approaches to depression. In R. Fieve (Ed.), *Depression in the 1970s*. The Hague: Excerpta Medica, 1970. Pp. 7–20.

Chapter 7

THE OLDER SCHIZOPHRENIC

Ivan N. Mensh

DEFINITIONS: SCHIZOPHRENIA, PARAPHRENIA, "LATE PARAPHRENIA"

The discussion, evaluation, and understanding of the older schizophrenic have been confounded by the lack of precise definition of schizophrenia, and there is further confusion when age is added to the diagnostic and behavioral variables. Even the epidemiology is little known; for example, Butler summarizes (1974) the state of affairs: "We can only guess at the extent of mental disorders of all types among the elderly, since so many older persons live outside the purview of medical, psychiatric, and social programs."

Within the past decade, there have been major attempts to clarify the concepts and diagnostic criteria of schizophrenia, namely, the United States–United Kingdom cooperative study (Cooper, Kendell, & Gurland, 1972) and the International Pilot Study of Schizophrenia (IPSS) (Carpenter, 1976). The former, for example, has demonstrated that the observed large differential rates in first admissions to British and U. S. mental hospitals for schizophrenia, manic depressive disorders, and psychoses with cerebral arteriosclerosis, "were due primarily to differences in diagnostic habits of the psychiatrists rather than to differences in the patients." The nine-nation IPSS utilized a large sample (over 1200 initially, but data on 83 patients, 6%, were dropped because it was not possible to clearly state whether the patients were schizophrenic or not). It also used systematic and uniform data collection and data on

PSYCHOPATHOLOGY OF AGING

patients with diverse psychiatric and cultural backgrounds. The cooperating nations were China, Colombia, Czechoslovakia, Denmark, India, Nigeria, the Soviet Union, United Kingdom, and United States. From the Present State Examinations there were derived 230 symptoms and 130 signs, constituting 433 overlapping variables. The patients' data were randomized into two cohorts, 405 schizophrenics and 155 nonschizophrenics in each. An analysis of variance discriminated 69 nonoverlapping variables and discriminant analysis yielded the 12 most discriminating symptoms—restricted affect, poor insight, clouded thinking, absence of early waking, poor rapport, absence of depressed facies, absence of elation, widespread delusions, incoherent speech, unreliable information, bizarre delusions, and nihilistic delusions.

Unfortunately, the studies reported in the major gerontological and psychiatric journals and texts since 1965 (this cutting point generally was used by the author in order to provide the basis for a recent review for the present text) did not utilize the better, though still far from perfected, diagnostic discriminations from either the U.S.–U.K. or IPSS studies. What then may we understand about the older schizophrenic? First, many reports indicate only "mentally impaired aged" (typically, chronic brain syndrome, as far as can be distinguished), although later references in the reports suggest schizophrenia in at least some of the patients. Next, neither minority nor ethnic origin is indicated, both of which may be significant variables; nor is there much attention paid to age at admission, other than 60 and over, rather than the critical discrimination, at least by decade, that is, 60s, 70s, 80s, or 90s. Further, treatment and treatment outcomes are only referred to in vague terms, no doubt because only custodial care has been provided in the great majority of cases.

What numbers of older schizophrenics are we talking about—in hospitals, in outpatient programs, and in the community, diagnosed or undiagnosed? One study deals with 137 subjects of whom 29 are "normal," 31 are diagnosed schizophrenic, and 77 others are classed as having an affective or organic syndrome. Another study reviews 30 years of admissions of discharged mental hospital patients to a home and hospital for the aged, reporting on 45 patients, of whom 2 are diagnosed schizophrenic. Another looked at more than 600 long-term residents, all 65 or older, of mental hospitals and indicates that 36% were diagnosed schizophrenic. A nursing home study of psychiatric consultation to 40 patients, mean age 70, lists 3 as chronic schizophrenics. In a 1700-bed mental hospital, 4000 patients (cumulative total for a year), all 64 or older, were diagnosed chronic schizophrenic. Four of these patients were selected for operant procedures to increase their verbal behavior (4 of 4000!).

A followup study of nearly 2200 state-hospital patients transferred to other state hospitals reported that 71% of the patients were schizophrenic and that 14% were 70 years of age or older; however, who among the latter were schizophrenic was not indicated. A report of 62 randomly selected elderly patients among those discharged in 1 year from a private psychiatric hospital showed only 3% were schizophrenic. In another study, psychiatric consultations following 924 consecutive referrals from other services in a 400-bed general hospital (where approximately 25% of the patients were past age 60) diagnosed only 31 of the 924 as schizophrenic or having paranoid psychosis. These diagnoses were recorded for 6% of patients aged 60–69; there were no patients past age 70 in this group.

This sample of studies illustrates the confusion in reporting the numbers of older individuals (60 years or older) who are diagnosed schizophrenic. Clearly, the numbers vary as a function of type of institution, focus of the study or report, and unreliability of diagnosis; there is essentially no information on incidence or prevalence among noninstitutionalized elderly. This state of affairs induces the observer to note major national reporting, for instance, by Kramer and his colleagues (Kramer, 1976; Kramer, Taube, & Redick, 1973; Redick, 1973, 1975; Taube, 1974, 1975), in the Biometrics Branch of the National Institute of Mental Health (NIMH). There are, for example, data on the number of resident patients and resident-patient rates for state and county mental hospitals in the United States and changes during the 1955 1968 period (Kramer et al., 1973); there are also data on changes in the age, sex, and diagnostic composition of the resident population of state and county mental hospitals, 1964–1973 (Taube, 1974, 1975) and 1969–1973 (Redick, 1975).

Redick (1973) has developed the concept of patient-care episodes in reporting, not a true annual prevalence, since episodes rather than cases are counted. Patient-care episodes are defined as the number of residents in inpatient facilities at the beginning of the year (or the number on the rolls of non-inpatient facilities) plus the total additions to these facilities during the year, both new admissions and readmissions (this is a duplicate count of persons, therefore). In 1955 there were 1.7 million episodes, in 1965 the count was 2.6 million, and in 1971 the rate had doubled from the 1955 figure to 2056 per 100,000 population, or 4.2 million patient episodes. The 1955–1971 decline was mostly inpatients in state and county mental hospitals. General hospital-inpatient, psychiatric-unit population, patient-care episodes doubled, and outpatient episodes increased six-fold. Also, community mental health centers reported an increase from 4% to 19% of all episodes, both inpatient and outpatient. From 1966 to 1971 the number of episodes and rates per 100,000 population increased in every age group *except for patients 65 and older.* Of all patient-care episodes on psychiatric services in 1971 (over 4 million in total), 22% (men) and 23% (women) were diagnosed schizophrenic, with rates varying from 6% for patients under 18 to a peak of 29% in the 25–44 range, dropping off to 20% among patients 65 or older.

What about the years since 1971 and the decade of the 1980s? Kramer (1976) points out the excess mortality of patients diagnosed as schizophrenic (see also Babigan & Odoroff, 1969; and Yolles & Kramer, 1969) for both institutionalized and community-care patients; but he emphasizes that projections of the number of schizophrenics under care in 1985 in the United States indicate an increase in patients of age 65 years and over. This is because of the effects of improved medical, psychiatric, and social services for schizophrenic patients now under the care of outpatient clinics, community mental health centers, mental hospitals, and nursing homes. However, there remain many unknowns about the effects of cerebral arteriosclerosis, senile brain disease, and other chronic illnesses (e.g., cardiovascular diseases and cancer) on both the course of schizophrenia among older patients and the outcome of various interventions by psychological, medical, and social programs.

The course of schizophrenia (see also the summary in this chapter) among the elderly also has been debated for decades, that is, whether schizophrenia has preexisted in older patients who first are diagnosed in their later years, or whether there is, indeed, a "late" schizophrenia. Daniel (1972) reported a 5-year study (1965–1970) of nearly 700 "psychogeriatric admissions" in Queensland, Australia, many of these readmissions, stating that "schizophrenics constituted the heaviest readmission rate of any major [diagnostic] classification"—59% for men, 68% for women, ages 65–84; although the total numbers were only 67 readmissions, less than 10% of the 693 admissions studied. Honigfeld and Gillis (1967) offer a conclusion typical of much of the literature:

> The chronic schizophrenic may spend much of his time in a mental hospital. Is behavioral deterioration, so often reported with these patients, part of the aging process, or is it related to mental hospital life? . . . Decline is linked to the hospitalization process, age per se in chronic schizophrenic patients is associated with a trend toward improvement [with] continued

hospitalization. . . . [There is] a clear-cut negative relationship with favorable aspects of patient behavior.

Understandably, the meaning of schizophrenia at any age needs definition if we are to comprehend its meaning among patients past 60. Reid (1973) writes of the "possibly schizophrenic patient"; Reich (1975) urges the "spectrum concept," that is, "a number of psychopathologic states, both psychotic and nonpsychotic, may share some genetic basis with schizophrenia, and may therefore constitute, together with schizophrenia itself, a genetic spectrum of schizophrenic disorders"; and Butler and Lewis (1973), in discussing "late-life schizophrenia" (also called late paraphrenia or senile schizophrenia) state, "In our own experience it has been rare to see a newly developed schizophrenic disorder in an older person. Many older people have developed types of schizophrenia in earlier years and have carried them into old age." Zerbin-Ruedin (1975), quoting German studies, also holds this latter position.

A World Health Organization scientific group (1972) proposed that "late schizophrenia" be included in the classification of psychological disorders of old age. But this does not resolve the issue; for example, Kaneko (1975) reported a 15-year (1953–1967) study of aged, psychologically ill inpatients in Japan, with a "marked . . . increase in schizophrenia which seemed to be caused by the longevity of the . . . patients and not by an increase of late onset of schizophrenia or paraphrenia." In contrast, Juel-Nielsen (1975) of Denmark reported, after a 10-year study (1957–1967), that "the rates for schizophrenia in old age (65+) remained practically unchanged for males, while a definite increase can be seen for females" (men 297–301 per 100,000; women 347–416 per 100,000 population). Bergman (1975), in the same text, holds to the Kay, Post, Roth, and other English psychiatric view of "paraphrenia," that is,

> Schizophrenia beginning in old age is commonly called paraphrenia. The essential feature is a delusional state arising in clear consciousness. . . . Kay (1972) sums up the recent views concerning schizophrenia and schizophrenia-like states in the elderly and concludes that "chronic paranoid hallucinatory psychoses that arise late in life are schizophrenia from the descriptive point of view."

However, Busse and Pfeiffer (1973) state that

> The relationship of the paranoid psychoses of late life to the schizophrenias of younger years, particularly to paranoid schizophrenia, is not clear. In Post's study (1966) of some 93 patients with paranoid psychoses of late

onset . . . only about a third had the more or less classical symptoms of
schizophrenia . . . .

Sternberg (1975), of the U.S.S.R. Institute of Psychiatry and
Academy of Medical Sciences, concluded that

> Only in middle age are there the most typical signs of a defect [negative
> symptoms], and the most obvious diversity of development. . . . In
> schizophrenic psychoses of old age the range of expression of syndromes
> gradually narrows. Such conditions as florid hebephrenic and catatonic
> states, oneiroid changes of consciousness, and polymorphic terminal states
> are practically never encountered. . . . Schizophrenic personality disor-
> ders may be modified by nonspecific traits of accentuated aging and a mild
> organic decline of the personality. Such shifts have been seen in a rela-
> tively large number of clinical cases and are correlated with the age of
> onset.

Bergman (1975), arguing that both genetic and organic lesions are
etiologic variables, suggests that "in common with symptomatic
schizophrenias in earlier life, focal cerebral lesions may be of importance and . . . these accumulate in the senium. . . . There may be
favorable factors at work to postpone the illness until later life, including a lesser genetic susceptibility." The organic hypothesis of focal
lesions in early schizophrenias is not one that is widely held, to be sure,
unlike the stronger evidence for genetic contributions to the variance in
schizophrenia.

Although Fann, Wheless, and Richman (1976) seem to accept the
notion of late paraphrenia (Alexander, 1972) as "a form of schizophrenia
occurring late in life . . . [with] well-organized paranoid delusions,
accompanied by an intact personality," they also state that "Psychoses
other than those associated with senility or arteriosclerosis are seldom
diagnosed in patients over 65 years of age." Janzarik (1963) has summarized his clinical impressions of

> Psychoses resulting from intoxications, encephalitises, and other organic
> illnesses which cannot be distinguished from schizophrenia. With old age,
> these diagnostic difficulties increase. Distinguishing paranoid and queru-
> lous developments from schizophrenic psychoses in extremely old patients
> . . . can be difficult. . . . In old age, the precipitating factors play a far
> more important role than in schizophrenias of younger years.

Kay and Roth also noted (1963) that "The relationship of paraphrenic,
paranoid, and schizophrenic illness has long been disputed, and no
present view commands general acceptance. . . . 'Paraphrenia' . . . [is]
customarily distinguished from paranoid schizophrenia on the grounds

that typically schizophrenic symptoms are absent. . . ." Janzarik (1963), reviewing British and Swedish studies, summarized these by concluding that "late paraphrenia has to be regarded as the mode of manifestation of schizophrenia in old age." This conclusion assumes that the disorder was not present earlier in the individual's adjustment to life, but Verwoerdt (1969) and Hamilton and Cowdry (1971) support the more general view that schizophrenia "usually begins in early adulthood and may, of course, be carried over into old age. . . . There are various types of schizophrenia, and one of these, paranoid schizophrenia, may have its onset relatively late in life [Verwoerdt, 1969]." According to Hamilton and Cowdry (1971),

> Schizophrenia [is] infrequent in the geriatric population except for those patients in whom the disease process manifested itself much earlier in life. . . . The great majority of elderly schizophrenic patients are individuals who have been so identified for many years. *When what seems to be schizophrenia* occurs for the first time in old age, it is usually paranoid in type and . . . centers around a coordinated set of delusions.

Fish (1960) also observed that schizophrenia is uncommon in old age but further stated that late paraphrenia is not in fact schizophrenia but in general the result of paranoid depression and organic states.

It is also of interest that Herbert and Jacobson (1967) traced "paraphrenia" to Kraepelin's description of paranoid illness, "subsequently shown to be a late form of schizophrenia. . . . Paraphrenia was the term employed to cover schizophrenia . . . in the fourth and fifth decades. Kay and Roth (1961) extended it to cover the . . . seventh or eighth decades, and called it 'late paraphrenia'."

"NATURAL" HISTORY OF THE OLDER SCHIZOPHRENIC

In order not to further complicate the picture of schizophrenia in the elderly, this section will be confined primarily to a discussion of studies of those patients who apparently did not suffer from the disorder in their early or middle adult years. Thus, although the literature is replete with reports, little further mention will be made of such reports as typified by an evaluation of over 600 long-term mental-hospital patients, of whom 36% were diagnosed schizophrenic. The median age of these patients was 70, and the median length of hospitalization was 15 years in a range of 20% patients hospitalized less than 5 years to 2% hospitalized for more than 50 years.

Among the difficulties in sorting out the natural history of schizophrenia occurring for the first time after age 60 or 65 is that of determining what variance may be associated with "the consequences of superimposed cerebral arteriosclerosis, senile brain disease, and other chronic diseases [cardiovascular disease, cancer, etc.] on the course of schizophrenia . . . [Kramer, 1976]."

Although we seek objective criteria of the development of schizophrenia in its natural course, it is difficult to avoid bias, whether this is "dynamic," organic or neurologic, or genetic. Thus, Reid (1973) recommends a new classification, "symptomatic schizophrenia," for the "possibly schizophrenic" patient, in which the initial diagnosis would be "suffering from 'schizophrenia—symptomatic? idiopathic?' and we would then fall into the habit of thinking along the logical lines of the neurologist." Reich (1975) suggests that "a number of psychopathologic states, both psychotic and nonpsychotic, may share some genetic basis with schizophrenia and may therefore constitute, together with schizophrenia itself, a genetic spectrum of schizophrenic disorders." Zerbin-Ruedin (1975) restates the view that late schizophrenias "appear most often as paranoid psychoses but, not too seldom, show depressive symptoms. . . . The schizophrenic and paranoid disorders of old age clearly show genetic relations to the whole group of schizophrenias, but obviously heterogeneous and non-genetic factors play a more important role than in the early onset cases." As noted previously, Sternberg (1975) summarized the Russian experience up to 1969 in a comparative study of the clinical expression of schizophrenia at different stages of development.

> Only in middle age are there the most typical psychopathological syndromes, the most characteristic signs of a defect (negative symptoms), and the most obvious diversity of development. . . . In schizophrenic psychoses of old age the range of expression of syndromes gradually narrows. . . . Florid hebephrenic and catatonic states . . . changes of consciousness, and . . . polymorphic terminal states are practically never encountered. . . . Schizophrenic personality disorders may be modified by nonspecific traits of accentuated aging and a mild organic decline of the personality. Such shifts have been seen in a relatively large number of clinical cases and are correlated with the age of onset.

Bergman (1975) describes paraphrenia as schizophrenia beginning in old age.

> The essential feature is a delusional state arising in clear consciousness. . . . [It] may arise suddenly . . . [as] a primary delusion or, gradually, blend imperceptibly from an irritable, hostile paranoid personality

. . . to an undoubted delusional illness. . . . The prognosis . . . is poor . . . it persists without remission, but it does not affect the life-span of the patient, and preservation of the personality and capacity to cope is often found. Indeed, above average drive and ability may sometimes be evident.

Bergman and others also have reported the frequent presence of auditory hallucinations and deafness in these patients; for example, in Post's study (1966) of 93 patients with late onset paranoid psychoses (schizophrenia?) one-third were deaf. Busse and Pfeiffer (1973) point out, however, that one-third of the patients had paranoid auditory hallucinations but no other "classical symptoms of schizophrenia"; another third had paranoid delusions that were fairly easily understandable on the basis of adverse living situations and social isolation. "Only about a third had the more or less classical symptoms of schizophrenia, with autistic ideation, disorganized thought processes, and archaic symbolization and delusional formation." Another observation by Post suggests that onset of the paranoid states in at least a third of his patients may not in fact have come late in life, for these were described as having a lifelong pattern of suspiciousness, undue sensitivity, quarreling, and hostility.

Fann, Wheless, and Richman (1976) and Alexander (1972) characterize schizophrenia with onset late in life by the presence of well-organized paranoid delusions in "an intact personality." The former also point out that the initial cause is "most tempestuous . . . [and] the precipitating factors play a far more important role than in schizophrenias of younger years."

Kay and Roth (1963) conclude from their studies that the course of schizophrenias of old age "tends to be chronic, and changes of the schizophrenic type usually become more prominent," with the cumulative effects of difficulty and stress in social contacts and communication, deafness, family role, and lack of surviving relations contributing to the "final breakdown in old age." (The mean age of their patients was 70, with onset of symptoms after age 55 and less than 2 years prior to hospitalization. However, the range was from a few weeks to 20 years.) Apropos of the chronic delusional states, Dunn and Arie (1973) have commented that "chronic delusional states . . . usually paranoid, are common in old people" but do not progress to dementia. "They can often live with their delusions quite happily, though they may cause concern to others. With new physical illness the delusional state may become more severe or come to . . . notice . . . for the first time . . . ."

Mueller and Ciompi (1968) and Kral (1973) note that "chronologically old schizophrenics (onset at an advanced age of about 50 or 60) seem to be relatively immune to senile mental changes" but the "paranoid condition leads in a relatively short time to a schizophrenic-like deterioration, although it does not shorten the patient's life expectancy, an important differentiation from senile deterioration [Kral, 1973]." However, Hare, Price, and Slater (1971), in their study of a national sample of first admissions to British mental hospitals in 1965–1966 (22,974 for schizophrenia, 28,346 diagnosed neurosis, 2551 "mania," 58,594 depression, and 6316 personality disorder), after reviewing the 1951–1963 Bethlem-Maudsley findings and examining 9 age periods from 16 to 75 and over, concluded that "Brain damage might . . . explain the relative excess of schizophrenia (mostly of the paranoid type) over neurosis in old age, though a reluctance to diagnose neurosis in old people is not improbable." The data show 3161 schizophrenic patients 60 and older, in a total of 22,974 and 2992 neurotic patients in this age range, among a total of 28,376. Yet, the similarities in age distributions are more striking than the differences:

> There is a close similarity between the age-distribution curves of schizophrenia and neuroses, and also between those of mania and psychotic depression. . . . The suggestion is made that similarity in age-distribution reflects a similarity in environmental precipitating factors. Whatever the nature of such [environmental] stresses, it may be assumed that their virulence varies in any given culture with the age of the patient, for age will affect not only a person's biological resistance but also his social resistance in so far as social roles are allotted to various age groups. [Hare *et al.*, 1971].

About the same time as the Hare *et al.* (1971) study, Müller (1971) reported a study of 101 schizophrenics in advanced senescence and cited a number of other significant studies (Müller, 1959; Pause, 1967; Post, 1962, 1965). These deal mostly with patients hospitalized for many years (a mean of 25 years in Müller's 1971 report), and thus these studies tell little about the course of the disorder among patients first diagnosed as schizophrenic in their late years:

> The beginning of senescence in the sixties, when the psychological problems of aging are most acute . . . [the] advancing years . . . will not modify the schizophrenic to any great extent; [though in 53 of the 101 cases] senescence had no influence on the form of schizophrenia . . . in 48 there were suggestive changes, e.g., disappearance of delusions . . . amelioration in "sociability" . . . even [the show of] insight into their former pathological state.

Lawton (1972) also has remarked on the "less overtly deviant" behavior of schizophrenics after lengthy hospitalization and "notably reduced" symptom visibility. These changes may, however, be associated with the course of the disorder, aging, or "institutional leveling." In another study, although now more than 20 years old, Wolff's 1956 report on 220 state mental hospital patients (age range 58–91) in a building for geriatrics states a conclusion that is supported by those clinicians and investigators who espouse the organic view. "Although the individual diagnoses vary, as with most psychiatric groups, most of the patients display certain identical features due to the prevalence of brain damage."

Kay's (1975) description of schizophrenia and "schizophrenia-like states" in the elderly discriminates the latter ("persistent paranoid psychoses") from unrelated "senile or arteriosclerotic dementia," which arises for the first time after age 60 and suggests that these paranoid psychoses may be indistinguishable from paranoid schizophrenia. Unfortunately, it is not clear in Kay's evaluation whether schizophrenia differs significantly from "schizophrenic reactions" as a disorder and in its course.

TREATMENT OF THE OLDER SCHIZOPHRENIC

In 1959, Rechtshaffen reviewed the previous 30 years of psychological treatment of older patients. Although he did not specifically include treatment for the schizophrenic patient nor treatment other than psychotherapy, it is of interest to summarize his review for historical reasons, especially since it will be apparent that the past 50 years have not reflected major new directions. Rechtshaffen marks the 1929 beginning of the treatment era by noting the founding of psychologist Lillien Martin's Old Age Counseling Center in San Francisco. Since then, there have been psychoanalytic approaches, traditional on occasion but usually modified (historically, neither Freud [1924] nor Fenichel [1945] favored individual analysis for patients over 45, nor for those with psychoses), there has been Goldfarb's "brief therapy" (1953), Stiegletz's "how to live" (essentially a teacher–student relationship), Offenbach's dependent relationship technique, Rockwell's distributive analysis and synthesis (derived from Adolf Meyer's concepts), Mittelman's treatment of psychosomatic disorders, and group therapies. According to Rechtshaffen (1959):

> There was a wave of optimism about how accessible older people are to psychotherapy and about how much can be accomplished. In retrospect, much of this optimism seems to have been exaggerated. . . . [There are] unresolved issues. . . . (1) Systematic, controlled studies of the effective-

ness of various treatments of older people are lacking. . . . (2) [There is] debate as to the extent to which . . . impairments of intellect and learning ability . . . are determined by dynamic or . . . physiologic factors. . . . Research evidence favors the latter. . . . (3) [There is] very active disagreement regarding the extent to which old people are open to self-examination. . . . (4) [There is] the question of the goals of geriatric psychotherapy.

If one confines the focus to the treatment of the older person who apparently developed schizophrenia after age 60 or 65, there are indeed no studies explicitly devoted to this population sample. Rather, there is mention of the survival rate of older schizophrenics in and out of the hospital milieu and, at best, there is custodial care euphemistically labeled "milieu therapy." Thus, Markson and Cumming (1975) concluded from a study of nearly 2200 patients transferred from four state hospitals, which had closed down, to other state hospitals in the system, that there is "no evidence that forced relocation of a group of relatively physically healthy, chronic, predominantly schizophrenic, patients . . . is sufficiently stressful to have any effect on mortality experience." And Daniel's (1972) 5-year study of nearly 700 psychogeriatric admissions to the hospital observed that patients diagnosed alcoholic, affective disorder, or schizophrenic constituted the largest proportion of long-stay patients but "A favorable discharge rate and high readmission rate reflect the amount of outpatient and group care in this group." The high readmission rate is a disturbing note, however.

Neither Weinberg's (1956) discussion of psychotherapy for the aged person nor Goldfarb and Turner's (1953) "brief therapy" for this age sample indicate that schizophrenic illness was under treatment. Similarly, Busse and Pfeiffer (1973) are no more specific in their general discussion of mental disorders in later life and, in view of their concern with the relationship of the paranoid psychoses of late life to schizophrenia, we can only infer what application there may be for their "immediate therapeutic goals with paranoid patients," that is, "to reduce the anxiety which leads to the development of paranoid ideas . . . by three differing but related techniques—psychotherapeutic intervention, by reducing the threat from the external environment, and by anxiety-alleviating drugs."

Fann, Wheless, and Richman (1976), in their discussion of psychotropic drug treatment for the aged, indicated their preference for antipsychotic medication, for example, phenothiazines, thioxanthenes, butyrophenones, rauwolfia alkaloids, and lithium, for patients with the "form of schizophrenia occurring late in life. . . . Unless the paranoid reaction is a component of depression." They cautioned that, in the use of commonly used phenothiazines, 200–800 mg/day, the patient who is over 65 . . . "has a greatly reduced ability to metabolize, and hence to tolerate, the antipsychotic medications . . . clinical efficacy and side effects [may occur] at doses lower than expected." Also, tardive dyskinesia may develop, a syndrome characterized by involuntary choreo-athetoid movements of the face, mouth, tongue, extremities, and trunk muscle groups. The condition may persist for months or years after withdrawal of the medication. In some it is irreversible. "Because geriatric patients have a special susceptibility to phenothiazine-induced states of confusion and delirium, these states can be mistaken . . . for an increase in the intensity of psychiatric symptoms; as a result, the physician might increase the dosage of the offending agent." Dunn and Arie (1973) also report that, for the older person whose delusional state first is noted in the late years, phenothiazine therapy sometimes dramatically relieves the persecutory state. Gabriel (1974) recommended "prolonged" treatment with phenothiazines for those 7% hospitalized, aged patients with "so-called late paraphrenia. . . . Some patients can be kept out of hospital as long as someone is willing and able to care for them."

Hamilton and Cowdry (1971), in reviewing treatment procedures for what seems to be schizophrenia "occurring" for the first time in old age, are of the opinion that "it is usually paranoid in type and usually centers around a coordinated set of delusions . . . superimposed on a relatively intact personality." Because of this, the disorder may be "potentially more treatable than chronic schizophrenia" and, for patients whose paranoid states first developed in old age, electroshock may replace "these new and noxious patterns [with] older and more comfortable ones."

Arie's (1971) plan for psychogeriatric services and his data for Goodmayes and Claybury hospitals in Britain specified neither diagnosis nor treatment but received an evaluation by Pitt (1974) that restates the core of the problem in discerning what treatment effects may exist for older, hospitalized psychiatric patients. At Goodmayes, for example, a hospital serving an area with a population of 370,000, Arie's program produced a significant increase in referrals and admissions, an even greater rise in discharges, a fall in deaths, and discharge of 20% of the inpatients within 2 years. At Claybury, the waiting list was reduced from 40 to 4 patients, the admission rate increased, and discharge rate increased from 54% to 80%. These shifts occurred against the background of a 70-year history in England and Wales, from 5% of the population of 33 million over 65 to 12% of a 50 million population, and

45% of psychiatric and general hospital beds occupied by patients among the 12% 65 and older. Pitt (1974) brings the Arie studies into perspective by asking whether what Arie practiced at Goodmayes, or Felix Post at Bethlem, Klaus Bergmann at Newcastle, or Anthony Whitehead at Severalls, was universally applicable or whether it depended on where they were working, with whom, and on their own personalities. "Whitehead, and Duncan MacMillan at Mapperley, set great store by day treatment, yet Arie seems to get by with very little. Is it that the respective services deal with some problems rather better than others, or do enthusiasm and drive count for more than technique?"

Nobbs (1973) summarizes his view of the late schizoid type of mental disorder, often called paraphrenia, and their hospital treatment and outcome in observing that paraphrenia, although similar to schizophrenia in younger patients, has a poor prognosis because of the difficulty in returning older individuals to the community. Thus, again, this observation has to be reconciled with that reported by Arie. As with the definition and "natural history" course of schizophrenia first occurring in the 60s in an individual's adjustment, the treatment phase also involves the vagueness and uncertainties of this field of study. To paraphrase a centuries-old observation, medicine is a system in which we treat individuals about whom we know relatively little, with therapies about which we know even less.

SUMMARY

Schizophrenia has been a dominant theme in psychological and psychiatric literature for decades, occupying clinicians and investigators as they have tried, and continue to try, to define and understand the disorder. In the past decade, emphasis has been upon standardized and uniform evaluation and definition. Most of the literature concentrates upon age groups other than those of the later decades and, when there are reports of schizophrenia among patients 60 years of age and older, the majority deal with those individuals who have been chronically ill for periods ranging up to 50 years. The British school—Kay, Post, Roth, and their colleagues—has been the primary focus on schizophrenia among older patients where the disorder has been first noted in the late years but, even here, "paraphrenia" or "late paraphrenia" has been stressed rather than schizophrenia. The definition of the disorder has reflected a syndrome that is narrower than that noted in younger schizophrenics. If the characterizations of behaviors labeled paraphrenia or late paraphrenia are not comfortable ones to accept, and the review in the preceding pages suggests why this attitude is easily understood, then there may not be a disorder of schizophrenia that first appears in the late decades of an individual's adjustment to life stresses. Rather, there are symptoms and symptom complexes, some of which resemble the schizophrenias of younger patients and, therefore, the course of the disorder and its treatment relate to these similarities and differences and not to uniform descriptions accepted by most workers in the field. Clinicians and investigators will recognize that this is not a state peculiar to the schizophrenias of old age.

REFERENCES

Alexander, D. A. "Senile dementia": A changing perspective. *British Journal of Psychiatry,* 1972, *121,* 207–214.

Arie, T. Morale and planning of the psychogeriatric services. *British Medical Journal,* 1971, 3, 166–170.

Babigian, H. M., & Odoroff, C. L. The mortality experience of a population with psychiatric illness. *American Journal of Psychiatry,* 1969, *126,* 470–480.

Bergman, K. Nosology. In J. G. Howells (Ed.), *Modern perspectives in the psychiatry of old age.* New York: Brunner/Mazel, 1975.

Boyd, R. R., & Oakes, C. G. (Eds.). *Foundations of practical gerontology.* Columbia, S.C.: Univ. of South Carolina Press, 1969.

Busse, E. W., & Pfeiffer, E. (Eds.). *Mental illness in later life.* Washington, D.C.: American Psychiatric Association, 1973.

Butler, R. N. Mental health and aging: Life cycle perspectives. *Geriatrics,* 1974, *29,* 59–60.

Butler, R. N., & Lewis, M. E. *Aging and mental health.* St. Louis, Missouri: Mosby, 1973.

Carpenter, W. T., Jr. Current diagnostic concepts in schizophrenia. *American Journal of Psychiatry,* 1976, *133,* 172–177.

Cooper, J. E., Kendell, R. E., & Gurland, B. J. *Psychiatric diagnosis in New York and London* (Maudsley Monograph No. 20). London: Oxford Univ. Press, 1972.

Cowdry, E. V., & Steinberg, F. U. *The care of the geriatric patient* (4th ed.). St. Louis, Missouri: Mosby, 1971.

Daniel, R. A five-year study of 693 psychogeriatric admissions in Queensland. *Geriatrics,* 1972, *27,* 132–158.

Dunn, T., & Arie, T. Mental disturbance in the ill old person. *British Medical Journal,* 1973, 4, 413–416.

Fann, W. E., Wheless, J. C., & Richman, B. W. Treating the aged with psychotropic drugs. *Gerontologist,* 1976, *16,* 322–328.

Fenichel, O. *The psychoanalytic theory of neurosis.* New York: Norton, 1945.

Fish, F. Senile schizophrenia. *Journal of Mental Science,* 1960, *106,* 938–946.

Freud, S. On psychotherapy. In *Collected Papers* (Vol. 1). London: Hogarth Press, 1924.

Gabriel, E. Der langfristige Verlauf schizophrener später krankungen im Vergleich mit Schizophrenien aller Lebensalter. *Psychiatria Clinica,* 1974, *7,* 172–180.

Goldfarb, A. I., & Turner, H. Psychotherapy of aged persons: II. Utilization and effectiveness of "brief" therapy. *American Journal of Psychiatry,* 1953, *109,* 916–921.

Hamilton, J. A., & Cowdry, E. V., Jr. Psychiatric aspects. In E. V. Cowdry & F. U.

Steinberg (Eds.), *The care of the geriatric patient* (4th ed.). St. Louis, Missouri: Mosby, 1971.

Hare, E. H., Price, J. S., & Slater, E. T. O. The age-distribution of schizophrenia and neurosis: Findings in a national sample. *British Journal of Psychiatry*, 1971, *119*, 445–448.

Herbert, M. E., & Jacobson, S. Late paraphrenia. *British Journal of Psychiatry*, 1967, *113*, 461–469.

Honigfeld, G., & Gillis, R. The role of institutionalization in the natural history of schizophrenia. *Diseases of the Nervous System*, 1967, *28*, 660–663.

Howells, J. G. (Ed.). *Modern perspectives in the psychiatry of old age*. New York: Brunner/Mazel, 1975.

Janzarik, W. Diagnostic and nosological aspects. In R. H. Williams, C. Tibbitts, & W. Donahue (Eds.), *Processes of aging: I*. New York: Atherton Press, 1963.

Juel-Nielsen, N. Epidemiology. In J. G. Howells (Ed.), *Modern perspectives in the psychiatry of old age*. New York: Brunner/Mazel, 1975.

Kaneko, Z. Care in Japan. In J. G. Howells (Ed.), *Modern perspectives in the psychiatry of old age*. New York: Brunner/Mazel, 1975.

Kay, D. W. K. Schizophrenia and schizophrenia-like states in the elderly. *British Journal of Hospital Medicine*, 1972, *10*, 369–376.

Kay, D. W. K., & Roth, M. Environmental and hereditary factors in the schizophrenias of old age ("late paraphrenia") and their bearing on the general problem of causation in schizophrenia. *Journal of Mental Science*, 1961, *107*, 649–686.

Kay, D. W. K., & Roth, M. Schizophrenias of old age. In R. H. Williams, C. Tibbitts, & W. Donahue (Eds.), *Processes of aging: I*. New York: Atherton Press, 1963.

Kral, V. A. Psychiatric problems in the aged: A reconsideration. *Canadian Medical Association Journal*, 1973, *108*, 584–590.

Kramer, M. *Population changes and schizophrenia, 1970–1985*. Second Rochester International Conference on Schizophrenia, Rochester, New York, 1976.

Kramer, M., Taube, C. A., & Redick, R. W. Patterns of use of psychiatric facilities by the aged: Past, present, and future. In C. Eisdorfer, & M. P. Lawton (Eds.), *The psychology of adult development and aging*. Washington, D.C.: American Psychological Association, 1973.

Lawton, M. P. Schizophrenia forty-five years later. *Journal of Genetic Psychology*, 1972, *121*, 133–143.

Markson, E. W., & Cumming, J. H. The post-transfer fate of relocated mental patients in New York. *Gerontologist*, 1975, *15*, 104–108.

Mueller, C., & Ciompi, L. (Eds.). *Senile dementia*. Baltimore, Maryland: Williams & Wilkins, 1968.

Müller, C. *Über das senium der schizophrenen*. Basel: Karger Verlag, 1959.

Müller, C. Schizophrenia in advanced senescence. *British Journal of Psychiatry*, 1971, *118*, 347–348.

Nobbs, K. L. G. Mental disorders in the elderly. In K. Hazell, K. L. G. Nobbs, W. A. Hurr, & W. F. Anderson (Eds.), *Social and medical problems of the elderly* (3rd ed.). London: Hutchinson, 1973.

Pause, F. *Problematic therapie und rehabilitation der chronischen endogen psychoses*. Stuttgart: Enke, 1967.

Pitt, B. *Psychogeriatrics: An introduction to the psychiatry of old age*. London: Churchill Livingstone, 1974.

Post, F. *The significance of affective symptoms in old age: A follow-up study of one hundred patients*. London: Maudsley Monograph 10, 1962.

Post, F. The clinical psychiatry of late life. Oxford: Pergamon Press, 1965.

Post F. Persistent persecutory states of the elderly. London: Pergamon Press, 1966.

Rechtshaffen, A. Psychotherapy with geriatric patients: A review of the literature. Journal of Gerontology, 1959, 14, 73–84.

Redick, R. W. Patient care episodes in psychiatric services, United States, 1971 (Statistical Note 92). Survey and Reports Section, Office of Program Planning and Evaluation, Biometrics Branch, National Institute of Mental Health, August 1973.

Redick, R. W. Changes in the age, sex, and diagnostic composition of additions to state and county mental hospitals, United States, 1969–73 (Statistical Note 117). Survey and Reports Section, Office of Program Planning and Evaluation, Biometrics Branch, National Institute of Mental Health, June 1975.

Reich, W. The spectrum concept of schizophrenia. Archives of General Psychiatry, 1975, 32, 489–498.

Reid, A. A. Schizophrenia—Disease or syndrome? Archives of General Psychiatry, 1973, 28, 863–869.

Sternberg, E. Y. A contribution to nosology from the USSR. In J. G. Howells (Ed.), Modern perspectives in the psychiatry of old age. New York: Brunner/Mazel, 1975.

Taube, C. A. Utilization of mental health facilities, 1971. Analytical and Special Study Reports, National Institute of Mental Health, Mental Health Statistics, Series B, No. 5; DHEW Public. NIH-74-657, 1974.

Taube, C. A. Changes in the age, sex, and diagnostic composition of the resident population of state and county mental hospitals, United States, 1964–1973 (Statistical Note 112). Survey and Reports Section, Office of Program Planning and Evaluation, Biometrics Branch, National Institute of Mental Health, March 1975.

Verwoerdt, A. Psychiatric aspects of aging. In R. R. Boyd & C. G. Oakes (Eds.), Foundations of practical gerontology. Columbia, S.C.: Univ. of South Carolina Press, 1969.

Verwoerdt, A. Clinical geropsychiatry. Baltimore, Maryland: Williams & Wilkins, 1976.

Weinberg, J. Psychotherapy of the aged person. In J. E. Moore, H. H. Merritt, & R. J. Masse-Link (Eds.), The neurological and psychiatric aspects of the disorders of aging. Baltimore, Maryland: Williams & Wilkins, 1956.

Williams, R. H., Tibbitts, C., & Donahue, W. (Eds.). Processes of aging: I. New York: Atherton Press, 1963.

Wolff, K. Treatment of the geriatric patient in a mental hospital. Journal of the American Geriatric Society, 1956, 4, 472–476.

World Health Organization. Psychogeriatrics: Report of a W.H.O. scientific group (World Health Organization Tech. Rep. Ser., 1972, No. 507). Geneva, Switzerland.

Yolles, S. F., & Kramer, M. Vital statistics. In L. Bellak & L. Loeb (Eds.), The schizophrenic syndrome. New York: Grune & Stratton, 1969.

Zerbin-Ruedin, E. Genetics. In J. G. Howells (Ed.), Modern perspectives in the psychiatry of old age. New York: Brunner/Mazel, 1975.

Chapter 8

NEUROSIS IN THE OLDER ADULT[1]

June E. Blum and Marcella Bakur Weiner

*One sees yet again that the whole world of the second half of human
life generally consists of the habits acquired in the first half.*

—STAVROGIN IN F. DOSTOEVSKY; *The Possessed*

In the preceding passage, Dostoevsky gave affirmation to the continuity of mental processes and the tenacity of early patterns of human
behavior which may, as unresolved conflicts, be reflected in the neuroses of one's later years. In effect, his literary wisdom underscored the
postulation that a true psychoneurosis did not emerge in senescence
without latent underpinnings of a childhood neurosis (Berezin, 1965;
Freud, 1896; Slater & Roth, 1969; Waelder, 1960).

There are other concurring views such as Stekel's (1940), who
maintained that most neurotic manifestations of the present seem to
emanate from past infantile patterns; yet, in partial contrast, he questioned the validity of considering the symptomatology as being the
"subspecie" of early infantile experiences. Thus, the neurosis polemic
was positively addressed by Gutheil (1944), who indicated that even if
current behavior is an exact facsimile of the past, we may, with psychotherapeutic intervention, "arrest" a person's neurotic development.
It was Abraham (1919) who felt that it was the age of the neurosis rather
than a patient's age per se that made the difference in treatment outcome. Irrespective of age, the prerequisite for positive outcome resides
in what Fenichel (1945) terms "the co-operation of a reasonable ego
[p. 537]" coupled with motivation for change. In the recent literature,
Meyer (1974) has sharply delineated the wellsprings of "new" manifes-

[1] The material in this chapter has emerged in part from Grant No. MH 25258, funded
by the National Institute of Mental Health.

167

tations of psychoneuroses and neurotic reactions in the senium as the "psychogenetic responses to acute crises in living" and the "neurotic exacerbation of former character traits."

VICISSITUDES OF AGING

In essence, the preceding is addressed to functional integrity rather than age itself. The evaluation of an older person's functional physical, psychological, and social status is more indicative of his[2] capacities than chronological age. Bergmann (1978), in fact, in place of age, stresses personal vulnerability and physical health as the major contributors to late onset neurotic reactions. In this tradition, Neugarten (1968) emphasized the distinction between the "young–old" and "old–old" as further delineating the general concept of "old." This differentiating concept appears to have field utility in both diagnostic-descriptive and treatment frameworks.

Notwithstanding that the aging of today are not those of yesterday or tomorrow, there are general and fairly stable components of the aging process. A universal patterning of the process reveals (Jarvik, Eisdorfer, & Blum, 1972) a dissociation of cognitive stability from a relentless slowing down of psychomotor functioning, that is, other generalized aging trends include physiological changes and decrements in various degrees of the sensorium. The changes, while common to all, vary individually and are specific to an individual's genetic endowment and physical health status.

The crowning nemesis for the senescent patient resides particularly in the psychosocial variables that encompass ego threats and traumas. It lies in the narrowing of the interpersonal field engendered by reduced physical stamina, physical illness, loss of loved ones, involuntary retirement, forced relocation, and societal rejection. It is this totality of narcissistic blows that may culminate in shaking an individual's sense of autonomy. It may be conjectured that many vulnerable older persons could bear the ego assaults with greater fortitude if the aforementioned were shared with loved ones and/or friends of long standing. With the loss of close ties through death and the consequent narrowing of borders for receiving narcissistic supplies, loneliness may be experienced with fullest impact, along with a closer sense of the inevitability and imminence of dissolution and death.

[2] For the purposes of this chapter "his" is used in the generic sense.

A 73-year-old woman noted the following to her group members. "I have made many friends but have you noticed there is no one of the childhood days around. There's no one who knew me in high school!"[3]

Herein lies the essence that loss rather than isolation has the closer relationship to loneliness (Shanas, 1968). It is, perhaps, this loss that underlies the assaults experienced by the aging person.

As a result of these assaults, three major intrapsychic components emerge in direct proportion to the integrity of an elder's ego: grief, helplessness, and fears of abandonment. It is here, in the weakening of repressive defenses, that one can trace the reemergence of and regression to an early conflictual developmental level. While the developmental level of a senescent patient may become regressed to that categorized as the pre-oedipal need-gratifying stage, it is incumbent upon the gerontologist–geriatrician to understand that older patients are not simply repeating the phase as children. Viewing them as such would be considered antithetical to the therapeutic process, for in their regression they carry with them the experience of their years.

In addition, the increase in variability among people as they age warrants special consideration. The tendency, due to preconceived values and ideas, is to view a senior person as *"the aged"* (Blum, 1977a; Butler, 1969; Peck, 1956). In metaphorical terms, while the orchestra performs as a totality, the instrumentalists are individual players. The aging person ages, too, in idiosyncratic ways that expand and particularize over time. As one 87-year-old patient aptly stated during a psychotherapy session: "It seems that the older I get, the more I can't escape being me."

Aging implies a continuity and constancy of lifelong personality styles that tend to become more sharply defined with time. The aging process itself may be viewed as a slow-paced stress phenomenon that may elicit responses similar to those utilized in other stress situations such as accidents, illness, and psychological and social loss. The lifelong adverse response to certain kinds of stress by older neurotics is seen by Slater and Roth (1969) as being the prime differentiating variable between them and older persons who age well. The aging person's ability to handle stresses will be determined by his enduring adaptive abilities and coping styles. Thus, adaptive coping styles linked to the utilization of compulsive–obsessional defenses may lead to behaviors illustrated

---

[3] This and the clinical examples which follow are from the authors' clinical practice.

by the 90-year-old male who, during a group therapy session in a nursing home, told the group how he labeled his bureau drawer: "My drawer looks like a railroad terminal, for I have signs for where to find my socks, where my 'good shirts' are and where my 'everyday shirts' are. I read the labels and then take the track that will lead me to where I want to go."

Nonadaptive responses to stress (aging) may include shame over agressive impulses, fear of aggressivity, survivor guilt, fear of iden-tification or merger with others, and prolonged mourning. Selection and utilization of any of these responses will be determined by the effect of the merging of preexisting conflicts with the current one upon an individual's adaptive homeostasis (Freud's *constancy principle*, 1896). Thus, the newly retired older man who was the masterful execu-tive used to "running his own ship" may experience his enforced retirement as an ego blow to his self-esteem, which may, in turn, lead to pathological symptoms such as depression. Similarly, the narcissistic person seeking the nourishment provided by a nurturant environment is especially vulnerable to the ego blows in aging, involving the possi-bility of chronic ailments, physical limitations, and mental changes due to separations, loss and loneliness (Kernberg, 1975). Facing a world now depleted and lacking in love and human contact they hunger for, such individuals often have difficulty living with the emptiness inside them-selves.

> Stated an older woman in an individual session: "When the kids come to visit, I glow. After they leave, there is this hole inside of me."

Aging may thus be considered as a continuous process. This pro-cess, analagous to stress, has its foundation grounded in the individu-al's lifelong physical health status, functional abilities, emotional stabil-ity, and educational, occupational, ethnic, and cultural backgrounds. Significant changes in any of these variables may be experienced as undue stress. The responses mustered represent, as throughout life, a way of coping with and defending against stress. In addition, the ways in which these factors interact with each other and the ways in which each individual acts upon them will help to determine the definition, diagnosis, and the category assigned to that individual (Kalish, 1975). For example, the reduced opportunities for older persons, particularly older women, to engage in sex may lead some to seek out substitute means; still others may find solace in religion; still others may turn their libido toward charitable endeavors; while still others may displace unacceptable sexual feelings onto their bodies by hypochondriacal complaints.

Again, as the younger years provide the model for adaptation in the later years, satisfactory coping attempts will be best made by persons whose earlier life included a trusting relationship with another, which becomes internalized as trust of self. This, in turn, leads to autonomy, valued identity, and the ability to sublimate successfully.

While stress, as anxiety, may be viewed negatively, optimal amounts of tension preserve "the level of excitation" characteristic for a person (Freud, cited in Fenichel, 1945). Current research efforts might be directed toward determining the range of optimal tension levels in the adaptation of aging individuals.

Patterns of Adaptation

We will discuss three patterns of adaptation here. First, it is known that some older persons represent individuals whose neurotic symptomatology reveals recurring patterns. For example, the "D'Capa effect" or "playing the chorus again" (Hiatt, 1966), is illustrated by a 64-year-old man who constantly looked to others for validation and was but a reflection of what he felt someone else wanted of him. Part of the chorus concerned his submission to his mother's tears and admonition not to express angry feelings, for his actions caused her to cry. His subsequent "adjustment" to her and his wife was that of "handmaiden." His engagement to marry replicated his early capitulation: He did not love his intended bride, but when she wept upon hearing he did not want to marry her, he entered into a loveless marriage. His reactive dynamics were such that he "bounded" from one depression to another for 30 years. Through an analytically oriented intervention (combined group and individual), he is regaining his "right to be." He has a new lease on life, is on his own and alone, but not lonely, and his interpersonal relations reveal a freedom heretofore a stranger to him.

Second, there are marginal individuals who have emotionally survived into later years aided and abetted by the support system of career, family, and social network. However, the weight of the "cumulative deprivations" (Berkman, 1967) are such as to trigger the onset of a neurosis heretofore postponed.

This may be exemplified by the case of an attractive 66-year-old woman who entered treatment due to depression caused by knowledge of her husband's affair with a younger woman. For her, the affair represented a loss of her auxiliary ego. Until that time, her relationship with her husband had been one of self-denial. She was unaware of not thinking of what she wanted. He was her life. In therapy, she struggled to gain separation–individuation. She spilled fury and jealousy. She recalled past and present dreams of losing her pocketbook. As she progressed, she began to think for herself and reported a dream in which she found her pocketbook; upon opening it, she discovered money. The ongoing working through of the trauma and its components constituted a progressive developmental step toward maturity.

Third, there are those who have been living full, rich lives. Their strong sense of autonomy and inner resources have served them well in resolving problems and the vicissitudes of aging. They, too, are subject to age-specific changes and are not exempt from the narcissistic blows. However, they differ from their more fragile and vulnerable cohorts in being fortified by adaptive flexibilities and the capacity to follow Freud's 1920 quote of a poet "whither we cannot fly, we must go limping. The scripture sayeth that limping is no sin."

Based on the aforementioned, once again, a person's formative years emerge as the soil for developmental adaptations in the later years.

Diagnoses

Simon and Cohan (1963) refer to the doctrine of single diagnoses in many psychiatric settings as an impediment to understanding senescent patients. This pitfall may be circumvented for persons of all ages by the draft of Diagnostic and Statistical Manual of Mental Disorders (DSM) III (Spitzer, 1977), which allows for multiple categories to be coded on any one patient.

A complete evaluation of an older patient's distress is best achieved within a multidisciplinary team approach, one of whose requisites consists of obtaining his pharmaceutical regimen. What may appear as a primary psychological and/or physical disorder may, in fact, represent a drug reaction such as reserpine-induced depression found in hypertensive patients (DiMascio & Goldberg, 1976). Typically, the evaluation may include the psychiatric interview supplemented by the Mental Status Questionnaire (MSQ) (Kahn, Goldfarb, Pollack, & Peck, 1960) and the Face–Hand Test (Bender, Fink, & Green, 1951) evaluating organic integrity and a utilization of psychological measures to assess the patient's ego development, be it of neurotic, borderline, or psychotic structure. Tests such as Memory for Designs (Graham & Kendall, 1960) may also be included to test for organicity that may be present and often confounds a valid mental health diagnosis. An extensive medical examination, including a laboratory work-up, visual and auditory evaluations, as well as assessment of the quality of the patient's psychosocial field, is basic to sound diagnosis.

The neurotic may then be differentiated from other diagnostic categories by the degree to which he (*a*) has a sense of identity derived from differentiation of himself from others; (*b*) can tolerate frustration; (*c*) can use thought before action; and (*d*) utilizes adequate "reality testing" (Blanck, 1974). Further, the individual's solutions, although seemingly neurotic ones, are based upon interactions with the environment. While presumably having failed to resolve the oedipal conflict, the neurotic is yet one whose ego may be well developed and fairly intact (Bergmann & Hartman, 1976).

The neurotic adjustment dichotomies noted later in this chapter are delineated in terms of the predominant system constellations and are not presented as distinct entities. In the later years, as throughout the life cycle, a disorder may mask and/or coexist with others.

ANXIETY REACTIONS

Anxiety, which is experienced universally in various degrees, regardless of age, is a component of every neurosis and is the dominant one in Anxiety Neurosis. The anxiety continuum may extend from being free floating to confinement to a particular situation that symbolically represents an intrapsychic conflict. In the latter case, the defense of phobic avoidance is utilized to stem the anxiety.

The manifestations of anxiety are poignant in older persons. The more fragile senescents are the most prone. However, there are yet other sturdy individuals who, though utilizing neurotic tension and anxiety productively in earlier years, are not immune to anxiety in later life. Faced with physiological and biological changes compounded by "ageism," they may be forced into a passive state. As a result of the new alien ego position, feelings of helplessness may emerge and be expressed through anxiety reactions.

According to Zetzel (1965), the active defenses mobilized by the anxiety reaction in this instance are counter to maturity, demanding a basically passive acceptance of that which is painful and inevitable. It thus becomes incumbent that individuals be helped to work through the mourning process for losses (including a way of life and unfulfilled aspirations). This has been conceptualized as partial mourning.

Symptomatology

Anxiety reactions are predominantly of a somatic nature involving pathways utilized for discharge of tension. They may be expressed by any of the following, either alone or in combination: agitation, tremors, sleeping problems, perspiration, hyperventilation, increased heart activity, forgetfulness, and generalized, free-floating feelings of apprehension. These may be exhibited by the older adult in particular, since somatization is an "accepted" way of expressing anxiety related to the physical, psychosocial, and economic losses accompanying aging.

Psychodynamics

Freud (1926) referred to one of two ways anxiety may arise in later life: (*a*) as an involuntary, automatic, and quantitatively appropriate reaction to danger; or (*b*) where the ego "subjects itself to anxiety as a sort of inoculation, submitting to a slight attack of the illness in order to escape its full strength—with the unmistakable purpose of restricting that distressing experience to a mere indication, that is, a signal [p. 162]." This is sometimes referred to as "signal anxiety." Here the adaptive value of anxiety is noted as a safety valve by serving in the automatic release of excess tension that stays ego integration and impedes further regression; as a warning signal it may reflect an incipient physical problem.

The dynamics of psychic conflict in adult life as well as its origins in early childhood were postulated by Freud (Brenner, 1976) to include anxiety emanating out of one or more of the following: loss of object, loss of love, castration, and superego condemnation. A gestalt is emphasized here since the preceding are the intrapsychic issues that are subject to recrudescence in the later stages of life in those whose ego resources have been strained by the demand of the years.

The aforementioned is supported by Zetzel (1965), who views anxiety in the elderly, as in the very young, as rooted in the fear of loss and separation. She ascribes anxiety in the elderly to a relation with the outside world rather than "as a signal of instinctual intrapsychic danger." While cultural and societal impingements may well provide the impetus for anxiety in elderly persons, the evoked tears rekindle the early intrapsychic danger signals.

The experience of anxiety in the very old and in the young is differentiated by Cath's (1965) postulation of depletion anxiety in which an elderly person is threatened by "emotional exile or total annihilation based on a gradual depletion of inner self, outer objects and the operative capacity to remedy this state [p. 31]." In this analogy "somatic sources from which instinctual energies are derived undergo progressive attrition [p. 41]."

All individuals are faced with losses that are compounded with added years. However, the manner in which losses are faced is dependent upon the nature of the loss, the present physiological capacities, the strength of ego reserves, and the person's adaptive capacities. The minimization–pervasiveness continuum of an anxiety reaction resides in what Laughlin (1967) refers to as the "theory of antecedent conflicts." The manner in which anxiety is manifested is underscored by Blanck (1974) as revealing an aspect or aspects of ego development; in so doing, it may serve as a guide for therapeutic intervention.

Treatment Suggestions

The anxiety reaction is reflective of ego disequilibrium and, as such, causes undue individual suffering and frustrates those who could be of help. Therapeutic intervention should be prompt, for the symptoms may yet be fluid and unfixed in value in the earliest stage of development. The focus is to understand the nature of the reaction for the individual patient. The way for increased adaptation may be aided by concretizing schedules and coping measures. Understanding should be based upon an exploration of lifelong adaptation patterns and attained level of ego development. The Hopkins' Symptom Check List (Derogatis, 1973) is one of the useful primary differential diagnostic tools when medication is deemed advisable. In addition to the cautions stressed regarding somatic drug reactions of older patients, there needs to be awareness that medications that relieve anxiety may also serve to exacerbate a depression. It may be additionally noted (Verwoerdt, 1976) that medication such as the tricyclic antidepressants may cause agitation.

DEPRESSIVE NEUROSES

The depressive neuroses (reactive depression or depressive reaction) are noted as a predominant diagnosis of senescence (Goldfarb, 1974). There are findings that differ, such as those of Ciompi (1969), whose outcome study of previously hospitalized depressed patients indicated a decrease of depressive symptomatology. However, this investigation was specific to hospitalized patients and did not include psychoneurotic patients whose depressions usually do not require hospitalization.

Depression neurosis was the dominant diagnosis of subjects between the ages of 60 and 75 who applied for participation in research addressed to comparative treatments of emotional problems in aging.[4] In the majority of cases, the exacerbation of depression coincided with increased stress due to one of several factors: a death or progressive illness of a spouse; enforced retirement or the prospect of same; reduction in stamina; conflictual relationships with children; or general dissatisfaction with the status of interpersonal relations. The desire for change was succinctly expressed by a 72-year-old woman requesting psychotherapy who remarked, "While I'm alive, I want to live!"

Such patients have been referred to as the "walking wounded." Their depression is usually viewed as a legacy of the aging process. Gurland (1972) reports that subjects may complain about anxiety or verbalize self-deprecation rather than express a depressed mood. Seligman (1975) postulates personal helplessness as a manifestation of depression. Other covert manifestations include somatization, malnutrition, and alcoholism. The latter appears to be on the increase in older individuals (Zinberg, 1974).

Reactive depressions characterized by Meyer (1974) as "psychogenic reactions to acute life stress which occur *de novo* in the senium" can be well understood in terms of the "sturm und drang" of the later years. While the reactive depressions differ from "true psychoneuroses" in direct connection between the precipitating stress and psychological reaction, the individual's lifelong adaptational patterns determine the reaction in both kind and intensity.

Depressive Symptomatology

Generally, the depressed patient is, in various degrees and different combinations, sad, self-involved, and lacking in interest and vitality. Symptoms may include mild gastrointestinal involvement, complaints of constipation, dizziness, palpitations, and, in the older patient, agitation. Sleeping problems are reported, with early morning arising, which may indicate insomnia, or there can be a proneness to sleeping. While weight loss is generally noted, there are depressed persons who attempt to assuage themselves by eating. This dual dynamic is again demonstrated by the vitiation of sexual desire and activity with indications of frigidity or impotency. Conversely, there are reports of some seeking release in sexual activity which, for many older people, may be a return to self-stimulation.

    [4] Grant No. MH 25258 funded by the National Institute of Mental Health for research on comparative treatments of emotional problems in aging.

Psychodynamics

Psychodynamically, Busse and Pfeiffer (1973) report mild depressive episodes of the elderly are more concerned with loss of narcissistic supplies than with guilt and anger turned against the self as seen in depressed younger people. An exception to this formulation is suggested by Butler and Lewis (1977), who counterpose that age does not mitigate the reaction of guilt and that even if diminished self-regard contributes to the depression, the consideration that the more guilty are the more vulnerable is not negated. In this instance, Hamilton's (1942) differentiation between a reactive depression in people over 50 who report a dreary sense of futility, failure, old-age infirmities, and melancholia, which he categorized as aggressive self-hatred, may be of significance.

The number of theoretical postulations emerging from etiological considerations are representative of the heterogeneity of the depressive reactions. Endogenous and exogenous considerations continue to be explored and advanced (Mendelson, 1972), as is the psychoanalytic model as a framework for understanding the etiology of depression.

The psychodynamic etiology of the depressive neuroses, for theorists working within a psychoanalytic framework, is the pre-oedipal period where primary adaptations to loss occur (Freud, 1898; Jacobson, 1964; Mahler, 1966). In particular, the general predisposition to depression is described by Fenichel (1945) as "oral fixations which determine the reaction to narcissistic shocks" and that the "injury may create a depressive disposition, because it occurs early enough to still be met by an orally oriented ego [p. 405]."

Brenner (1973) does not negate the impact of the pregenital object relations stage where unconscious identifications with the lost object plays a definitive role in the formation of depression. However, Brenner (1974) stresses oedipal conflict as the decisive factor in depressive neuroses. To come full circle, Glatzer (1962) views oedipal conflicts as a mask and defense against unresolved pre-oedipal conflicts.

In this regard, the differences in relationship to depressions found in older adults are not paramount; a dynamic of the oedipal conflict is the sufferance of another kind of frustration and loss due to disappointment and renunciation. Thus, it may be that regardless of psychosexual-stage involvement, the experience of loss is a prominent common denominator.

The theme of loss is no stranger to the aging adult. As a consequence of cumulative losses and narcissistic insults, the older person inevitably feels helpless (Levin, 1965, 1975; Zetzel, 1965). It is this helplessness that emerges as the fulcrum in Bibring's (1953) definition that depression is "a human way of reacting to frustration and misery whenever the ego finds itself in a state of (real or imaginary) helplessness against overwhelming odds [p. 34]." The preceding characterizes the effects of the narcissistic intrapsychic and psychosocial impacts of the aging process. The reaction to loss and helplessness is determined in relation to the integrity of the older person's ego reserves and the nature of his adaptations to and resolution of loss and/or disappointments in his formative years.

As an adaptive maneuver, depression is ineffectual in its drive to force the symbolic return of lost objects. Yet, whether a depression is of long standing or one that has emerged due to the impact of aging, its adaptational aspects cannot be minimized (Engel, 1962; Klerman, 1975). It may thus serve as signal functions in assessing behavior or represent Goldfarb's (1974) "search for aid."

Treatment Suggestions

In order for older persons to sustain narcissistic onslaughts, they should be encouraged to do the work of mourning (Freud, 1917). This should be emphasized despite the concerned attempt of those around them who may try to abort this period. Many individuals can come to terms with the losses by effecting ongoing "partial mournings" that help prepare for the final separation—death. The partial mournings include coming to terms with unrealized dreams and expectations of self. Included here would be the working through of the conscious and unconscious expectation of returns from children and others for what the patient may have done for them in the past. In coming to terms with the past, the older person will be freer to handle what is, and to entertain options for himself. Antidepressants may be prescribed to relieve the more debilitating depression. The medication as a sole recourse, however, does not meet the needs of the patient for expressing himself.

SUICIDE

Not only does depression emerge in the diagnosis for the majority of old persons who commit suicide, but the rate is at its peak for men in their 80s. Among those of 65 years plus, the rate doubles that of depressed younger groups, reaching a peak at 50 years of age in women and over 70 years of age in men, whose rate at that time is quadruple that of women (Kramer, 1972; Payne, 1975).

Psycho-socio-physiological explanations have been advanced regarding the preceding phenomena. Among those that warrant consideration is the conceptualization of an unconflictual wish to die akin to Freud's "ego letting itself die," (cited by Bibring, 1953). The unconflictual states may arise from the decreased ego reserves, feelings of helplessness, and a state of exhaustion in the more fragile senescent. Farberow and Schneidman (1970) have also noted the phenomena of the wish to die as a factor in elderly suicides. Linking suicide to decreased sexual activity in aging persons, Leviton (1973) suggests that where sexuality among the aged is intense, the desire for death, epitomized by suicide, is weak. Sexuality, here, is defined broadly as a "by-product of a loving relationship with another."

Treatment Suggestions

Prevention of suicide in the older population resides in early detection of depression and an alertness to the vulnerability for suicide upon the lifting of the depression in all who had previously attempted it. With the persistence of stresses, the suicide risk may be a continuous one in a highly dependent, elderly person whose initial attempt was aborted. Kiev (1975) and Litman (1970) note the need for appropriate medication and underscore the empathetic qualities of the therapist. Further, a passive stance is of less importance; the therapeutic intervention would involve those close to the patient and, in many cases, environmental manipulation and the available social services. Thus, obtaining knowledge of the critical variable or variables is of primary concern and aid. In the psychosocial sphere, the expansion of outreach programs for older people living alone could serve as an additional deterrent, for approximately 42% of those 65 or older are in this category.

Philosophical considerations of the right to die are complicated. However, clinical reports suggest that where there have been psychosocio-medical interventions into suicidal intent, patients for the most part have responded positively, utilizing options residing in living.

SEXUALITY

The spirit of the times is such that research in sexuality among younger adults has been extended to older adults. Of the many investigations, those cited by Butler and Lewis (1976), contrary to prejudicial ideas, revealed sexual desire, capacity, and resourcefulness to be the more typical picture of the senescent. In one study (Pfeiffer & Davis,

1972), past experience was noted as a determinant of sexual activity in the later years. For women, the quality of enjoyment emerged as a predictor for sex in the later life rather than frequency of contact. Other variables included physical health, social class, educational level, and availability (for women especially) of socially acceptable partners. The latter is of particular concern for older women, since they outnumber older men. For the older woman to be with a younger man may evoke societal criticism, yet the older man in the company of a younger woman wears a positive symbolic badge. In either case, both older men and women are sexually deprived. It may be noted that the nature of sexual expression is the degree to which a neurosis is present for neurotic individuals suffer from a disturbance of their sexuality which in their unconscious has an infantile significance (Fenichel, 1945).

Psychodynamics

Psychodynamically, the stereotypical attitudes regarding sexual expression of older individuals is understandable in terms of oedipal determinants. Indeed, many older men and women are themselves recipients of the adaptational asexual oedipal label which, when younger, they attributed defensively to their elders.

In this writing, sexuality is viewed in the full psychoanalytic sense postulated by Freud (1910) that the concept of what is sexual comprises not only coitus but "all the activities of tender feeling even when the impulses become inhibited in reference to the original sexual aim or have exchanged this aim for another which is no longer sexual [p. 222]."

Berezin (1972) emphasized this tenet by indicating that many of the studies on sex in older persons did not refer to the expression of tender feelings and object relationships that comprise the complete psycho-sexual picture. Validation of this is supported by more recent writings indicating that sex for older persons needs to be redefined as more than coitus per se (Starr & Weiner, in preparation). A regressive adaptation to restriction of sexual expression resides in Hamilton's (1942) "compensatory regression" or Schur's (1955) "regressive somatization" by self-stimulation, including masturbation and preoccupation with bodily sensations. The former, Kahn (1971) observes, may arise in treatment as masturbatory guilt.

Treatment Suggestions

Therapy for unsatisfactory sexuality, as indicated, is not of an isolated nature but is viewed in terms of the patient's total adaptational milieu. Specifically, counseling for the older patients will provide aid for the working through of long-standing conflicts. In addition, educational parameters are introduced; for instance, a male patient prescribed medication should be alerted to the possibility of impotence as a side effect. Similarly, a female patient should be informed of the age-related possible thinning of the vaginal walls and decrease in lubrication that may be ameliorated by prescribed lubricants. In addition to pharmacological side effects and physiological changes, psychodynamic components, as noted, press for relief.

> A 65-year-old woman announced to her group members that she was concerned about her lack of sexual feeling for her friend. She had been responsive with other men and could not understand why she was no longer so. The insight emerged that her feelings were repressed due to unresolved anger. Her friend reminded her of her father who left her in Poland upon his emigration to America. Her anger was compounded by the fact that her mother kept talking against him. "She didn't allow me to love him." Amidst anger and tears, she remembered her mother being there for her. As therapy progressed, this woman became more relaxed and increasingly able to give of herself and to receive love.

As Leviton (1973) noted, sexual expression in its full sense may be a deterrent against suicide. In the later years, it may thus be life-extending.

> This factor is well illustrated by the case of a 76-year-old woman who entered the hospital in a depressed state for an exploratory work-up. After a few days of painful procedures, the nursing staff questioned how could she possibly be so much happier. She replied, "Until a few days ago, no one touched me in years."

HYPOCHONDRIASIS

Hypochondriasis and depression are among the outstanding clinical entities noted in older adults. Diagnostically, each may be a component of the other. Thus, hypochondriasis, depression, and anxiety are noted for their ubiquity in other clinical states such as anxiety reactions, obsessional neurosis, various psychoses, and an aspect of organic brain syndrome.

Differentiation is noted (Nunberg, 1955) between hysterical hypochondriasis, where "objects in the external world retain objects of the libido," and in hypochondria where the subject's own body or parts become, more or less, cathected, leading to an adaptation that is noted in the incipient schizophrenic reaction. Hypochondriasis can also be a nonpathological reaction to traumatic episodes encountered in the normal process of aging.

Symptomatology

The hypochondriac is concerned with self-observation and is preoccupied with physical functions and bodily processes in regard to the status of his physical health. The patient is prone to iatrogenic ailments, in which he seizes upon minor pain, harmless symptoms, or "lesions" visible only to him as signs of serious disease or disorder.

The complaint patterns are such that geriatricians are caught between the Scylla of underdiagnosis or the Charybdis of overdiagnosis. In this instance, Butler and Lewis (1977) cite Meyersberg's investigation of hypochondriasis in which he describes the alienation of the geriatrician in the face of treatment defeat. This sense of defeat may be attributed to patients expressing hypochondriacal complaints and the ensuing difficulties of dealing with patients who cloak the therapist with omnipotence while supporting a contention that no one cares.

Patients suffering in this manner represented over one-half of those over 60 in Busse's study (1965). The majority were women whose symptoms, in part, may have represented a displacement of complaints arising from a sufficient lack of return from children and close ones.

It has been suggested that many women in the 40–70 age range regress to "miserable hypochondriasis" upon the reemergence of previously renounced ambitions with ensuing reduction of family dependency needs (Zetzel, 1965). This, again, may be viewed as a displacement phenomenon.

According to Slater and Roth (1969), more men may be involved in the hypochondriacal reaction than the data reveal. This may be due to a tendency to overlook the reaction in those men who are forced to limit their physical fitness regimen due to the exigencies of aging. The symptoms noted in both older men and women may well represent unfulfilled sexuality.

In a study assessing body image in a geriatric population, findings indicated that a person's bodily worries and discomforts may not be related to age per se, but may, rather, reflect special life circumstances (Plutchik, Weiner, & Conte, 1971). The study, which utilized measures testing various geriatric populations as well as younger ones, revealed that the population scoring highest on measures of bodily worries and discomforts were those receiving little attention by others and were those not actively involved with others.

Psychodynamics

The manner in which an aging person copes with changing life circumstances is largely dependent on his premorbid personality. Some meet the changes as they have lived in the world, exercising options; others maintain object cathexis by life review and savoring the worn suitcase filled with loving memoirs; still others narcissistically withdraw along a continuum to preoccupation and self-absorption in bodily concerns.

Hypochondriasis in older persons is not without its adaptive purposes:

1. It may represent a displacement of anxiety from a more threatening psychic concern, such as a retreat from fear of society's criticism regarding reduced proficiency, loss of status, and curtailed activities to the acceptable "sick role," and thereby be a bid for the sympathy, forgiveness and help of others.
2. The physical symptoms may gratify guilt feelings by serving as an atonement for unacceptable hostile feelings against close ones (Busse, 1977; Fenichel, 1945).
3. The reaction may also serve as a defense against further regression to schizophrenia.
4. It may exemplify "regressive autoeroticism" where narcissistic pleasure is derived from caring for the body. This is referred to by Verwoerdt (1976) as the secondary gain of hypochondriasis.

Treatment Suggestions

The nonpathological–pathological hypochondriasis continuum for older persons is such as to warrant sensitivity of diagnosis. In view of the adaptational aspect of hypochondriasis as a displacement, atonement, or means of fending off increased emotional debilitation, confronting the patient with his actual state of health would, in the majority of cases, spell the death knell of the intervention and serve to strengthen the feeling, "no one cares or understands" (Blum, 1977b).

The establishment of a patient–therapist working alliance is the cornerstone for both reestablishing and strengthening tenuous object relations. While the therapist may feel drowned in the flood of complaints, the patient's continuous testing, and the tenacity of the defensive adaptation, the pay-off resides in the possibility of the opening of horizons to outside interests. This is accomplished by the uncritical acceptance of the patient and the therapist's sensitive responsiveness to his expressed suffering.

OBSESSIVE–COMPULSIVE REACTIONS

The Obsessive–Compulsive reactions share an attention-absorption defense with the hypochrondriacal reaction. Laughlin (1967) writes of Sullivan's observation that in the obsessional state the person is so frightfully busy doing that he does not have time to suffer some of the greatest pains of life. Among the true obsessives are those who find free time so disconcerting that with retirement their defense structure is severely strained. They develop what has euphemistically been called the "Sunday neurosis."

Those persons whose obsessive–compulsive traits are less rigid are aided in their adaptation in later years by profiting from being steady and orderly.

> A case in point is that of an 84-year-old woman of stable ego integrity who complained of her forgetfulness. However, she bounced back saying, "You know, dear, I'm such a creature of habit that even though I've forgotten where I put something, I know I'll find it in its usual place."

Meyer (1974) observed a diminishing of the obsessive–compulsive neurosis with age. The authors believe this observation could represent the dividends of the zeitgeist supporting "relaxing of the guards" and a diminution of the strength of impulses which, in later years, may mitigate stern repression. This explanation is supported by Müller (in Ciompi, 1969) as the "beneficial influence of old age on obsessional illness." He writes of cultural factors relaxing the ego ideal, such as increased freedom from responsibilities and duties, permission to do things that they would not have considered in the past and, in part, a reduction of social demands.

Symptomatology

Obsessive–compulsive symptoms comprise grossly exaggerated aspects of "normal" behavior, including precise repetition, inflexible uniformity, rigid taboo and harsh self-punishment, and the ageless reaction formations of exaggerated caution, phobic-like reactions to specific people or situations, renunciations, self-doubts and expiations of a compulsive nature (Cameron, 1963; Nunberg, 1955). In addition, the obsessive is concerned with guilt in response to being good or bad.

Rigidity of manner is expressed by military posture, social awkwardness, and persistence in a course of action that has lost its raison d'être. The ensuing intellectual rigidity, as noted by Shapiro (1965), may simulate the concreteness in organic brain damage often observed in elderly patients. However, the obsessive–compulsive is not handicapped as is the person with cerebral loss. He is not stimulus-bound nor is he unable to use free will in shifting attention, although his defenses are such that his attention, while sharp, is limited in freedom of action and scope. In addition, his persistence in accomplishing a goal often leads to nuances and fringe joys going unnoticed.

Psychodynamics

The psychodynamics of the obsessive–compulsive adaptation resides in repression being inadequate to contain anxiety generated by the genital libido position. The inadequacy of the repression leads to a retreat from the genital impulses to regression or to fixations at the anal-sadistic state of development. Defense mechanisms to block libidinal strivings are brought to the fore. While instinctual danger is, in part, thwarted, the flight becomes one of renunciation of real gratification and adaptation (Nunberg, 1955). Therefore, rather than being free, the obsessive is driven. High priority is placed on the "shoulds" and "oughts" in life to ensure warding off anxiety and remaining distant from his emotional life.

As in all adaptations, the continuum ranges from the "normal" to the pathological. To prevent disequilibrium, the obsessive utilizes the following defenses singly or with others in combination: displacement, substitution, isolation, projection, reaction formation, rationalization, repression, denial, symbolization, and undoing. The preceding are in the service of reaching solutions or compromises to allay anxiety and restore ego equilibrium. Specifically, the adaptive aspects of repression for older individuals as an extension of Kris' concept of "regression in the service of the ego" is addressed by Zinberg and Kaufman (1963). As noted previously, the adaptive aspect rests upon the stability that is achieved.

This adaptation may often prove to be the "bane of existence" to those around them. In particular, unknown to them, hostile or caustic remarks may often elude the defense fortress leaving the older obsessive person bewildered by the outburst reaction of others. Nevertheless, the adaptation prevents further ego debilitation and in the case of the older adult may hinder regression to "paraphrenia" or a psychosis (Slater & Roth, 1969).

Isolation, compartmentalization, and denial are used adaptively in regard to sustained losses. Zetzel (1955) cautions not to regard the elder person as being without feeling or remorse. In actuality, the defenses aid him to cope by protective indifference.

Nonpathological aspects of the obsessive–compulsive adaptation can be in the service of the older person's ego in today's world by helping to make order out of what could well appear to be chaos. Thus, a sense of security is maintained at an important time of life.

Treatment Suggestions

The focus of treatment, as always, is dependent upon the patient's ego development and resources. To remove a defense of an obsessive–compulsive may undermine achieved homeostasis. Thus, awareness need not mandate interpretation. Treatment may extend from the analytic to supportive, designed to soften the harshness with which the patient treats himself. Hopefully, this will pave the way for increased flexibility. Once again, the working alliance establishes that trust and understanding become the groundwork for growth and change.

HYSTERIA

Hysteria has the laudatory position of being the first neurosis to be studied by Freud (1898). Its specific defense mechanism is repression that is more pervasive than in the other neuroses. Hysteria and obsessive neurosis are often compared, for they share a common bond in defending against libidinal strivings. However, there are many differences. The obsessive, by regressing as well as repressing, adds the stringent defenses of the pregenital, anal stage to his structure. As a result, Nunberg (1955) notes the obsessive is always on the defense, with renewed symptomatology, whereas the hysteric's symptoms are relatively specific and constant.

Symptomatology

Two groupings are subsumed under hysteria. There is the classical conversion reaction that converts the psychic conflict into a symbolic physical symptom akin to body language. In this case, related symptoms such as hysterical blindness, hysterical parasthesia, or globus hystericus do not involve an organic basis. When they do occur, despite the discomfort, the hysteric's attitude is one of *la belle indifférence*. Conversely, the second group, the dissociative reaction, resembles an organic brain syndrome. Here, increasing anxiety may lead to states of identity confusion such as amnesia, fugues, and sleepwalking. In either reaction, the symptoms generally represent substitutes for a repressed affect or impulse.

Hysterics are described as being suggestible, emotionally labile, mimicking, seductive, distractible, naive, and shallow in affect. In contrast to the obsessive, the hysteric usually makes friends with ease and is high spirited, full of life, and responsive. While rapid shifts may occur, the hysteric's general good humor ensures a ready welcome not extended to the obsessive.

> The picture is well drawn by a 73-year-old hysteric who said, "I've always loved everything glossy."

Psychodynamics

Aging usually comes as a shock to hysterics, whose neurosis becomes less effective. With age, the hysteric's eroticized approach is no longer seductive, and it becomes increasingly difficult to replace an audience. Consequently, the older hysteric is confronted with progressive object loss and ineffectual behavior. As a result, Ciompi (1969) proposes that the elevated defensive struggle of the older hysteric may capitulate to regressive reactions, in particular, depression, hypochondriasis, or exaggeration of illnesses.

Adaptively, the regression may help the hysteric to allay anxiety and derive secondary gains from the extra attention and help of others. This unconscious attempt is to replace objects and gratify dependency needs. The aforementioned is supported by Laughlin's (1967) observations that what appears to be a sexual need in the hysteric is often a cover for other needs and particularly by Glatzer's (1962) conclusion that early pregenital issues underlie the conflicts of the oedipal stage for the most part.

Treatment

The treatment of choice for the older hysteric, as for the younger one, depends upon the dynamics of the presenting patient. The focus, through objective, empathic understanding, is to help the patient to decrease "cognitive shifting" (Horowitz, 1976) as a primary means of avoiding anxiety and to mitigate vulnerability by replacing the hysteric's mask with increased self-esteem.

DIFFERENTIAL DIAGNOSIS

Precision of differential diagnosis is most essential. Depressive symptomatology may mask an organic brain syndrome or a physical illness or be a concomitant of both. Similarly, symptoms of apathy, mental confusion, and irritability may elicit a diagnosis of organic brain syndrome (OBS), but which, in fact, may prove to be a depressive reaction. This may sometimes be highly situational in nature and caused by an acute decrease of environmental stimulation or sensory input (Weiner, Brok, & Snadowsky, 1978). Further, as noted previously, depressive features may indeed be reflective of a medication reaction.

The preceding emphasizes the need to avoid an exclusive reliance on symptoms for diagnosis. Rather, there should be an encouragement of interdisciplinary involvement such that diagnosis would include a description of the genetic and dynamic aspects of a patient's conflict. A diagnosis, rather than being a static concept, reflects an ongoing process of change. It is, after all, a positive change in diagnosis that suggests that there has been successful therapeutic intervention, at any age.

TREATMENT OVERVIEW

Although there has been an increased awareness of the psychological problems of the aging process, there has been a reluctance of people in their 60s and beyond to seek psychotherapy. This reluctance may be attributed to the fact that many older persons are less knowledgeable about psychological interventions; they have not as yet sought aid as readily as younger persons due to the stigma perceived by them and their cohort group in obtaining such help.

Other deterrents may include physical handicaps, difficulties in obtaining transportation, and monetary problems. Coupled with the present hesitancy of older adults to obtain therapeutic help is a concomitant hesitation of therapists to accept aging patients. While it is not within the province of this chapter to delve into this issue, two facets may be noted. The first may reflect a "phobic" attitude of some therapists who have not come to terms with their own aging and finiteness of being. The second may be due to the fact that therapy with older persons is sometimes demeaned by the erroneous assumption that such treatment requires less training. Rationale for this may originate in an ageist assumption that unconscious conflicts are to be less explored. A third facet may be the knowledge that there is less left to life to warrant any kind of extended therapeutic process; the therapist may feel, "why bother if . . ."

If the therapist treating younger persons needs to listen with the well-known "third ear," this is more than equally true for one treating the older person. In assessing the intrapsychic strengths of the individual and his environmental support system, the therapist works at two levels. His objective is to help establish a harmony between these inner and outer realities. Only the well-trained person can listen to the harmony and dissonance in this orchestration of life. Hence, in wanting more than survival, the older neurotic is a likely candidate for therapeutic intervention. The positive view of treatment and prognosis has been well documented (Blum & Tross, 1979; Grotjahn, 1955; King, 1974; Krasner, 1977; Linden, 1957; Meerloo, 1955).

The treatment of choice for neurosis in the older adult as for the younger ones depends on a holistic evaluation of the patient's intrapsychic strengths and external impingements upon these strengths. Therefore, the treatment range is a broad one. It may be analysis, analytically oriented psychotherapy, supportive psychotherapy or counseling on an individual or group basis. As noted, older people who apply for treatment are interested in increased psychic freedom and the working through of conflictual encumbrances. Resistances, which are evident, are part and parcel of this working through process. As early as 1898, Freud suggested that there are times when the "customary methods are to be set aside [p. 245]." In particular with older patients, parameters of eliciting interdisciplinary involvement may be called upon. Knowledge of intrapersonal and interpersonal issues now facing the older adult are crucial to treatment, as is respect for each person's individual pattern of adaptation and autonomy.

Observing the therapeutic process at work undermines the shibboleth that it is unsatisfying to treat patients who are in their later years. It is precisely this aspect of chronology that encourages the older adults to undertake the working-through process of enduring phenomenological problems such as grief, helplessness, feelings of abandonment, and the final separation—death. Essentially, this process is made possible by the continuity of mental processes as reflected in therapeutic sessions. Psychodynamically, in working through, the older patient, like all patients, is engaged in the ongoing task of separation–individuation and reinforcement of object constancy.

> A 66-year-old woman who had been somewhat resistant to group questioned a member in surprise—"Lydia, don't you think about us at all during the week? When I have a problem I think about what you all have said here and it helps me to do something about it."

The treatment process, as with any patient, reflects the aging person's adaptational style and, as such, is congruent with his needs.

Thus, knowledge of the patient's neurosis continuum will determine the patient's capacity for self-examination, tolerance of delay, and willingness to seek and/or make changes. Similarly, this knowledge, in conjunction with the status of external factors, will determine therapeutic goals and expectations. Therefore, while an older neurotic may be helped, as may one of any age, he may or may not be a perspective analytic or psychoanalytic-oriented psychotherapy candidate. This aspect will be determined not primarily by age, per se, but, as has been the focus of this writing, by the unique characteristics of the aging individual. It is to this uniqueness that the therapist attends.

As a result, the therapist who frees himself of judgments and prejudices can realize that the process of change and the working for a resolution of conflicts is not agebound. He may then recognize the continuity of mental processes, use himself creatively, and approach all patients, regardless of age, with hope (Blum & Tallmer, 1977).

IMPLICATIONS FOR THE FUTURE

In terms of predictions for the future, the societal trends suggest that the potential patient is changing. The authors' experience indicates that the older adult who now seeks psychotherapy in private and/or clinical settings is most often diagnosed as neurotic. Conversely, it is generally reported by most therapists that the typical young patient seen privately and/or in clinic settings is assigned a diagnosis such as borderline or narcissistic personality. Thus, the contemporary older patient, more integrated, manifests intrapsychic maturity, including a superego structure that encourages the person to create clear guidelines for behavior with delineated "do's and don'ts." This is often in contrast to the younger person's superego, considered to be less able to offer direction, or less clearly delineated.

Were the contemporary young person to seek psychotherapy in his later years, it seems likely that core problems would be ones of internal self-regulation and self-direction. It is also likely that the future older patient raised in a more permissive milieu will be freer to demand more for himself.

Were treatment to be based on the preceding, it would do the following: focus on the development of inner controls; offer a strong sense of direction; foster an identity; help one to choose a feasible direction; and help create a climate of explorations for that which is still possible and open as against finite and closed.

SUMMARY

This chapter has been addressed to neuroses in the later years. The major tenet is a belief in the continuity of mental processes. Neuroses were suggested as emerging at any time in the life span when stresses are such as to revive preexisting problems of adaptation. Aging is thus perceived as a stress phenomenon with individual, lifelong adaptive patterns determining reactions.

Since older persons may reveal a range of reactions to aging phenomena, evaluation is to be determined by interdisciplinary measures. While the single diagnosis has been considered to be as specious as the concept of "the aged," for classification purposes, neuroses are specifically delineated with attention to the implications of medication as a variable in emotional and physiological reactions. Differential diagnoses, psychodynamic understanding, the symptomatology of neuroses, as well as the defenses utilized by older persons are emphasized. Treatment suggestions are noted, attention being given to the particular nature of the neurosis in question and the importance of a holistic evaluation of a patient is stressed.

The vicissitudes of various physiological, social, and economic components upon the older person may, at times, call for treatment parameters to include family, family surrogates, and/or social services.

It is postulated that the reluctance of many older persons to seek psychotherapy may be based upon a lack of knowledge or the stigma involved in obtaining psychological help. Further factors related to health, economics, and transportation are realities of concern.

The reluctance of therapists to treat the older person is also noted. This reluctance may be rooted in the ageist attitudes in our society. Thus, it is concluded that coming to terms with one's finiteness, ageism, and specific phenomenological problems is most essential to the acceptance of the aging person as a psychotherapy candidate.

Implications for the future suggest that the older person of 20 years hence may present a different diagnostic picture. Positive treatment considerations stress that one meets the needs of the individual. The essential consideration continues to be the therapist's belief that the process of change and the working toward resolution of conflicts is not agebound.

REFERENCES

Abraham, K. The applicability of psychoanalytic treatment to patients at an advanced age (1919). In *Selected Papers of Karl Abraham*. London: Hogarth Press, 1968.

Bender, M. B., Fink, M., & Green, M. Patterns in perception in simultaneous tests of the face and hand. *Archives of Neurology and Psychiatry*, 1951, *66*, 355–362.

Berezin, M. Introduction. In M. Berezin & S. H. Cath (Eds.), *Geriatric psychiatry: Grief, loss, and emotional disorder in the aging process*. New York: International Universities Press, 1965.

Berezin, M. Psychodynamic considerations of aging and the aged: An overview. *American Journal of Psychiatry*, June 1972, *128*(12), 1483–1491.

Bergmann, K. Neurosis and personality disorder in old age. In A. D. Isaacs & F. Post (Eds.), *Studies in geriatric psychiatry*. New York: Wiley, 1978. Pp. 41–77.

Bergmann, M. S., & Hartman, F. *The evolution of psychoanalytic technique*. New York: Basic Books, 1976.

Berkman, P. L. Cumulative deprivation and mental illness. In M. F. Lowenthal & P. L. Berkman, *Aging and mental disorder in San Francisco*. San Francisco: Jossey-Bass, 1967.

Bibring, E. The mechanism of depression. In P. Greenacre (Ed.), *Affective disorders*. New York: International Universities Press, 1953.

Blanck, G., & Blanck, R. *Ego psychology: Theory and practice*. New York: Columbia University Press, 1974.

Blum, J. E. Clinical gerontology. In W. D. Gentry (Ed.), *Geropsychology: A model of training and clinical services*. Cambridge, Massachusetts: Ballinger, 1977. (a)

Blum, J. E. Aging: Non-organic disorders. In B. B. Wolman (Ed.), *International Encyclopedia of neurology, psychiatry, psychoanalysis and psychology. Section VIII: Maturity and Aging*. Boston: Aesculapius Publishers, 1977. (b)

Blum, J. E., & Tallmer, M. The therapist vis-à-vis the older patient. *Psychotherapy: Theory, research and practice*, *14*(4), Winter 1977.

Blum, J. E., & Tross, S. Psychotherapy with the elderly: A holistic approach. In C. Eisdorfer (Ed.), *Annual review of geriatrics and gerontology*. New York: Springer, 1979.

Brenner, C. *An elementary textbook of psychoanalysis*. New York: International Universities Press, 1973.

Brenner, C. The concept and phenomenology of depression with special reference to the aged. *Journal of Geriatric Psychiatry*, 1974, *10*(1), 6–20.

Brenner, C. *Psychoanalytic technique and psychic conflict*. New York: International Universities Press, 1976.

Busse, E. W. Research on aging: Some methods and findings. In M. Berezin & S. H. Cath (Eds.), *Geriatric psychiatry: Grief, loss, and emotional disorders in the aging process*. New York: International Universities Press, 1965.

Busse, E. W., & Pfeiffer, E. (Eds.). *Mental illness in later life*. Washington, D. C.: American Psychiatric Association, 1973.

Busse, E. W., & Pfeiffer, E. *Behavior and adaptation in later life*. Boston: Little, Brown, 1977.

Butler, R. N. Ageism: Another form of bigotry. *Gerontology*, 1969, *9*, 243–246.

Butler, R. N., & Lewis, M. *Aging and mental health*. St. Louis, Missouri: C. V. Mosby, 1977.

Butler, R. N., & Lewis, M. *Sex after sixty: A guide for men and women for their later years*. New York: Harper & Row, 1976.

Cameron, N. *Personality development and psychopathology: A dynamic approach*. Boston: Houghton Mifflin, 1963.

Cath, S. H. Some dynamics of middle and later years: A study in depletion and restitution. In M. Berezin & S. H. Cath (Eds.), *Geriatric psychiatry: Grief, loss, and emotional disorder in the aging process.* New York: International Universities Press, 1965.

Ciompi, L. C. Follow-up studies on evolution of former neurotic and depressive states in old age. *Geriatric Psychiatry*, 1969, *3*, 90.

Derogatis, L. R. The Hopkins symptom checklist (HSCL): A manual of primary symptom dimensions. In B. Pichot (Ed.), *Psychological measurement: Modern problems in pharmacopsychiatry*, 1973.

DiMascio, A., & Goldberg, H. L. *Emotional disorders: An outline guide to diagnosis and pharmacological treatment.* Oradell, New Jersey: Medical Economics Co., 1976.

Engel, G. *Psychological development in health and disease.* Philadelphia: W. B. Saunders, 1962.

Farberow, N. L., & Schneidman, E. S. Suicide and age. In E. S. Schneidman, N. L. Farberow & R. E. Litman (Eds.), *The psychology of suicide.* New York: Science House, 1970. Pp. 165–174.

Fenichel, O. *The psychoanalytic theory of neurosis.* New York: Norton, 1945.

Freud, S. *Heredity and the aetiology of the neuroses* (1896). Standard Edition (Vol. 3). London: Hogarth Press, 1962. Pp. 141–156.

Freud, S. Sexuality in the aetiology of neuroses (1898). In *Collected Papers* (Vol. I). London: Hogarth Press, 1950.

Freud, S. *Wild psychoanalysis* (1910). Standard Edition (Vol. 11). London: Hogarth Press, 1957. Pp. 219–227.

Freud, S. *Mourning and melancholia* (1917). Standard Edition (Vol. 14). London: Hogarth Press, 1957. Pp. 239–258.

Freud, S. *Beyond the pleasure principle* (1920). Standard Edition (Vol. 18). London: Hogarth Press, 1959. Pp. 7–64.

Freud, S. *Inhibitions, symptoms and anxiety* (1926). Standard Edition (Vol. 20). London: Hogarth Press, 1959. Pp. 75–172.

Glatzer, H. T. Handling narcissistic problems in group psychotherapy. *International Journal of Group Psychotherapy*, October 1962, *12*(4), 448–455.

Goldfarb, A. I. Minor maladjustment of the aged. In S. Arieti (Ed.), *American handbook of psychiatry.* New York: Basic Books, 1974.

Goldfarb, A. I. Depression in the old and aged. In F. F. Flach & S. C. Draghi (Eds.), *The nature and treatment of depression.* New York: Wiley, 1975.

Graham, F. K., & Kendall, B. S. Memory for designs test. *Perceptual and Motor Skills*, Mono. Suppl., 1960, *7*(2), 147–188.

Grotjahn, M. Analytic psychotherapy with the elderly. *Psychoanalytic Review*, 1955, *42*, 419–427.

Gurland, B. J. *Age differentiation in depression: Diagnostic and descriptive aspects.* Paper presented at meeting of the Gerontological Society, Puerto Rico, December 1972.

Gutheil, E. A. Psychoanalysis and brief psychotherapy. *Journal of Criminal Psychopathology*, October 1944, *6*(2), 207–230.

Hamilton, G. V. Changes in personality and psychosexual phenomena with age. In E. V. Cawdry (Ed.), *Problems of aging* (2nd ed.). Baltimore, Maryland: Williams & Wilkins, 1942.

Hiatt, H. Dynamic psychotherapy of the aged. In J. H. Masserman (Ed.), *Handbook of psychiatric therapies.* New York: Science House, 1966.

Horowitz, M. J. *Stress response syndromes.* New York: Jason Aronson, 1976. Pp. 141–185.

Jacobson, E. *The self and the object world.* New York: International Universities Press, 1964.

Jarvik, L. F., Eisdorfer, C., & Blum, J. E. *Intellectual functioning in adults.* New York: Springer, 1972.

Kahn, R. L. Sex and senility: The dilemma of the cute little old lady and the dirty old man. *The Academy,* 1971, *15,* 13–15.

Kahn, R. L., Goldfarb, A. I., Pollack, M., & Peck, A. Brief objective measures for determination of mental status in the aged. *American Journal of Psychiatry,* 1960, *117,* 326–328.

Kalish, R. A. *Late adulthood: Perspective in human development.* Belmont, California: Wadsworth Publishing Co., 1975.

Kernberg, O. *Borderline conditions and pathological narcissism.* New York: Jason Aronson, 1975.

Kiev, A. Psychotherapeutic strategies in the management of depressed and suicidal patients. *American Journal of Psychotherapy,* 1975, *29*(3), 345–354.

King, P. H. M. Notes on the psychoanalysis of older patients: Reappraisal of the potentialities for change during the second half of life. *Journal of Analytical Psychology,* 1974, *19*(1), 22–37.

Klerman, G. L. Overview of depression. In A. M. Friedman, H. O. Kaplan, & B. J. Sadock (Eds.), *Comprehensive textbook of psychiatry.* Baltimore, Maryland: Williams & Wilkins, 1975.

Kramer, M., Pollack, E. S., Rechik, R. W., & Locke, B. Z. *Mental disorders: Suicide.* Cambridge, Massachusetts: Harvard Univ. Press, 1972.

Krasner, J. Treatment of the elder person. In B. Fabrikant, J. Barron, & J. Krasner (Eds.), *To enjoy is to live.* Chicago: Nelson Hall, 1977.

Laughlin, H. P. *The neuroses.* Washington, D.C.: Butterworths, 1967.

Levin, S. Discussion: Grief and depression. *Journal of Geriatric Psychiatry,* 1974, *7*(1).

Levin, S. Depression in the aged. In M. A. Berezin & S. H. Cath (Eds.), *Geriatric psychiatry: Grief, loss and emotional disorders in the aging process.* New York: International Universities Press, 1965. Pp. 203–247.

Leviton, D. The significance of sexuality as a deterrent to suicide among the aged. *Omega,* Summer 1973, *4*(2), 163–173.

Linden, M. E. *The promise of therapy in the emotional problems of aging.* Paper presented at Fourth Congress of International Association of Gerontology, Merano, Italy, July 1957.

Litman, R. E. Treatment of the potentially suicidal patient. In E. S. Schneidman, N. L. Farberow, & R. E. Litman (Eds.), *The psychology of suicide.* New York: Science House, 1970. Pp. 405–413.

Mahler, M. S. Notes on the development of basic moods: The depressive affect in psychoanalysis. In R. M. Loewenstein, L. M. Newman, M. Schur, & A. J. Solnit (Eds.), *Psychoanalysis: A general psychology.* New York: International Universities Press, 1966.

Meerloo, J. A. M. Transference and resistance in geriatric psychotherapy. *Psychoanalytic Review,* 1955, *42,* 72–82.

Mendelson, M. *Psychoanalytic concepts of depression.* New York: Spectrum Publications, 1972.

Meyer, J. E. Psychoneuroses and neurotic reactions in old age. *Journal of the American Geriatrics Society,* 1974, *22*(6), 254–257.

Neugarten, B. L. *Middle age and aging.* Chicago: Univ. of Chicago Press, 1968.

Nunberg, H. *Principles of psychoanalysis.* New York: International Universities Press, 1955.

Payne, E. C. Depression and suicide. In J. G. Howells (Ed.), *Modern perspectives in the psychiatry of old age.* New York: Brunner/Mazel, 1975.

Peck, R. Psychological developments in the second half of life. In R. Anderson (Ed.), *Psychological aspects of aging*. Washington, D. C.: American Psychological Association, 1956.

Pfeiffer, E., & Davis, G. C. Determinants of sexual behavior in middle and old age. *Journal of the American Geriatrics Society*, 1972, *20*(4), 151–158.

Plutchik, R., Weiner, M. B., & Conte, H. Studies of body image. I: Body worries and body discomforts. *Journal of Gerontology*, 1971, *26*(3), 334–350.

Schur, M. Comments on the metapsychology of somatization. *Psychoanalytic study of the child* (Vol. 10). New York: International Universities Press, 1955. Pp. 119–164.

Seligman, M. E. P. *Helplessness—on depression, development and death*. San Francisco: W. H. Freeman, 1975.

Shanas, E., Townsend, P., Wedderburn, D., Henning, F., Milhoy, P., & Stehouwer, J. *Old people in three industrial societies*. New York: Atherton, 1968. Pp. 258–287.

Shapiro, D. *Neurotic styles*. New York: Basic Books, 1965.

Simon, A., & Cohan, R. The acute brain syndrome in geriatric patients. In W. M. Mendel & L. J. Epstein (Eds.), *Acute psychotic reaction: Psychiatric research report No. 16*. Washington, D.C.: American Psychiatric Association, 1963.

Slater, E., & Roth, M. *Clinical psychiatry*. Baltimore, Maryland: Williams & Wilkins, 1969.

Spitzer, R. L. *Diagnostic and Statistical Manual of Mental Disorders III Draft*. Washington, D. C.: American Psychiatric Association, April 1977.

Starr, B., & Weiner, M. B. *Sex forever: A survey of sexuality in older persons*. London: Paddington Press, in preparation.

Stekel, W. *Technique of analytic psychotherapy*. New York: Norton, 1940.

Verwoerdt, A. *Clinical geropsychiatry*. Baltimore, Maryland: Williams & Wilkins, 1976.

Waelder, R. *Basic theory of psychoanalysis*. New York: International Universities Press, 1960.

Weiner, M. B., Brok, A. J., & Snadowsky, A. M. *Working with the aged*. New York: Prentice-Hall, 1978. P. 58.

Zetzel, E. R. Dynamics of the metapsychology of the aging process. In M. Berezin & S. H. Cath (Eds.), *Geriatric psychiatry: Grief, loss, and emotional disorder in the aging process*. New York: International Universities Press, 1965.

Zinberg, N. E., & Kaufman, I. Introduction. In N. E. Zinberg & I. Kaufman (Eds.), *Normal psychology of the aging process*. New York: International Universities Press, 1963. Pp. 17–71.

Zinberg, S. The elderly alcoholic. *The Gerontologist*, 1974, *14*, 221–224.

Chapter 9

THE MENTALLY RETARDED
IN LATER LIFE[1]

Alexander J. Tymchuk

There has been an increasing awareness of the special needs of various groups within society including the mentally retarded and the aged. Both of these groups have been seen as distinct groups when, in fact, such is not always the case. Efforts in response to needs of the aged or the retarded have been slow in coming and minimal; efforts on behalf of the aged mentally retarded have been almost nonexistent.

There are historical reasons for minimal efforts on behalf of the older retarded person and on behalf of any retarded person, but an understanding of complexities in the area of mental retardation is needed to grasp fully the special concerns of the older retarded person.

THE NATURE OF MENTAL RETARDATION

Historically, the mentally retarded individual has been seen as one who has significantly impaired intellect. At present, as a result of the recognition of the fact that many people with lowered intelligence, as measured by intelligence tests, can and do function adaptively within society, the definition of mental retardation has changed. Currently, mental retardation refers to significantly lowered intellect coupled with poor social adaptation that are present during the developmental period (Grossman, 1973). This definition excludes those people who develop disorders later in life that impair their intellectual and social function-

[1] The author's work is supported in part by Maternal and Child Health Grant No. 927.

197

ing. For the aged, those with psychotic, acute, or chronic brain or personality disorders would not be considered mentally retarded.

Mental retardation can be characterized as being on a continuum of severity ranging from profound through severe and moderate to mild. This continuum from profound to mild, however, uses only intelligence test scores and begins two standard deviations below the mean. This continuum does not incorporate deficits in social adaptation, although generally at the more severe levels there is a clear relationship between lowered intelligence and impairment in social functioning.

The causes of mental retardation are varied but fall into two large etiological groups, organic and nonorganic. Organic etiologies include those related to chromosomal, biochemical, neurological, viral, and other identifiable physiological reasons for the retardation. Generally, those individuals with more severe impairment have an organic basis for their retardation, whereas those who are included in the mild range of retardation do not have any identifiable physiological reason for their retardation. Rather, the assumption has been made, and corroborated to a great extent, that the concomitants of poverty, including inadequate nutrition and poor living conditions, lack of developmental stimulation and cultural differences, constitute the nonorganic bases for retardation. The nonorganic type of mental retardation has sometimes been termed sociocultural retardation. There has been a great deal of discussion related to the use of the term sociocultural retardation particularly regarding whether or not those who are considered socioculturally retarded should be considered retarded at all or whether these people are really at the lower end of the intellectual continuum. In this view only those with an identifiable organic disorder would be considered to be retarded. Even among the socioculturally retarded, however, there may be minor physiological problems caused by prematurity, lead poisoning, and malnutrition, each of which is related to poverty.

The prevalence of mental retardation is usually taken to be 3% of the population; however, this figure is statistically based and when determined by epidemiological surveys, the figures are somewhat lower, ranging from 1.5% to 2.5%. In the United States, the incidence of about 5 million mentally retarded people is large, with approximately 25% having an organic basis for the retardation and 75% a nonorganic basis.

Historical Emphasis upon the Child

Mental retardation affects a considerable portion of the population within the United States, but before 1960, the problem had attracted only limited attention. President Kennedy appointed the President's Committee on Mental Retardation and the members' report in 1962, which included recommendations that research and clinical training centers be set up, provided the impetus for more extensive efforts in the study of mental retardation. As a result of this initial report and of the continued support by the federal government and later by state governments, clinical and educational services for the mentally retarded as well as research on etiology, treatment, prevention, and other areas were developed and continued.

Most of the early efforts, however, both in the clinical–educational and in the research areas, focused upon the younger retarded person, particularly the school and preschool-age child. The genesis of this focus can only be guessed at, but it probably derives from the emphasis upon prevention and working with the younger person as well as deriving from the fact that more mildly retarded people are identified during school years. During the school years there is an emphasis upon the development of cognitive and academic abilities rather than upon the development of social–adaptive abilities, which tends to emphasize the mildly retarded person's cognitive deficits. The moderately retarded child has more severe cognitive deficits, but during the school years, these children participate in special educational programs that emphasize social–adaptational survival skills rather than cognitive–academic skills.

Mental retardation then is not a unitary concept; it is a very heterogeneous concept with consideration of age, severity of impairment, and etiology being important variables in any discussion of the area.

The Problem

Although there is an emphasis upon resources for the younger and school-age mentally retarded person, less emphasis has been placed at the opposite end of the age continuum and, as a consequence, much less is known about the adult or aged mentally retarded. A similar lack of information regarding the geriatric person in general exists, but this is much more pronounced in relation to the mentally retarded elderly person. This lack of information then makes a definitive statement on the mentally retarded in later life almost impossible. With this in mind, the remainder of this chapter will present a review of what is currently known about the older retarded person and attempt to outline what additional information is needed.

ISSUES IN THE STUDY OF THE OLDER MENTALLY
RETARDED PERSON

Definition

One of the difficulties in speaking of the mentally retarded person in later life is in determining what constitutes "later life." In relation to the normal person, age 65 is often taken to define the lower limit of old age, since it marks a clear change in living patterns from a working to a retirement life style. Age 65, however, is an arbitrary age physiologically, since many people of that age may still be able to work, and 65 is a more socially convenient age. For the mentally retarded, age 65 appears to be too high, since from what little is known of older retarded persons, they appear to age much more quickly than normal people. Whether the retarded person in fact ages more quickly than the normal person must be established empirically. Thus, two ages have been used as the lower limit of old age for the retarded, 40 and 55 years, both of which have been arbitrarily chosen (Kriger, 1975).

A second difficulty relates to the definition of mental retardation in later life. Although there is little information about the cognitive and behavioral characteristics of the aged normal person, there appear to be some similarities between the aged normal and what is known currently about the retarded person, especially where there is deterioration in abilities in the former. Strict adherence to the American Association on Mental Deficiency's (AAMD) definition of mental retardation excludes those who exhibit low intelligence and poor social adaptability later in life. The researchers who study the older retarded must determine that the members of this population have in fact been mentally retarded all of their lives. A similar difficulty occurs, both for research and epidemiological purposes, in relation to the phenomenon that a person may be considered to be retarded during the school years, but he may not be once he has completed school. He has difficulty in academic tasks while in school but can work and be self-sufficient once out of school. This phenomenon accounts for the lowered prevalence of mental retardation after the school years. What has not been considered is that some of these people as they age may once again exhibit intellectual and social impairment and may once again be considered retarded for research, epidemiological, or programatic purposes. In my opinion, these people probably are similar to a normal aged population, but again, similarities or differences should be determined through empirical study. I raise the issue of difficulty in definition to demonstrate the rather arbitrary nature of *who* is to be considered retarded as well as to point out the need for agreement among researchers.

Epidemiology

A second major issue relates to just how many older retarded people there are and what their demographic characteristics are. There are few studies that provide data related to the older retarded, regardless of which age is taken to signify the lower limit of old age. Tarjan, Wright, Eyman, and Keeran (1973) for example, in their study of institutional patterns, used age categories of 0–5, 6–11, 12–17, and 18 and over. These data do not tell us specifically how many older retarded people there were in the institution studied, but they do indicate that there was a significant shift in the age groups from 1950 to 1967 that were present within the institution. Over the period studied, there was a decrease in the percentage of retarded people over the age of 18, which suggests that more adults are being placed within the community.

Although there are no studies that give an exact prevalence of the older retarded person, an estimate can be derived from census figures. In 1970 the general population of the United States was 215,588,000. There were approximately 23 million persons between the ages of 45 and 54; 20 million persons between 55 and 64; and 21 million 65 and over (Eisdorfer & Lawton, 1973). If a 2% prevalence rate is used as an estimate, there would be approximately 1.2 million retarded people over the age of 45 years excluding those who might develop personality disorders in later life. With increased longevity, this figure will also increase. Although older retarded people do not represent a large proportion of all people over the age of 45, they have significant needs that should be met.

Just as it is difficult to determine the exact number of older mentally retarded people, it is difficult to determine their mortality rate. For the mildly retarded person, the mortality rate probably is similar to that of the general population. For the more severely retarded, the rate is higher. Lilienfeld (1969), in an epidemiological study of people with Down's syndrome, found that the mortality rate was about 6% higher than that of the general population. Even though those with Down's syndrome may die at an earlier age than do people in the general population, there is no indication that the aging process is speeded up in the former. Death among people with Down's syndrome is usually a result of respiratory or congenital heart problems associated with the syndrome rather than a result of deterioration of tissues. Whether there is a higher mortality rate among other etiological groups is yet to be determined.

A critical issue then is to determine just how many retarded older people there are. A related issue is whether or not the aging process is similar between retarded and nonretarded people. For the normal person, aging may mean some loss of sensory abilities, including the need for eyeglasses or hearing aids; aging may mean a curtailment in mobility, and it may mean changes in activities. Adaptation to these changes is sometimes difficult for the normal person, and support systems are being made available for them. For the mentally retarded, adaptation may be more difficult and even more and different support systems may be needed. At present, there do not seem to be any support systems specifically for the older retarded person.

NEEDS OF THE OLDER RETARDED PERSON

There has been relatively little written about the older retarded person, and what has been written is in the form of surveys rather than in systematic research (e.g., Hamilton & Segal, 1975; Segal, 1977). These surveys focus upon identification of needs of the older retarded person and are restricted to a small geographical area, usually a state, city, or the jurisdiction of an agency. Because of these restrictions, it is difficult to be definitive; rather general statements will be made that draw from these studies.

Specific Therapeutic Needs of the Older Retarded Person

Support Systems

Since the older retarded person has not previously been a focus of therapeutic efforts, there is a need for support systems to which these people can turn. These systems include recreational facilities, special social services, medical–dental services, and legal services. Such services are similar for all older people, but for the retarded, because of their learning difficulties, more detailed and followup assistance may be required. As more retarded people are returned to the community, they will need help in their transition to and maintenance in the community.

Another support system relates to friends and companions. In a survey of retarded people over the age of 40 within one area of Ohio,

Kriger (1975) found that almost all of the people desired a friend, and only a few had anyone close to them or anyone visiting them.

Counseling

Historically, mentally retarded individuals were seen as people without much of anything, including feelings or emotions. Such a view was based more on lack of information than upon fact, because few people ever addressed the retarded person's feelings. Currently, studies have shown that the retarded person has a very definitive emotional life and can enunciate very clearly emotional conflicts that occur (e.g., Gan & Tymchuk, 1977; Lorber, 1974). Some of these conflicts relate specifically to the retarded person's recognition and degree of acceptance of the fact that he is retarded, and counseling is required to help the retarded in handling these conflicts.

Another conflict relates to how the retarded person perceives how he has been treated by society. Such treatment generally has been very punitive, and especially for the retarded person who is re-entering the community after having been placed within an institution, such a return may be frightening. Counseling of the older retarded person then is especially needed because he will be the one returned to the community.

Related to the retarded person's acceptance of his abilities and potential is his acceptance of his aging. There are few therapeutic counseling programs for the retarded and none that relate to helping the retarded person accept aging and its consequences. Programs for counseling older people in general have been established with the recognition that people have difficulty in understanding and adjusting to aging. Presumably, the retarded have similar difficulties, but programs are nonexistent for them. Whether or not the retarded have as severe adjustment problems as normal people must be determined through research. Their adjustment problems may not be as great because retarded persons tend to live in situations where some degree of care is provided for them, few have jobs, few are married, and few would change their life style either after retirement or after the death of a marital partner. For the normal person, the change in life style can be difficult after either of these, and adjustments must be made. In the future, as more retarded people work and live independently, more difficulties may occur in their adjustment to aging, and counseling programs should be set up to aid them. Such counseling, however, may have to be given at a different age for the retarded if in fact the aging process is speeded up in mentally retarded persons.

Within the normal population there is a disproportionate ratio of women to men over the age of 65 (1.39:1) (Cottrell, 1974). A similar situation seems to exist among the retarded if data from Ohio can be extrapolated to the remainder of the United States (Kriger, 1975). If such a situation exists, then counseling for the retarded would have to take into consideration the differential needs of the male and female retarded person. One study offers some support for this. Edgerton (1967) studied persons who left a large California institution for the retarded and found that almost three times as many females as males were married out of a total sample of 20 males and 25 females. Although there has not been a followup of married retarded people as they age and a mate dies, Edgerton's data suggest that differential counseling would be needed for older retarded women and men.

Other Needs

There are other needs of the older mentally retarded person that are similar to those of any older person, including special medical and nutritional services. There are also needs that may be similar to those for a normal aged population, but that are more critical for the older retarded person.

Vocational and Recreational Training

Once a mentally retarded person leaves the public school setting, he faces several areas of need. Two critical ones are vocational and recreational training. Most of the vocational opportunities for the retarded exist within supervised workshop situations. Only a few more innovative opportunities exist where a few retarded people work in less restricted environments. For the older retarded person, few are maintained in any type of vocational setting. This leaves a great deal of time free for other activities. However, neither younger nor older retarded persons have been trained in how to use their leisure time. Stanfield (1973) found that among moderately retarded adults time spent outside of the workshop was typically solitary and consisted of watching television, playing cards, and looking at magazines or walking alone around the neighborhood. A similar situation probably exists for the older retarded person. Kriger (1975) found that of her sample, most lived in a group home, but few had friends, and the remainder lived alone or in a rest home. The leisure activities were solitary, the major one being viewing television. Another important finding was that only 12% were self-supporting, whereas 54% were on welfare and 25% were on welfare and worked as well. The remainder were supported by private funds. In terms of housing, once in a place, few people moved and those who did, did so either because the home closed or because they could not get along with neighbors or the landlord.

Participatory Citizenship

Another critical area for older retarded persons relates to their participation within society as citizens. Both the American Association on Mental Deficiency (AAMD) and the National Association for Retarded Citizens (NARC) have enunciated statements on the basic rights of the retarded, one of which is the right to participate fully in society as citizens. Unfortunately, enunciation of this right does not guarantee full expression of it. For the older retarded person especially, there is a lack of awareness that rights exist or that training can be received in how to express these rights. Gozali (1971), for example, found that few mildly retarded people knew how to vote and fewer still voted. Only recently have the nonretarded aged developed activist groups and selected representatives to participate within the political arena where policies that might effect them are made. For the mentally retarded in general, regardless of level of deficit, there is not a similar opportunity to participate in policymaking.

Related to participatory citizenship is the older retarded person's need to have access to the judicial system for protection of his or her legal rights. Whereas any citizen has the right to sue as well as to be granted a public defender if they are charged with a crime and cannot afford to pay for their own attorney, the older retarded person does not have the inherent ability to take advantage of either. An advocate system has been initiated by some agencies, and for the older retarded person, advocates are essential, but few really are available.

Similarly, the older retarded person needs assistance in management of his or her resources, particularly social security.

Training Needs

Professional Training Needs

Not only are there specific needs for the older retarded person that must be responded to, there are also professional training needs. Although there is an increasing number of programs being offered for the training of health care professionals in geriatrics, there are only cursory efforts in relation to the older retarded person. Clearly, professionals need to be aware of the areas of concern for the older retarded; they need to be able to utilize or to develop services for this population, and they have to be trained in therapeutic and counseling techniques to be used with this population. In my own experience, there are some differences and similarities in methods used for counseling the aged normal person and the older retarded person, but there is no known study that enumerates or describes these similarities or differences. Whereas both the retarded and normal older person may benefit from more structured and repetitive therapeutic techniques, the latter may benefit more than the former from insight-oriented techniques. Again, however, such differences and similarities should be established empirically.

Public Training Needs

The mentally retarded generally have been viewed with prejudicial attitudes. Although these attitudes are becoming more positive, negative attitudes still do prevail. There are some similar prejudicial attitudes toward aging and the aged both by younger people and the aged themselves (Bennett & Eckman, 1973). An argument can be made then that attitudes toward the older mentally retarded may be even more negative; again, however, this would need to be examined empirically. For now, regardless of the strength of these attitudes and regardless of the fact that their existence is accepted, their immutability is not. Negative attitudes held by undergraduate students toward the mentally retarded have been shown to become more positive after the students had participated in a course on mental retardation (Shaw & Gilling, 1975). Although the durability of such attitude changes was examined for only a short period after the course, education about and familiarization with the aged mentally retarded may also foster long-term positive attitudes. Fostering positive attitudes toward the older mentally retarded is critical for fostering the development of services for and the integration of the older mentally retarded into the community, since negative attitudes interfere with effective integration. Such integration probably would be with the aged nonretarded, but paradoxically, it appears that although the aged normal person is viewed prejudicially by the younger, the aged themselves may have prejudicial attitudes toward the older retarded (Allardice & Crowthers, 1975).

Research Needs

Since there are so few formal studies of the older mentally retarded from which conclusions can be drawn about this population, a great deal of effort must be expended so that careful program development can proceed. There are particular research problems related to the older retarded person, such as in the three following areas.

Epidemiology

One clear need is to identify how many retarded people there are at older ages both in community and in institutional settings so that programatic needs can be determined. Such epidemiological studies also could answer specific questions about the aged retarded population including whether more women survive than men and whether longevity is different for other etiological groups or for institutionalized persons versus noninstitutionalized older retarded persons. An adjunct area of research would be to determine whether there is a premature aging process in the retarded or if their noticeable physical deterioration is due to poor medical and health care.

Behavioral Development

Another important area of research pertains to the behavior of the older retarded person to determine whether or not the behavioral manifestations are different from those of the normal aged or from those of the aged who are mentally ill. If patterns of behavior were similar, perhaps similar treatment facilities could be used for all three or any of two of the populations. A critical factor would be to determine whether some of the behaviors in the older retarded that appear sooner than in the normal aged, could be remediated through training programs.

Other aspects of behavior that should be studied are the various stages through which the retarded proceed developmentally. Whereas the normal person proceeds in an orderly manner through the developmental stages, the retarded seem to jump from young adulthood to old adulthood quite quickly. Whether this is a sociological phenomenon related to poor care needs to be determined.

Cognition

Much research has been done to clarify various aspects of cognitive behavior in the retarded child, including language development, short- and long-term memory, and abstracting abilities. None has been done with the older retarded. Particularly relevant for study would be a comparison between the retarded and a normal aged population of the maintenance or loss of various cognitive abilities.

CONCLUSIONS

In 1945 Kaplan discussed the state of knowledge and the various needs regarding the older mentally retarded person. His comments and conclusions in large part still hold true some 30 years later. Specifically, there has been a limited amount of effort related to studying the older retarded person. There were historical reasons for this lack of effort in relation to the mentally retarded generally. Since 1962, however, there has been more effort on behalf of the younger retarded person, but still very little has been done on behalf of the older retarded person.

There are several areas in which there is a need for training and research. The training efforts should be focused not only upon the older retarded person, but also upon the professional. Training and counseling programs are almost nonexistent for the older retarded person, and there is a similar lack in preparing professionals to work with this population. Research efforts, therefore, should focus upon epidemiology and upon the behavioral and cognitive development of the older retarded person.

REFERENCES

Allardice, M., & Crowthers, V. *The role of the practitioner in serving the elderly mentally retarded.* Unpublished paper, Senior Center, Inc., Detroit, 1975.

Bennett, R., & Eckman, J. Attitudes toward aging: A critical examination of recent literature and implications for future research. In C. Eisdorfer & M. Lawton (Eds.), *The psychology of adult development and aging.* Washington, D. C.: American Psychological Association, 1973.

Cottrell, F. *Aging and the aged.* Dubuque, Iowa: Brown, 1974.

Edgerton, R. *The cloak of competence.* Berkeley: Univ. of California Press, 1967.

Eisdorfer, C., & Lawton, M. (Eds.). *The psychology of adult development and aging.* Washington, D.C.: American Psychological Association, 1973.

Gan, J., & Tymchuk, A. Mentally retarded adults: Their attitudes toward retardation. *Mental Retardation,* 1977, *15,* 5–9.

Gozali, J. Citizenship and voting behavior of mildly retarded adults: A pilot study. *American Journal of Mental Deficiency,* 1971, *75,* 640–641.

Grossman, H. (Ed.). *Manual on terminology and classification in mental retardation.* Washington, D.C.: American Association on Mental Deficiency, 1973.

Hamilton, J., & Segal, R. (Eds.). *The gerontological aspects of mental retardation.* Proceedings of a conference, Univ. of Michigan, Ann Arbor, April 1975.

Kaplan, O. The aged subnormal. In O. Kaplan (Ed.), *Mental disorders in later life.* Stanford, Calif.: University Press, 1945.

Kriger, S. *Life styles of aging retardates living in community settings in Ohio.* Columbus, Ohio: Psychologia Metrika, 1975.

Lilienfeld, A. *Epidemiology of mongolism.* Baltimore, Maryland: Johns Hopkins Press, 1969.

Lorber, M. *Consulting the mentally retarded: An approach to the definition of mental retardation by experts.* Unpublished doctoral dissertation, University of California, Los Angeles, 1974.

President's Committee on Mental Retardation. *Report.* Washington, D.C.: U.S. Government Printing Office, 1962.

Segal, R. Trends in services for the aged mentally retarded. *Mental Retardation, 1977, 15,* 25–27.

Shaw, S., & Gilling, T. Efficacy of a college course for regular class teachers of the mildly handicapped. *Mental Retardation, 1975, 13,* 3–6.

Stanfield, J. Graduation: What happens to the retarded child when he grows up? *Exceptional Children, 1973, 34,* 548–552.

Tarjan, G., Wright, S., Eyman, R., & Keeran, C. Natural history of mental retardation: Some aspects of epidemiology. *American Journal of Mental Deficiency, 1973, 77,* 369–379.

Chapter 10

ALCOHOL-RELATED PSYCHOPATHOLOGY IN THE AGED

Marc A. Schuckit and Paul A. Pastor, Jr.

As recently as 1970, this chapter could probably not have been written. Alcohol has been a problem for the elderly for as long as people have brewed spirits, but most societies have tended to ignore it. In recent years there has developed a growing literature on the ubiquitous effects of alcohol on the body and psychologic functionings. The aging body, with its decrease in physical and mental reserves, is more vulnerable to adverse effects of alcohol than the younger one. These facts, along with the concomitant increased level of awareness of substance abuse and geriatric problems in the United States, have combined with the new activism for our older citizens to result in people asking questions about alcohol-related health care needs for the older population.

Alcoholism or drinking problems are part of the differential diagnosis of psychopathology in all age groups, as heavy, continued ethanol intake can present a variety of pictures, including depression, paranoia, organicity, and asthenia. To help the reader gain a broader overview of mental problems in geriatric patients, we will present a background on alcohol problems in the elderly. We will first review the literature on the topic, then synthesize some conclusions, and hope that the reader will use this as a starting point for continued interest and more in-depth readings in this area.

EPIDEMIOLOGY

Our relative ignorance of alcohol problems in elderly individuals is unfortunate, since without a high level of awareness of the problem

211

health professionals tend to miss the diagnosis of alcoholism more often in geriatric populations than in younger ones (Rosin & Glatt, 1971). Estimates of alcohol problems or alcoholism in general populations range from 2% to 10%, with higher rates for widowers and, of course, people having difficulty with the police (Bailey, Haberman, & Alksne, 1965; Siassi, Crocetti, & Spiro, 1973). Reviews of nursing homes indicate a problem rate of approximately 20% (Graux, 1969), whereas studies of psychiatrically ill older patients show rates of between 5% and 50% (Busse, 1973; Daniel, 1972; Gaitz & Baer, 1971; Kramer, 1969; Simon, Epstein, & Reynolds, 1968). Surveys of general medical wards show rates of alcoholism in the same range as those for younger patients (Barchha, Stewart, & Guze, 1968; McCusker, Cherubin, & Zimberg, 1971; Moore, 1971), with slightly lower rates for outpatients. Looking at the problem from another standpoint, it has been estimated that about 10% of alcoholics in treatment are age 60 or older (Glatt, 1961; Rosin & Glatt, 1971).

We have recently analyzed two samples in an attempt to determine the extent of geriatric alcohol problems. In the first, 113 consecutive general medical and surgical patients at the La Jolla Veterans Administration Hospital were given a structured interview to determine any general problems in psychopathology (Schuckit & Miller, 1976). The alcoholic was defined as a person having a major life problem related to alcohol (two or more nontraffic arrests; *or* the loss of a job related to alcohol; *or* physical evidence that alcohol had harmed health). Almost 20% of the men met the definition of alcoholism during their lives, with 9 of the 20 actively drinking at the time of interview.

The second evaluation involved analysis of all men for whom alcohol was given as a primary drug of abuse and who were listed in the 1975 Washington State Client Oriented Data Acquisition Process (CODAP) tapes. Almost 10% of the alcoholics were age 60 or over, with a rate of problems in the elderly much higher than for a comparable sample of drug abusers (Schuckit, 1976).

A unique population at reported high risk for alcohol problems are the elderly people living in disadvantaged areas, such as skid row. This population will be discussed in a separate section later in the chapter.

In short, alcohol problems do occur in elderly individuals. Anyone carrying out a clinical practice dealing with older patients will encounter alcoholics at a rate that is probably somewhere between 10% and 20%. The actual prevalence will depend upon the specific population being seen, but the disorder will be there no matter what subgroup is involved. Unless we look for the problem, we will miss it, with the likelihood of improper diagnosis and inadequate care.

Now that we have established that the disorder exists in elderly populations and occurs in an incidence high enough to be of concern, we will progress to a discussion of some of the clinical pictures involved. We will first deal with possible subtypes of clinical pictures and then go on to a discussion of generalizations that can be made about most elderly alcohol abusers.

POSSIBLE SUBTYPES OF ALCOHOLISM IN THE ELDERLY

No clinical population is homogeneous. When we are dealing with a problem pattern in a population that heretofore has not been well understood, it is important to look for various subgroups. This will help to establish possible prognostic differences among patients and might better allow adequate evaluation of treatment patterns and help clarify issues in research on etiology.

Age of Onset

A number of investigators feel that the elderly alcoholic is probably the young alcoholic grown old (Fillmore, 1974; Patterson, Abrahams, & Baker, 1974; Rathbone-McCuan & Bland, 1974); whereas others feel that alcoholism develops de novo in advanced age (Pascarelli, 1974; Stotsky, 1972). In one study (Pascarelli, 1974; Zimberg, 1974), at least one-third of a group of old-age alcoholics in San Francisco had begun abusing alcohol after the age of 60.

Our own data indicate that both phenomena occur. The Veterans Administration Hospital sample of elderly alcoholics fell into two patterns of age of onset of drinking problems—one beginning at age 40 or younger (including almost all of the alcoholics who were not actively drinking at the time of the study) and another, an almost equal-sized group with an onset of alcohol problems at age 41 or older (including almost all individuals who were actively drinking at the time of study). In the group of individuals who began drinking later in life, seven had their first alcohol problem while they were in their 40s, two while they were in their 50s, and two when they were age 60 or above (Schuckit & Miller, 1976).

The early onset and later onset alcoholics differed in a number of ways. The man who began his drinking problems later in life tended to be slightly younger at the time of study (70 versus 72 years), was more likely to be separated or divorced at the time of interview (55% versus

22%), but less likely to be widowed (9% versus 33%). He was also more likely to live alone (44% versus 22%), but he appeared to be no different from the earlier onset individual with regard to occupational or educational level. Our review of psychiatric history showed that the men with later ages of onset of drinking problems had a much higher rate of organic brain syndrome (OBS) at the time of study (36% versus 11%) (Woodruff, Goodwin, & Guze, 1974) and were much more likely to be active heavy smokers (60% versus 22%) and less likely to have spent time in jail (55% versus 78%). The older onset alcoholic also had a greater chance of reporting serious health difficulties (91% versus 41%). The earlier onset group had a higher rate of job problems, but there were similar rates of police difficulties. The CODAP-tape studies in the state of Washington, which analyzed data from 1975, also demonstrated that approximately one-half of the elderly alcoholics began to have drinking problems after age 40.

Organic Brain Disease

Another rubric divides alcoholics based on the presence or absence of an organic brain syndrome. Signs of organicity are common in the alcoholic but tend to be temporary pictures related to withdrawal. Compared with alcoholics without an OBS, the organically impaired alcoholic is younger (Gaitz & Baer, 1971; Simon et al., 1968), has a higher rate of nursing needs, and has an elevated 2-year mortality rate (Daniel, 1972; Schuckit & Miller, 1976; Simon et al., 1968).

The Veterans Administration Hospital study yielded some further data in this area. While the sample was quite small, the authors were able to compare the trends in the 5 alcoholics who showed an organic brain syndrome, with the 15 who showed none. The OBS alcoholics were slightly younger, reported less education (40% with less than eighth-grade educations versus 0% for the other group), had a lower occupational level, and a greater tendency to live alone (60% versus 23%). There were also differences in alcoholic background: While about the same percentage of the OBS and non-OBS alcoholics had been in jail, and they both reported a mean of three serious alcohol problem areas, the OBS patients reported fewer nontraffic, police problems (40% versus 60%), fewer job problems (0% versus 40%), and a much higher rate of serious health problems unrelated to organicity (100% versus 60%). Based on the literature cited previously, it is our estimate that the OBS patients will have a much worse prognosis, and a followup is presently being carried out.

These data suggest that there are both treatment and prognostic reasons for identifying OBS in elderly alcoholics. Those with organicity are more likely to have serious medical problems than the non-OBS alcoholics, despite their similar ages. They also will show some major differences in background. One can imagine that their prognosis is different and, of course, they will require more vigorous and long-term nursing care than the average alcoholic.

Sample Origin

The subdivision by sample origin is obvious. The data on the course, prognosis, and even causes of most diseases indicates characteristics that vary over demographic categories. Alcoholism in the elderly is no exception.

The average elderly alcoholic will probably in many ways resemble the average younger alcoholic: a blue-collar or white-collar worker who has many strengths in his life in addition to his alcohol problems. The average elderly alcoholic, then, is *not* a resident of skid row, and it is likely that only about 10% of all alcoholics are skid-row residents (Haglund & Schuckit, 1977). The public, nevertheless, tends to view the skid-row alcoholic as typical of alcoholics in general.

The data reported thus far in this chapter have tended to focus on the more common, middle-class elderly alcoholic. The following section deals with the less common but nonetheless important skid-row subtype.

Elderly Skid-Row Alcoholics

Skid-row districts are found in every major metropolitan area (Bouge, 1963). These districts are slum areas characterized by deteriorating buildings, cheap service establishments, and a population of homeless men (Bahr, 1973, Chapter 5; Bouge, 1963, pp. 1–4; Wallace, 1965, pp. 13–25). Demographic research indicates that skid-row populations contain from three to six times the number of persons over 65 as are found in the general population (Bahr, 1973, p. 104; Bouge, 1963, p. 10).

Among the most visible aspects of skid row are drinking and public drunkenness. Several writers state that drinking is the ultimate basis of skid-row subculture (Wallace, 1965, pp. 23–24); that skid-row institutions and norms are all structured around excessive alcohol consumption (Bahr, 1967a; Straus & McCarthy, 1951; Wiseman, 1970); and that obtaining, consuming, and recovering from the effects of alcohol are the focal points of life on skid row.

Although alcohol certainly permeates life on skid row, to equate skid row with alcoholism or to characterize all skid-row inhabitants as alcoholics is erroneous. Several studies indicate that approximately one-third of the skid-row inhabitants are either teetotalers or light drinkers; another one-third are moderate drinkers; and a final one-third may be classed as heavy drinkers either due to heavy daily intake or periodic heavy intake during drinking sprees (Bahr, 1969, pp. 649–650; Bahr & Caplow, 1973, pp. 248–249). One major study concludes that the alcoholic image may be particularly inappropriate for the elderly skid-row resident, since this group contains the fewest heavy drinkers (Bouge, 1963, p. 172).

While not all skid-row residents exhibit heavy alcohol intake, nearly all are improverished and socially isolated (Bahr & Caplow, 1973, p. 14; Blumberg, Shipley, & Moor, 1971, p. 928; Wallace, 1968, p. 93). These two attributes are important not only with regard to distinguishing the skid-row way of life from others, but also in recruitment into skid row: Skid-row living is cheap—a fact frequently cited when skid-row residents are asked why they live on skid row (Bahr & Caplow, 1973, p. 46; Bouge, 1963, p. 46; Wiseman, 1970, p. 11). The elderly skid-row resident is especially likely to cite inadequate pensions and unemployment due to age or a specific disability (Bahr & Caplow, 1973, p. 21; Bouge, 1963, p. 483). Social isolation also contributes: The lack of social supports makes it less likely that economic decline will be interrupted and leaves few alternatives to skid row. Alcoholism as well as other psychiatric and physical conditions can precipitate social isolation, downward economic mobility and, ultimately, arrival on skid row. With regard to the role of alcoholism, two patterns of arrival have been described (Bahr & Caplow, 1973, pp. 260–263; Pittman & Gordon, 1958, pp. 130–136). The first, the "early-skid" pattern, is characterized by: (a) the onset of heavy drinking and drinking-associated life problems in the subject's early 20s to early 30s; (b) poor occupational and marital adjustment in early adulthood; and, according to one source, (c) arrests for non-drunkenness-related offenses. The second, or "late-skid" pattern, is characterized by (a) stability in occupational and marital roles until approximately age 40 or older, at which time instability ensues; and (b) increasingly heavy drinking with the onset of drinking-related problems at approximately age 40 or older. It is not clear, however, whether heavy drinking generates or is generated by instability and maladjustment. Nor is it clear what proportion of elderly skid-row alcoholics are products of "early-skid" or "late-skid" patterns. But given the effects of long periods of heavy drinking and the hazards of skid-row life, it is likely that relatively few "early-skidders" survive to old age. Thus, it would be expected that most elderly skid-row alcoholics are products of the late-skid pattern.

Hazards of skid-row life exist for nondrinkers and alcoholics alike. Substandard housing that is inadequately protected against fire (Bouge, 1963, pp. 82–90; Wiseman, 1970, pp. 21–23), combined with exposure to contagious diseases such as tuberculosis (Blumberg, Shipley, & Shandler, 1973, pp. 112–114; Olin, 1966; Rhodes & Hudson, 1969), and the increased risk of trauma (whether from accidents or from assaultive robberies) (Blumberg *et al.*, 1971, p. 922; Brickner, Greenbaum, Kaufman, O'Donnell, O'Brian, Scalice, Scandizzo, & Sullivan, 1972, p. 567; Olin, 1966) all tend to make life tenuous. Finally, the suicide rate among skid-row men is reportedly over five times that for males in the general population (Bouge, 1963, p. 228). These and other aspects of skid-row life result in a reduced life expectancy for skid-row residents: It is estimated that the years of life remaining to any skid-row man is less than one-half the number of years one would estimate from general population statistics (Bouge, 1963, p. 225).

Several commentators have noted that skid row, as a unique sociogeographic entity, is declining (Bahr, 1967b; Rubington, 1971; Vander Kooi, 1973) because of urban renewal and renovation projects. The central location and deteriorated condition of skid-row areas make them prime targets for such projects. Another factor contributing to the decline of skid row is the increase in government-subsidized housing programs for the elderly, which offer the indigent elderly alternatives to skid row. The combined effect of these factors is to disperse skid-row populations. Sometimes this results in the emergence of new skid rows, but more frequently, the population is scattered over several low-rent areas (Bahr, 1967b, p. 44; Blumberg *et al.*, 1973, pp. 3–7; Vander Kooi, 1973, p. 69).

This phenomenon of dispersal may have certain beneficial implications from the standpoint of health. Specifically, the housing in non-skid-row areas may be cleaner, safer, and warmer; the chance of contact with contagious disease may be reduced; and the probability of falling victim to violent crime is lessened.

The effect on alcoholism and other psychiatric illness, however, is less clear. Removed from the skid-row environment, the average elderly skid-row resident undergoes no miraculous change. He or she remains indigent and isolated and subject to the social, medical, and psychiatric problems common among the thousands of other low-income elderly.

COURSE AND PROBLEMS OF
THE ELDERLY ALCOHOLIC

Psychopathology

The two following sections deal with the overall course of elderly alcoholics and the special problems of those on skid row. Before launching into those discussions, we will present a brief overview of the psychological pictures that can be seen in alcoholics. This is important, since alcoholism can mimic a number of other psychiatric pictures.

Depression is almost uniformly present in actively drinking alcoholics—a result of the pharmacologic effects of alcohol and the social stresses generated by an active drinking life style. While in some instances this depressed mood reflects a bona fide affective disorder deserving antidepressants or electroshock therapy (Woodruff et al., 1974), most alcoholics will snap back into a normal mood after a few days of abstinence (Gibson & Becker, 1973; Warren & Raynes, 1972). Therefore, in alcoholics sadness does not necessarily mean affective disorder, and antidepressant treatment should not be begun until after withdrawal is completed and mood has had a chance to return to normal.

Alcoholics can also present us with clinical pictures that mimic schizophrenia but carry a very good prognosis (Scott, Davies, & Malherbe, 1969). The occurrence of auditory hallucinations and/or delusions in a clear sensorium (alcoholic hallucinoses or alcoholic paranoia) appears to result from alcohol abuse but clears within 3–21 days following cessation of drinking. Here again, the clinician should take care before assigning a poor prognosis and jumping into long-term antipsychotic medications.

A third common picture in alcoholics, especially those of advanced age, is confusion and disorientation. The organic brain syndrome (OBS) occurring during alcoholic withdrawal carries a good prognosis and usually clears in 3–5 days of general supportive care (Gross, Lewis, & Hastey, 1974). Other OBS pictures can develop in response to vitamin deficiencies (especially thiamine), trauma, or general ill health and usually clear with nutrition and supportive care. As with any elderly patient, it is most important to avoid assigning a diagnosis of "senility" to an OBS picture without careful evaluation to rule out more treatable problems.

General Course

The older alcoholics in the Veterans Administration Hospital study were compared with a control group of the remaining medical and surgical patients age 65 and over who were hospitalized during the time of the study. Compared with the remaining subjects, the alcoholics reported a higher rate of suicide attempts (5% versus 1%), and there were more signs of organicity (OBS diagnoses for 25% of the alcoholics versus 22% of the remainder). Alcoholics were also more likely to be living alone (33% of the alcoholics versus about 25% of the remainder), less likely to be married (40% of the alcoholics versus approximately 65% of the remainder), and less likely to have been living at their present address for 5 or more years (25% of the alcoholics versus 50% of the remainder).

The rates of specific problems and difficulties with psychopathology were, as would be expected, higher for the presently active-drinking elderly alcoholics than for the remainder of the sample. Thus, the figure of 70% for health problems for the whole group of alcoholics included 89% for active versus 55% for the inactive; the 45% of marital problems included 56% for the active and 36% for the inactive; the 40% rate of alcohol-related driving problems included 44% for the active and 36% for the inactive; and the 60% rate of other problems, including life adjustment, included 67% for the active and 55% for the inactive (Schuckit & Miller, 1976).

The average practicing alcoholic was drinking 6 out of 7 days a week, with an average intake of four drinks per day—a rate lower than that reported for younger alcoholics. He also reported a mean of three serious alcohol problems having occurred at some time during his life.

It is interesting to note that the findings on smoking generally paralleled those on alcohol. Alcoholics were less likely to abstain from smoking and more likely to be heavy smokers as compared with the remaining population (25% versus approximately 10% of the remainder smoking one or more packs a day). The finding was even more marked for active alcoholics, 44% of whom smoked one or more packs per day as compared with 10% of the inactive men (Schuckit & Miller, 1976).

The primary medical diagnoses for the alcoholics were also compared with the remaining groups. While 25% of the alcoholics reported chronic obstructive lung diseases, the same was true for only about 15% of the remaining subjects. Also, while only 15% of the alcoholics had a primary admitting diagnosis related to heart disease, the same was true for approximately 27% of the remaining subjects. The study groups, however, tended to have similar rates of pneumonia (about 13%) and cancer (between 25% and 30%).

Data on clinical history was also carried out in the CODAP study. Compared with younger alcohol abusers in that study, the elderly alcoholic was more likely to be male, Caucasian, and have a lower level of education. Probably reflecting on his advanced age and thus his lowered level of physical reserve, he was more likely to be treated in a hospital and less likely to receive antabuse (disulfiram—a drug that causes vomiting when combined with alcohol) (Schuckit, 1976). There were no major differences in histories of prior treatment between the older and younger alcoholics. Compared with his younger counterpart, the older alcoholic was more likely to drink daily, but apparently had a better response to treatment, with 73% completing therapy (versus 40% for younger individuals) and only 15% (versus 38% for the younger men) leaving therapy before it was completed.

The data from the two studies were consistent with the literature (Schuckit & Miller, 1976). It demonstrated, among other factors, that: many active elderly alcoholics began drinking relatively late in life; a high percentage of them had organic brain disease; they are more likely than younger alcoholics to be hospitalized when they present with problems; and, also probably due to their decreased physical reserve, they are less likely to receive antabuse once they enter treatment. They present with less social stability, more frequently living alone, since many are either unmarried or divorced, are more likely to present with medical problems centering around lung disease, probably related to their heavy smoking, but they seem to be more stable in their response to treatment, staying in therapy longer than is true for their younger counterparts.

Skid Row

The character and course of alcoholism and related conditions on skid row are a function of preexisting pathology, the skid-row environment, life style, and the access of skid-row residents to medical care. Studies indicate that skid-row residents often display signs of serious physical and psychiatric problems prior to taking up residence on skid row (Bouge, 1963, p. 197). As was indicated previously, physical or psychiatric disability may result in downward economic mobility and, ultimately, arrival on skid row. In implicating disease in downward mobility, however, it should be noted that for most skid-row residents, the downward drift is not dramatic: Most have lower-class origins (Bahr & Caplow, 1973, p. 85; Bouge, 1963, p. 329; Rubington, 1962, p. 148). A single injury or an extended period of ill health may be sufficient to push these individuals out of their already tenuous economic roles. Their origins may even predispose them to ill health: Lower-class groups traditionally show higher rates of physical psychiatric problems and have less access to medical care (Herman, 1972; Hollingshead & Redlich, 1958; McKinlay, 1975; Petras & Curtis, 1968).

There is evidence that preexisting pathology in skid-row populations differs over age categories. Younger and middle-aged men, for example, show the highest rates of psychiatric illness (Bouge, 1963, p. 208). The elderly, as might be expected, show the highest rates of degenerative disease, including cardiovascular problems, genito-urinary conditions, and impaired hearing and vision (Bouge, 1963, p. 208).

With regard to alcoholism, the evidence indicates that it, too, is a preexisting condition. For both the early-skid and late-skid patterns described earlier, heavy drinking antedates arrival on skid row. For the elderly, however, alcohol consumption need not be heavy to precipitate difficulties. Given the decreased tolerance for alcohol in most elderly persons, and given the fact that elderly people are more likely to be receiving medication than are other groups, the ingestion of even modest amounts can cause intoxication or more serious effects. Thus, isolated, indigent elderly individuals who begin drinking even small amounts on a regular basis may present a unique type of late-skid pattern.

Alcoholism compounds the hazards of housing and generally poor health and presents hazards of its own. The medical complications of skid-row alcoholism are many, leading one author to list a common medical profile that he calls the "skid row syndrome" (Olin, 1966). The profile includes body weight at least 10 pounds less than average; fractures or amputations of limbs; skull fracture; tuberculosis, pneumonia, and other respiratory diseases; history of venereal disease; hepatic abnormality; and clinical evidence of brain damage (Olin, 1966). To this list may be added body lice infestations; anemia; peptic ulcers; and, of course, alcoholic withdrawal (Blumberg *et al.*, 1973, p. 112; Rosenblatt, Gross, Broman, Lewis, & Malanowski, 1971). As might be expected, the number and seriousness of the conditions making up this profile increase with the subject's level of drinking (Blumberg *et al.*, 1973, p. 112) and probably with increasing age.

Another very common condition in skid-row alcoholics is nutritional deficiency. This is usually due to eating infrequently or simply neglecting to consume any food other than alcoholic beverages over extended periods. Factors that contribute to this condition include the depressing effects of alcohol on the appetite, the desire to increase the alcohol high by fasting (Mello & Mendelson, 1971), and the fact that skid-row alcoholics often have little money, most of which is spent on alcohol or lost during periods of intoxication. Nutritional deficiency contributes to various pathological conditions by lowering resistance to infection and impeding healing. "Wine sores" (i.e., superficial cutaneous ulcers), a common condition of skid-row alcoholics, are directly attributable to poor nutrition (Journal of the American Medical Association, 1969).

With regard to psychiatric disease on skid row, the evidence indicates that the younger and middle-aged residents display not only more psychiatric disease, but also more serious pathology than elderly residents. In terms of particular diagnostic categories, schizophrenia and personality disorders are most frequently found in the younger residents, whereas affective disorders are more common in the elderly (Brisolara, Bishop, Bossetta, & Gallant, 1968; Goldfarb, 1970). In addition, psychiatric disease would appear to occur more often and in more serious forms among nondrinkers and light drinkers than among moderate and heavy drinkers (Bouge, 1963, p. 390). It has been suggested that psychopathology is a major reason these individuals take up skid-row residence (Bahr, 1973, pp. 100–102; Bouge, 1963, p. 390).

Limited access to medical care is another major factor affecting the character and course of alcoholism and related problems on skid row. A combination of circumstances contribute to this situation, including the fact that access to medical care and quality of care is a function of economic position: The economically privileged generally have more access than others (Herman, 1972; Mechanic, 1972, pp. 92–96). The social isolation of skid-row residents is another factor, as the availability of medical care is in part dependent on access to social networks that facilitate and reinforce health care seeking (Chrisman, 1976; Robinson, 1971; Zola, 1971). Socially isolated individuals are, by definition, estranged from these networks.

Yet another factor affecting access to medical care is the fact that skid-row residents and skid-row alcoholics in particular are often regarded as undesirable patients (Blumberg et al., 1971, p. 926; Goldfarb, 1970). There are several reasons for this. First, these individuals neglect personal hygiene: Many look and smell unpleasant. Second, their medical problems are often chronic and yield slowly, if at all, to the practitioner's efforts. Finally, the practitioner may regard the alcoholic as at least partly responsible for his or her condition.

One factor that has traditionally affected the character and course of alcoholism and related conditions on skid row is the criminal justice system's involvement in drunkenness control. In most jurisdictions, municipal ordinances and state statues prohibit public drunkenness (Grad, Goldberg, & Shapiro, 1971; Pastor, 1976, pp. 61–64). These laws have recently come under attack (Nimmer, 1971; President's Commission, 1967, pp. 1–6). Those opposed to the criminal status of public drunkenness note that the recidivism rate for drunkenness arrests is very high: Most of those arrested are repeat offenders (Pittman, 1967, p. 8; Rubington, 1966; Stern, 1967, p. 153). The critics argue that these repeat offenders are alcoholics and that arresting and incarcerating these individuals is tantamount to punishing them for their illness (Stern, 1967). Defenders of the traditional approach reply to these critics by stating that medicine is no better equipped to deal with the problem than is the law (Kittrie, 1971, pp. 285–296) and that periodic arrest and incarceration provides public inebriates with a period of enforced abstinence that allows them to regain their health.

In several jurisdictions, the arguments against the traditional criminal-law approach to public drunkenness have prevailed: These jurisdictions have decriminalized public drunkenness (Pastor, 1976, pp. 3–4). Some of these have replaced criminal justice processing with medically supervised alcohol detoxification programs (Nimmer, 1971; Pastor, 1976, pp. 79–84). These programs, which the public inebriate enters voluntarily, not only provide alcohol detoxification and care for various medical problems, but also frequently offer alcoholism counseling and postdetoxification referral to alcoholism treatment programs and housing as well. There is very little information available on the clientele of these programs and how they compare with those processed under the traditional criminal justice approach. Data from one recent study that compared police and detoxification agency processing, however, indicate that the detoxification agency is more likely then the police to process elderly public inebriates and those who are ill or injured (Pastor, 1976, pp. 152–154, 165–166).

In summary, the elderly skid-row alcoholic is at a particular disadvantage as compared with his or her non-skid-row counterpart, displaying more physical and psychiatric pathology throughout life. Once on skid row, these people live under more hazardous conditions and the access of these individuals to medical care is comparatively limited.

The trend toward decriminalization of public drunkenness and the substitution of medical care for legal sanction may serve to improve the health of the elderly skid-row alcoholic by (*a*) increasing access to general medical care; and (*b*) confronting and attempting to intervene in his alcoholism. The nationwide decline of skid-row areas will tend to disperse these individuals so that they are less easily recognized as a distinct epidemiological population. Removed from the skid-row environment, they will probably become largely indistinguishable from other indigent, socially isolated, elderly individuals.

CONCLUSIONS AND REFLECTIONS ON TREATMENT

Alcoholism exists in the elderly as it does in any age group. The cause and prognosis for alcoholism differs with different clinical or historical features of the patient. The combination of any of the factors of decreased physical reserve, poverty, living in blighted areas, poor nutrition, and heavy alcohol intake combine to make up the final clinical picture and dictate the therapeutic needs.

We have not had the time or the space to delve into treatment for the elderly alcoholic. The health care approach is a combination of the common-sense lessons applicable to alcoholism and geriatric medicine. Alcoholism is approached through the usual methods of confrontation, prophylaxis against development of an abstinence syndrome, and rehabilitation. At the same time, the brittle medical status is carefully evaluated, and the common social problems of poverty, isolation, and the need for coping with failing health are recognized and treated. Perhaps even more than with younger alcoholics, one must take care to consider alcoholism as a possible explanation for any psychopathology in the aged. If you do not look for alcoholism, you will not find it.

REFERENCES

Bahr, H. M. Drinking, interaction and identification: Notes on socialization into skid row. *Journal of Health and Social Behavior,* 1967, *8,* 272–285. (a)

Bahr, H. M. The gradual disappearance of skid row. *Social Problems,* 1967, *15,* 41–45. (b)

Bahr, H. M. Lifetime affiliation patterns of early- and late-onset heavy drinkers on skid row. *Quarterly Journal of Studies on Alcohol,* 1969, *30,* 645–656.

Bahr, H. M. *Skid row: An introduction to disaffiliation.* New York: Oxford Univ. Press, 1973.

Bahr, H. M., & Caplow, T. *Old men drunk and sober.* New York: New York Univ. Press, 1973.

Bailey, M. D., Haberman, P. W., & Alksne, H. The epidemiology of alcoholism in an urban residential area. *Quarterly Journal of Studies on Alcohol,* 1965, *26,* 20–40.

Barchha, R., Stewart, M. A., & Guze, S. The prevalence of alcoholism among general hospital ward staff. *American Journal of Psychiatry,* 1968, *125,* 681–684.

Blumberg, L., Shipley, T. E., Jr., & Moor, J. O., Jr. The skid row man and the skid row status community. *Quarterly Journal of Studies on Alcohol,* 1971, *32,* 909–941.

Blumberg, L., Shipley, T. E., & Shandler, I. W. *Skid row and its alternatives: Recommendations from Philadelphia.* Philadelphia: Temple Univ. Press, 1973.

Bouge, D. J. *Skid row in American cities.* Chicago: Community and Family Study Center, Univ. of Chicago, 1963.

Brickner, P. W., Greenbaum, D., Kaufman, A., O'Donnell, F., O'Brian, J. T., Scalice, R., Scandizzo, J., & Sullivan, T. A clinic for male derelicts: A welfare hotel project. *Annals of Internal Medicine,* 1972, *77,* 565–569.

Brisolara, A. M., Bishop, M. P., Bossetta, J. R., & Gallant, D. M. The New Orleans "revolving door" alcoholic: Degree of severity of illness and financial expense to the community. *Journal of the Louisiana Medical Society,* 1968, *120,* 397–399.

Busse, E. W. Mental disorders in later life—organic brain syndrome. In E. W. Busse & E. Pfeiffer (Eds.), *Mental illness in later life.* Baltimore, Maryland: Garamond/Pridemark Press, 1973.

Chrisman, N. J. American patterns of health care seeking behavior. In W. Arens & S. P. Montagne (Eds.), *The American dimension: Cultural myths and social realities.* Port Washington, N. Y.: Alfred Publishing Co., 1976.

Daniel, R. A five-year study of 693 psychogeriatric admission in Queensland. *Geriatrics,* 1972, *27,* 132–155.

Fillmore, L. M. Drinking and problem drinking in early adulthood and middle age. An exploratory 20-year follow-up study. *Quarterly Journal of Studies on Alcohol,* 1974, *35,* 819–840.

Gaitz, C. M., & Baer, P. E. Characteristics of elderly patients with alcoholism. *Archives of General Psychiatry,* 1971, *24,* 372–378.

Gibson, S., & Becker, J. Changes in alcoholic's self-reported depression. *Quarterly Journal of Studies on Alcohol,* 1973, *34,* 829–836.

Glatt, M. M. Drinking habits of English alcoholics. *Acta. Psychiatrica Scandanavia,* 1961, *37,* 88–113.

Goldfarb, C. Patients nobody wants: Skid row alcoholics. *Diseases of the Nervous System,* 1970, *31,* 274–281.

Grad, F. P., Goldberg, A. L., & Shapiro, B. A. *Alcoholism and the law.* Dobbs Ferry, N. Y.: Oceana, 1971.

Graux, P. Alcoholism of the elderly. *Review Alcoholsme,* 1969, *15,* 46–48.

Gross, M. M., Lewis, E., & Hastey, J. Acute alcohol withdrawal syndrome. In B. Kissin & H. Begleiter (Eds.), *The biology of alcoholism.* (Vol. 3). Clinical pathology. New York: Plenum Press, 1974. Pp. 191–263.

Haglund, R. M. J., & Schuckit, M. A. The epidemiology of alcoholism. In N. Estes & E. Heineman (Eds.), *Alcoholism: Psychological and physiological basis.* St. Louis, Missouri: C. V. Mosby, 1977.

Herman, M. W. The poor: Their medical needs and health services available to them. *Annals of American Academy of Political and Social Science,* 1972, *399,* 12–21.

Hollingshead, A. B., & Redlich, F. C. *Social class and mental illness.* New York: Wiley, 1958.

Journal of the American Medical Association. Pathogenesis of wine sores, *JAMA,* 1969, *209,* 566.

Kittrie, N. N. *The right to be different: Deviance and enforced therapy.* Baltimore, Maryland: Johns Hopkins Univ., 1971.

Kramer, M. *Patients in state and county mental hospitals* (Public Health Service Publication No. 1921). Chevy Chase, Md.: U.S. Department of Health, Education, & Welfare, National Institute of Mental Health, 1969.

McCusker, J., Cherubin, C. F., & Zimberg, S. Prevalence of alcoholism in general municipal hospital population. *New York State Journal of Medicine,* 1971, *71,* 751–754.

McKinlay, J. B. Health-seeking behavior of the poor. In J. Kosa & I. K. Zola (Eds.), *Poverty and health: A sociological analysis.* Cambridge, Massachusetts: Harvard Univ., 1975. Pp. 224–273.

Mechanic, D. *Public expectations and health care: Essays on the changing organization of health services.* New York: Wiley, 1972.

Mello, N. K., & Mendelson, J. H. A quantitative analysis of drinking patterns in alcoholics. *Archives of General Psychiatry,* 1971, *25,* 527–539.

Moore, R. A. The prevalence of alcoholism in a community general hospital. *American Journal of Psychiatry,* 1971, *128,* 638–639.

Nimmer, R. T. *Two million unnecessary arrests: Removing a social service concern from the criminal justice system.* Chicago: American Bar Foundation, 1971.

Olin, J. S. Skid row syndrome: A medical profile of the chronic drunkenness offender. *Canadian Medical Association Journal,* 1966, *95,* 205–214.

Pascarelli, E. F. Drug dependence: An age-old problem compounded by old age. *Geriatrics,* 1974, *29,* 109–115.

Pastor, P. A., Jr. *The control of public drunkenness: A comparison of the legal and medical models.* Unpublished doctoral dissertation, Department of Sociology, Yale University, 1976.

Patterson, R. D., Abrahams, R., & Baker, F. Preventing self-destructive behavior. *Geriatrics,* 1974, *29,* 115–121.

Petras, J. W., & Curtis, J. E. The current literature on social class and mental disease in America: Critique and bibliography. *Behavioral Science,* 1968, *13,* 380–395.

Pittman, D. J. Public intoxication and the alcoholic offender in American society. In President's Commission on Law Enforcement and the Administration of Justice, *Task force report: Drunkenness.* Washington, D.C.: U. S. Government Printing Office, 1967.

Pittman, D. J., & Gordon, C. W. *The revolving door: A study of the chronic police case inebriate.* New York: Free Press, 1958.

President's Commission on Law Enforcement and the Administration of Justice. *Task force report: Drunkenness.* Washington, D. C.: U.S. Government Printing Office, 1967.

Rathbone-McCuan, E., & Bland, J. *Diagnostic and referral considerations for the geriatric alcoholic and aging problem drinker.* Paper presented at Gerontological Society's 27th Annual Meeting, Portland, Oregon, October 28–November 1, 1974.

Rhodes, R. J., & Hudson, R. M. A follow-up study of tuberculosis skid row alcoholics. *Quarterly Journal of Studies on Alcohol,* 1969, *30,* 119–128.

Robinson, D. *The process of becoming ill.* London: Routledge & Kegan Paul, 1971.

Rosenblatt, S. M., Gross, M. M., Broman, M., Lewis, E., & Malanowski, B. Patients admitted for treatment of alcohol withdrawal syndromes: An epidemiological study. *Quarterly Journal of Studies on Alcohol,* 1971, *32,* 105–115.

Rosin, A. J., & Glatt, M. M. Alcohol excess in the elderly. *Quarterly Journal of Studies on Alcohol,* 1971, *32,* 53–59.

Rubington, E. "Failure" as a heavy drinker: The case of the chronic drunkenness offender on skid row. In D. J. Pittman & C. R. Snyder (Eds.), *Society, culture, and drinking patterns.* New York: Wiley, 1962.

Rubington, E. The "revolving door" game. *Crime and Delinquency,* 1966, *12,* 332–338.

Rubington, E. The changing skid row scene. *Quarterly Journal of Studies on Alcohol,* 1971, *32,* 123–135.

Schuckit, M. A. *An overview of alcohol and drug abuse problems in the elderly.* Testimony before the Subcommittee on Alcoholism and Narcotics and Subcommittee on Aging of the Senate Committee on Labor and Public Welfare, Washington, D.C., June 7, 1976.

Schuckit, M. A., & Miller, P. L. Alcoholism in elderly men: A survey of a general medical ward. *Annals of the New York Academy of Sciences,* 1976, *273,* 558–571.

Scott, D. F., Davies, D. L., & Malherbe, M. E. L. Alcoholic hallucinosis, *International Journal of the Addictions,* 1969, *4,* 319–330.

Siassi, I., Crocetti, G., & Spiro, H. R. Drinking patterns and alcoholism in a blue-collar population. *Quarterly Journal of Studies on Alcohol,* 1973, *34,* 917–926.

Simon, A., Epstein, L. J., & Reynolds, L. Alcoholism in the geriatric mentally ill. *Geriatrics,* 1968, *23,* 125–131.

Stern, G. Public drunkenness: Crime or health problem? *The Annals of the American Society of Political and Social Science,* 1967, *374,* 147–156.

Stotsky, B. A. Social and clinical issues in geriatric psychiatry. *American Journal of Psychiatry,* 1972, *129,* 117–126.

Straus, R., & McCarthy, R. G. Non-addictive pathological drinking among homeless men. *Quarterly Journal of Studies on Alcohol,* 1951, *12,* 601–612.

Vander Kooi, R. Skid row revisited. *Society,* 1973, *10,* 64–71.

Wallace, S. E. *Skid row as a way of life.* Totowa, New Jersey: Bedminister, 1965.

Wallace, S. E. The road to skid row. *Social Problems,* 1968, *16,* 92–105.

Warren, G. H., & Raynes, A. E. Mood changes during three conditions of alcohol intake. *Quarterly Journal of Studies on Alcohol,* 1972, *33,* 979–989.

Wiseman, J. P. *Stations of the lost: The treatment of skid row alcoholics.* Englewood Cliffs, N.J.: Prentice Hall, 1970.

Woodruff, R. A., Jr., Goodwin, D. W., & Guze, S. B. *Psychiatric diagnosis.* New York: Oxford Univ., 1974.

Zimberg, S. Two types of problem drinkers: Both can be managed. *Geriatrics,* 1974, *29,* 135–138.

Zola, I. K. Pathways to the doctor: From person to patient. In P. McEwan (Ed.), *Problems in medical care.* London: Tavistock, 1971.

Chapter 11
DRUG PROBLEMS IN THE ELDERLY

Marc A. Schuckit and Margaret A. Moore

Drug abuse in the elderly is not widely discussed (Batalden, 1974; Morrant, 1975), yet the misuse of medications in this age group is probably common. This topic is of special importance because the circumstances of growing old with failing health *both* make the elderly vulnerable to the overuse of drugs and give them less tolerance for the effects of the misuse. The physical and mental results are a part of everyday practice, and it is our aim to review briefly this topic. In this introduction, we will discuss some of the reasons for drug overuse and some factors behind adverse reactions to drugs in the elderly.

Of course, the older person is more likely than the young one to be sick, making him or her more likely to take medication. Some 86% of Americans over 65 years of age have one or more chronic conditions: heart disease, diabetes, arthritis, visual impairment, or cancer, etc. (Phillipson, 1976). Furthermore, the extent and intensity of physical disability increase sharply with age.

It is not surprising, therefore, that the elderly consume a lot of drugs and as a group are the largest consumers of legal medications. Persons over 60 years of age are presently 10% of the population in the United States, yet they are receiving 25% of all prescribed drugs (Batalden, 1974). Although largely due to the increased incidence of chronic disease, the hazard to abuse also exists because of the sheer quantity of drugs prescribed (Pascarelli, 1974). Despite this, health care for the elderly is fragmentary, as older people tend to get medical treatment from a variety of sources with inadequate communication between the

229

agencies (Morrant, 1975; Pascarelli & Fischer, 1974). Also, the elderly are perhaps more likely to delay getting care until a crisis arises due to the inaccessibility of offices or clinics, the lack of transportation to facilities (Gault, Rudwal, & Redmond, 1968), and from a fear that admitting that one is ill means admitting that one is going to die.

Perhaps related to these factors, the elderly frequently self-medicate (Lenhart, 1976). They tend to hoard outdated medications and share prescriptions with friends (Gibson & O'Hare, 1968). They also tend to use over-the-counter drugs and to combine them with alcohol (Capel & Stewart, 1971).

Older individuals have fewer life supports to ensure that they receive treatment when they need it. At the same time, they may have increased life stresses: adapting to life without work, adjusting to income maintenance, to reduction in physical vigor and motor performance, to physical disabilities, to reduced expectations with a drop in activity level, as well as to loss of companions and/or spouse, lowered social status, substandard housing, and social isolation from their family, neighbors, and community (Batalden, 1974; Pascarelli, 1974). With equilibrium potentially this brittle, it is difficult to regain balance after a drug-reaction crisis.

In general, the elderly are twice as likely to react adversely to medications in even normal doses (Cooper, 1975; Glick, 1974; Raskind & Eisdorfer, 1978), and they experience side effects from a wider variety of medications than is true in younger populations (Morrant, 1975; Shader, 1972). Also, the metabolism of drugs slows down as people get older. Loss of body weight, loss of fluid, and reduced reserves impair all phases of pharmacodynamics: absorption, distribution, excretion, and metabolism (Lenhart, 1976).

In aging, the pattern of detoxification is not uniform (Leathern, 1972; Batalden, 1974). Older persons demonstrate an increased half-life and higher blood levels for many drugs as compared with younger populations (Raskind & Eisdorfer, 1978). Other sources of influence on drug metabolism that differ with age could be drug history, drugs currently used, nutritional condition, disease history, drug combinations, and combinations of nicotine, caffeine, and alcohol (Phillipson, 1976).

In summary, the life situation inherent in many older people makes drug misuse a huge potential problem. This chapter will discuss both deliberate and inadvertent misuse of prescription and over-the-counter drugs, as well as abuse of street narcotics in elderly groups. We first outline the abuse of narcotics in older age. This problem affects many fewer individuals than prescription or over-the-counter drugs, but it does exist and is worthy of note.

ABUSE OF NARCOTICS

The elderly opiate abuser is not highly visible in official statistics. For example, for 38 white long-term opiate users (mean age, 59), an average of 9 years had lapsed since their last arrest (Capel, Goldsmith, Waddell, & Stewart, 1972). In another study, 85% of 44 addicts over 50 years of age had no arrests in the past 5 years (Capel & Stewart, 1971).

Related to this is the feeling that elderly opiate abusers are not seen because the younger addicts either die or "mature out" of their abuse (Winick, 1962, 1964). Winick's public record search (1962, 1964) reported that 65% of the known addicts in New York City may have matured out, but this was based on the erroneous assumption that the addict life style automatically attracted the attention of the authorities. Snow (1973), in an attempt to duplicate Winick's study, found that only 23% of the known addicts in New York City may have matured out of their addiction. A recent study (Capel & Stewart, 1971) shows that illegal activity of older opiate abusers usually centers on panhandling or minor con games, and thus they are only reluctantly taken in to the criminal justice system by the police (Bergman & Amir, 1973).

Although persons over age 45 tend to disappear from narcotic registers and police records, they do exist in increasing numbers (O'Donnell, 1969), which may become more apparent as the opiate abusers of the 1960s grow older. Within the next decade, some predict a six-fold increase in this population, and a twenty-fold increase in the next two decades (Pascarelli, 1974).

Clinical Course

The clinical picture of the elderly addict differs from the younger counterpart in several ways. Usually they are "survivors": long-time narcotic users with over 15 years of addiction—36 years was the mean length of addiction among 44 addicts over 50 years of age (Capel & Stewart, 1971). The age of onset of drug use other than marijuana is 22.5 years on the average, with nearly one-third (32%) beginning between the ages of 25 and 29 (Capel et al., 1972).

The observed number of deaths among older narcotic addicts exceeds the expected by a ratio of 2.5 to 1 for men, 3 to 1 for women (Capel & Stewart, 1971). Yet few deaths are attributable to narcotic use directly, since there is insufficient evidence to indicate that long-term use of opiates, in and of itself, is related to any major medical condition. Two in a sample of 31 chronic opiate users died during hospitalization from subarachnoid hemorrhage and cardiac failure, but there was no reason to relate this to opiate use (Ball & Urbaitis, 1970). The percentage of

deaths from overdose is small in addicts over 50 years of age (O'Donnell, 1969).

The use of drugs is less frequent in the elderly than in the younger
opiate abuser, perhaps due to their decreased physiological need. They
often use less drugs than is considered addicting by most medical
standards (Capel *et al.*, 1972). Of 38 white long-term opiate users not in
treatment the following was found: 47% used drugs daily; 37% four
times weekly; 11% three times weekly; 5% twice weekly. However,
street users grown old maintain their identity as drug users.

Most elderly addicts are single; many never marry, others are
separated or divorced. Surprisingly, over one-half of the elderly opiate
abusers hold employment (51% full-time, 14% part-time), enabling
them to support a small habit (Capel & Stewart, 1971). They are generally reluctant to seek help from existing programs, but if they choose to
do so, they often join a methadone maintenance program. Most older
addicts have had some experience with treatment (a mean of 24 admissions per individual in one Lexington, Kentucky, sample) (Ball & Urbaitis, 1970).

Most elderly abusers in treatment have already switched to a narcotic other than heroin several years prior to joining methadone maintenance treatment. This change in drug type is due to several reasons—
more reliable dosage, fewer impurities, a standarized strength, as well
as the option to take these drugs orally. The inability of the older opiate
abusers to hustle may also necessitate a compromise on drugs of choice
(Capel *et al.*, 1972; Pascarelli, 1974). The other opiates used by older
persons are morphine, codeine, and paregoric with drug of choice
varying with what is available. Demerol was the preferred drug to
replace heroin in New York (Capel & Stewart, 1971); diluadid was
preferred in a New Orleans sample (Capel *et al.*, 1972). Reports indicate
that these patients occasionally have patterns of multiple drug use.
Methadone patients may concomitantly use barbiturates, diazepam
(Valium), cocaine, and alcohol. Most abuse occurs in depressant
categories, little occurs with stimulants or hallucinogens in this older
population (Pascarelli, 1974). It has been conjectured that the main use
of auxilliary drugs is to produce euphoria, which methadone maintenance does not provide.

Treatment and Recommendations

Despite the older narcotic abusers' increased treatment needs, their
slower life style and lower crime rate provide camouflage from public
recognition. The tendency to treat their narcotic abuse as a legal, rather

than social, medical, or physiological problem, also encourages self-protection in the older abuser (Bean, 1974).

The main treatment modalities currently available for older abusers are methadone maintenance and total abstinence; both are unattractive to the older addict. There appears to be a general trend for outpatient treatment for the elderly addict in community-based programs, perhaps because they are less of a threat to society than younger addicts (Subby, 1975). Placement in long-term facilities, geriatric residences, and nursing homes is difficult even now (Pascarelli, 1974), and a prison setting offers no benefits (Bergman & Amir, 1973).

Capel and Stewart (1971) feel that methadone maintenance does not appear appropriate, since the side effects of the drug are more pronounced in older patients—constipation, weight gain, myoclonic jerks, and nausea on intake. Some authors advocate maintenance therapy using diluadid, demerol, or codeine, because there is no evidence that small, regular doses aggravate or cause physiological harm (Capel & Stewart, 1971). Other authors still recommend methadone maintenance as the most acceptable of all treatments for actively abusing elderly addicts (Glick, 1974; Pascarelli & Fischer, 1974).

An elderly person in maintenance treatment presents a variety of special problems: housing conditions are poor, general health may be marginal, and medical problems are common, making multimodality services important in accommodating these specialized needs. Advantages of any maintenance program for the elderly narcotic abuser, whether outpatient or institutionalized, are the regularity of schedule, proper nutrition, good medical care, and a reduction in petty crime for the community.

In summary, the older opiate abuser does exist. He is usually the younger addict who, with increasing age, slows down his frequency of drug intake and illegal activities. The usual treatment modality is outpatient methadone maintenance, but these programs should take cognizance of the special treatment needs of this group.

We will now proceed to a discussion of a more frequently observed drug misuse pattern among the elderly—one involving prescription drugs. This will be followed by a section on over-the-counter drug problems.

ABUSE OF PRESCRIPTION DRUGS

Two subpopulations appear to abuse prescription drugs—deliberate and inadvertent abusers. Some older persons seek out drugs to abuse, obtaining medications from a variety of sources. Others, abusing inadvertently, fail to take medications as prescribed, perhaps through ignorance, confusion, or poor prescribing practices. We will discuss deliberate and inadvertent abuse in the same section because of the similarities in consequences and the difficulty in establishing the motive for intake.

Surveys in Australia and the United States show that the chance of abusing prescription drugs increases with age for both men and women (Abrahams, Armstrong, & Whitlock, 1970; George, 1972; Swanson, Weddige, & Morse, 1973). The chance for misuse also increases with the increasing number of drugs and the complexity of instructions (Hemminki & Heikkila, 1975), but unfortunately, both problems occur regularly. A sample of 86 elderly occupants of an in-residence hotel in Manhattan were found to be taking 17 regular prescription drugs, including 105 psychoactive drugs, with 19% of these individuals receiving two or more psychoactive drugs (Pascarelli, 1974). In another study of 236 geriatric patients who were visited in their homes, 77 were taking barbiturates despite the fact that most already had some impairment in cerebral circulation; and 46 of 58 patients taking diuretics were not on potassium, resulting in a number of them being lethargic, dehydrated, and constipated (Gibson & O'Hare, 1968). The problem is worldwide, as a survey of 217 persons averaging 70 years of age in Finland showed; one-third had ingested four or more different kinds of drugs during one week, including one-half using psychotropic drugs, with 20% using more than one psychotropic drug (Hemminki & Heikkila, 1975).

While frequently the case, noncompliance is not always toward excessive use. Some 53% of the elderly receiving precriptions were taking less drugs than prescribed because (according to their stated reasons) they did not feel the need for the drugs any longer, it did not help, it caused unpleasant side effects, or the drugs were too expensive (Hemminki & Heikkila, 1975).

Leading classes of drugs of abuse for persons over age 50 are barbiturates and benzodiazepine tranquilizers (Pascarelli, 1974). The most frequently misused specific drugs, according to the frequency of their abuse, are: diazepam (Valium), barbiturate mixtures (Tuinal), phenobarbital, and propoxyphene (Darvon) (Petersen & Thomas, 1975).

The sleeping pills (hypnotics) and antianxiety medications have special dangers in the elderly. Because they decrease alertness, their use in even normal doses can result in confusion (Johnson, 1972). As the elderly metabolize drugs slowly, the organic brain syndrome might continue to be misdiagnosed as one of the senile brain diseases with resultant misprescribing and misplacement and subsequent increased mortality (Kidd, 1962). Other hazards related to decreasing alertness include hypotension, which can precipitate falls. A related problem is lethargy and apparent sadness and depression, which can be mislabeled and mistreated. This can also lead to immobility with its own complications.

Thus, the elderly patient who either receives too much of these drugs from a physician or who deliberately or inadvertently abuses the drugs, can develop serious difficulties in both psychiatric and physical spheres.

Treatment and Recommendations

Apart from ignorance by the elderly themselves, careless prescribing habits lead to the misuse of powerful drugs. Often practitioners fail to relate the symptomatic conditions of their patients to the drug therapy, which is itself a possible cause (Gibson & O'Hare, 1968). Automatic prescriptions are issued with no attention to present drug therapy or previous drug intake. Obtaining a good drug history should be mandatory and made available to appropriate health team colleagues.

The best policy in prescribing for the elderly population is simplicity: the fewest possible drugs in the simplest way (Gibson & O'Hare, 1968; Hemminki & Heikkila, 1975). Basic rules for proper drug therapy might include: Know the pharmacological action of the drug, use the lowest dosage possible, use the fewest drugs possible, do not treat symptoms without attempting to know the cause, and regularly review the drugs that have been prescribed (Hall, 1973). Noncompliance is not necessarily bad: Underuse is one way for the patient to avoid ingesting excessive quantities of drugs.

In summary, abuse of prescription drugs in the elderly is especially acute for depressant drugs like hypnotics and antianxiety medications. Both deliberate patient abuse and physician overprescribing can be avoided through good history taking and the observation of some common-sense rules.

ABUSE OF OVER-THE-COUNTER DRUGS

Use of over-the-counter drugs by the elderly has been influenced in several ways. Advertising creates a demand for both prescribed and over-the-counter drugs (Cooper, 1975). Misleading claims increase sales and develop a false sense of security regarding the safety of over-the-counter drug use (Stewart, 1973). Many of the health problems common in elderly populations (e.g., arthritis, gastrointestinal complaints, skin problems, stiffness) are usually temporarily improved by nonprescription medication. Many elderly rely on their own self-medication measures, and it is not surprising that utilization patterns are heavy.

Difficulty in diagnosing over-the-counter drug abuse occurs due to deception by the patient, reticence in the relatives to acknowledge the problem, and the lack of awareness by the family doctor (Carney, 1971). Three of the most abused drugs in elderly populations are not widely abused by younger people: aspirins and aspirin compounds, bromides, and laxatives. We will give further information on these three categories, as well as discuss other miscellaneous over-the-counter drugs.

Analgesic Abuse

Consumption of analgesics (aspirin, aspirin compounds, phenacetin, and caffeine) has doubled in a 10-year period in the United States, Canada, Denmark, and Switzerland (Gault et al., 1968). Trends suggest that analgesic consumption is increasing two to three times as fast as the population growth rate (Murray, Greene, & Adams, 1971). In one survey of 2921 individuals, 15% of the women and 8% of the men ingested aspirin daily (Gillies & Skyring, 1972); another survey showed that 12% of 639 randomly selected households used analgesics daily (George, 1972). Frequently, analgesic abusers also take alcohol and other drugs, and often give a history of past psychiatric disorders (Murray et al., 1971). In one sample, 18 of 32 analgesic abusers had been patients on a psychiatric ward at some point (Gault et al., 1968).

Aspirin alone may result in gastrointestinal upsets, bleeding, gastric ulcers, asthmatic attacks, and skin reactions. The salicylates can also produce excitement, confusion, or delirium and hallucinations when taken in a high dosage (Johnson, 1972). Many elderly are unaware of the associated dangers of other drugs frequently used in combination with aspirin in nonprescription remedies. Abuse of compound analgesics may result in serious complications, including anemia, peptic ulcer, upper gastrointestinal bleeding, and renal disease—difficulties the elderly will not be able to tolerate.

Chronic use of phenacetin has been implicated as a cause of kidney prolems and can produce a state of chronic intoxication with impairment of concentration, irritability, depressed moods, and psychotic or hallucinatory experiences (Gault et al., 1968; Lenhart, 1976). Dextropropoxyphene hydrochloride (Darvon) and paracetamol mixtures can give rise to euphoria and physical dependence. Other analgesics (e.g., pentazocine or Talwin) occasionally produce hallucinations or disorientation with disturbed behavior (Johnson, 1972). The decreased cerebral circulation and lack of rapid healing powers in the elderly may mean they are high-risk candidates for these problems.

Bromide Abuse

Patients seeking relief from anxiety and tension or gastrointestinal complaints may be predisposed to chronic use of bromides, which are still present in some over-the-counter medications, such as Nytol, Sominex, and Bromo Seltzer (Morrant, 1975). Bromide dependence may be superimposed on other disorders (epilepsy, hypothyroidism, anxiety) for which it was originally prescribed (Hunter, 1956).

The bromide ion is slowly excreted by the kidney, with a half-life of 12 days. Therefore, it tends to accumulate when taken for prolonged periods or when it is used by patients with decreased renal function (Stewart, 1973). But even the short-term use of bromide can cause cerebral impairment (Johnson, 1972).

Differential diagnosis of bromide intoxication is wide. Protean symptoms increase the difficulty of diagnosing, and, as stated earlier, bromism often coexists with another condition (Carney, 1971). Bromide intoxication should be suspected in patients who have unexplained neurologic manifestations and behavior disorders, particularly of recent onset. Bromism is clinically characterized by mental changes, usually confusion (occasionally psychosis), depression, a skin rash, and a variety of neurological abnormalities, including tremor, sensation of spinning, midline headache, ataxia, tendon reflex changes, loss of power, dysarthria, paraphasia, and extensor plantar responses (Carney, 1971, Johnson, 1972; Stewart, 1973).

Wider realization that bromism still occurs and stricter control of the sale of bromide preparations without prescription have been advocated (Carney, 1971). Pharmacists ideally could help advise patients on the safe and effective use of these nonprescription drug products (Stewart, 1973).

Laxative Abuse

The taking of laxatives is entrenched in Western culture. More than 30% of people over 60 years of age take a weekly does of a cathartic. It is well recognized that excessive laxative consumption may have grave consequences.

Many laxatives contain phenolphthalein which, when absorbed systematically, may cause cardiac and respiratory distress in susceptible individuals (Lenhart, 1976). Classical features of laxative misuse include diarrhea, abdominal pain, thirst, muscular weakness and cramps due to hypokalemia, melanosis coli, and characteristic radiological appearances of the colon (Cummings, Sladen, James, Sarnes, & Misiewicz, 1974; Morrant, 1975). Mineral oil retards gastric emptying and may impede the absorption of some minerals and fat-soluble vitamins. It also presents a real danger of aspiration pneumonia in the debilitated patient, while saline cathartics may result in dehydration and electrolyte imbalance (Lenhart, 1976).

Diagnosis is difficult due in part to the patients' concealment of their own laxative use. It is also nearly impossible to detect laxatives in the body with the chemical tests now available (Cummings *et al.*, 1974).

Many elderly persons develop a dependence on laxatives. Special attention to proper diet and fluid intake can reduce the need for chemical stimulation (Lenhart, 1976). Unless the health care deliverer asks about laxative abuse patterns in *all* elderly patients, the diagnosis will be missed.

Abuse of Other Over-the-Counter Drugs

Although analgesics, bromides, and laxatives are most frequently abused, other over-the-counter drugs may also be misused by the elderly patient. *Cough mixtures* may contain phenylpropanolamine, which could produce hypotention/hypertension, and psychiatric symptoms such as visual disturbances, nervousness, or dizziness (Johnson, 1972). The elderly patient's response to *antihistamines* can be agitation, excitement, and mild concentration difficulties (Johnson, 1972; Morrant, 1975). *Sleep-producing agents* should be used carefully by anyone with glaucoma, since they often contain scopolamine (Lenhart, 1976), which can increase intraocular pressure. Scopolamine can also create an organic brain syndrome in elderly individuals.

Vitamins can have side effects when usage patterns are heavy, a problem seen especially among the affluent elderly. For example, vitamin D in large doses may cause hypercalcemia, weakness, fatigue, headaches, nausea, and diarrhea. One gram or more a day of vitamin C can cause diarrhea and the precipitation of uric acid crystals in the urine, potentially forming stones (Lenhart, 1976).

In summary, a variety of facts are responsible for abuse of over-the-counter drugs by the older age group. While all medications are at risk, analgesics, bromides, and laxatives are most commonly used.

Health care specialists need to be aware of these problems as part of the differential diagnoses of psychiatric problems in the aged.

CONCLUSIONS

We have presented a very serious problem: abuse of a variety of medications by a population vulnerable to side effects and lacking the physical reserve to survive an adverse reaction once it begins. Drug misuse can contribute much to the psychopathological picture in the elderly. Treatment starts with the recognition that problems do exist and that our elderly patients are in no way immune to these difficulties.

Control of the drug abuse and misuse patterns can be approached through a variety of mechanisms. First, the possible role of drugs as causative agents in almost any medical or psychiatric picture in the elderly should be recognized. Unless one thinks of it, one will miss the diagnosis.

Second, in evaluating new patients, all past prescriptions and all health care agencies involved in their care should be noted. Patients should be encouraged to throw out old drugs. Long-term patients should undergo periodic reviews of what medications are being received by prescription, over-the-counter, and through friends.

Third, prescriptions should be kept to a minimum and instructions kept as simple as possible.

Finally, there are areas of public actions that should be considered. New controls on over-the-counter drugs and their advertising might be needed. Education programs covering special drug problems in the elderly have great potential benefit for physicians in practice and those in training, as well as for pharmacists and nurses. Public interest groups, including medical and older age organizations, should consider sponsoring drug education campaigns aimed at reaching and informing older people.

Two additional drug-related problems in the elderly must also be recognized. The elderly opiate abuser is not highly visible but does exist and has some important special health care needs. Also, the rate of alcoholism in older people is almost equal to that of younger age groups (see Chapter 10 of this volume). Unless these problems are recognized and treated, many perplexing physical and emotional crimes will occur. Good early identification and treatment will save both the patient and health provider many future problems.

We have used this chapter to increase readers' awareness of drug problems in elderly populations. We hope that readers will use the references listed here and employ their own clinical practice to learn more about these important problems.

REFERENCES

Abrahams, M. J., Armstrong, J., & Whitlock, F. A. Drug dependence in Brisbane. *Medical Journal of Australia*, 1970, *2*, 397–404.

Ball, J. C., & Urbaitis, J. C. Absence of major medical complications among chronic opiate addicts. *British Journal of the Addictions*, 1970, *65*, 109–112.

Batalden, P. B. *Working with older people*. (Vol. 2). *Biological, psychological and sociological aspects of aging*. (DHEW Publication No. HRA 74-3117, formerly HSM 72-6006, Public Health Service Publication No. 1459-Vol. 2). Washington D.C.: Government Printing Office, 1974.

Bean, P. *The social control of drugs*. New York: Halstead Press, 1974.

Bergman, M. S., & Amir, M. Crime and delinquency among the aged in Israel. *Geriatrics*, 1973, *28*, 149–157.

Capel, W. C., Goldsmith, B. M., Waddell, K. G., & Stewart, G. T. The aging narcotic addict: An increasing problem for the next decades. *Journal of Gerontology*, 1972, *27*, 102–106.

Capel, W. C., & Stewart, G. T. The management of drug abuse in aging populations: New Orleans findings. *Journal of Drug Issues*, 1971, *1*, 114–120.

Carney, M. W. P. Five cases of bromism. *Lancet*, 1971, *2*, 523–524.

Cooper, J. W., Jr. Implications of drug reactions—recognition, incidences and prevention. *Rhode Island Medical Journal*, 1975, *58*, 274–280, 287–288.

Cummings, J. H., Sladen, G. E., James, O. F. W., Sarner, M., & Misiewicz, J. J. Laxative-induced diarrhea: A continuing clinical problem. *British Medical Journal*, 1974, *1*, 537–541.

Gault, M. H., Rudwal, T. C., & Redmond, N. S. Analgesic habits of 500 veterans: Incidence and complications of abuse. *The Canadian Medical Association Journal*, 1968, *98*, 619–626.

George, A. Survey of drug use in a Sydney suburb. *Medical Journal of Australia*, 1972, *2*, 233–237.

Gibson, S. S. J. M., & O'Hare, M. M. Prescription of drugs for old people at home. *Gerontologica Clinica*, 1968, *10*, 271–280.

Gillies, M. A., & Skyring, A. P. The pattern and prevalence of aspirin ingestion as determined by interview of 2921 inhabitants of Sydney. *Medical Journal of Australia*, 1972, *1*, 974–979.

Glick, M. A. Elderly addicts are treatable. *Journal of Addiction Research Foundation of Ontario*, 1974, *4*, 151–159.

Hall, M. R. P. Drug therapy in the elderly. *British Medical Journal*, 1973, *3*, 582–584.

Hemminki, E., & Heikkila, J. Elderly people's compliance with prescriptions, and quality of medication. *Scandinavian Journal of Social Medicine*, 1975, *3*, 87–92.

Hunter, D. (Ed.). *Price's textbook of the practice of medicine*. London: Oxford, 1956.

Johnson, D. A. W. The psychiatric side effects of drugs. *Practitioner*, 1972, *209*, 320–326.

Kidd, C. B. Misplacement of the elderly in the hospital. A study of patients admitted to geriatric and mental hospitals. *British Medical Journal*, 1962, *2*, 1491–1495.

Leathern, J. H. Endocrine changes with age. In A. M. Ostfeld & D. C. Gibson (Eds.),

Epidemiology of aging. Washington, D.C.: U.S. Government Printing Office, 1972. Pp. 180–193.

Lenhart, D. G. The use of medications in the elderly population. *Nursing Clinics of North America, 1976, 11,* 135–143.

Morrant, J. C. A. Medicines and mental illness in old age. *Canadian Psychiatric Association Journal, 1975, 20,* 309–312.

Murray, R. M., Greene, J. G., & Adams, J. H. Analgesic abuse and dementia. *Lancet, 1971, 2,* 242–245.

O'Donnell, J. A. *Narcotic addicts in Kentucky* (Public Health Service Publication, No. 1891). Washington, D.C.: 1969, 258–260.

Pascarelli, E. F. Drug dependence: An age-old problem compounded by old age. *Geriatrics, 1974, 29,* 109–115.

Pascarelli, E. F., & Fischer, W. Drug dependence in the elderly. *International Journal of Aging and Human Development, 1974, 5,* 347–356.

Petersen, D. M., & Thomas, C. W. Acute drug reactions among the elderly. *Journal of Gerontology, 1975, 30,* 552–556.

Phillipson, R. *Drugs and the aged: Policy issues and utilization of research findings.* Paper presented at the American Association for the Advancement of Science, Boston, 1976.

Raskind, M., & Eisdorfer, C. The use of psychotherapeutic drugs in geriatrics. In L. L. Simpson (Ed.), *The use of psychotherapeutic drugs in the treatment of mental illness.* New York: Raven Press, 1978.

Shader, R. I. *Psychiatric complications of medical drugs.* New York: Raven Press, 1972.

Snow, M. Maturing out of narcotic addiction in New York City. *International Journal of the Addictions, 1973, 8,* 921–938.

Stewart, R. B. Bromide intoxication from nonprescription medication. *American Journal of Hospital Pharmacology, 1973, 30,* 85–86.

Subby, P. *A community-based program for the chemically dependent elderly.* Paper presented at North American Congress on Alcohol and Drug Problems, San Francisco, December 1975.

Swanson, D. W., Weddige, R. L., & Morse, R. M. Abuse of prescription drugs. *Mayo Clinic Proceedings, 1973, 48,* 359–367.

Winick, C. Maturing out of narcotic addiction. *Bulletin on Narcotics, 1962, 14,* 1–7.

Winick, C. The life cycle of the narcotic addict and of addiction. *Bulletin on Narcotics, 1964, 26,* 1–11.

Chapter 12

DEVIATE SEX BEHAVIOR IN THE AGING: SOCIAL DEFINITIONS AND THE LIVES OF OLDER GAY PEOPLE

Myra T. Johnson and James J. Kelly

OLDER PEOPLE AS "DECREPIT" AND "SEXLESS": THE IMPACT OF PREVALENT SOCIETAL ATTITUDES ON THE STUDY OF AGING

Gerontological Publication: "The Language of Despair"

Gerontological theorists have long been plagued by what is often fragmented and contradictory data couched in what Kutner (1962, p. 6) has termed "the language of despair." One possible explanation for this dilemma has been advanced by Berger and Luckmann (1967), who posit that learning and scientific research are deeply affected by the culture in which they are produced. From this perspective a racist nation is likely to produce scientific theory tinged with, and implicitly based on, racial prejudice; an ageist society is, similarly, likely to produce theory, social definitions, and empirical findings based on the premise that aging is a "decremental process" (Lansing, 1952) or "a flight of irregular stairs" (Howell, 1953).

It is now becoming widely acknowledged that prejudice and negative attitudes have underscored the field of gerontology, and new definitions are being phrased and research conducted from fresh perspectives. However, this period of rethinking and reexamination constitutes a very new phenomenon. The traditional viewpoint was, unfortunately, manifested not only in theory and definition, but also in what was and

243

was not considered "researchable" or "important." For example, 10 years ago Feigenbaum commented that after reviewing the published programs of the Gerontological Society for the 5 previous years he was unable to find even *one* reference concerning the sexual attitudes of senior citizens (Feigenbaum, 1967, p. 42).

Research in Aging Sexuality:
A Compendium of Taboos

The reservations of physicians and researchers in probing the sex lives of people old enough to be their parents have been cited by Berezin (1969, p. 132). Informal societal taboos against older people engaging in sex also impede research.[1] "Often, when subjects do volunteer, relatives find out and insist that they leave the study [Pfeiffer, 1972, p. 17]." Research suffers both from the hesitation of older persons to serve as research subjects and because of the hesitation of doctors and other researchers to ask questions:

> In one study at Duke University, young doctors found it difficult to inquire into the sex lives, past or present, of aged women who had been single all their lives. There were fourteen such women in the study, and on only four of these were any sexual data obtained [Pfeiffer, 1972, p. 18].

There is a paucity of research data on the sexuality of either older men or older women, and the lack seems clearly most acute in regard to older women.[2] Kinsey, Pomeroy, Martin, and Gebhard, for instance, dealt, in only a very limited way, with sexuality and aging in *Sexual Behavior in the Human Female* (1953); with only one expection the data published described women under 60. "Look through any bibliography on aging and you will discover that older women are practically nonexistent" say a group of librarians compiling material on women and aging in 1976, suggesting that the amount of research available on older women is still insufficient (NOW Task Force on Older Women, 1976, p. 1).

Some factors that may help to account for the particular taboo

[1] Definitions of "old" and "older" tend to be subjective and influenced by individual attitudes as illustrated by Neugarten's 1968 study of "age norms, age constraints, and adult socialization." To permit maximum use of relevant data the terms are operationalized, in this chapter, to include anyone 50 or over.

[2] Christenson and Gagnon (1965) propose that one reason the older male is a more popular research subject is simply that most researchers have been males and that these male researchers have had a vested interest in studying impotence and other topics related to aging in the male.

against sex research about older women have been suggested by Margaret Hellie Huyck in her article "Sex and the Older Woman" (1977). The concept that the purpose of sex, and the purpose of women, is for "procreation," women's cultural definition as sex objects for men, the notion that older women are unattractive and therefore sexually unmarketable and a subtle extension of the incest taboo all operate as negative prohibitions against sex research involving older women.

Research on the sexuality of older adults has also suffered by an implicit presumption, sometimes made, that older people are "sexless" and can be lumped together in categories such as "the elderly" or "senior citizens." When this presumption underlies research, older men and women lose not only their sexuality, but also their gender. Much valuable information is necessarily lost (Christenson & Gagnon, 1965; NOW Task Force on Older Women, 1976).

The dilemma confronted by gerontologists now is that, until recent years, information about the sex lives of older persons was not socially defined as "valuable." The professional "language of despair" made sex, for the most part, a taboo, or seemingly nonsensical, research topic for gerontologists. Older people were thought too "decrepit," too "frail and near to God" to engage in sexual behavior and, as has been illustrated in the case of women, therefore thought to have outlived their reproductive ability and consequently their usefulness. This socially prescribed sexlessness may be linked to broader stigmatization of older people as "undesirable," and, if they engage in sexual relations, as sexually deviant.

DIRTY OLD MEN AND WITCHES: OLDER PEOPLE AND SEXUAL DEVIANCE

The Social Construction of Sexual Deviance

Just as definitions of aging and age-appropriate behavior shift, definitions of what constitutes sexual deviance may also be socially constructed.[3]

---

[3] Some social scientists (Gagnon & Simon, 1967; Hunt, 1974) favor defining sexual deviance as a concept relating to deviation from statistical "normalcy" or "conformity." However, there is usually some reference in their writing to the "conflict" between sexually deviant acts and the "social order" (Gagnon & Simon, 1967, pp. 4–11; Hunt, 1974, p. 297). Goode and Troiden (1974, p. 16) clarify the linkage between the social order and deviance in their definition: "Deviance . . . is simply behavior which some people in a society find morally offensive, and which excites in these people—or would, if it were discovered—disapproval, condemnation, censure, hostility [p. 16]."

Religious, social, and legal convention has, for several thousand years, at least, favored the married, baby-producing, heterosexual, creating what has been termed a "sexual elite" (Gochros, 1977). In political terms, elite groups tend to have privilege and control. For the heterosexual "elite" this control has included the power to define, denigrate, and attempt to cure "deviance," sexual deviants being condemned for engaging in extragenital or nonreproductive sexual practices (Zubin & Money, 1971, pp. 203–209).

This definition encompasses a wide range of not only handicapped, gay, and autoerotic people and people who prefer sex with children or animals but, in fact, all people past their childbearing years. Guilt in older persons who desire to continue "evil, erotic" sexual activities in later years has been cited by Stokes (1971), Pfeiffer (1972), and Leaf (1973), illustrating the power of the elite's negative sanctions.

Sexual Deviance and Social Undesirability

Negative sanctions applied to one area of life sometimes extend, through stereotypes, to stigmatize the personalities and life styles of entire groups of people. The mentality that stereotypes sexual activity and interest as inappropriate for older people also seems to suggest that older people are somehow "undesirable." The old in general are often stereotyped (Hickey & Kalish, 1968; McTavish, 1971; Palmore, 1968) and a number of myths, stigmas, negative societal beliefs, and definitions tend to be attached to older persons. In modern times, elderly persons have been generalized to be "politically reactionary," "senile," and "fanatically religious" (Bengtson, 1973, p. 27). There is also evidence that older people are viewed as childlike. For example, while only about 20% of professionals who work with older people have had training in gerontology, many have been trained to work with children (Kleyman, 1974, p. 37). This orientation is evident in the activities planned in many senior centers and nursing facilities. (Interestingly, both older persons and children have been thought to have little sexual interest and both have also been considered incapable of full participation in the adult world.)

The Myth of the "Dirty Old Man"

The stereotype of the old man who makes sexual advances to younger people, especially children, is a common one despite considerable evidence to the contrary. West (1965, p. 421) suggests that "elderly pedophiles are less common in clinical practice than the frequent references to them in the literature might lead one to suppose." Cohen and Boucher (1972, p. 62) explain that while the only classification of sexual "offenders" to have an average "older" age range are the pedophiles, most of the members of this group have had a long interest in this activity rather than first engaging in it as older adults.[4]

Despite evidence to the contrary, the persistence of the popular image of the elderly sex offender seems to fit with the idea of a reproducing sexual elite. Whiskin (1967), for example, appears to espouse this viewpoint when he writes: "It is not difficult to see an element of attempting to prove 'I am still a male' plus some attempt to obtain a more passive kind of sexual gratification [p. 17]."

The Post-Menopausal Woman as "Witch"

Historically, one of the most damning of all images has been that of the aging woman as "witch." In the 1961 edition of Webster's Dictionary (Gove, 1961), the second definition of witch is "an ugly old woman; crone, hag." The association of older women with witches is explained by scholarly agreement that women persecuted as witches were usually "isolated, eccentric, mostly old, widowed or single." In essence, women accused of witchcraft were often not part of the "sexual elite" and, in many instances, appear to have been persecuted for their nonconformity (Grimstad & Rennie, 1975, p. 197; Szasz, 1970).

A Double Stigma: Aging in Sexual Minority Groups

Closely associated with the persecution of older people for nonconformity is the notion that people who engage in sexually deviant activities when young become particularly strange in old age. Studies of the politics of aging indicate that membership in any other minority group further lowers status in aging (Binstock, 1972; Kleyman, 1974).[5] For example, in sexual terms, people who have faced society's stigmatization for years, such as gays, face a double stigma when they grow older.

"The aging homosexual tends to become distinctly odd . . . living

---

[4] Older people tend to be poorer (Kleyman, 1974), and the poor tend to be more visible to public authorities. It could be hypothesized, therefore, that they are more likely to be observed in pedophilic activity than are younger men.

[5] Older black people, according to Binstock (1972) are about twice as "badly off" as the rest of the aged population. It has also been estimated that 14% of women over age 65 have no income (Kleyman, 1974, pp. 47–51).

in the Bowery, seeking oblivion in handouts and cheap wine . . .
regress[ing] to a point where he preys on small children" (Allen, 1961,
pp. 95, 258–259). Statements like these, part of respected nonfiction
literature 17 years ago, still continue to influence and inform much of
public opinion, especially in an area where so little is written.

The public's attitudes toward sexual minorities are influenced not
only by available literature, but perhaps more insidiously by films. *Boys
in the Band, Staircase,* and *The Killing of Sister George* are just three
examples of films portraying gay men and women as old or as confronting the "problems" of aging (Tyler, 1973). Altman wrote in 1971 (p. 51):
"To the best of my knowledge no film depicting homosexuals as anything but pitiful and scarred or at least pathetic and ridiculous has come
out of Hollywood . . ." While a handful of movies have portrayed gay
people more positively since, few of these films have dealt with aging.
Moviegoers are left with a "gay is evil—old is evil" double whammy.

Viewing the person who is simply beyond childbearing age as
undesirable or deviant may have its roots in historical times when few
people outlived their reproductive ability. The old witch and the elderly
child molester are both ancient stereotypes. However, modern
psychiatry has bolstered the popular stereotype of the "unfortunate"
aging members of sexual minority groups with the term "psychopathological."

PSYCHOPATHOLOGY AND THE AGING:
A DEFINITIONAL CONTROVERSY

Focus on Gay People

Among the sexual preference groups that are not part of the sexual
elite, and are therefore labeled "deviant," gays probably form the
largest percentage. Kinsey's (1948) research revealed that about 50% of
the men he studied had been involved in homosexual activity at some
time in their lives. Kinsey's researchers estimated that approximately
12–13% of the women studied had experienced orgasm with another
woman at some point during adulthood (Kinsey *et al.*, 1953, pp. 481–
482), and the recent Hite Report indicates that 8% of women responding were primarily lesbian (Hite, 1976, p. 261). Statistics on other sexual
deviations are spottier, but research seems to suggest that the percentages of people involved are relatively small. For this reason, focus
throughout the rest of this chapter will be primarily on middle-aged
and older gay men and women.

The "Psychopathology" Label: Counterarguments

As the theme of this book is "psychopathology and the aging," this analysis first counters the notion that gay people, or older gay people, are psychopathological.[6] Until fairly recently most gay people led highly secret private lives in order to avoid possible social–legal penalties. In this context, gays were only "available for study" when entering law enforcement or psychiatric systems (Hooker, 1967). In addition, many researchers (Collins, 1975; Goldfarb, 1965) undertaking studies of the general public have overlooked the possibility of gay subsamples in populations that they somehow "assume" to be totally heterosexual. Also, bias may enter into the reporting when samples do include, or are composed of, gay people. The controversy and emotionalism surrounding the topic of gayness creates the potential for researchers bias in the work of both gays and heterosexuals. As Dr. Richard C. Pillard (Pillard, in White, 1972) states in a Boston University School of Medicine lecture: "One reason mental health professionals continue to think of homosexuality as an illness is that most research about the subject has been done by heterosexuals who may approach the subject with prejudice [p. 46]."

A number of eminent therapists and researchers in psychological fields (Chesler, 1972; Halleck, 1971; Saghir & Robins, 1973; Szasz, 1970), as well as the American Psychiatric Association, have now rejected stereotypes of gay people and notions that they are "mentally ill."

Labels and the Attitudes of Older Gay People

However, Tripp (1971, p. 49) refers to therapists who may continue to gain money and legitimacy by "frightening the patient with the image of the aging, lonely homosexual." Indeed, there is a popular belief, common both among heterosexuals and within the gay community, that while it may be delightful to be "young and gay," the older gay person is rejected and subsequently becomes "pathological."

Weinberg (1970) summarizes the tone of the societal attitudes and opinions he recorded while researching age-related variations in the social and psychological characteristics of gay males:

> The older homosexual is often described by homosexuals themselves and in the literature . . . [as] isolated from the exciting aspects of homosexual life, alone and lonely, anxious and lacking in self-esteem due to the social

---

[6] According to Hinsie and Campbell's *Psychiatric Dictionary* (1970, p. 618) "psychopathology" is that "branch of science that deals with morbidity or pathology of the psyche or mind."

and sexual rejection experienced. Most people speak of his general unhappiness and depression and his generally low state of psychological well-being [Weinberg, 1970, p. 528].

In 1974 Kelly, co-author of this chapter, conducted a study of 241 gay men between the ages of 16 and 79 in the Los Angeles metropolitan area. At the time of this study a review of English language social science literature uncovered little material—four journal articles and no books—devoted directly to the subject of aging gay men.[7]
Kelly sought to explore his subjects' attitudes, stereotypes, and characteristics in reference to aging, and much of his material is relevant to the "psychopathology" issue. Few of the gay men studied indicated that they, themselves, feared aging. No one who was over 56 years of age feared what he was coming to know, his own older years.

A Look at the Lives of Some Older Gay Men

Well, I know so many who call me on the telephone and they're lonely and they don't know what is going to become of them and all this kind of stuff. Well, I yell at them. If you want to be loved, LOVE. Love somebody. Love many. I write letters to people and call people and people call me. Because you got to be active, just like a good doctor says, if you want to keep your sex life active. The thing that you don't use, you lose. So, if you want a friend or if you want to be loved, be a friend, and be loving [interview by Kelly, 1974, p. 169].

In order to know something about the real tenor and depth of life for those living with the double stigma of being old and gay, Kelly conducted intensive taped interviews with 16 men over age 65, 5 between the ages of 75 and 79. The quotation that opens this discussion was selected because it seems to reflect the life philosophies of the majority of these older men.

Stigma and Strength through Mastery of Crisis

The adaptational patterns of aging of all but one of these men could be classified as "reorganizing," "focused," or "holding on."[8] The

---

[7] See Calleja, 1967; Francher and Henkin, 1973; Hader, 1966; Weinberg, 1970.

[8] Havighurst, Neugarten, and Tobin have defined a "pattern of aging [as] a coherent complex of behavior, including social interaction and use of free-time, achieved by an individual through the interaction of his personality with his social setting [Havighurst *et*

majority described themselves as socially and sexually active and satisfied in interpersonal relationships.

The comment of one older man suggests a focus for further exploration of gay adaptational patterns of aging:

> I used to feel depressed, but it's a social approval thing. Everybody wants to have self-esteem. . . . I found out when I was going to college, people would always walk by and say, "Oh, he's gay." I think all gay persons have to go through that shit, you know . . . "he's a faggot; he's a freak." . . . So they try to condemn you . . . social approval is a bitch at times, especially being gay [interview by Kelly, 1974, p. 170].

Weinberg (1970), Simon and Gagnon (1969), and Tripp (1971, 1975) all suggest that the gay man tends to adapt well to aging, at least partially because he usually faces the crisis of handling his stigmatized identity early in life.

However, in terms of the "strength through mastery of crisis" hypothesis, gays in the current "over 65" cohort may have endured particular hardships that later generations may be less likely to face. For example, 2 of the 16 interviewees over age 65 mentioned having spent time in prison on sodomy charges.

> Then trouble came on, they found out and I spent ten years in the penitentiary. Over being gay. I'd known this friend for over a year . . . and he, well, we parted and he tried to blackmail me. And when I wouldn't go for it, he turned me in. . . . The judge decided . . . because I was so respectable he was going to make an example of me so he threw the book at me. He gave me ten years [interview by Kelly, 1974, p. 172].

Loneliness and Isolation: Lifelong Patterns

Tripp's remark (1975) that gays who are lonely old men were isolated and guilt ridden when young seems supported by the words of the one older respondent interviewed whose adaptational pattern seemed "disorganized".[9]

---

al., in Bengtson, 1973, p. 37]." There are a limited number of patterns which can be discovered empirically.

These authors conceptualize the "reorganizing" pattern of aging as characterized by high role activity, life satisfaction, and integrated personality. The "focused" pattern is seen as similar but involving a "medium" level of social activity. The "holding on" pattern, while still involving high life satisfaction and medium social activity, differs in the introduction of the "armored–defended" personality type (Bengtson, 1973, p. 38)

[9] The "disorganized" pattern of aging is defined as including a low role activity level, medium to low life satisfaction, and an "unintegrated" personality type (Bengtson, 1973, p. 38).

I'm very unhappy, miserably unhappy, because I'm alone. I used to work so hard all my life; I wasn't able to make friends. My mother, her side of the family, seems to be like that. It may be because we are reserved or something like that. For me it's a tough situation. Sometimes for days I don't speak to a soul [interview by Kelly, 1974, p. 171].

In other portions of the interview, this individual seemed to have internalized considerable guilt and stigma over his sexual preference (defining it as a "pathological state"), yet he linked his unhappiness, ultimately, not to his sexuality, but to personality traits developed over the life span.

Friendship and Other Supports

Simon and Gagnon (1969) cite friendship supports in the gay community as an additional contributing factor in the successful adaptation of many gays to aging. Friendship ties also seemed to be a source of strength for some of the men studied: "I have a host of friends. They brought me through my grief with Wally. If I didn't have those, I would have never made it. I'm sure. They were strictly friends . . . very comfortable people [interview by Kelly, 1974, p. 172]."

Other older gays mentioned such phenomena as the so-called lack of a "male menopause" as contributing to an easier process of aging: "I did hear on TV not so long age [that] the male menopause in the heterosexual man is a form of vanity, fear of losing your virility. Of course, I don't have to worry about that [interview by Kelly, 1974, p. 172]."

Self-Concept: "An Exception to the Rule"

There may, in fact, be a relationship between stigmatization and discrimination and a mind-set that pervaded many of these older men's conversations.

In the first quotation in this section the respondent talks about giving advice to "so many who call me on the telephone and they're lonely . . ." This theme, that "most *other* older gays have difficulty adapting while *I* do not," was repeated, in some form, by over half of the gays interviewed over age 65.

Interviewer: How do you feel about growing older?
Interviewee: I don't mind it at all. I'm having a good time so why apologize.
Interviewer: How do you think most gays feel about growing old?
Interviewee: They dread it.

Interviewer: Any reasons why you say that?
Interviewee: Yes, because it offends their ego. It disturbs their egos. . . .
Interviewer: What happens to old gays?
Interviewee: They get lonely and desperate. And they just kind of waste
             away.

                                  [interview by Kelly, 1974, p. 174]

As documented by Kelly's research, many older gay people seem unable to account for or accept the success of their lives except by seeing themselves as "exceptions to the rule." The "deviance–psychopathology" label is so pervasive that gay people who have grappled with it for a lifetime take it for granted as "sound," in a generalized sense. It is accepted as a constant, a fact, and the proliferation of negatively phrased literature about both gays and aging and about older gays serves to "document" these "facts," making them appear to be "real" and "tangible."

THE LIVES OF OLDER LESBIANS: A LITERATURE REVIEW

Social Definitions and "Happiness" Measures

Most of the men Kelly studied seemed satisfied with their lives and few mentioned experiencing symptoms of psychopathology. This is not to suggest that all older gays are enjoying life to the fullest. Del Martin and Phyllis Lyon (1972) recommend, on the basis of many years' experience counseling lesbian women, that researchers abandon the practice of attempting to measure the lesbian's happiness or her "psychopathology." Because of the deviance and "sickness" imputed to lesbians, many older gay women have faced years of job discrimination, blackmail, lack of understanding of their personal needs and commitments, and, as a result, sometimes, self-hate, anger, and/or depression.

The Older Lesbian: Overlooked

While Martin and Lyon's (1972) insight seems equally applicable to both gay men and gay women, it must be noted that there are many crucial differences in life style between the two groups. Social scientists have sometimes counted and analyzed gay women and men together and have occasionally suggested that findings that apply to gay men (the more frequently studied group) apply equally to gay women (Martin & Lyon, 1972, p. 7).

Since most researchers in the social sciences are still men, gay men are still much more frequently studied than are gay women. Research on both gay women and gay men, also, tends to focus on the young and on the correctly or incorrectly ascribed "exotic activities" of the young: bar hopping, dating, and gay movement activism (Simon & Gagnon, 1967). While research on the older lesbian continues to be virtually nonexistent, enough is known to counter the long popular images of older lesbian women as cold, cruel entrepreneurs and child molesters.[10]

A handful of studies aimed at the younger gay adult have included some material relevant to lesbianism and aging. For example, Saghir and Robins (1973, pp. 311–312) posed the question "How do you feel about aging?" in their survey of the life styles of gay men and women. Women's responses indicated that growing old alone was apparently not as great a source of apprehension as was for the men studied, although more women desired to grow old with a lover.

Most studies of the sexuality of older women tend to ignore the lesbian (Christenson & Gagnon, 1965; Gubrium, 1975). However, Christenson and Johnson (1973) report 8 lesbian women in a sample of 71 never-married, white women over 50. All 8 had experienced heterosexual coitus, with most of the women seeming to turn to heterosexual behavior after experiencing lesbianism in their youth. Shere Hite's (1976, p. 349) comment, "The sexual revolution did not include older women," may help to explain this pattern.

Acknowledgment of Lesbian Feelings: The Pressure of Social Definitions

During the young adult years of most women who are now "middle-aged" or "aging," pressures to assume socially defined wife–mother roles were so great that many women never found outlets for lesbian feelings or abandoned outlets under social pressure to marry. Many of these women now find themselves deviating from this life pattern in middle age, when children are grown, or with the advent of menopause.[11] Linkage of a shift in roles and a shift in hormonal balance spells an awakening or resurgence of lesbian interest in some women (Hite, 1976; Huyck, 1977; Martin & Lyon, 1972).

[10] According to Martin and Lyon (1972, pp. 15–16) instances of lesbian child molestation are so rare that, since helping to found the Daughters of Bilitis in the early 1950s, they have not been confronted with a single case.

[11] Medical evidence suggests that the increase in androgen production, combined with other physiological changes and diminution of inhibition may cause women to feel increased sexual desire at menopause (Hite, 1976; Huyck, 1977).

For women who are now middle aged, historical developments (the women's liberation movement and changes in role definitions for women) have facilitated the identification and acknowledgment of lesbian feelings. Women who might have earlier chosen to ignore such feelings are now "coming out."

The fact that much of the material currently available on the older lesbian is in the form of personal essays (Gidlow, 1976), novels (Arnold, 1975), and open-ended interviews (Galana & Covina, 1977; Tavris, 1977) may be related to this sense of release from oppressive social definitions.

Lesbian Aging: "Changing the Negative into the Positive"

Carol Tavris (1977), who interviewed several lesbian couples in their 50s and 60s for the *Redbook Report on Female Sexuality* reports that older gay women seem to have much the same concerns as straight women in the same age brackets. The fears and complaints voiced by the older gay women focused around being alone in old age and doubting their attractiveness to younger women, both concerns similar to those voiced by a large number of the straight women Tavris interviewed (Tavris, 1977, p. 65).

Other lesbian writers seem to differ with these findings, suggesting that the older lesbian is *not* just like older straight women, and as might be hypothesized, thereby "absolved" of any stigma of pathology by virtue of association. Poet Elsa Gidlow (1976) sees aging as an *easier* process for the lesbian because of her insulation from concern about male emphasis on youth and physical attractiveness. (She suggests that the sexual selection process in the lesbian community may be based on other criteria, a statement contrary to Tavris's findings.)

Martin and Lyon (1972) stress that the older lesbian has been molded by her responses and adaptations to social oppression, and that the older lesbian cannot be analyzed in a vacuum, apart from the culture that has "defined" her.

Galana and Covina (1977), after traveling for 3 months to interview lesbians across the country, found that the women exhibited an "overwhelming ability to change the negative into the positive." They indicated that only two couples, out of approximately 300 women interviewed, engaged in "butch"–"femme" role playing. The great majority of women, when asked how they felt about being lesbian, responded with positive self-definitions.

A sense of "strength through mastery of crisis," similar to that observed by Kelly, runs through the interviews Galana and Covina did with older women, typified in one with a 44-year-old woman who admitted, for the first time, in the course of the interview, her pride in her lesbianism (Galana & Covina, 1977, p. 128).

Toward a New Definition of "Deviance"

The psychiatrist who defines the misery of the older person and/or the older gay person as "illness" may, according to Halleck (1971, p. 113), be helping "to perpetuate a vicious form of oppression." Instead of diagnosing "pathology," Halleck recommends concentrating on analysis of factors that contribute to happiness and a sense of well-being.

Guilt over sexual behavior socially defined as "deviant" or "wrong" can interfere with adjustment and interpersonal relations at every stage of the life cycle. The issue, however, may well be the "guilt" and not the "behavior" itself.

The problem may lie with the currently accepted definitions of deviance. Perhaps it is time to redefine the term, not in relation to nonconformity with society's standards, but to describe a turning away from deep inner feelings, a denial of the reality and truth of one's self.

REFERENCES

Allen, C. The aging homosexual. In I. Rubin (Ed.), *The third sex*. New York: New Book, 1961.

Altman, D. *Homosexual oppression and liberation*. New York: Avon, 1971.

Arnold, J. *Sister Gin*. Plainfield, Vermont: Daughters, Inc., 1975.

Bengtson, V. L. *The social psychology of aging*. New York: Bobbs-Merrill, 1973.

Berezin, M. A. Sex and old age: A review of the literature. *Journal of Geriatric Psychiatry*, 1969, *2* (2), 131–149.

Berger, P. L., & Luckmann, T. *The social construction of reality* (Anchor ed.). New York: Doubleday, 1967.

Binstock, R. H. Interest group liberalism and the politics of aging. *The Gerontologist*, Autumn 1972, p. 265.

Calleja, M. A. Homosexual behavior in older men. *Sexology*, August 1967, pp. 46–48.

Chesler, F. *Women and madness*. New York: Avon, 1972.

Christenson, C. V. & Gagnon, J. H. Sexual behavior in a group of older women. *Journal of Gerontology*, 1965, *20*, 351–356.

Christenson, C. V., & Johnson, A. B. Sexual patterns in a group of older never-married women. *Journal of Geriatric Psychiatry*, 1973, *6* (1), 80–98.

Cohen, M., & Boucher, R. Misunderstandings about sex criminals. *Sexual Behavior*, March 1972, pp. 57–62.

Collins, M. *Age and ageism: Report of a study on ageism experienced by older women.*

Portsmouth, New Hampshire: The Institute for the Study of Women in Transition, 1975.

Feigenbaum, E. Sexual attitudes in the elderly. *Geriatrics,* July 1967, pp. 42–59.

Francher, J. S., & Henkin, J. The menopausal queen: Adjustment to aging and the male homosexual. *American Journal of Orthopsychiatry,* 1973, *43,* 670–674.

Gagnon, J., & Simon, W. (Eds.). *Sexual deviance.* New York: Harper & Row, 1967.

Galana, L., & Covina, G. *The new lesbians.* Berkeley, California: Moon Books, 1977.

Gidlow, E. A view from the seventy-seventh year. *Women: A Journal of Liberation,* 1976, *4,* (4), 32–35.

Gochros, H. L., & Gochros, J. *The sexually oppressed.* New York: Association Press, 1977.

Goldfarb, A. I. Foreword. In I. Rubin (Ed.), *Sexual life after sixty.* New York: Basic Books, 1965.

Goode, R., & Troiden, R. *Sexual deviance and deviants.* New York: Morrow, 1974.

Gove, P. B., & Merriam-Webster Editorial Staff. *Webster's third new international dictionary of the English language, unabridged.* Springfield, Massachusetts: G. & C. Merriam, 1961.

Grimstad, K., & Rennie, S. (Eds.). *The new woman's survival sourcebook.* New York: Knopf, 1975.

Gubrium, J. F. Being single in old age. *International Journal of Aging and Human Development,* 1975, *6,* 29–41.

Hader, M. Homosexuality as part of our aging process. *Psychiatric Quarterly,* 1966, *40,* 515–524.

Halleck, S. L. *The politics of therapy.* New York: Science House, 1971.

Hickey, T., & Kalish, R. A. Young people's perception of adults. *Journal of Gerontology,* 1968, *23,* 215–219.

Hinsie, L. E., & Campbell, R. J. *Psychiatric dictionary.* New York: Oxford Univ. Press. 1970.

Hite, S. *The Hite report.* New York: Macmillan, 1976.

Hooker, E. The homosexual community. In J. H. Gagnon & W. Simon (Eds.), *Sexual deviance.* New York: Harper & Row, 1967.

Howell, T. H. *Our advancing years.* London: Phoenix, 1953.

Hunt, M. *Sexual behavior in the 1970s.* Chicago: Playboy Press, 1974.

Huyck, M. H. Sex and the older woman. In L. E. Troll, J. Israel, & K. Israel (Eds.), *Looking ahead: A woman's guide to the problems and joys of growing older.* Englewood Cliffs, New Jersey: Prentice-Hall, 1977. Pp. 43–59.

Kelly, J. J. *Brothers and brothers: The gay man's adaptation to aging.* Unpublished doctoral dissertation. Ann Arbor, Michigan: University Microfilms, 1974.

Kinsey, A. C., Pomeroy, W. B., & Martin, C. E. *Sexual behavior in the human male.* Philadelphia: Saunders, 1948.

Kinsey, A. C., Pomeroy, W. B., Martin, C. E., & Gebhard, P. *Sexual behavior in the human female.* Philadelphia: Saunders, 1953.

Kleyman, P. *Senior power.* San Francisco: Glide, 1974.

Kutner, B. The social nature of aging. *Gerontologist,* 1962, *2,* 5–8.

Lansing, A. I. (Ed.). *Cowdry's problems of aging.* Baltimore, Maryland: Williams & Wilkins, 1952.

Leaf, A. Every day is a gift when you are over 100. *National Geographic,* January 1973, pp. 93–118.

Martin, D., & Lyon, P. *Lesbian/woman.* San Francisco: Glide, 1972.

McTavish, D. G. Perceptions of old people: A review of research methodologies and findings. *Gerontologist,* 1971, *11* (4), 90.

Neugarten, B. L. Age norms, age constraints, and adult socialization. In B. L. Neugarten (Ed.), *Middle age and aging*. Chicago: Univ. of Chicago Press, 1968.

NOW Task Force on Older Women. *Age is becoming: An annotated bibliography on women and aging*. San Francisco: Glide, 1976.

Palmore, E. The effects of aging on activities and attitudes. *Gerontologist*, 1968, *8*, 259–263.

Pfeiffer, E. Sex and aging. *Sexual Behavior*, October 1972, pp. 17–21.

Saghir, M. T., & Robins, E. *Male and female homosexuality*. Baltimore, Maryland: Williams & Wilkins, 1973.

Simon, W., & Gagnon, J. H. Femininity in the lesbian community. *Social Problems*, 1967, *15* (2), 212–221.

Simon, W., & Gagnon, J. H. Homosexuality: The formulation of a sociological perspective. In R. W. Weltge (Ed.), *The same sex*. Philadelphia, Pilgrim, 1969.

Stokes, W. R. Sexual pleasure in the late years. *Professional Psychology*, Fall 1971, pp. 361–362.

Szasz, T. S. *The manufacture of madness*. New York: Delta, 1970.

Tavris, C. The sexual lives of women over 60. *Ms.*, July 1977, pp. 62–65.

Tripp, C. A. "Debate: Can homosexuals change with psychotherapy?" *Sexual Behavior*, July 1971, pp. 42–49.

Tripp, C. A. *The homosexual matrix*. New York: Signet, 1975.

Tyler, P. *Screening the sexes: Homosexuality in the movies*. Garden City, New York: Anchor, 1973.

Weinberg, M. S. The male homosexual: Age-related variations in social and psychological characteristics. *Social Problems*, 1970, *17*, 527–537.

West, D. J. Clinical types among sexual offenders. In R. S. (Ed.), *Sexual behavior and the law*. Springfield, Illinois: C. C. Thomas, 1965.

Whiskin, F. E. The geriatric sex offender. *Geriatrics*, October 1967, pp. 168–172.

White, D. Changing attitudes on homosexuals. *Boston Globe*, December 12, 1972. P. 42.

Zubin, J., & Money, J. *Contemporary sexual behavior: Critical issues in the 1970s*. Baltimore, Maryland: Johns Hopkins University Press, 1971.

Chapter 13

CRIMINALITY AND THE AGING

Charles P. McCreary

INTRODUCTION AND DEFINITIONS

A review of the literature in the area of criminality and the aging does not reveal an extensive body of theory or research. This sparsity of scientific effort contrasts markedly with the extensive body of literature in the field of juvenile delinquency. However, there have been investigators who have examined certain key issues such as the types of crimes that older people commit, changes in the incidence of illegal behavior associated with increasing age, and the special needs of the elderly law offender.

The first task of this chapter is to clarify what is meant by criminality. Criminality is defined as patterns of behavior that are regarded by society as illegal. Causes of criminal behavior are certainly complex. Most experts in this field now tend to de-emphasize past beliefs in the etiological significance of heredity or physical characteristics and, instead, stress the importance of social and psychological factors such as poverty, discrimination, and family disturbance.

Regardless of the cause of criminality, this behavior seems to be related to certain personality characteristics (low frustration tolerance, rebelliousness, lack of empathy, etc.). This chapter will discuss the overt criminal behavior of the aging and it will review the underlying attitudes and inclinations that characterize older people who engage in illegal behavior. The present chapter will use the term *criminality* when referring to overt behavior and will utilize the term *antisocial traits* when referring to underlying characteristics.

259

One hurdle in the attempt to examine criminality and the aging is the dilemma of how to regard the complex social behaviors of alcoholism and drug abuse. It should be recognized that society, including behavioral scientists interested in these problems, is not clear on whether these complicated behaviors should be regarded as "crimes," as a "disease," or as emotional disturbances. This chapter will not attempt to explore these problems in depth but will note them when they involve illegal activities. Also, we shall not discuss suicide, even though it has been regarded as illegal by many people. The kinds of criminal behavior discussed here include property offenses (theft, burglary, embezzlement), violent offenses (homicide, rape, assault, robbery), sex offenses, nuisance offenses (vagrancy), and substance-abuse offenses (drunkenness, narcotics violations) and do not include minor offenses such as traffic violations.

The Crimes that Older People Commit: A Review of Findings

In general, there is some consensus that the overall crime rate declines with age. Riley and Foner (1968) note that crime rates typically decline over the middle and later years after a peak in adolescence or early adulthood. They point out that basically similar declines have occurred both in the United States as well as in many of the European countries. These authors also maintain that the rate of recidivism (reconviction for a new crime) declines with increasing age.

Epstein, Mills, and Simon (1970) did a thorough investigation of the frequency and causes of arrest of individuals 60 years old or older living in San Francisco. They conducted extensive interviews of a sample of persons arrested for drunkenness. They obtained permission from the San Francisco Police Department to examine data from the city jail arrest ledger. They found that during the period under investigation there were 2429 arrests of persons 60 years of age or older in San Francisco, which amounted to only 5.3% of all persons 18 years of age or older arrested in that period. This figure is much lower than the percentage of the total population that is 60 years of age or older, both in San Francisco as well as in the United States as a whole.

Although there is agreement that the overall crime rate declines with age, there is a lack of agreement about the relative preponderance of specific types of criminal behavior associated with aging. This lack of agreement may be partially explained by differences in the samples under study. Whiskin (1968) studied elderly persons referred by the courts for psychiatric evaluations. He reported that these older offenders committed more minor sex offenses, such as child molestation and exhibitionism, in relationship to other age groups, and he found that over half of the cases involved child molestation, whereas only two offenders were involved in overt assaultive acts. On the other hand, Keller and Vedder (1968) surveyed patterns of criminal behavior in the entire sample of offenders (reported in the FBI Uniform Crime Reports); they found that older offenders commit a disproportionately higher number of drunkenness and vagrancy offenses. Furthermore, the previously described study by Epstein et al. (1970) showed that 80% of the arrests in San Francisco of persons over the age of 60 were for drunkenness, whereas only 50% of all adult arrests were for this offense. In summary, previous researchers tend to agree that there are fewer offenses in the aging that involve stealing and assault, many more offenses involving drunkenness and vagrancy, and possibly more minor sex offenses such as child molestation.

AGE AND ARRESTS IN 1975

I have analyzed the data collected by the U.S. Federal Bureau of Investigation (1976) in order to assess the most recently available findings regarding patterns of criminal behavior associated with aging. The FBI produces a yearly summary of information from cooperating individual police departments in the United States regarding patterns of criminal behavior. It should be noted that there is variability among the states in terms of procedures of reporting crimes and in the actual definition of certain offenses. The federal government has been encouraging development and implementation of mandatory state uniform crime reporting programs in order to reduce the numbers of communities not represented in the FBI crime reports. Caution must be taken in using the FBI data to make interpretations about changes in crime rates or patterns over time since such changes may, in part, reflect improved reporting practices.

The true occurrence of illegal behavior can be measured only indirectly. Estimates can be derived from an examination of conviction rates, crimes that are prosecuted, or arrests. The FBI chooses to use arrests as an index of the incidence of illegal behavior. These figures produce larger numbers than would be shown in terms of court records of convictions, yet they may actually underestimate the actual occurrence of illegal behavior, since many crimes are either not reported to authorities or no potential perpetrator is identified by the police.

Most likely, the pattern of age differences in illegal behavior would be basically the same if another index of criminality were utilized. However, it should be noted that the rates of prosecution and conviction differ according to various types of crimes. Finally, it should be noted that 76% of persons arrested in 1975 were male and 51% were white.

Table 13.1 summarizes the total arrest figures at various ages and corresponding figures for the total population of the United States. It is apparent that the arrest rate is more than double the population figure in the younger ages up to age 34, has shifted to equal the expected population rate at the 35- to 44-year age range, and has begun to show a dramatic decrease by age 55. In fact, those persons over age 65 are arrested at a much lower rate than would be expected. Only 1.2% of persons arrested are 65 and above, whereas this age group comprises over 10% of the population of the United States.

Table 13.2 presents the total number of persons arrested for various kinds of crimes and the percentages of arrests at several age ranges for the different types of illegal behavior. This table gives the relative preponderance of patterns of criminal behavior within each age grouping. For persons 65 years and above, the incidence of arrest for the following crimes is very close to their rate of arrest for all crimes: homicide, negligent and nonnegligent manslaughter, aggravated assault, sex offenses, weapons possession, driving under the influence, and disorderly conduct. Their relative rate of arrest is much higher for offenses such as drunkenness, vagrancy, and gambling. It is much

TABLE 13.1
Total Population and Arrests at Various Ages in 1975

Age in years	Population (%)	Arrests (%)
Under 11	19.1[a]	1.0
12–17	12.0[a]	24.9
18–24	12.9	31.0
25–34	14.4	19.3
35–44	10.7	10.8
45–54	11.1	8.1
55–64	9.3	3.6
65+	10.5	1.2
Total *N*	213,137,000	8,013,645[b]

[a] Prorated estimates, since figures published by the U.S. Bureau of the Census (1976) do not include these ranges.
[b] Obtained from communities having an estimated total population of 179,191,000.

TABLE 13.2
Percentages of Various Categories of Arrest by Age in 1975

Type of arrest	Age range							Total (N)
	Under 18	18–24	25–34	35–44	45–54	55–64	65+	
Homicide and nonnegligent manslaughter	9.5	35.3	29.5	13.4	7.3	3.2	1.6	16,484
Negligent manslaughter	12.1	36.5	24.5	11.9	7.3	3.9	1.8	3,041
Forcible rape	17.6	40.4	28.4	9.3	3.2	.8	.3	21,963
Aggravated assault	17.6	32.0	26.2	13.3	7.1	2.7	1.0	202,217
Robbery	34.3	42.8	17.7	3.8	1.1	.3	.1	129,788
Burglary	52.6	32.6	10.6	2.8	1.0	.3	.0	449,155
Larceny and theft	45.1	29.4	13.6	5.1	3.3	1.6	.9	958,938
Motor-vehicle theft	54.5	30.0	10.5	3.2	1.2	.3	.1	120,224
Assault—other	19.8	32.1	26.0	12.6	6.5	2.1	.7	352,648
Fraud, etc.[a]	5.9	35.7	35.5	14.7	6.3	1.5	.3	213,358
Sex offenses[b]	21.4	25.5	24.4	12.3	7.6	3.4	1.4	50,837
Stolen property	32.6	39.1	17.9	6.3	2.8	.9	.3	100,903
Arson	53.0	21.8	13.1	6.7	3.5	1.5	.5	14,589
Vandalism	65.4	20.6	8.3	3.3	1.6	.5	.2	175,865
Weapons—possessing	16.3	34.9	25.7	12.3	6.9	2.8	1.0	130,933
Prostitution— commercial vice	4.7	61.2	24.8	5.4	2.6	.9	.3	50,229
Drunkenness	3.5	20.4	20.8	20.3	20.8	10.7	3.3	1,176,121
Narcotics	24.2	52.9	18.0	3.5	1.1	.2	.0	508,189
Vagrancy	9.0	23.2	19.4	18.9	18.3	6.8	3.5	59,277
Gambling	3.6	15.3	24.6	22.1	18.7	10.6	5.0	49,469
Offenses against family and children	11.8	30.2	32.3	17.1	6.8	1.5	.3	53,332
Driving under the influence	1.9	25.1	27.2	20.4	16.2	7.3	1.8	908,680
Disorderly conduct	19.0	38.4	21.6	10.4	6.8	2.7	1.0	632,561

[a] Fraud, embezzlement, forgery, and counterfeiting.
[b] Other than forcible rape and prostitution.

lower for forcible rape, robbery, burglary, motor vehicle theft, fraud, vandalism, narcotics violations, prostitution, and offenses against families and children.

When the percentage of arrests of persons 65 and above for each type of crime is compared with the rate for the total sample of persons arrested (see Table 13.3), some interesting patterns emerge. First of all, violent offenses (homicide, forcible rape, robbery, aggravated assault, and assault) comprise 9% of arrests of the total group of offenders and

TABLE 13.3
Percentage of Arrests and Types of Crimes for Total Sample of Persons Arrested and for Those 65 Years Old and Above

Type of arrest	Total group		Ages 65 and above	
	Percentage	Rank	Percentage	Rank
Homicide and nonnegligent manslaughter	.2	26.5	.3	17.5
Negligent manslaughter	.0	29	.057	27
Forcible rape	.3	25	.058	26
Robbery	1.6	14.5	.2	20
Aggravated assault	2.5	11	2.2	8.5
Assault—other	4.4	8	2.6	6.5
Burglary	5.6	7	.4	15.5
Larceny—Theft	12.0	3	9.0	3
Motor vehicle theft	1.5	16	.1	23
Fraud	1.8	13	.6	13
Forgery and counterfeiting	.7	19	.1	23
Embezzlement	.1	28	.07	25
Stolen property, receiving and possessing	1.3	17	.3	17.5
Arson	.2	26.5	.02	28
Vandalism	2.2	12	.4	15.5
Weapons possession	1.6	14.5	1.4	11
Prostitution and commercial vice	.6	22	.2	20
Sex offenses	.6	22	.8	12
Gambling	.6	22	2.6	6.5
Narcotics violations	6.3	6	.5	14
Drunkenness	14.7	1	40.9	1
Driving under the influence	11.3	4	17.5	2
Liquor law violations	3.3	10	1.8	10
Offenses against family and children	.7	19	.2	20
Disorderly conduct	7.9	5	6.9	5
Vagrancy	.7	19	2.2	8.5
Curfew and runaway	3.8	9	.00	29
Suspicion	.4	24	.1	23
Other	12.9	2	8.6	4

only 5.3% of the arrests of those persons 65 years and above. Therefore, it seems that these offenses are about half as common in those aging persons who are arrested than in the total group of persons arrested.

Theft offenses even more dramatically reveal the lack of involvement on the part of the aging. The base rate for theft offenses (burglary, larceny, motor vehicle theft, fraud, forgery, embezzlement, possession

of stolen property) is 23% whereas c
are arrested for these offenses (see
motor vehicle theft predominate i·
offenders arrested for these crimr
less than 1% of these offenders
forgery, counterfeiting, and en.
to 34-year age range. Some 71%
people in this age range who comprise ⸺

Clearly, offenses that do not involve .
dominate in the aging. Drunkenness, driving
gambling, and vagrancy stand out as crimes that inv.
the age of 64. Among persons over 65, are 63.2% are arre⸺
offenses, whereas only 27.3% of all persons arrested have been ⸺
in these offenses. However, because of the low crime rate in c.
persons, even these offenses are relatively infrequent in terms of absolute numbers. For example, although over 40% of persons arrested who
are 65 years of age and older are arrested for drunkenness, only 3.3% of
all persons arrested for drunkenness are in this age group. In summary,
our findings substantiate the impression that the aging infrequently
engage in illegal behavior, and when they do, they are arrested for less
"antisocial" crimes such as those involving drunkenness and vagrancy.

CHANGES IN ANTISOCIAL TRAITS ASSOCIATED WITH AGING

Weiss (1973) did an extensive study to determine if antisocial traits
or behavior, or both, were related to changes in age. His subjects
consisted of a group of 532 adult patients referred to a midwestern
university medical center for outpatient or short-term, inpatient
psychiatric care. The narrative contents of the medical records of these
patients were analyzed in order to discover descriptive statements that
indicated antisocial attitudes or behavior. In addition, the patients were
administered the Minnesota Multiphasic Personality Inventory (MMPI)
in order to evaluate for personality traits related to antisocial inclinations. Weiss found that of the eight MMPI clinical scales, the only one
that statistically differentiated the age groups was the depression scale
(D); scores on depression increased in each successive age group. Although not finding clear statistical significance, he also noted that the
psychopathic deviate (Pd) scale, commonly regarded as indicating antisocial attitudes (impulsivity and rebelliousness), decreased with age
for males and tended to decrease with age for females. Mean

w scores for males on this scale were 27.37 (under 20 years
6.95 (20–44 years group), 24.45 (45–64years), and 18.33 (65
e and older). If Weiss had compared his oldest group with all
s, the difference on the Pd scale probably would have been
nt statistically. The relative rank of this scale among the eight
clinical scales showed a clear decrease with age. In males, Pd was
second highest scale in the youngest age group and the second
est in the oldest age groups. In females the Pd scale was first in the
oungest age group and seventh in the oldest age group. An analysis of
mean profiles (combinations of scale scores) for the various age groups
suggested that antisocial traits tended to be less common in each suc-
ceeding age group.

When Weiss performed an analysis of the patients' records, he
found that current antisocial characteristics (resentment of authority,
impulsivity, lack of reliability, rebelliousness) were found in 88% of the
youngest group and tended to be virtually absent in the oldest groups.
This was not so true for women. An analysis of past antisocial behavior
revealed that even a history of antisocial behavior decreased with age.
Statements indicating a past history of impulsivity, trouble with the
law, or hostile behavior were found in 62% of the youngest group and
were virtually absent among the two oldest groups. Weiss (1973) concludes that the clinical anecdotal viewpoint that antisocial attitudes
persist as lifelong patterns was not supported by his study. Rather, his
findings indicated that, at least among midwestern adult psychiatric
patients, both antisocial behavior (reported by the patients and observed by others) and antisocial attitudes (indicated by statements and
performance on a psychological test) do tend to decrease with age,
especially among men. He maintains that the age-related decrease in
antisocial behavior does not represent a physical, emotional, or en-
vironmentally determined inability to act upon psychopathic attitudes
that have been retained as basic personality characteristics. Rather, the
decrease in criminal behavior in the aging is associated with fundamental personality reorganization.

One of the disadvantages of the Weiss study (1973) was that the
subject population consisted of psychiatric patients rather than law
offenders. McCreary and Mensh (1977) studied personality differences
(including antisocial inclinations and attitudes), measured by the
MMPI, associated with aging in a sample of law offenders. They were
especially concerned about examining the characteristics of older law
offenders, since the stereotypes and generalizations about the geriatric
offender had not been verified by objective description of their per-

sonalities based upon the systematic administration of quantitatively scored personality inventories. The subjects in this study were 362 male misdemeanor offenders referred to a university-affiliated legal-psychiatry clinic for a postconviction, presentencing dispositional evaluation. Only males were studied, since the number of females referred for an evaluation over the age of 60 was extremely small. Offenders were divided into six age groups (18–19 years, 20–29, 30–39, 40–49, 50–59, 60–85 years). In contrast to Weiss, who only found statistically significant age differences on the depression scale, McCreary and Mensh found that as the age difference between groups increased, the number of significant differences on the various MMPI scales also increased. There were slight increases on the hypochondriasis and hysteria scales associated with age and large decreases on the schizophrenia and mania scales. Thus, the increases associated with age were in the "neurotic" direction and the corresponding decreases were indicative of fewer "psychotic" characteristics in the older offenders. Furthermore, there was an abrupt decrease in the oldest group of offenders on the scale assessing impulsivity and psychopathic tendencies (Pd). This study also utilized Goldberg's (1972) Categorization System, which differentiated psychiatric from sociopathic MMPI profiles. Only the oldest group of offenders scored in the psychiatric range on this index: all other offenders scored in the sociopathic range. The authors conclude that their results are consistent with earlier findings of more neurotic and less psychotic symptomatology in the elderly, and their results indicate less antisocial attitudes and traits among those offenders over the age of 60.

In a study of aged domiciled male veterans, Apfeldorf, Scheinker, and Whitman (1966) used the MMPI in an attempt to discriminate between those veterans having a history of disciplinary offenses (noted in domiciliary and police records) and a "nonoffense" group. The latter group was also rated on a special scale by domiciliary personnel in order to detect subjects who may have escaped official recording. The authors expected that the Pd scale would be higher in the offender group but did not find the two groups to be significantly different from each other on this scale. Although the authors of this study did not report the actual Pd scores of their subjects, their statements suggest that both groups did not differ from the norm on this scale. They refer to a study by Levy, Southcombe, and Cranor (1952), which found that younger criminal groups showed peaks on the Pd scale above a t score of 70 (two standard deviations above the average), while criminal groups 46 years of age or older did not. It appears that in a number of studies older offenders consistently demonstrated a relative absence of the pattern of antisocial characteristics typically found in younger offenders.

CONCLUSIONS AND RECOMMENDATIONS

There is clear evidence that older people are less likely to engage in illegal behavior. This decrease in criminal activity among the aging appears to reflect basic personality reorganization in the direction of greater socialization and does not seem to represent only the lack of opportunity to commit crimes.

When older people do engage in illegal behavior, they tend to commit less serious crimes than the younger population of offenders. They are less likely to engage in assaultive or property offenses and more likely to commit crimes involving drunkenness and vagrancy. Older offenders referred for a psychiatric evaluation are more likely to have committed minor sex offenses such as child molestation. This latter finding probably reflects society's relative intolerance of sexual activity in the aging. Either older people (predominantly male) with no outlets for sexual expression find children less threatening or any sexual behaviors in the aging, including overtures toward children, are regarded by society as unacceptable and, therefore, referred to the criminal justice system for redress. More likely, both processes account for the relative increase in minor sex offenses among the aging.

In general, older offenders themselves are not as antisocial as their younger counterparts. They are not as impulsive and rebellious and they tend to demonstrate patterns of emotional disturbance that are more neurotic and correspondingly less psychotic than younger criminals. Finally, the older a person is when he commits a crime, the less likely he is to commit another one.

The preceding conclusions have many implications for how older offenders should be handled by the criminal justice system. First of all, one should recognize that there is great concern about increasing criminal activity in our present society. Much of this concern focuses on the dramatic increase in assaultive and theft offenses among the very young. Those concerned about this development often suggest that potential and new juvenile offenders be identified and diverted from typical handling that too often involves labeling, incarceration, and identification with "hard-core" prisoners, which seems to increase the vicious spiral toward greater criminal activity in the young. Although this emphasis on prevention and diversion for the youthful offender is appropriate and justifiable, an unfortunate, untested, and unjustifiable policy becomes indirectly associated with it. Older offenders tend to be neglected or regarded as "too old" to benefit from similar efforts toward rehabilitation and diversion.

Older offenders, as discussed previously, are less antisocial and, probably, their criminal behavior reflects more of a response to current environmental stressors than results from longstanding personality characteristics. Therefore, special efforts seem needed to alleviate the impact of those stressors (e.g., lack of employment, loss of close relatives) on the aging.

Also, large numbers of older offenders are arrested for drunkenness and vagrancy and are often put in jail to protect them because there are no alternatives. Jail personnel typically realize that these people are not "criminals" and may attempt to treat them with some measure of compassion (Epstein *et al.*, 1970). Mental health facilities generally do not accept responsibility for caring for these kinds of intoxicated or vagrant elderly people. Halfway houses are needed that would be designed to treat the immediate physical problems of these offenders as well as the more complex and refractory psychological and social problems. However, would society invest the money and effort to serve the needs of such people stereotyped as "useless, harmless, and lazy"?

There would be more interest in dealing with other types of older offenders, such as child molesters, because they are not regarded as harmless but are looked upon with great alarm. Treating these people becomes especially complicated when the victim is not a total stranger to the aging offender. The mental health system should develop programs to treat the offenders themselves and to help the victim and his/her family cope with this traumatic experience. In addition to meeting the emotional needs of the victims, this attention may help to lessen the impact of the elderly offender being labeled as "dangerous" and further ostracized by the community.

Finally, more research is needed in order to assess the special needs of the aging offender. Procedures need to be developed to help differentiate older offenders responding primarily to current stressors from those whose illegal behavior reflects more of a characterological disturbance. Careful evaluation research is necessary in order to find the most effective and efficient programs and facilities to help the aging offender become or remain constructive members of our society.

REFERENCES

Apfeldorf, M., Scheinker, J., & Whitman, G. MMPI responses of aged domiciled veterans with disciplinary records. *Journal of Consulting Psychology*, 1966, *30*, 362.

Epstein, L., Mills, C., & Simon, A. Antisocial behavior of the elderly. *Comprehensive Psychiatry*, 1970, *11*, 36–42.

Goldberg, L. Man versus mean: The exploitation of group profiles for the construction of diagnostic classification systems. *Journal of Abnormal Psychology*, 1972, *79*, 121–131.

Keller, O. J., & Vedder, C. B. The crimes that old persons commit. *Gerontologist*, 1968, *8* (Part I), 43–50.

Levy, S., Southcombe, R., Cranor, J., & Freeman, R. Outstanding personality factors among the population of a state penitentiary: A preliminary report. *Journal of Clinical and Experimental Psychopathology*, 1952, *13*, 117–130.

McCreary, C. P., & Mensh, I. N. Personality differences associated with age in law offenders. *Journal of Gerontology*, 1977, *32*, 164–167.

Riley, M., & Foner, A. *Aging and society* (Vol. 1). *An inventory of research findings*. New York: Russel Sage Foundation, 1968.

U. S. Bureau of the Census. *Statistical abstracts of the United States* (97th ed.). Washington, D. C.: Government Printing Office, 1976.

U. S. Federal Bureau of Investigation. *Crime in the United States, 1975, Uniform Crime Reports*. Washington, D. C.: Government Printing Office, 1976.

Weiss, J. The natural history of antisocial attitudes: What happens to psychopaths? *Journal of Geriatric Psychiatry*, 1973, *6*, 236–242.

Whiskin, F. E. Delinquency in the aged. *Journal of Geriatric Psychiatry*, 1968, *1*, 243–252.

Chapter 14

THE OLDER SOCIOPATH[1]
Eugene Ziskind

Do old sociopaths differ from other old people in their capacity to adjust to aging? There has not been enough scientific research on the subject to permit quantitative or categorical responses to that question. Nevertheless, I have been engaged in extensive research on the nature of sociopathy and the treatment of sociopaths so that a statement of my observations and tentative conclusions may help to enlighten others about the process of adjusting to old age.

In regard to my personal experience, there were distinct shortcomings. Although my research group examined about 100 sociopaths and a somewhat smaller number of controls, ranging in age from 15 to 85 years, no systematic observations were made on their adjustment to aging. However, experiences with a special population of compulsive gamblers permit comments on some aspects of aging in this group of sociopaths.

The major feature of this chapter, therefore, is a description of a selected group of compulsive gambler sociopaths from Gamblers Anonymous (GA) who have abstained from gambling for 5 to 20 years. This special group lends support to the hypothesis that such sociopaths have an enhanced capacity for adjusting to the aging process.

To elucidate this thesis, I offer a case report and some background materials in this chapter.

[1] This study was supported in part by the Andrew Norman Foundation, the Joe D. Bain Foundation, the Roy and Eva Markus Foundation, and also the UCLA Biomedical Sciences Support Grant No. 1-S05-FR-07009-05.

271

THE GATEWAYS RESEARCH PROJECT
ON SOCIOPATHY

For the last 6 years, my colleagues and I have been associated in a research project on sociopathy. The team had three psychologists, Irving Maltzman, co-principal investigator, also head of the Department of Psychology at the University of California, Los Angeles (UCLA), Karl Syndulko, and David Parker; we had three psychiatrists, Ruth Jens, Rodger Farr, and myself, as principal investigator; we also had a social worker, Anne Cahn, and a law student with sociologic training, Margaret Tan. All engaged in the behavioral multidisciplinary collaborative study in sociopathy, assisted by Eulalia Giguette, clinical psychologist and George Maison, professor of pharmacology and psychiatrist, both from the Gateways Forensic Clinic. Although there are several research programs involving sociopaths at Gateways, the present research centers chiefly on compulsive gambler sociopaths.

The research at Gateways was an outgrowth of our participation in the National Institute of Mental Health–Veterans Administration Hospitals collaborative researches on the use of lithium in the affective psychoses, 1968–1972. The research population consisted of patients with "manic" and "depressive" attacks. These turned out to be of three groups. One contained the circular manic-depressives with free intervals of normality. The other two groups, in free periods between manic and depressive episodes, showed either schizophrenia or sociopathy (antisocial personality disorder). Early research was devoted to the effects of lithium upon the recurrent manic and depressive attacks. In one instance of residual sociopathic behavior between mood swings, the family of the patient offered me a research grant for the study of the personality disorder. The first patient had a drug addiction and her special nurse served as the normal control in the original examination by Maltzman. This led to a study of conditioning and evoked responses in sociopaths. The findings of Maltzman on such conditioning and responses supported the contentions of Hare as to differences in conditioning and the extinction of the orienting reflex between sociopaths and controls. There followed researches at Gateways Hospital over the past 8 years. The later studies highlighted an interdisciplinary approach. This will be further discussed in the section on GA after the following case study.

Interdisciplinary Approach

Research on sociopaths lends itself very well to interdisciplinary study. Humans are bio-psycho-social beings. Hence, stresses in various areas call for the collaboration of biological, psychological, and social scientists. In addition, the interdisciplinary approach has other merits for studies in sociopathy. Psychiatry, conceived of as a branch of the science of behavior, helps to do away with the misunderstandings of eclecticism (although the definition in Webster's unabridged dictionary is quite explicit). All behavior is multidetermined, and that of human beings is no exception.

The presence of many behavioral facets does not preclude the presence of specific etiologic factors. Not infrequently there is one cause that is specific, the sine qua non, the one factor without which the disorder cannot occur. This enlarges the scope of the interdisciplinary approach. It includes the so-called medical model, which uses scientific methods to look for specificity of biological, psychological, or social factors in sociopathic behavior. This is the approach we use at Gateways.

However, in the absence of such a demonstrable proven cause, one may set up hypotheses to test for specific biological, psychological, or social stresses. This we have done also. Consequently, we have not only a therapeutic program based on multiple, helpful, plausible methods, but also another with a heuristic approach favoring specific chemical etiologic substances, for example, the peptides.

When scientists are confronted with problems that cannot be measured objectively, they turn to theorizing. The inability to establish adequate hypotheses for testing makes it necessary to resort to the heuristic approach. Measurement is replaced by logic or common sense. This is a wide departure, of course, from the experimental method. Theoretical considerations will later often be proven or disproven. With this disclaimer, we still use the heuristic approach whenever necessary.

I shall present special problems encountered and our experimental strategies in confronting them.[2]

Definition of the Sociopath

The diagnostic designation of the sociopath abounds in difficulties, as is true for all other major diagnostic categories in the classification of

---

[2] Currently, the research team is involved in six different projects. The first is the diagnosis of sociopathy, which the author shares with two other psychiatrists. The second is the psychophysiological laboratory project in sociopaths and controls for measurement of autonomic and electrocortical paramaters. The latter includes (*a*) EEG power spectrum; (*b*) evoked potentials (EP); and (*c*) contingent negative variation (CNV). The third and fourth projects are focused on treatment, and the fifth and sixth involve field studies by the author on GA and Gam-Anon. Gam-Anon is the organization for the mates of compulsive gamblers.

mental diseases. To begin with, the terms psychopath, sociopath, and antisocial personality are all used synonymously. The last term appears in the latest International Classification of Diseases (ICD-9)—and in the American Psychiatric Association Diagnostic Statistical Manual (DSM-III)—now being readied for publication. The term *antisocial personality disorder* is currently preferred. It is particularly propitious because it avoids some of the stigma attached to the terms psychopath and sociopath. There are many different types of antisocial behavior among sociopaths. That of the compulsive gambler, especially when associated with membership in GA, has special research advantages.

A Research Definition

In order to select a homogeneous group of sociopaths, a research definition was formulated.[3] The diagnostic dilemma in sociopathy, as well as in most of the major psychiatric categories, arises from the fact that many of the criteria are not objective. A clinical definition serves several purposes, such as communication with colleagues, labeling patients, and statistical compilation. A research definition can be stricter in its criteria, even eliminating questionable subjects in order to attain homogeneity in the population selected for study. This we accomplished through the use of a rating scale and criteria for selection and exclusion.

A Rating Scale

To overcome the lack of objective measurement for personality traits, we defined five characteristic traits of sociopaths and rated subjects for each characteristic along a scale from 1 to 7 (from almost never to extreme). The selection of subjects for a homogeneous population was made stricter and more accurate by insisting that the subjects chosen have all traits in the pathological range designated as 5 = distinct, 6 = marked, or 7 = extreme. A lesser rating in even one trait was sufficient to exclude the subject. This means that some sociopaths were excluded, but those selected should have greater homogeneity for diagnostic reliability.

The definition of the sociopath in this research is characterized by five inclusions and five exclusions. The sociopath was defined as a person with antisocial behavior who shows the five following traits:(*a*) impulsivity; (*b*) irresponsibility in major social roles; (*c*) superficiality

---

[3] *A research definition.* Because there are numerous definitions of sociopathy, our team has chosen one based on the clinical descriptions by early psychiatrists and criminologists. Pritchard (1837) gave his description more than 150 years ago.

of affect with impairment of empathy; (*d*) inability to profit from past experience, either in the form of punishment or reward; and (*e*) impairment of conscience. Excluded were five classes of psychiatric disorder: (*a*) mental retardation; (*b*) organic brain syndromes or severe brain damage; (*c*) psychoses; (*d*) neuroses; and (*e*) situational maladjustment.

The exclusions are based on that feature found in most clinical classifications of mental diseases which utilizes progressive dichotomies for diagnostic groupings. The first dichotomy divides all the patients into two groups, those with mental deficiency or retardation and the others. From the latter, the second dichotomy separates those with organic brain syndromes from the rest. From the latter, the third dichotomy separates the patients with psychoses from those remaining. From the latter, the fourth dichotomy separates the patients with neuroses from those that remain. The final dichotomy separates persons with situational maladjustments from the rest. The remainder we have called sociopaths.

The Results of the Gateways Research

Following are the results of the Gateways research.

1. It demonstrated defective conditioning in the laboratory of sociopaths as compared with controls.

2. It established a research definition for selecting a homogeneous population of sociopaths for study. Its validity and replicability have been statistically demonstrated.

3. The research established measures for the reduction of the dilemma of diagnosis of sociopathy. A task force formulation for continued work on this goal has been instituted.

4. Clinical differences between sociopaths and controls have been demonstrated for the incidence of: (*a*) hyperkinesis in infancy and childhood; (*b*) specific learning disabilities; (*c*) enuresis; and (*d*) nailbiting.

5. The heuristic argument supporting a specific biologic etiology for sociopathy was formulated.

6. The research showed that mixed simultaneous and sequential combinations of sociopathy, manic-depressive, and schizophrenic syndromes frequently obscure both diagnosis and treatment.

7. Currently, the studies have led to the consideration of pilot treatment experiments to include: (*a*) the effect of administration of peptides prior to the laboratory conditioning experiment; (*b*) naloxone treatment of the "addictive" symptoms of compulsive gamblers; and (*c*) the use of peptides for the treatment of sociopaths.

THE SPECIAL EXPERIENCE WITH COMPULSIVE
GAMBLER SOCIOPATHS

Characteristics of Compulsive Gambling

Most sociopaths have had a great many stresses throughout their lives. Their antisocial behavior has led them into much difficulty. They have developed unusual techniques for keeping out of trouble. They utilize such techniques for long periods of time, but finally they are caught up in the devastation that is common to the lives of most sociopaths.

In the group of compulsive gambler sociopaths, one can observe a most extraordinary commitment to gambling and a profound alteration of life experiences from this circumstance. The individual not infrequently finds a position or a type of work where he can complete his occupational responsibilities rather early in the day. This leaves time open to gamble for many hours, at the racetracks, or in casinos, or in other betting practices involving various sports. Hence, it is not uncommon that these persons are traveling salesmen or have other jobs that can be disposed of in the morning, with the remaining hours available for gambling. They gamble for many hours at the racetracks, near and far, or at local casinos until they are closed. Usually, by day's end they have sustained considerable losses; so they must spend part of the night conning relatives or friends for additional financial resources in order to gamble the next day.

It is quite common for them to sleep only 4 or 5 hours a night. They demonstrate an unusual physical capacity to devote themselves to their compulsive gambling.

It has sometimes been said that the sociopath's major trouble is that he is poorly motivated. It would be more accurate to say that he is a highly motivated person, but his motivations are unconventional. Whatever low motivation he seems to have is for conventional standards of behavior.

The ability that the confirmed sociopath shows in having an unusual resistance to fatigue and various privations must mean that he has developed a resistance to much stress—an aspect of survival of the fittest, as it were.

My personal experience with the specially selected population of compulsive gamblers to be described has been mostly with persons between 50 and 80 years of age. Of the compulsive gamblers, some have been in remission for 5 to 20 years. They are now functioning at better levels of adjustment than are many controls.

Do these people really have a greater capacity for handling stress and, therefore, are they able to survive in circumstances not endured by others who have not had such hardening experience? A case study follows.

THE CASE STUDY

A 70-year-old male had gambled compulsively between ages 26 and 52. He is the oldest of four children of parents in the lower middle class. Both parents ran a fruit and vegetable market and later a general notions store. The subject and his siblings were cared for by a maid. His health was generally good, although he suffered from allergies.

His mother was a strict disciplinarian who criticized and rejected him in favor of his siblings. She demanded that he show gratitude for sacrifices she was forced to make for the family. The subject rejected this attitude openly, which caused his mother to refer to him as a "most miserable child."

At 16 years, our subject moved away from his family in the Midwest to his grandmother's home in Los Angeles. The grandmother disagreed with the mother's opinion of him. She found him so cooperative that she insisted on his remaining with her after the rest of his family moved across the street from her. He helped in his parents' business until he was 21, even while studying at college. Before graduation, he quit school and married.

His gambling history began as a youngster, when he would often play the third hand in his parents' card games at home. At the age of 12 years, he was a better pinochle player than his father. The subject admits no problems with gambling during this period. An indication of his early compulsiveness in gambling, however, was his slavish commitment to slot machines. He tells further of his thirteenth birthday party at which there were two poker tables, each for eight boys.

The Santa Anita racetrack opened when he was 26, and he soon found himself "hooked" on gambling. He gambled daily and compulsively. On Sundays, when the local racetracks were closed, he paid one of his employees to go to Mexico to place bets at the racetracks there.

During this period, he changed jobs frequently. This caused some financial deprivation. For 16 years, his wife held steady jobs to keep the family from going without basic necessities. Despite his erratic employment history, including the loss of two businesses and daily gambling, he was able to hide the nature and extent of gambling from his wife and family for 22 years. The gambling activities remained secret only through many machinations, such as the use of bookies, the prompt covering of bad checks, regular attendance for daily meals, and appearances at special family functions.

Despite apparent concern for his family's welfare, he describes himself as being quite selfish during these years, compared with his self-image of decency and goodness during the precompulsive gambling years. As evidence of selfishness, he tells of going into bankruptcy every 7 years ("the law did not allow it more often").

In his opinion, most members of GA who stop gambling have been "good guys." Those so categorized have stayed out of trouble with the law and have remained close to their families. "A compulsive gambler must have money, the good guys are no exception." Therefore they all lie, cheat, con, and engage in illegal activities.

After age 48, his compulsive gambling was exposed to his wife. They had six major quarrels concerning this. At 52, he sustained his greatest financial loss. He then liquidated all remaining assets and turned to gambling to recoup. This effort was to no avail, for he lost everything. His wife's deprivations at this point were so great that she initiated divorce action. Subsequently, the subject's wife allowed him to return home in response to interventions by their daughter and her family doctor. At this time, he heard of Gamblers Anonymous (GA) and arranged to join the program.

When he joined GA, he encouraged his wife to join Gam-Anon, an organization for the spouses of compulsive gamblers, and they both actively participated. As a newly reformed compulsive gambler, he was adamant in informing his former gambling associates that he no longer gambled, had joined GA, and considered their urging him to return to gambling as a personal insult. He still avoids all gambling establishments, for they continue to produce a "tingle" in him as he passes by. He even refrains from a simple flipping of a coin for coffee. Even though he is quite strict as to his own encounters with the gambling world, he insists that his wife continue her social gambling and trips to Las Vegas, although he does not allow himself to accompany her.

In addition to this radical change in life style, the subject threw himself completely into the GA activities. During the first year, he established an unprecedented record for drawing in 20 new members. Every afternoon and evening he made himself available for answering the GA phone calls from new members, sometimes spending a whole day with a troubled member or taking him into his own home overnight. He has been a member for 18 years. During this period, he has helped to establish five new GA chapters and serves on the Board of Regents.

He attributes his refraining from gambling to a firm policy of following the program one day at a time. He believes that a declaration never to gamble again, or to refrain for a sustained block of time, would have resulted in failure. Other compulsive gamblers often have difficulty in sustaining the resolve for even one day at a time.

He is now semiretired and runs an auto repair service on a half-time basis. He shares the business with a fellow former compulsive gambler whom he induced to join GA and stop gambling. Semiretirement allows a full social life shared with wife, family, friends, and members of the GA organization. He feels comfortable in the present situation. "I have returned to being the good, decent guy I was before compulsive gambling began."

This case report is typical of an individual who has fulfilled the general requirements of Gamblers Anonymous. He is a remitted compulsive gambler sociopath who had gambled for nigh 20 years. He has undergone unusually severe stresses and has been able to weather them. He did not ruin his chances for spontaneous remission since he was essentially a "decent person." In addition, he joined GA and was actively engaged in their program. The frequently observed tendency of sociopaths in midlife to undergo spontaneous remission constitutes an intriguing "experiment of nature." Hence we have asked ourselves, is the attainment of 5 to 20 years of abstinence seen in the lives of some members of Gamblers Anonymous an expression of this phenomenon? Does the remitted compulsive gambler sociopath of midlife have a high rating of "survival in the school of hard knocks" based on his earlier life style of deprivations and stresses characteristic of many compulsive gamblers?

Two features in our subjects aided in the selection of our special group for study: (*a*) they showed a tendency to spontaneous remissions at or beyond midlife; and (*b*) they profited in the GA organization by having sustained a period of abstinence from gambling for 5 to 20 years.

THE TENDENCY TOWARD SPONTANEOUS REMISSION OF SOCIOPATHS

The two definite features known clinically for a long time about sociopaths are first, they do not respond to the usual types of psychiatric care, and second, they tend to undergo spontaneous remission in midlife. Not all sociopaths show a spontaneous remission. However, probably many more would do so, if they had not, early in life, already ruined the opportunity for such remission. Conditions that tend to interfere with spontaneous remission are (*a*) imprisonment with long periods of solitary confinement; (*b*) alcoholism; and (*c*) drug addiction.

Clinicians frequently plead, whenever possible and practical, for the prevention of incarceration. They also advise against ejections from the home by the family and from schools by teachers. Young children are traumatized by isolation from peer groups and by police arrests and detention. These all tend to interfere with normal development and later midlife spontaneous improvement.

The tendency to spontaneous remission lends support to the idea that sociopathy represents a delayed maturation in the nervous system. Several symptoms, more common in the early life of the sociopath than in control subjects, are known to undergo spontaneous remission. Among these are (*a*) the hyperkinesis of childhood; (*b*) specific learning disabilities, such as reading, spelling, and mathematics; (*c*) enuresis of the severest type, often extending into puberty and beyond; (*d*) nail-biting, very severe in sociopaths and two or three times more frequent than in matched controls. Such symptoms are likely to be of bio-psycho-social origin.

THE MULTIFACETED GAMBLERS ANONYMOUS (GA) ORGANIZATION

The GA organization is a multifaceted fellowship, details of which can only be appreciated from direct observation of its numerous activities. The literature of the organization includes many publications, but these hardly do justice to the ongoing, ever-revised, local, autonomous actions of the separate chapters. The profound character of these activities is now being evaluated by me. Over the last 2 years, I have been making field observations to ascertain what can be relayed to psychiatrists, medical schools, and society that will explain why this organization accomplishes more for the compulsive gambler than any other therapy.

The idealism of the GA fellowship seemingly transcends the interest and devotion among members seen in other fraternal orders. This is true even if there is not much financial support given to members in GA. What is given in greater intensity is the time devoted to personal contacts, taking "hurting" persons into their homes overnight, frequent sessions for discussions, numerous phone calls, "twelfth step" calls, the pressure committees, fraternization at after-meeting sessions, round robins, conferences, sharing in official roles, sponsorships, marathon listening at meetings, and team games (baseball, bowling). The weekly group therapy held at Gateways includes compulsive gamblers, manic-depressives, sociopaths, and those with still other types of psychopathology. Our special type of confrontation reinforces the GA program.

The GA program includes, in addition, many supportive activities: there is soul searching, interest in the younger members, taking of inventories, making of retributions, search for other aids such as "marriage encounter," close partying to avoid the temptations encountered constantly in usual social settings, such as card playing and social gambling, with our without drinking; there is an attempt to displace all the hours of temptation to gambling by constructive activities; there is also faith in a "higher power" with its religious or even nonreligious connotations; there is moralistic and idealistic promotion of the "Twelve Steps;" the Serenity Prayer; and there is the concept of working the program a day at a time. All of these, too complicated to impart here, encompass the program.

Many religions render services akin to those of GA and Alcoholics Anonymous (AA), which indeed, in themselves, parallel some religions. I know of nothing in the secular world, or even in religious organizations, that gives as much personal time and service on an ongoing basis as GA (and AA) offer.

Of course, there are some shortcomings, such as the tendency to engage in rigid ritual; the hazards of inculcation; the ingrown tendency to settle down to restricted life patterns; the failure to recognize what the fellowship can do and cannot do; the tendency to interpret all happenings in terms of the primary disorder, and hence, the failure to recognize other disorders and to get help for them (such as manic and endogenous depressive illness); and the failure to recognize the harm of wrong or poor sponsors.

Not all compulsive gamblers are sociopaths—some are and some are not. The presence of both in GA may be an advantage. Possibly nonsociopaths are more altruistic. The latter are social gamblers who may have compulsive personalities but not the antisocial disorder. Many of the antisocial characteristics of the primary sociopath may be countered by the normal character structure of the "social gambler." The group as a whole might just profit by the presence of both compulsive and social gamblers in GA.

Although the absence of antisocial behavior in the early or pregambling years may not be an adequate differential diagnostic feature between the nonsociopath and sociopath compulsive gambler, the fact is that among those compulsive gamblers with 5 to 20 years of gambling abstinence, the number without an early life history of sociopathy is small.

In general, patients with various types of pathology are known to die at earlier ages than those without major pathologies. On this score, one would suspect a lesser longevity for sociopaths than matched normal controls. Even the heightened resistance to stress that I have assumed for the sociopath—at least, the remitted sociopath—may not be warranted.

The foregoing would be true for sociopaths not having the hardened resistance and aid from the GA organization. The original assumption could still be true for the heightened resistance of these sociopaths. It may not be true for those with lesser resistance for the age group of 50 years and older. Quantitative aspects are highly variable and measurements inadequate, so that much of this discussion must be speculative. Be that as it may, I have been very much impressed with the adjustment of many of the remitted sociopaths.

On closer scrutiny, it may well be that such remitted sociopaths still have more restricted lives than others who are not compulsive gamblers. Although they are now better husbands and fathers, has the impoverishment of their earlier lives still remained with them? Does the dedication to the GA program replace for them the broader cultural and less restricted lives of nongamblers?

Even if this possible limitation is so, to what extent is it displaced by a zeal and dedication to the new goals and activities of our remitted sociopaths? How many other persons have the same socializations, the same devotions, and the same discussions of the problems with their friends and social contacts? The question still is, Does GA give its members a stimulus and experience that helps in the adjustment to the aging process?

The self-help group of GA has been able to influence compulsive gamblers (as AA has helped alcoholics) more effectively than any other treatment resource. Although this is not as widely appreciated as it should be, my personal experience, gained from attending numerous sessions of GA in various chapters, has confirmed my strong belief that such is the case. The fact that not all compulsive gamblers (nor all compulsive alcoholics) are helped by these organizations does not detract from the contention. The GA experience strongly reinforces the potential for spontaneous remission.

ORGANIC FACTORS IN THE AGING PROCESS

A word should be said about the organic factors in the aging process. Aging itself is primarily an organic process manifesting itself in a slow but progressive impairment of the physiochemical, the psychological, and the sociocultural functions of human beings. In addition, physical stresses and diseases have frequently accelerated this process. In a practical way, adequate geriatric treatment consists in seeing that nutrition and basic hygienic measures of living are sustained. The presence of physical illnesses, particularly those impairing the general health (e.g., circulatory disease and arteriosclerosis), lead to early signs of brain deterioration. Diffuse involvement of the brain produces the acute and chronic brain syndrome. As far as we know, these processes occur in sociopaths and normal individuals with the same pernicious influence. Hence alcoholism, drug abuse, and the poor conditions of living in prisons should all present the same effects on aging in sociopaths and nonsociopaths.

The only saving grace may be in the hardened life process beyond the spontaneous remission of these sociopaths. Perhaps the biometricians, in their statistics, may have some data on this subject in the different occupations. The remission rates are so low even in GA compulsive gambler sociopaths that only special studies comparing those with nonremitting gambler sociopaths might demonstrate the difference.

Certainly, those in the group of compulsive gambler sociopaths showing 5 or more years of remission appear to be handling aging better than those not so fortunate. This still leaves the quantitative answers unknown. The tale of successful GA compulsive gambler sociopaths at least is a saga that raises interesting questions.

A look is warranted at individual cases of secondary sociopaths, those excluded from our study because of mental retardation, organic brain syndrome, psychosis, neurosis, and situational maladjustment. Those with demonstrable organic etiology, particularly with chronic brain syndrome, have a substantially lower longevity and also have lesser capacities for adjustment. There are prognostic studies reported by Glaser (1978) showing differences in the various types of criminal behavior. The greater degrees of alcoholism, drug abuse, and violence in sociopaths would lead one to suspect lower longevity and lessened capacity for adjustment. The literature, in general, bears this out. But again, so many variables are present, including the diagnosis of sociopathy, that definite conclusions are often difficult to arrive at.

DISCUSSION

The impression that the older sociopath adjusts differently to the aging process than others has been my personal, selective experience.

An objective study of the problem has not yet been done. Involved researches might or might not be conclusive.

The personal experience reported here is not an adequate pilot sample for an objective study. It highlights a number of special features of the sociopath: the specific type of spontaneous remission; a special type of stress; and the life style of the compulsive gambler. It indicates a hardening to stress. It emphasizes, for compulsive gambling in general, and for members of GA in particular, the freedom from drugs and usually from alcohol. The fellowship of GA points up the possibilities for therapeutic support and occasional "cure." Finally, the usefulness in all these for the life adjustment has been delineated.

However, all sociopaths are not compulsive gamblers or compulsive alcoholics. Not all belong to such self-help organizations as GA or AA. The effect on longevity and late adjustment also varies widely. Only a minority have sustained remissions. In other words, most sociopaths have not had good prognostic features. Both longevity and the capacity for adjustment in later life may not be any better for these people, they may be even less so than in other normal or pathological groups. The special results depicted for our selected group of old remitted sociopath gamblers reported in this chapter, however, warrant contemplation and further study.

There are a number of problems that warrant more detailing. As previously stated, this is not merely a report on a highly selected group bearing on the adjustment to aging by sociopaths and others. Because the understanding of this problem is intimately bound up with factors not generally known or readily found in the literature and experiences, it might be helpful to pose some of the questions arising from our researches (particularly since much of what has been written in this chapter is idiosyncratic to me):

1. How robust are the findings of abnormality of conditionability in sociopaths? Our results show highly significant differences between a mixed group of sociopaths and a group consisting largely of compulsive gambler sociopaths. The question has been raised by us and others as to whether compulsive gamblers are ever, or often, characteristic sociopaths. In our opinion, they often are—especially those who have met our diagnostic criteria. The compulsive features are only an additional aspect of the heterogeneous syndromes that comprise any group of sociopaths at large.

2. A second question warrants inquiry. Is our remitted compulsive gambler the result of the tendency to spontaneous remission in sociopathy? Or could he have improved from the therapeutic effects of

GA? The very small number of GA members who undergo this type of remission does not permit an answer to this question. However, remissions occurring earlier than midlife might suggest a "treatment" effect. This would require further investigations.

3. A further question is pertinent. Is the case report characteristic? Or is it an accidental contrivance? To date we have seen several such cases. There are persons with prolonged remissions who have not been "good guys." A more intensive research of all the subjects available with and without such remissions would yield some worthwhile answers. It would be quite time absorbing, but it is certainly warranted.

Obviously many more questions could be raised. Answers are needed before we can write with scientific certainty about the enhanced capacity for adjustment to aging in sociopaths.

SUMMARY AND CONCLUSIONS

The compulsive gambler sociopath who while a member of GA has had from 5 to 20 years of abstinence from gambling has the potential for an increased capacity for adjustment to aging in the later years of life. Reference has been made to a small group of such cases with a detailed report on one such person.

Contributory conditions in our small group of sociopaths include: (a) a history of sustained abstinence from gambling at midlife for 5 to 20 years; (b) membership in GA; (c) freedom from legal incarceration; and (d) maintenance of marriage and family.

Which of these conditions are necessary or how many are sufficient is unknown.

It is suggested that the earlier life style of the compulsive gambler with the conquering of stresses and deprivations of the years of compulsive gambling is a hardening process, a survival of the fittest. This serves the individual to adjust better to later vicissitudes of aging.

More definitive research is necessary to establish the foregoing interpretations.

Even should the findings be true only for our particular group of compulsive gambler sociopaths, they still constitute a definite addition to knowledge about abnormal personality disorders. They raise the important issue of whether they are a "marker" for compulsive gambler sociopaths or for the larger group of sociopaths in general. The question is not yet answered as to whether the temporal gradient of fear (Hare, 1965; Tharp, Maltzman, Syndulko, & Ziskind, in press) constitutes an objective set of findings that can be utilized as a "marker" for either of these conditions. A "marker" has long been sought, and our subsequent research will continue to explore this matter.

ACKNOWLEDGMENTS

Many aided in the writing of this chapter. For this I thank Helen Zimnavoda, Esther Somerfeld-Ziskind, my wife, and David Ziskind, my brother. Particular gratitude is due Pearl Glaser and her husband, Dan Glaser, Professor of Sociology at the University of Southern California, for their reorganization and rewriting of much of the original manuscript. I also wish to extend my thanks to Eulalia Giguette for scoring the MMPIs for me.

REFERENCES

Cleckley, H. *The mask of sanity*. St. Louis, Missouri: C. V. Mosby, 1964.

Diagnostic and statistical manual of mental disorders: DSM-III. Washington, D. C.: American Psychiatric Association, in preparation.

Gamblers Anonymous (3rd ed.). Los Angeles: G. A. Publishing Co., 1977.

Glaser, D. The classification of offenses and offenders. In D. Glaser (Ed.), *Handbook of criminology.* Chicago: Rand McNally, 1974.

Glaser, D. *Strategic criminal justice planning.* NIMH Center for Studies of Crime and Delinquency, Monograph Series. Washington, D.C.: US Government Printing Office, 1975.

Glaser, D. *Crime in our changing society.* New York: Holt, Rinehart and Winston, 1978.

Gough, H. *California psychological inventory.* Palo Alto, California: Consulting Psychologists Press, 1975.

Hare, R. D. Temporal gradient of fear arousal in psychopaths. *Journal of Abnormal Psychology*, 1965, *70*, 442–445.

Hare, R. D. Psychopathy, autonomic functioning, and the orienting response. *Journal of Abnormal Psychology*, 1968, *73*, (3), Pt. 2.

Hare, R. D. *Psychopathy.* New York: Wiley, 1970.

Hare, R. D. Electrodermal and cardiovascular correlates of psychopathy. In R. D. Hare & D. Schalling (Eds.), *Psychopathic behavior.* London: Wiley & Sons, 1978.

Hare, R. D., Frazelle, J., & Cox, D. N. Psychopathy and physiological responses to threat of an aversive stimulus. *Psychophysiology*, 1978, *15*, 165–172.

International classification of diseases (9th rev. ed.). Geneva: World Health Organization, 1978.

Langfeldt, G. The significance of a dichotomy in clinical psychiatric classification. *American Journal of Psychiatry*, 1959, *116*, 537.

McCallum, W. C., & Walter, W. G. The effects of attention and distraction on the contingent negative variation in normal and neurotic subjects. *Electroencephalography and Clinical Neurophysiology*, 1968, *25*, 319–329.

Parker, D., Syndulko, K., Jens, R., Ziskind, E., & Maltzman, I. Psychophysiology of sociopathy: Autonomic measures. *Research Communications in Psychology, Psychiatry and Behavior*, 1977, *2*(2), 81–90.

Pritchard, J. C. *A treatise on insanity and other diseases affecting the mind*. Philadelphia: Haswell, Barrington & Haswell, 1837.

Robins, L. N. *Deviant children grown up: A sociological and psychiatric study of sociopathic personality*. Baltimore, Maryland: Williams & Wilkins, 1966.

Smith, R. J. *The psychopath in society*. New York: Academic Press, 1978.

Spielberger, C. C., Gorsuch, R. L., & Lushene, R. *Manual for the state-trait anxiety inventory*. Palo Alto, California: Consulting Psychologists Press, 1970.

Stainbrook, E. Some historical determinants of contemporary diagnostic and etiological thinking in psychiatry. In P. H. Hock & J. Zubin (Eds.), *Current problems of psychiatric diagnosis*. New York: Grune & Stratton, 1953.

Syndulko, K., Parker, D., Jens, R., Maltzman, I., & Ziskind, E. Psychophysiology of sociopathy: Electrocortical measures. *Biological Psychology*, 1975, *3*, 185–200.

Tecce, J. J. Contingent negative variation (CNV) and psychological processes in man. *Psychological Bulletin*, 1972, *77*, 72–108.

Tharp, V. K., Maltzman, I., Syndulko, K., Ziskind, E. Autonomic activity during anticipation of an aversive tone in noninstitutional sociopaths. *Psychophysiology*, in press.

Weiss, J. M. A. *The natural history of antisocial attitudes: What happens to psychopaths?* From report at Third International Symposium on Social Psychiatry, Slantcher Brugan, Bulgaria, October 20–22, 1971.

Ziskind, E. *Psychophysiologic medicine*. Philadelphia: Lea & Febiger, 1954. Pp. 189, 210–213, 282–289.

Ziskind, E. The maturational lag hypothesis for sociopaths: Some research strategies. Paper presented to the Society for Biological Psychiatry 25th Annual Meeting, San Francisco, May 8–10, 1970.

Ziskind, E. The maturational lag hypothesis for sociopathy. Paper presented to the AAAS Meeting, Washington, D. C., December 26–31, 1972.

Ziskind, E. The diagnosis of sociopathy. In NATO Advanced Study Institute on Psychopathic Behavior, Les Arcs, France, September 5–12, 1975. Chichester, England: John Wiley & Sons, 1977.

Ziskind, E., Jens, R., Maltzman, I., Parker, D., Slater, G., & Syndulko, K. Psychophysiological, chemical, and therapeutic research on sociopaths: A search for a homogeneous population. *World Congress of Psychiatry, Proceedings V*. Mexico City: La Prensa Medica, Mexicana, 1971.

Ziskind, E., Syndulko, K., & Maltzman, I. Evidence for a neurologic disorder in the sociopath syndrome: Aversion conditioning and recidivism. In C. Shagass, S. Gershon, & A. J. Friedhoff (Eds.), *Psychopathology and brain dysfunction*. New York: Raven Press, 1977.

Chapter 15

SEX DIFFERENCES IN SUICIDE AMONG OLDER WHITE AMERICANS: A ROLE AND DEVELOPMENTAL APPROACH

Warren Breed and Carol L. Huffine

The single most challenging question about suicide and aging in the white population of the United States is the enormous contrast by sex (see Figure 15.1 and accompanying Table 15.1). The rate for males rises from youth and increases steadily after age 35 into the decade of the 80s. The rate for females peaks before age 50 and declines steadily after that. In the age bracket 45–49 the suicide ratio is about 2:1, male to female; at age 75 and over the ratio approximates 7:1.

This chapter focuses primarily on these differences. A valid explanation of this striking contrast would require solid data. Ideally we should have several hundred detailed social-psychological autopsies of persons who killed themselves at an advanced age, to compare with similar data of younger suicides. Unfortunately, comparative data are scarce and little research has been devoted specifically to suicide among the aged, although an innovative step is provided by Marshall (1975).

Given this tantalizing problem and the scarcity of data, we have proceeded in a rather unusual way. We set as our goal the "explanation" of the facts and proceeded to take cautious first steps toward a solution. From theory and existing empirical evidence, we have selected certain variables that we feel are related to suicide among older people. Surveying studies of the process of human aging provided data on how these variables are related to living elderly persons and provided clues to other factors or processes that might be important in future investigations.

In this work we have made some assumptions that we want to

289

make explicit. We have assumed that suicide potential is inversely related to level of life satisfaction as measured in many studies of aging. We have also assumed that morale—a less specific measure sometimes found in the research literature—is inversely related to suicide. From this we assume that factors found to be related to high life satisfaction or morale will be related to low suicide rates and vice versa.

We hope that this "detective" kind of scholarship will provide clues to other scholars in the field. Our work should be considered as an early attempt to "narrow down" those factors that make suicide rates among older women low, and among older men high.

To provide a frame of reference, we will comment briefly on suicide patterns by age bracket, sex, race, marital status, and over time. We will then review existing data about suicide among aging populations. To integrate these data into a cohesive model we have drawn upon developmental psychology and role theory to illuminate structural arrangements that operate in such a way as to leave men more vulnerable to suicide than women. More than *presenting* sociological and psychological factors, then, our goal is to *integrate* them to emphasize their interaction and interdependence upon each other.

PATTERNS OF SUICIDE[1]

Age, Sex, Marital Status, and Race

The suicide rate of white males in the United States is much higher than that of white females (see Figure 15.1). The difference increases with age as the male rate climbs steadily and sharply and the female rate peaks in middle age and then decreases almost as sharply as it had previously increased. (The detailed data are shown in Table 15.2.)

In the past 40 years the suicide rate of older white men has declined sharply. This is not true of other categories of people. Rates have remained relatively stable for middle-aged white men and have in-

[1] In this presentation we are using data provided by the U.S. Public Health Service or individual investigators. We are familiar with the criticisms of such data (Douglas, 1967) and have ourselves wondered whether reporting of suicide in the elderly might be more or less reliable than in the young. We feel that, important as such questions are, they are not so problematic as to legitimate halting all analysis until some standards of validity and reliability are assured. We are also aware of the conceptual difficulties presented by implicit suicides—those deaths that occur, for instance, from some act of omission rather than commission. Not eating or failing to take life-maintaining medication are examples. These might be more numerous among the elderly than the young but, of course, their enumeration is beyond us at present.

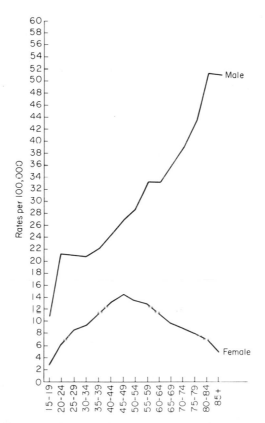

FIGURE 15.1 United States White Suicide Rate per 100,000 by Sex, 1970–1974.
(*Source:* National Center for Health Statistics, 1976.)

creased some for middle-aged women and nonwhite persons. Among the young—particularly male—there have been, since the early 1960s, substantial increases in suicide rates.

Marital status is consistently found to be related to suicide. As the data in Table 15.3 show, nonmarried persons at all ages are more likely to commit suicide than are their married age peers.[2] The divorced are particularly disadvantaged relative to the married, and widowhood is apparently most devastating in early life. The data also confirm Durkheim's (1951) somewhat surprising discovery that marriage is more important to the survival of males than it is to females.

[2] We have limited presentation of the data to age groups beyond 39, partly because the focus of our attention in this paper is older age groups, but also because there are so few young widowed people that rates of suicide calculated for them may be quite misleading.

TABLE 15.1
Suicide Rates by Age and Sex, United States, 1970–1974

Age	Male	Female
15–19	10.8	2.9
20–24	21.5	6.1
25–29	21.4	8.4
30–34	20.7	9.4
35–39	22.0	11.7
40–44	24.3	13.4
45–49	27.0	14.2
50–54	28.6	13.5
55–59	33.5	13.1
60–64	33.5	11.3
65–69	35.9	9.7
70–74	39.3	8.8
75–79	43.8	7.9
80–84	51.4	6.8
85+	51.0	4.7

Generally, suicide rates among nonwhite people are much lower than among whites. An exception is seen in young males, where the rate for nonwhites is possibly higher; "possibly" because of the census underenumeration of young blacks (Linden & Breed, 1976). There is, however, great diversity among the racial groupings incorporated in the category "nonwhite." For instance, compared with rates of whites, those of Chinese-Americans are higher at all ages, but those of American Indians are higher only in youth (Kramer, Pollack, Redick, & Locke, 1972). A single nonwhite suicide rate does not reliably reflect the picture presented by any of the individual racial groupings and suggests that any attempt to assess differences between nonwhite and white rates is of questionable value. For that reason, and the small number of suicides in any one racial category, we have excluded analysis of suicide among nonwhites.

FACTORS ASSOCIATED WITH SUICIDE AMONG OLDER PEOPLE

We have seen that suicide is related to the demographic factors of age, sex, race, and marital status. Existing evidence indicates further relationships. We will limit ourselves, in discussing that evidence, to studies focused upon or data drawn from older subjects as opposed to samples that are very heterogeneous with regard to age.

TABLE 15.2

United States White Suicide Rates per 100,000, 1968–1977

	Year	15–19	20–24	25–29	30–34	35–39	40–44	45–49	50–54	55–59	60–64	65–69	70–74	75–79	80–84	85+
Male	1977	15.3	30.8	28.8	24.3	25.4	24.0	26.9	27.7	29.8	32.2	34.5	41.3	48.9	47.7	49.9
	1976	11.9	27.0	24.1	23.1	23.2	24.0	27.3	28.1	31.3	32.0	34.5	38.6	44.3	47.8	49.9
	1975	13.0	26.8	25.1	23.5	22.8	26.1	29.1	30.2	32.0	32.3	35.0	37.6	44.9	44.6	50.3
	1974	11.9	24.5	23.8	22.8	24.1	23.5	27.7	28.9	32.4	31.7	32.2	38.7	44.6	48.3	48.5
	1973	11.4	24.3	22.1	21.4	21.7	23.9	27.6	29.2	32.1	32.8	35.5	39.0	46.4	46.1	54.6
	1972	11.1	20.5	21.0	20.7	21.3	24.5	29.8	29.6	32.1	35.2	38.0	39.1	42.1	58.0	54.5
	1971	10.3	19.0	20.1	18.5	21.0	25.2	27.7	29.5	36.2	32.8	36.6	39.4	43.6	53.1	51.8
	1970	9.4	19.3	19.8	20.0	21.9	24.6	28.2	30.9	34.9	35.0	37.4	40.4	42.2	51.4	45.8
	1969	9.0	17.0	18.4	18.2	20.4	24.2	27.8	29.6	33.0	37.3	36.5	37.7	44.5	50.6	52.2
	1968	8.3	15.0	16.3	18.3	22.0	24.2	27.0	30.8	35.8	36.5	35.6	37.0	42.5	47.2	56.8
Female	1977	3.5	7.5	8.7	10.0	10.0	12.4	13.5	13.6	12.0	10.2	9.9	8.8	7.8	7.1	4.4
	1976	3.3	6.6	7.8	9.7	10.5	11.6	13.7	13.9	13.3	10.7	9.2	8.5	8.1	7.4	5.8
	1975	3.1	6.9	8.0	10.0	11.4	13.9	14.0	13.6	12.7	10.6	9.6	7.3	7.8	7.7	4.7
	1974	3.3	6.4	8.4	9.0	10.7	13.5	14.4	13.9	12.0	10.0	8.9	8.0	8.2	6.0	4.0
	1973	3.2	5.5	8.0	9.1	11.2	13.2	14.2	13.2	13.2	10.6	9.3	8.7	8.3	6.9	4.4
	1972	2.7	6.6	8.8	9.9	12.3	12.8	14.6	12.2	14.0	12.5	10.0	8.2	8.1	7.2	5.9
	1971	3.0	6.2	8.3	9.5	12.2	13.8	14.3	14.8	13.3	11.8	10.9	9.5	7.5	6.9	3.6
	1970	2.9	5.7	8.6	9.5	12.2	13.8	13.5	13.5	13.1	11.5	9.4	9.7	7.3	7.2	5.8
	1969	2.6	5.0	7.3	8.9	11.9	13.4	13.1	13.4	12.2	11.4	10.6	8.8	7.7	7.1	4.5
	1968	2.2	4.8	7.0	8.1	10.6	12.3	13.1	13.9	12.3	10.7	8.3	8.0	7.2	5.4	4.9

Source: National Center for Health Statistics. Annual Reports on Deaths by Suicide. U.S. Department of Health, Education and Welfare. Washington, D.C.

TABLE 15.3
Ratios of Suicide Rates of Unmarried to Married Persons by Age and Sex, 1959–1961

Age	Married	Single	Widowed	Divorced
Male				
40–44	1	1.90	4.57	5.14
45–49	1	1.75	3.65	4.26
50–54	1	1.72	3.30	3.64
55–59	1	1.68	2.65	3.54
60–64	1	1.74	2.51	3.61
65–69	1	1.92	2.25	2.88
70–74	1	2.21	2.35	3.24
75–79	1	2.28	2.16	3.39
80–84	1	1.96	1.81	2.53
85+	1	1.68	1.91	2.36
Female				
40–44	1	1.48	1.84	3.36
45–49	1	1.19	2.06	2.62
50–54	1	1.12	1.73	2.53
55–59	1	1.09	1.82	2.05
60–64	1	1.12	1.64	2.52
65–69	1	1.09	1.38	2.65
70–74	1	1.61	1.79	2.36
75–79	1	.87	1.65	4.45
80–84	1	1.06	1.54	3.91
85+	1	1.24	1.67	5.03

Source: U.S. Department of Health, Education, and Welfare, 1967.

Social Factors

Suicide among the aged appears to be more common among lower-class than among middle- and upper-class males (Bock & Webber, 1972; Gardner, Bahn, & Mack, 1964; Sainsbury, 1963; Stengel, 1964; Weiss, 1968), but the relationship is far from clear. For instance, evidence has been provided by Breed (1963) and Gardner *et al.* (1964) that some men occupied middle-class positions but "skidded" into lower-class ones prior to suicide. Future studies, using interview data should pursue this lead.

Suicide among the aged has also been linked to social isolation. In a subsample of white, Cook County, Illinois males over the age of 49 who were unmarried or separated, Maris (1969) found that about half lived alone. Most of them had no dependents and their contact with relatives had been minimal (see also Bock & Webber, 1972; Gardner *et al.*, 1964; Sainsbury, 1963). Social isolation may also be related to findings that loss of a significant other is associated with suicidal behavior (Moss &

Hamilton, 1956); that suicide is less common among the rural elderly than among their urban counterparts (Gardner *et al.*, 1964; Sainsbury, 1963); and that the foreign-born have higher suicide rates than the native-born (Kramer *et al.*, 1972).

A final, more hypothetical social factor involves a relational process built around the societal definition of the old person as "doomed." Two interview studies (Cameron, 1972; Connell, 1972) found that people of all ages feel less opposed to suicide when commited by old people. This suggests that the social controls regarding suicide are relaxed when old people are involved. Related to but going beyond this apparent consensus about aging are the thinly veiled messages sometimes found in individual psychological autopsies. We are referring to such behaviors by relatives and others as making guns available to depressed elderly invalids. While we have no way of knowing how many suicides are preceded by such actions, we suggest that their effect is to confirm the person's fears of being a burden and perception of death as a desirable alternative.

Psychological Factors

The psychological condition most frequently reported as characteristic of suicidal old people is depression (Barraclough, Bunch, Nelson, & Sainsbury, 1974; Batchelor, 1955; Bennett, 1973; Benson & Brodie, 1975; O'Neal, Robins, & Schmidt, 1956). Sainsbury (1963) has, however, called attention to sex and social differences in the incidence patterns of depression and suicide. Among the complications of attempts to relate these two phenomena is the number of clinical entities subsumed under the general term, *depression*. These apparently have differing incidence patterns (Silverman, 1968), so there is every reason to expect them to relate variously to suicide. On the other hand, the diagnosis of depression is arrived at in different ways from study to study. At times it is post hoc and based on reports of family and friends. At other times it refers to the diagnosis applied during a hospitalization prior to the suicide. The validity and reliability problems of psychiatric diagnoses made under the best of conditions are well known. When one's task is to utilize data obtained in such diverse ways as diagnoses of suicide victims, the problems are greatly multiplied.

The overall motivation for suicide appears to vary by age. Farberow and Shneidman (1957) applied the Menninger scheme to a large number of suicide notes. They classified 57% of the notes left by elderly males and 75% of those by elderly females in the category "wish to die." Younger suicides (aged 20 to 39) had only 23% and 21% "wish to die" notes (male and female, respectively) but many notes classified as "wish to kill" and "wish to be killed." In other words, many older suicides signal "resignation" from life.

One of the most intriguing psychological characteristics related to suicide and aging, in our opinion, is *the ability to adjust, cope, and adapt.* Provocative insights in this area come from Wolff's (1969) study of aging male veterans. Those men with "significant evidence of suicidal ideation or attempts" were characterized by compulsivity and rigidity, showing great difficulty in adjusting to new circumstances. Their life patterns focused around ambition, hard work, and perfection. Depressive feelings were combined with resentment and anger against themselves and others. They were able, however, to repress, sublimate, and/or deny their hostile feelings and their "anal" character through compulsive work. When aging weakened their controls over aggressive impulses, they could not express hostility against others, so they introjected them.

Studies relating suicide in the elderly with adjustability or flexibility are not definitive, but rather suggest directions for research involving more systematic definition of terms as well as sampling and measurement. Something akin to a capacity to adjust to the new role of "aged"—and to leave identification with work behind—seems particularly promising for the understanding of the high suicide potential of a certain kind of man.

Physical Factors

Physical illness or disability is generally cited as among the factors associated with suicide (Butler, 1975; Resnik & Cantor, 1970). Sainsbury (1963) has noted a high incidence of physical illness among suicide victims, particularly those aged 60 and over. Among those suicide victims who leave notes (approximately 15%) persons over the age of 60 are more likely than younger people to refer to physical illness in connection with their actions (Capstick, 1960).

Attempted Suicide

Among the elderly, the ratio between suicide attempts and completed suicides is not so large as among younger people. Older people apparently are less likely than the young to make suicide attempts, but when they do, they employ more lethal methods and so are more likely to kill themselves. For instance, the proportion of self-inflicted deaths caused by poisoning generally decreases with age, whereas the proportion caused by hanging and, among men, gun shot increases (see also Dublin, 1963; Weiss, 1968).

DEVELOPMENTAL THEORY AND RESEARCH

On an individual level we propose that the suicide rates we have described are, in large measure, a function of adaptation to old age. As mentioned earlier, it is our assumption that indicators of successful adjustment will, by opposition, suggest precursors to high suicide risk. Therefore, we turn now to a review of the findings from research on aging and to the formulation of a model based upon socialization and role theories whereby measurable constructs such as level of life satisfaction serve to link social indicators like socioeconomic status with the suicide of individuals.

For a variety of reasons, the research on aging tells us more about successful than unsuccessful aging. When a group of elderly people is compared with a younger group—a common method for assessing adjustment to age—a unique bias may be introduced. The former may be an elite group in that they possess special qualities enabling them to survive, whereas the younger group may be heterogeneous with regard to those qualities. For instance, one finds proportionately fewer smokers and heavy drinkers among a group of elderly people than among a younger group due to the effects of smoking and drinking on the life span. To the extent that these behaviors are associated with other characteristics of individuals (personality variables, life style, etc.) comparison of two groups will be distorted by the nonrandom distribution of these characteristics.

Longitudinal studies in which one might hope to overcome some of the difficulties of cross-sectional studies are plagued with the problem of attrition and the evidence that attrition is not a random process. Cumming and Henry (1961) noted that attrition in their study was greater among respondents with low rates of social interaction.

Even though researched groups of aged persons may be biased samples, they still include a range of personal characteristics and level of satisfaction with life. Such variation and data from studies comparing well-adjusted and poorly adjusted aged persons provide us with clues to factors associated with "unsuccessful" aging and, presumably, with suicide.

Factors Associated with Satisfaction in Advanced Age

There is evidence that older people have fewer emotional experiences—positive or negative—than younger people (Lowenthal, Thurnher, & Chiriboga, 1975; Riley, Foner, Moore, Hess, & Roth, 1968) and that emotional cathexes toward persons and social objects decrease with age (Neugarten *et al.*, 1964).

Life satisfaction in later years tends to be associated with doing what one prefers in regard to work. That is, retirement is satisfying to those who choose to retire or who are willing to retire in due course, but it is less often satisfying to those who are retired against their wishes (Maas & Kuypers, 1974; Thompson & Streib, 1958). Not surprisingly, economic security is related to life satisfaction among the aged (Riley *et al.*, 1968) but the most important factor is probably health status. Finally, adjustment to aging appears to be related to one's attitudes about aging and aged people (Riley *et al.*, 1968).

Factors Influencing Adaptation to Age

Several individual characteristics influence adjustment to age and, therefore, level of life satisfaction. An obvious category is that of mental illness—particularly depression (Lowenthal & Berkman, 1967). Of more central importance to our task is the evidence that adjustment to age depends in large measure on long-established personality characteristics and life styles. Of the two poorly adapted groups of older men described by Reichard, Livson, and Petersen (1962), for instance, the "angry men" were characterized as aggressive, having difficulty with impulse control, utilizing nonadaptive defense mechanisms, having few hobbies—social or recreational—and being seclusive, rigid, and unable to tolerate doubt and uncertainty. The other group—"the self-haters"—turned their aggression inward as self-blame; they lacked ego strength and were depressed and relatively constricted in their thinking (see also Maas & Kuypers, 1974; Neugarten, Havighurst, & Tobin, 1968). The self-haters are clearly high suicide risks. We predict that the angry men would become high risks if they lost the ability to maintain their defenses.

Finally, there is evidence that during the latter part of middle age, people undergo changes that facilitate the transition to old age. A major modification of disengagement theory emerged from Neugarten and her associates' (1964) evidence that psychological disengagement precedes the disengagement of the individual from social interaction described by Cumming and Henry (1961).

There is also evidence of change in values or orientations that would tend to facilitate functioning in roles in later years. Many men mellow and become more concerned with warm, interpersonal relations, whereas women become more assertive and less dependent (Livson, 1976; Lowenthal *et al.*, 1975; Neugarten *et al.*, 1964). A study by Haan (1976) resulted in an apparent integration of these findings. She found that while there are core consistencies in personality organization of well-functioning people at different ages, there are suggestive differences. Her data reveal that young people are socially assertive and that they actively engage situations. Older people, by contrast, tend to more tender, intimate interpersonal involvements. There is also evidence of differences in experiencing the self. The personality organization of younger people indicate "considerable cognitive investment" and display of capability, whereas that of older people suggest that the "preservation of the self's integrity and integration" is more important (Haan, 1976).

Finally, some men late in their middle years, prepare themselves for retirement by reducing their level of interest in their work and by viewing retirement in more positive terms than in younger years (Lowenthal et al., 1975). The changes described for men prepare them for adaptation to a situation in which instrumental skills, developed and treasured for years, are no longer relevant, whereas interpersonal skills and relations take on increasing importance. Men who fail to make changes such as these are, we suggest, relatively high suicide risks. The changes described for women would obviously facilitate their adjustment to widowhood.

FACTORS INFLUENCING SOCIALIZATION, DEVELOPMENT, AND STATUS IN OLD AGE

We turn now to the discussion of three "master" variables—physical health, social rank, and sex—which are statistically associated with suicide and which may influence processes of socialization and development in such a way that they affect an individual's adaptation to aging and thereby his or her chances for suicide.

Health

The first of these variables, physical health, is the most simple and straightforward. Health status is related to suicide indirectly as well as directly. It is, for instance, associated with emotional disturbances (Lowenthal et al., 1967) which, in turn, may predispose a person to suicide. Health status, as mentioned previously, is directly associated with level of life satisfaction among the aged and it probably also plays an *indirect* role in level of satisfaction by virtue of its effects on options. For instance, illness or disability may necessitate retirement and limit social and voluntary activities, thereby exerting a negative influence on the individual's level of satisfaction with his/her life.

Social Status

Although the suicide data are not as complete and consistent as one might like, we have cited evidence that suicide is inversely related to social status. We suggest that there are sound bases for predicting this because of the impact one might expect social class to have on adaptability and level of life satisfaction in advanced age. The middle-class and upper-class individual is, relative to the lower-class person, more likely to be economically secure in retirement. More importantly perhaps, middle- and upper-class men are likely to have more options open to them with regard to work and retirement. By virtue of the nature of their work they are more likely to be physically able to continue working, to have the option to do so, and to have alternatives for full- or part-time work available if forced out of their jobs by compulsory retirement programs. Such choices, as we have seen, are associated with life satisfactions.

Finally, studies of the socialization practices of families at varying socioeconomic strata have provided data suggesting that the middle- and upper-class man may be more likely to possess the personal characteristics associated with adaptability. For instance, Kohn's (1969) data show that working-class parents place high value on conformity to external authority in their children. Middle-class parents place more emphasis on self-direction. A tentative conclusion one might draw from these data is that the working-class child is more likely to grow into an adult whose guiding principle is rigid obedience to external authority, whereas the middle-class child is more likely to become an adult attuned to his or her own (as well as to others') internal dynamics. For the vast majority of people, the authority of the social order is articulated through role demands and expectations. However, there are relatively few demands and expectations the retired person is supposed to meet, and there is no formal social mechanism through which social authority may be articulated to the retiree. Dependency on external authority may, then, make retirement particularly stressful to the working-class man who is unable to adapt to its loss.

Sex

Most of the factors discussed up to this point are affected by sex, the best single predictor of an individual's suicide potential. For instance, there is woman's well-known physical advantage. She lives longer and, although older women are more likely than older men to have and report illness, the men are more likely to be limited in the amount or kind of major activity in which they can engage (Carpenter, McArthur, & Higgins, 1974; Cole, 1974).

The differences in socialization experiences of males and females in this society have been subject to a great deal of discussion (see Maccoby & Jacklin, 1974 for extensive review of this area). Rather than review the work already done, we will draw suggestions from the literature that are particularly relevant for our topic and the argument we are constructing.

Those personality characteristics that are so frequently viewed as psychologically and intellectually crippling to the woman may also be influential in her ability to survive. That is, the passivity, suggestibility, and malleability of women may, ironically, translate into adaptability. While the little girl learns not to make waves, she may well be learning to ride out a gale without being capsized.

Furthermore, the little girl in our society is reinforced for coping mechanisms that may be more adaptive than many the little boy perceives in his role models or is encouraged to develop (Block, 1973). For instance, the boy is less likely to be discouraged from aggressively expressing emotion, he is more likely to be discouraged from seeking comfort and solace, and he is more likely to see his role models using alcohol to cope with stress. The woman reflects the coping mechanisms she was taught to develop in her greater use of institutionalized sources of help—doctors, therapists, clergy, etc. (Gurin, Veroff, & Feld, 1960). One might also interpret as evidence of this differential socialization, the survey data on substances used by Americans to cope with emotional distress. In the older age group (60–74), as at all ages, the use of medically prescribed psychotherapeutic drugs is more common among women and the use of alcohol is much more common among men (Mellinger, Balter, Parry, Manheimer, & Cisin, 1974). Another outcome of these sex differences in socialization may well be differences in ability to adapt to significant change in later years.

An ambitious attempt to relate socialization practices *directly* to suicide was made by Hendin (1964), who focused on the nature of the mother–child relationships in three Scandinavian countries. A subsequent test of Hendin's conclusions illustrates the importance of sex in socialization. Block and Christiansen (1966) found that the socialization experiences described by Hendin were characteristic of girls in each of the three countries but not of the boys. It is possible that Hendin's data came disproportionately from females, which would help explain the disparity between his findings and those of others who attempted to replicate them.

THE AGING PROCESS

It is likely that the *process of aging* differs for the sexes. The average American woman has experienced major qualitative role changes throughout her adult life. While the birth of the first child has been studied as a crisis situation for both parents, the event does not signal major changes in the new father's day-to-day activity. He typically does not have to stop or shift role activities. The reverse is true of the woman. There is very little about her diurnal activity that does not change with motherhood. As the child progresses through the developmental stages—entering school, achieving independence, leaving home—the demands of the mother's role qualitatively shift and change. In addition, during this period of mothering, the woman may well be in and out of the labor market, further varying her roles.

The average American male experiences role changes of a different order. His central role—work—is more likely to change quantitatively as he experiences advancement and increased responsibility. He is not likely to experience major qualitative change after the first few years of adulthood and marriage. In his developmental process, each stage prepares him for the next, and the demands and expectations on him are consistent throughout—he is expected to be assertive, to seek mastery over his environment, and to strive for achievement.

When the man's work role *does* change at retirement, the change is abrupt and dramatic. From full-time work, he goes to no work at all. From interpersonal relations with many job associates, few remain. From feelings of accomplishment, achievement, or at least involvement in a task that he (or others) considers worth doing, there is nothing. The individual response to this drastic shift varies, of course, but for many it is a wrenching loss.

Most readers are familiar with the concept of role, but there is one aspect of it not so well known. This is the sequential nature of roles. Our belief is that men experience greater sequential role conflict than women do, and that this has important bearing on the contrasting suicide rates by sex.

Before a role can be played satisfactorily (especially an achieved role) the person must do several things. He must qualify for entry, learn the requirements, and somehow "practice" it. This takes time. The more central roles (like work for men) are those that one occupies for a long time; these are often subject to anticipatory socialization; the teenager aspires to be a doctor, a craftsman, an executive. He takes such a role in imagination. And as he moves into the role, he relates to it in his own way, develops attitudes toward it, and identifies with it. Most men hold attitudes (positive or negative) toward their work, attitudes that form an important part of the self.

Further, what one learns in one role may help one's performance in later roles. Most men engage in increasingly responsible and demanding role activities as they advance through the years. This is what is meant by the sequential nature of roles.

Let us return now to the position of the retired man. The "role question" asks, "What is expected of me?" The retiree—unless he has carefully planned for retirement—is typically uncertain about his answer. Another question, "What roles am I about to undertake?" Again, uncertainty. And, "Will my experience in work prepare me for my roles in retirement?" The answer is that often the instrumental skills learned at work no longer apply. There is no such role as "vice-president old person" to aspire to. There are no other people to admire one's work and offer promotions. Now, in the instrumental sense at least, there is "nowhere to go." The next roles facing the man have names like "retired man," "old man," "senior citizen," "patient," and eventually, "deceased."

Sequential role conflict means that the person must unlearn patterns imposed on him in earlier years and learn new—often contradictory—patterns, not an easy task for many people. Kutner, Fanshel, Togo, and Langner (1956) found, for instance, that a substantial number of people were disappointed in their retirement and that the morale of retirees tended to be lower than that of age peers who were still working. Just over 15% of the men studied by Cumming and Henry (1961) experienced the loss of their instrumental role as a disadvantage. It must be emphasized, however, that most men cope with this sequential conflict and do *not* commit suicide. Our point is that the differential response to retirement and aging is partly an individual matter and partly one influenced by sociocultural forces. The relatively few men who cannot adapt to retirement and who have the other deficits that we have discussed constitute the high suicide risks. It is to the risk variables that we mean to point in this chapter.

The picture we are painting has a visual analogy. The developmental process of the male is like a steeply inclined, narrow, and confined path. The man has relatively little choice other than to follow the path, moving forward toward goal achievement, and at the end of the path there may be just that—an end—retirement. The process of the woman is more like an open field in which she may range from place to place, but the places are not hierarchically structured nor are they necessarily on line with one another. We suggest that these differences require and reinforce adaptability in the woman to a far greater degree than in the man. The analysis by Maas and Kuypers (1974) of the adult lives of 142 people is consistent with this suggestion. They found women to be more responsive than men to environmental factors and to have had more variation in their life styles over time. They suggest that the life-style changes of the women shaped and/or reinforced personality dispositions consistent with successful adaptation. The men, relatively unresponsive to their environment, had shown considerable consistency in life style over the years. "It is as though the trajectory for our fathers' ways of living were established early in their adult lives" (Maas & Kuypers, 1974, p. 130).

The one apparently discordant note with our line of reasoning consists of findings that women nearing retirement anticipate the transition less positively than do their male counterparts (Lowenthal *et al.*, 1975; Streib & Schneider, 1971). In both studies, reluctance to retire is particularly high among widowed and divorced women. This suggests a desire to avoid the isolation that may lie in a solitary retirement. We suggest that although she may resist retirement, the woman's identity is generally not so intimately and inexorably intertwined with her work that the level of her life satisfaction or her will to live are seriously affected by retirement. In fact, data suggest that, although the morale of recently retired women tends to be low, it rises as time passes. This is unlike the data for men, who apparently become increasingly demoralized (Kutner *et al.*, 1956).

It is plausible that the problematic stage for women is not old age but the middle years when suicide rates for women peak. These are years during which most women experience multiple changes that may bear significantly on their identity and self-esteem. Their children leave home, depriving them of the structure imposed by their roles as mothers. They change physically, losing not only the ability to reproduce, but also the beauty and sexual allure that society valued them for. In fact, the evidence suggests that instead of finding these middle years distressing, *most* women experience increased freedom (Cumming & Henry, 1961). They have time to devote to themselves and to develop latent talents and capacities (Neugarten, 1968). Nonetheless, for *some* women the onset of middle age has been likened to forced retirement for the man (Public Broadcasting System, 1977).

We have, in the preceding pages, outlined an argument that says, in effect, that the number of factors that influence *adaptation* to old age and thereby suicide potential are, in turn, influenced by major "master" variables that are chance factors and relatively immutable to change. However, the *influence* is not inevitable, and we may see change as the current assault on American mores continues and future generations experience different patterns of socialization and development. This is not to presume that all change will be good. It is possible that increased assertiveness and achievement orientation in women will result in higher suicide rates. Reports of high suicide rates among professional women (Steppacher & Mausner, 1974) would suggest this, but there are also analyses suggesting that women are better able to cope with adverse professional change (Rice, 1976).

If future generations of men are less achievement oriented, more responsive to their social environment, and more receptive to available help in coping with crises, they may reap the benefit of lower suicide rates. Ideally, an optimal balance is possible—that women can be encouraged to express themselves vocationally and socially without giving up all the qualities that facilitate their adaptive abilities. Also, men can learn to cope with stress in non-self-destructive ways and develop adaptive and interpersonal skills without forfeiting all the characteristics motivating them to achieve and produce. Thus, both men and women can seek liberation.

DISCUSSION AND CONCLUSIONS

Several years ago, Breed (1972) proposed a "basic suicide syndrome" containing numerous factors, of which five are paramount: commitment, failure, shame, isolation, and rigidity (see also Miller & Goleman, 1970). To summarize this briefly, the person is committed to a role, aspires to success in that central role, fails at it, and feels shame. If the person is also isolated and rigid—cannot change roles and goals—his or her suicide risk is very high. Although the five components emerged from study of the suicides of 264 persons between the ages of 18 and 60 years, they may contribute to an understanding of suicide among the aged.

Commitment to a role, such as that of breadwinner, is vital to success in that role. But retirement requires disengagement from the commitment to work and adaptation to quite different role expectations. Developmental psychologists, principally Erikson (1963), describe the final stage of life as a time for reflection upon one's past. Recognizing successful accomplishments in the preceding stages facilitates realization of the integrity that is the positive culmination of a life. However, if in reviewing one's life, the individual sees failure, particularly in the preceding—generative—stage, despair is likely. The failure that, at the time, brought shame, now leads to despair as the individual recognizes that rectification is no longer possible—there is no time to find alternative paths to integrity.

The other two components suggested by Breed are straightforward. Isolation is recognized by all as a major factor in suicide, and it is, of course, to some degree or another inevitable in old age. Rigidity may be viewed as the polar opposite of the characteristic we have repeatedly pointed to as essential in the smooth transition from one life stage to another—adaptability.

Since adaptability is a major factor in our model, we must be clear about the term. Biologists use the concept of adaptation in reference to species survival. Our usage refers to the ability of the individual to survive major life changes not only physically, but also psychologically and socially. It is the ability of a person to maximize the benefits of and minimize the costs exacted by crisis situations. We have focused here on the crisis of retirement when the individual faces challenges along several dimensions. A suggestive compilation of these has been developed by Clark and Anderson (1967), who argue that when a person enters retirement, five adaptive tasks must be faced:

1. The perception of aging and definition of instrumental limitations. The person must accept the physical situation, not deny it.
2. A redefinition of the physical and social life space. Some roles and activities must be relinquished.
3. The substitution of alternative sources of need satisfaction. New roles, activities, and interests can be "tried on" so that the person can maintain a measure of control over his or her life.
4. A reassessment of the criteria for evaluating the self. This requires, for example, that the retired man drop his identification with his work role and seek involvement with other roles.
5. The reorientation of values and life goals. The person must become "committed" to values appropriate to the new age status.

In our attempts to clarify some of the issues related to suicide among the elderly we have, in the preceding pages, argued that adaptability is the primary factor enabling individuals to survive crises of all kinds, including the transition to old age. We have presented data from a wide variety of sources to demonstrate that adaptability is a function of socialization and developmental experiences. These, in turn, are influenced by certain master variables—sex, social status, and physical health. It is our position that the master variables may be related to suicide rates directly but that generally the relationship rests upon the effect of the master variables on socialization and developmental experiences. One of the master variables—sex—has been the focus of our attention. We have attempted to show that differential socialization experiences will result in greater adaptability among girls in this society than among boys. These differences tend to be reinforced by typical adult role patterns of men and women and are ultimately reflected, we believe, in differential suicide rates.

Adaptability is, we have argued, a characteristic of individuals that enhances their ability to survive, socially and psychologically, as well as physically. Its opposite is rigidity or inflexibility—the inability to change roles and goals. The rigid individual will have difficulty dealing with transitions and situational change. Such a person becomes a high suicide risk to the extent that other basic elements are present—such as social isolation and failure in a role to which he or she is deeply committed. The failure brings with it, as an immediate consequence, shame. It may have the long-term consequence of causing despair if the failure is not rectified or if the commitment is not attenuated to cushion the impact of the failure.

Our model of suicide stresses the interaction between psychological and social factors. We do not presume that we have incorporated all the important factors. Self-image and role taking, for instance, are clearly related to the theme we have followed. Further exploration might show how these and other elements could be incorporated into the model to strengthen its explanatory power and enhance its utility in research and therapy.

REFERENCES

Barraclough, B., Bunch, J., Nelson, B., & Sainsbury, P. A hundred cases of suicide: Clinical aspects. *British Journal of Psychiatry,* 1974, *125,* 355–373.

Batchelor, I. R. C. The management and prognosis of suicidal attempts in old age. *Geriatrics,* 1955, *10,* 291–293.

Bennett, A. E. Psychiatric management of geriatric depressive disorders. *Diseases of the Nervous System,* 1973, *34,* 222–225.

Benson, R. A., & Brodie, D. C. Suicide by overdose of medicine among the aged. *Journal of the American Geriatric Society,* 1975, *23,* 304–308.

Block, J. H. Conceptions of sex role: Some cross-cultural and longitudinal perspectives. *American Psychologist,* 1973, *28,* 512–526.

Block, J. H., & Christiansen, B. A test of Hendin's hypotheses relating suicide in Scandinavia to child-rearing orientations. *Scandinavian Journal of Psychology,* 1966, *7,* 267–288.

Bock, E. W., & Webber, I. L. Social status and the relational system of elderly suicides. *Life-Threatening Behavior,* 1972, *2,* 145–159.

Breed, W. Occupational mobility and suicide among white males. *American Sociological Review*, 1963, *28*, 179–188.

Breed, W. Five components of a basic suicide syndrome. *Life-Threatening Behavior*, 1972, *2*, 3–18.

Butler, R. N. *Why survive? Being old in America*. New York: Harper & Row, 1975.

Cameron, P. T. Suicide and the generation gap. *Life-Threatening Behavior*, 1972, *2*, 194–208.

Capstick, A. Recognition of emotional disturbance and the prevention of suicide. *British Medical Journal*, 1960, *1*, 1179.

Carpenter, J. O., McArthur, R. F., & Higgins, I. T. The aged: Health, illness, disability and use of medical services. In C. L. Erhardt & J. E. Berlin (Eds.), *Mortality and morbidity in the United States*. Cambridge, Massachusetts: Harvard Univ. Press, 1974.

Clark, M. M., & Anderson, B. G. *Culture and aging*. Springfield, Massachusetts: Thomas, 1967.

Cole, P. Morbidity in the United States. In C. L. Erhardt & J. E. Berlin (Eds.), *Mortality and morbidity in the United States*. Cambridge, Massachusetts: Harvard Univ. Press, 1974.

Connell, M. Attitudes toward suicide of three American sub-populations. In L. Miller (Ed.), *Fourth International Congress of Psychiatry: Abstract of papers*. Jerusalem: AHBA Coop., 1972.

Cumming, E., & Henry, W. E. *Growing old: The process of disengagement*. New York: Basic Books, 1961.

Douglas, J. *The social meanings of suicide*. Princeton, New Jersey: Princeton Univ. Press, 1967.

Dublin, L. I. *Suicide*. New York: Ronald Press, 1963.

Durkheim, E. *Suicide*. New York: Free Press, 1951.

Erikson, E. H. *Childhood and society* (2nd ed.). New York: W. W. Norton, 1963.

Farberow, N. L., & Shneidman, E. S. Suicide and age. In E. S. Shneidman & N. L. Farberow (Eds.), *Clues to suicide*. New York: McGraw-Hill, 1957.

Gardner, E. A., Bahn, A. K., & Mack, J. Suicide and psychiatric care in the aging. *Archives of General Psychiatry*, 1964, *10*, 547–553.

Gurin, G., Veroff, J., & Feld, S. *Americans view their mental health*. New York: Basic Books, 1960.

Haan, N. Personality organizations of well-functioning younger people and older adults. *International Journal of Aging and Human Development*, 1976, *7*, 117–127.

Hendin, H. *Suicide and Scandinavia*. New York: Grune & Stratton, 1964.

Kohn, M. L. *Class and conformity*. Homewood, Illinois: Dorsey Press, 1969.

Kramer, M., Pollack, E. S., Redick, R., & Locke, B. Z. *Mental disorders/suicide*. Cambridge, Massachusetts: Harvard Univ. Press, 1972.

Kutner, B., Fanshel, D., Togo, A. M., & Langner, T. S. *Five hundred over sixty*. New York: Russell Sage Foundation, 1956.

Linden, L. L., & Breed, W. The demographic epidemiology of suicide. In E. S. Shneidman (Ed.), *Suicidology*. New York: Grune & Stratton, 1976.

Livson, F. B. *Coming together in the middle years: A longitudinal study of sex role convergence*. Paper presented at 29th Annual Meeting of Gerontological Society, New York, 1976.

Lowenthal, M. F., & Berkman, P. L. *Aging and mental disorder in San Francisco*. San Francisco: Jossey-Bass, 1967.

Lowenthal, M. F., Thurnher, M., & Chiriboga, D. *Four stages of life*. San Francisco: Jossey-Bass, 1975.

Maas, H. S. & Kuypers, J. A. *From thirty to seventy*. San Francisco: Jossey-Bass, 1974.

Maccoby, E. E., & Jacklin, C. N. *The psychology of sex differences.* Stanford, California: Stanford Univ. Press, 1974.

Maris, R. W. *Social forces in urban suicide.* Homewood, Illinois: Dorsey, 1969.

Marshall, J. R. *Suicide among aged Americans, 1947–1968.* Paper presented at the 70th Annual Meeting of the American Sociological Association, San Francisco, September 1975.

Mellinger, G. D., Balter, M. B., Parry H. J., Manheimer, D. I., & Cisin, I. H. An overview of psychotherapeutic drug use in the United States. In E. Josephson & E. E. Carroll (Eds.), *Drug use: Epidemiological and sociological approaches.* New York: Hemisphere Publishing Corp., 1974.

Miller, D., & Goleman, D. J. Predicting post-release risk among hospitalized suicide attempters. *Omega,* 1970, *1,* 71–84.

Moss, L. M., & Hamilton, D. M. Psychotherapy of the suicidal patient. *American Journal of Psychiatry,* 1956, *112,* 814–820.

Neugarten, B. L. The awareness of middle age. In B. L. Neugarten (Ed.), *Middle age and aging.* Chicago: Univ. of Chicago Press, 1968.

Neugarten, B. L. *et al. Personality in middle and late life: Empirical studies.* New York: Atherton, 1964.

Neugarten, B. L., Havighurst, R. J., & Tobin, S. S. Personality and patterns of aging. In B. L. Neugarten (Ed.), *Middle age and aging.* Chicago: Univ. of Chicago Press, 1968.

O'Neal, P., Robins, E., & Schmidt, E. H. A psychiatric study of attempted suicide in persons over sixty years of age. *Archives of Neurological Psychiatry,* 1956, *75,* 275–284.

Public Broadcasting System's Documentary Showcase. *Going Past Go.* Produced by WGBH-Boston, aired over KQED-San Francisco, January 16, 1977.

Reichard, S., Livson, F., & Petersen, P. G. *Aging and personality.* New York: Wiley, 1962.

Resnik, H. L. P., & Cantor, J. M. Suicide and aging. *Journal of the American Geriatric Society,* 1970, *18,* 152–158.

Rice, R. E. *Dreams and actualities: Danforth fellows in mid-career.* Unpublished manuscript, Stockton, California, University of the Pacific, 1976.

Riley, M. W., Foner, A., Moore, M. E., Hess, B., & Roth, B. K. *Aging and society* (Vol. 1). *An inventory of research findings.* New York: Russell Sage Foundation, 1968.

Sainsbury, P. Social and epidemiological aspects of suicide with special reference to the aged. In R. H. Williams, C. Tibbitts, & W. Donahue (Eds.), *Processes of aging: Social and psychological perspectives* (Vol. 2). New York: Atherton, 1963.

Silverman, C. *The epidemiology of depression.* Baltimore, Maryland: Johns Hopkins Press, 1968.

Stengel, E. *Suicide and attempted suicide.* London: Penguin, 1964.

Steppacher, R. C., & Mausner, J. S. Suicide in male and female physicians. *Journal of the American Medical Association,* 1974, *228,* 323–328.

Streib, G. F., & Schneider, C. J. *Retirement in American society: Impact and process.* Ithaca, New York: Cornell Univ. Press, 1971.

Thompson, W. E., & Streib, G. F. Situational determinants: Health and economic deprivation in retirement. *Journal of Social Issues,* 1958, *14,* 18–34.

U.S. Department of Health, Education, and Welfare. *Suicide in the United States: 1950–1964* (Public Health Service Publication No. 1000, Series 20, No. 5). Washington, D.C.: Government Printing Office, 1967.

Weiss, J. M. A. Suicide in the aged. In H. L. P. Resnik (Ed.), *Suicidal behaviors.* Boston: Little, Brown, 1968.

Wolff, K. Depression and suicide in the geriatric patient. *Journal of the American Geriatric Society,* 1969, *17,* 668–672.

SUBJECT INDEX